ARTHURIAN STUDIES LIV

A COMPANION TO THE *LANCELOT-GRAIL CYCLE*

ARTHURIAN STUDIES

General Editor: Norris J. Lacy

ISSN 0261–9814

Previously published volumes in the series
are listed at the back of this book

A COMPANION TO
THE *LANCELOT-GRAIL CYCLE*

Edited by Carol Dover

D. S. BREWER

First published 2003
D. S. Brewer, Cambridge

D. S. Brewer is an imprint of Boydell & Brewer Ltd
PO Box 9, Woodbridge, Suffolk IP12 3DF, UK
and of Boydell & Brewer Inc.
PO Box 41026, Rochester, NY 14604–4126, USA
website: www.boydell.co.uk

A catalogue record for this book is available
from the British Library

Library of Congress Cataloging-in-Publication Data
A companion to the Lancelot-Grail cycle / edited by Carol Dover.
p. cm. – (Arthurian studies)

1. Lancelot (Legendary character) – Romances – History and criticism.
2. Grail – Romances – History and criticism.   3. Arthurian romances.
I. Dover, Carol, 1943–   II. Series.
PN2071.I5C66 2003
809.93351 – dc21   2003005121

This publication is printed on acid-free paper

Contents

PART III: POSTERITY

Acknowledgements

This volume owes many significant debts, not least to its contributors for their diligence in completing their chapters. Special thanks are due to the valuable editorial assistance provided by three of my undergraduate students, Cate Poole, Alison Heller, and Patricia Stumpf, under the auspices of the Georgetown University Research Opportunities Program. Thanks are also due to the Georgetown University Graduate School for a grant-in-aid to support in part the publication of this volume.

The Contributors

RICHARD BARBER   Director, Boydell & Brewer Ltd

EMMANUÈLE BAUMGARTNER   Professor in Medieval Literature, Université de Paris III – Sorbonne Nouvelle

FANNI BOGDANOW   Professor Emeritus, Manchester University

FRANK BRANDSMA   Associate Professor of Comparative Literature (Medieval), Utrecht University

MATILDA TOMARYN BRUCKNER   Professor of French, Boston College

CAROL J. CHASE   Professor of French, Knox College

ANNIE COMBES   Maître de Conférences in Medieval Literature, Université de Nantes

HELEN COOPER   Fellow of University College, Oxford

CAROL DOVER   Associate Professor of French, Georgetown University, Washington, D.C.

MICHAEL HARNEY   Associate Professor of Spanish and Portuguese & Comparative Literature, University of Texas at Austin

DONALD L. HOFFMAN   Professor of English, Northeastern Illinois University

DOUGLAS KELLY   Professor Emeritus, University of Wisconsin, Madison

ELSPETH KENNEDY   Emeritus Fellow of St. Hilda's College, Oxford

NORRIS J. LACY   Professor of French, Pennsylvania State University

ROGER MIDDLETON   Honorary Research Fellow in French, University of Nottingham

HAQUIRA OSAKABE   Professor Emeritus, Universidade de Campinos, São Paolo

HANS-HUGO STEINHOFF   Professor of German, Universität Paderborn

ALISON STONES   Professor of History of Art and Architecture, University of Pittsburgh

RICHARD TRACHSLER   Maître de Conférences in Medieval Literature, Université de Paris IV – Sorbonne

Abbreviations

BBIAS	*Bibliographical Bulletin of the International Arthurian Society*
BL	British Library
BNF	Bibliothèque nationale de France
Lacy	*Lancelot-Grail: The Old French Arthurian Vulgate and Post-Vulgate in Translation*, ed. Norris J. Lacy, 5 vols. (New York and London, 1996)
LK	*Lancelot do Lac: the non-cyclic Old French Prose Romance*, ed. Elspeth Kennedy, 2 vols. (Oxford, 1980)
LM	*Lancelot: roman en prose du XIIIe siècle*, ed. Alexandre Micha, 9 vols. (Geneva and Paris, 1978–83)
MHG	Middle High German
PMLA	*Publications of the Modern Language Association of America*

A *Note on the* Lancelot-Grail Cycle

The title *Lancelot-Grail Cycle*, as used in this volume, refers to the ensemble of five prose works consisting of the *Estoire del Saint Graal*, the *Estoire Merlin* and its continuation (*Suite*), the *Lancelot*, *Queste del Saint Graal*, and *Mort Artu*. Together they correspond to the seven-volume *Vulgate Cycle of the Arthurian Romances* published by H. Oskar Sommer in 1908–13, excepting the *Livre d'Artus* which Sommer included but which belongs to the *Post-Vulgate Cycle*. The name *Vulgate Cycle*, invented by Sommer, is still in common use and is used occasionally in this volume where circumstances require it (Sommer's is still the only edition of the complete *Cycle*), but generally it has been replaced by *Lancelot-Grail Cycle*. The full complement of five works was achieved with the composition of the *Estoire del Saint Graal* and the *Estoire Merlin*, the last components to be included. They were added to form the prequel to an existing trilogy consisting of the *Lancelot – Queste del Saint Graal – Mort Artu*, which is also sometimes referred to as a cycle and also called the *Prose Lancelot*. To add to the confusion, *Lancelot*, the *Lancelot-Grail Cycle*'s huge centerpiece, has also been called the *Lancelot Proper* to differentiate it within the trilogy and to avoid confusion with Chrétien de Troyes' Lancelot verse romance (*Le Chevalier de la Charrette*) which critics and readers habitually referred to as the *Lancelot*. In this volume, *Lancelot* is the prose story of Lancelot that forms the centerpiece of the *Lancelot-Grail Cycle* and corresponds to volumes III–V of Sommer.

Introduction

CAROL DOVER

The early thirteenth-century French *Lancelot-Grail Cycle* (or *Vulgate Cycle*) brings together the stories of Arthur with those of the Grail, a conjunction of materials that continues to fascinate the Western imagination today. It is a vast compendium of Arthurian literature whose importance for the development of European fiction is finally being appreciated. Representing what is probably the earliest large-scale use of prose for fiction in the West, it also exemplifies the taste for big cyclic compositions that shaped much of European narrative fiction for three centuries. Dante admired the meandering seductiveness of the *Cycle*'s storytelling, Malory relied on it in large part for his fifteenth-century Arthuriad, and it spawned a progeny of adaptations in other languages. Despite its impressive medieval pedigree, the *Lancelot-Grail*'s sixteenth- and seventeenth-century critics pronounced it soporific, boring, worthless, while it fared no better with 'scientific' nineteenth-century critics who berated it for being repetitive, derivative, unfocused, and prosaic. Scholarship on the work was hampered until recently by the complexity of its manuscript tradition, the compilatory nature of the *Cycle*, its gigantic size, and its complex artistry. However, modern critical editions of all five branches of the *Cycle* have fanned scholarly interest in this vast text, while on a broader front the recent English translation of Sommer's *Vulgate Cycle* under the general direction of Norris J. Lacy (*Lancelot-Grail: the Old French Arthurian Vulgate and Post-Vulgate in Translation*, 5 vols. [New York: Garland, 1993–96]) opens up this medieval bestseller to a much wider audience of scholars, students, and general readers.

This volume attempts to convey to modern readers the appeal that such an unwieldy text must have had for its medieval audiences, and the richness of composition that made it compelling. The *Lancelot-Grail Cycle* could be described summarily as an anonymous text comprising at least five different works, possibly by five different authors, a text with no clear provenance although the majority of its manuscripts come from the north-east corner of France and what is now Belgium and Flanders. This description of the *Cycle* in terms of what it does not have, has the advantage of compelling us to focus largely, though not exclusively, on the text itself as our primary source of documentation.

Manuscript evidence suggests that the *Cycle* existed initially as a mini-cycle, the *Lancelot – Queste – Mort Artu* trilogy, which narrates the biography of Lancelot and the glory and downfall of the Arthurian kingdom. The subsequent addition of the *Estoire del Saint Graal* and the *Estoire Merlin – Suite*, however, gave the mini-cycle a new historical and religious foundation. The manuscript context of the *Cycle* is an evolving field of investigation made more complex by the enormous size of the *Cycle* (it was rarely contained in a single manuscript book), manuscripts totaling more than a hundred, and the considerable variance among them; all of which has complicated the task of reuniting the *membra disjecta* and determining the relationships among them. Exciting ongoing research on all the known manuscripts (whole or partial) of the *Cycle* promises to fill large gaps in our current knowledge, as well as opening up fresh areas of investigation concerning, for example, the relationship between text and image, for many of these manuscripts are richly and profusely illuminated.

Modern scholarship has investigated the links between genre and time, and underlined the difficulty of distinguishing between history and story, since these were designated by the same word (*estoire*) and seemed to be interchangeable in the early thirteenth-century. However, the distinction is sharpened by the fact that the *Cycle*'s historical perspective is not that of dynastic succession and power but the time-line of universal history, beginning with Christ's Passion and ending with the Revelation and the Apocalypse. It embraces the beginning and the end of all things. The work retains the mystery essential to romance writing while revealing the starkness of known history, for if Galahad takes the secrets of the Revelation with him at his passing, the apocalyptic end of Arthur's kingdom is poignantly and powerfully narrated.

Epic in scope but decidedly romance in tone and artistry, the *Cycle* exploits its audience's familiarity with characters, landscapes, and motifs from twelfth-century Arthurian verse romance, and we might well ask how accessible its prose narrative would be without the support of such a cast of 'reappearing characters.' It is this laudable medieval process of re-writing – recycling existing material, polishing it to produce something new and better, with a subtle dose of subversion – that the *Cycle* exemplifies. The variety of its sources reflects its project of combining a Grail story and an Arthurian story: Robert of Boron's trilogy of Grail romances (*Joseph–Merlin–Perceval*), Arthurian romances by Chrétien de Troyes and others, Celtic Merlin legends, 'historical' works such as Geoffrey of Monmouth's *History of the Kings of Britain* and Wace's *Roman de Brut*, and the Bible (Old and New Testaments, the Apocrypha) and perhaps other works that were 'in the air.' But recent attention to the *Cycle*'s rewriting, allied with its intertextuality, has shifted scholarly attention to the realm of poetics and opened up to view some of the imaginative creative processes that went into fashioning such a complex opus.

The popularity of King Arthur and Arthurian chivalric romance in the twelfth century can be attributed to their promotion by Henry II of England, who claimed Arthur as a worthy ancestor, but countervailing forces underpin the production of the *Cycle* with narratives that progressively question the viability of Arthurian chivalry as a role-model. If Arthurian chivalry has indeed lost its moral compass and is reduced to slaughter, as Perceval's mother claims it has in Chrétien's *Conte du Graal*, the *Lancelot-Grail* pursues this perspective. The contribution of Arthurian chivalry is insufficient to complete the new challenges, its image of perfection is steadily undermined through moralization and contrasted unfavorably with a new, spiritual chivalry, but the one is nevertheless generated by the other, like father and son. As the earthly quest gives way to the spiritual quest for the Holy Grail, the *Cycle* offers a new Gospel for chivalry.

For many readers the *Lancelot-Grail Cycle* is synonymous with interlaced narrative and prose for large-scale fiction, its two signal innovations. Recent scholarship has traced the complex interlacing of key themes, and further insights into the choice of prose and interlace suggest the two are strange bedfellows indeed. If the prose exploits the medium's connection with didactic narrative, truth-telling, and historiography, it is a richly poetic prose that works in concert with interlace to harbor secrets within the fragmented narrative.

The *Companion* is, to my knowledge, the first comprehensive volume devoted exclusively to the entire *Lancelot-Grail Cycle*. This first step is therefore intended to introduce today's reader to the greatness of the *Cycle* in an accessible and systematic form. The volume is divided into three sections. The first section offers perspectives from which to understand the social and ideological contexts that gave rise to the work, to its stages of growth, its literary and cyclic environments, the interconnections between its time, genre, and history. The second and largest section provides a sense of the rich diversity of the five texts, as stories for pleasurable reading and as texts to be delved into for further investigation. Each one of these central chapters brings out important structures and developments within one of the five works, while an additional chapter is reserved for the *Lancelot* and one chapter is devoted to manuscript illumination. The third and final section testifies to the remarkable reception and influence of the *Cycle*, measured by efforts to re-create all or part of the work in different areas of medieval Europe. A further important chapter traces the movement of manuscripts of the *Cycle* in England and Wales, and the section closes with a glance at the modern use of *Cycle* material in film. There is in addition a select bibliography and an Index. I wish the reader much pleasure in delving into this fascinating and elusive medieval text known as the *Lancelot-Grail Cycle*.

PART I

THE *LANCELOT-GRAIL CYCLE* IN CONTEXT

1

Chivalry, Cistercianism and the Grail

RICHARD BARBER

The *Queste del Saint Graal* is a remarkable feat of the imagination. It is a deeply religious story, yet it has little basis in the received history and teachings of the Church, and is embedded as an integral part in a series of romances which have quite other, secular values. Despite the unofficial nature of its material, the theology it contains is complex and subtle; yet at the same time it succeeded in appealing to the courtly audience for whom the romances were created. We may well wonder how these disparate themes of chivalry, mysticism and apocryphal stories of the Crucifixion were welded into one.

Chivalry itself was of course a primarily secular movement. The rise of the knightly class in the tenth and eleventh centuries, and the emergence of a specific ethos attached to the concept of knighthood, is a vast and difficult theme in itself. Who or what a knight was depended on the language you spoke: the Latin *miles* means soldier, the German *Ritter* and the French *chevalier* a horseman, the English *knicht* a man who serves a lord. Only in English can we distinguish between chivalry and knighthood.[1]

What we can say is that the knights were key players in the evolving feudal world of this period, and that somehow, from the newly developed arms and tactics of the period, an *esprit de corps* emerged which came to transcend immediate social rank. It can be seen in the conduct of war and in the introduction of restrictions aimed at mitigating the risks of war for the knightly classes.[2] There is evidence for organized training in the use of knightly weapons on horseback – spear, shield and sword – developing from the early eleventh century onwards into a violent form of sport, mock fights where war to the death was prevented by a series of rules and restraints. This in turn developed in the mid-twelfth century into a spectator sport, with distinguishing badges and commentators: heralds and heraldry were needed to make it possible for the onlookers to make out what was going on, and the emblems of opposing sides in war became individual coats of arms marking the prowess of the single knight.[3]

---

[1] The main general works on chivalry are: Maurice H. Keen, *Chivalry* (London and New Haven, 1984); Richard Barber, *The Knight and Chivalry*, 2nd ed. (Woodbridge, Eng., and Rochester, NY, 1995); Jean Flori, *L'Essor de la Chevalerie, XIe–XIIe siècles* (Geneva, 1986).

[2] Matthew Strickland, *War and Chivalry: The Conduct and Perception of War in England and Normandy, 1066–1217* (Cambridge, Eng., and New York, 1996), pp. 330–4.

[3] Noël Denholm-Young, *History and Heraldry, 1254–1310: A Study of the Historical Value of the Rolls of Arms* (Oxford, 1965), p. 5.

The primacy of the individual over the concept of the order of knighthood is probably the defining moment of chivalry, making it possible for the anonymous knight to become the named hero, and thus to join the ranks of those celebrated in literature. Great warriors had always been thus commemorated, but only for their deeds in actual warfare. Now it was possible to earn fame off the battle-field, and for the poets to create a world where the court and the knight became synonymous, and where fighting mock-battles won not only fame, but also women's hearts.

These concepts, widely differing in origin, converged in the mid-twelfth century to produce the first secular romances of chivalry. The romance genre was not new; late classical literature had a flourishing repertory of such stories, and they were to be found in contemporary Byzantium. But the vital element was provided by yet another genre, the troubadour love lyrics of southern France.[4] The complex secular ideology contained in these poems, drawing on concepts from religion, philosophy and the Arab world to create images and arguments which ranged from the dazzlingly simple to the deeply obscure, came through into the romances in a much simplified form: the idea of love-service. Just as a knight served his lord in the political world, so in the world of the emotions, he should serve his lady. His lord would reward him with lands and riches; but – and here the subtlety of the troubadours creeps in – the question of physical reward from the lady was much more ambiguous. Where the troubadours had been able to conceive of love almost as an intellec-tual game, and the question of its physical consummation, let alone marriage, was not their central concern (if indeed it was ever envisaged), the writers of romance addressed a less sophisticated audience.

The result was that the early romances were either about the winning of a bride or are frankly adulterous, and later writers try to evade the issue – the love potion becomes an excuse for Tristan's love for Iseult, while Lancelot's love for Guinevere is justified because it is never consummated. The driving force behind the stories is clear, a kind of Darwinian selection which matches the most accomplished (and handsome) knight with the most courtly (and beautiful) lady.

But a simple framework of tournaments and battles as the background to these love-stories would never have captured the imagination of a knightly audience sufficiently. The last element in the secular romances is that of the quest and its adventures. There is evidence that the idea of setting out to seek adventures was an early component of knighthood: a Norman knight declared to the Byzantine emperor in 1099, during the First Crusade:

> I am a pure Frank and of noble birth. One thing I know; at a crossroads in the country where I was born is an ancient shrine; to this anyone who wishes to en-gage in single combat goes, prepared to fight; there he prays to God for help and there he stays awaiting the man who will dare to answer his challenge. At that crossroads I myself have spent time, waiting and longing for the man who would fight – but there was never one who dared.[5]

4   See Peter Dronke, *The Medieval Lyric*, 3rd ed. (Cambridge, Eng., and Rochester, NY, 1996) for
    an overview of the lyric.
5   *The Alexiad of Anna Comnena*, trans. E. R. A. Sewter (Harmondsworth, 1979), p. 416.

The framework and setting for such episodes within the romances came from an unexpected source, the world of Celtic folktale and myth, with which the Norman conquerors of Britain had come into contact by the early twelfth century. The transmission of these tales to continental France is an enigma equal to that of the origins of the concept of courtly love. But the marvels and magic of the Celtic tales combined admirably with the quest for prowess; only the best knight in the world could break this or that spell, and the ultimately repetitive victories in tournaments or single combat could be given variety by these magical tests, which added a vital element of suspense and drama as well. In the hands of an artist such as Chrétien de Troyes, the stories become not only psychologically convincing, but they hold our attention as the hero encounters new terrors and dangers at each turn. By comparison, the contemporary chansons de geste, with their endless accounts of feuds and battles, seem heavy going indeed.

The Church's Attitude to Knighthood

The rise of a secular ethos such as knighthood, with its own set of values, particularly when combined with an exaltation of the individual and a fondness for violence, even under controlled conditions, was viewed with alarm by the Church. The values that the new 'order' promulgated seemed conducive to pride and adultery, and tournaments – called 'detestable fairs' by the Council of Clermont in 1130[6] – could lead to manslaughter or worse. Yet there were positive moral elements about knighthood. It had, at least in part, its origins in the Church's attempts to involve itself in all elements of secular life, in the services of blessing when a new warrior received his arms.[7] These had originally been little more than a variant on the blessings accorded to the tools of each trade, but the ambivalent nature of the knight's weapons led the Church to take more interest where the knighting ceremonies were concerned, particularly in view of the rank of those involved. The prayer on the occasion of giving of arms involved the idea that such power should only be used in a just cause:

> Hearken, we beseech Thee, O Lord, to our prayers, and deign to bless with the right hand of Thy majesty this sword with which this Thy servant desires to be girded, that it may be a defence of churches, widows, orphans and all Thy servants against the scourge of the pagans, that it may be the terror and dread of all evildoers, and that it may be just both in attack and defence.[8]

This particular prayer may in fact have been used at the investiture of a lay lord who pledged himself to defend a particular monastery, and became its *advocatus*;

---

6   Karl Joseph von Hefele and Henri Leclercq, *Histoire des Conciles, d'après les documents originaux* (Paris, 1912), 5.i,729.
7   Flori, *L'Essor de la Chevalerie*, pp. 90–2.
8   *The Pontifical of Magdalen College, with an Appendix of Extracts from other English MSS. of the Twelfth Century*, ed. H. A. Wilson (London, 1910), p. 255.

but it illustrates exactly the Church's problem in harnessing violence to its own ends.

The idea that warfare could in some way be restrained, as exemplified in the distinction between tournaments and real war, also owed something to the Church's influence; the movement known as the 'truce of God' attempted to limit the timescale of warfare by excluding holy days and indeed much of each week, and to regulate its conduct. It originated in southern France in the late tenth century, and spread throughout western Europe during the eleventh century. As local warfare diminished, and secular rulers established their authority, its usefulness decreased, but a principle had been established, that warfare could be controlled and its excesses curbed.

From controlling warfare, and setting certain ideals for the warriors who fought in it, the Church turned to harnessing the power of the knights for its own ends. The interplay of forces which led to the First Crusade is still much debated by historians: did the crusaders respond piously to an appeal by the pope, were they landless adventurers in search of territory to conquer, or were they even part of a popular movement fired by religious enthusiasm which the Church later brought under its aegis?[9] In whatever way the movement began, the First Crusade brought the Church and knighthood together in a fashion which neither had foreseen. The scenes of religious exaltation – and religious excess – at Antioch and at the fall of Jerusalem in 1099 were to have practical results, in the foundation not only of the largely secular and colonial Frankish state in Palestine, but also of the military orders, who combined the ideals of monasticism and the ideals of knighthood.

The impetus for the creation of the military orders was in the main secular: the first of them was devised for the purely practical purpose of defending pilgrims on the journey to Jerusalem, and the knights' function was not unlike that of the *advocati* of a monastery, sworn to defend a religious institution. It was only when the search for a more formal basis to the enterprise began that the idea of forming an order seems to have come into play. The initial impetus was undoubtedly from the secular side: in about 1120 Hugh of Payns and a group of companions took vows of poverty, chastity and obedience under the auspices of the patriarch of Jerusalem, but very much at their own instigation.[10] The political situation in the kingdom meant that they were rapidly enlisted not simply to defend pilgrims, but the state itself. When, in 1127, Hugh of Payns came to the West to seek support for his order, he was able to persuade the prelates assembled at the Council of Troyes to approve a formal rule. Among his supporters was Bernard of Clairvaux, to whom he may have been related, but it was only after some hesitation that Bernard wrote his famous epistle in support of the new institution, *De laude nove militie* (In praise of the new knighthood). The

9 On the idea that the crusade began as a popular movement, see Jean Flori, *Pierre l'Ermite et la première croisade* (Paris, 1999).
10 Alan Forey, *The Military Orders from the Twelfth to the Early Fourteenth Centuries* (London and Toronto, 1992), pp. 6–17; Malcolm Barber, *The New Knighthood: A History of the Order of the Temple* (Cambridge, Eng., and New York, 1996), p. 49.

stumbling-block, even after the events of the first Crusade, was the Church's attitude to warfare: put simply, opponents of the new idea held that 'to devote oneself to fighting against the enemies of the faith was wrong,' an attitude which stemmed from the eternal debate over the question of a 'just war.'[11] But, after three requests from Hugh of Payns, Bernard overcame his reservations on this score, and his hesitation about such an innovative idea. *De laude nove militie* was to be the defining text of Cistercian attitudes to knighthood; if the military orders are seen as one way of harnessing the energies of the warrior in the service of religion, the implication is that there could be others.

Cistercian involvement with the military orders was not limited to propaganda on their behalf and letters of support. The Templars made an immediate impact in Spain, where their potential usefulness for the wars of the reconquista was realized; Alfonso I of Aragon named the order as one of three heirs to his kingdom in 1131. The Templars, however, wanted revenue and resources for the Holy Land, not new commitments. When, in 1158, the frontier fortress at Calatrava was in danger of being abandoned, it was the nearby Cistercian monastery at Fitero who took over the task of organizing its defense in response to an appeal from the Archbishop of Toledo, a move which led to the establishment of a new military order bearing the castle's name.

The traditional story of the foundation of Calatrava relates that the King of Castile offered the castle to anyone who would hold it, with sufficient lands to pay for its defence. The heralds proclaimed the offer three times, without success. At court, there was a monk of Fitero, Fray Diego Velazquez, who had once been a soldier; and it was he who persuaded the Abbot of Fitero to undertake the enterprise.[12] What this episode underlines is the close contact between the Cistercians and the knightly class; indeed Bernard of Clairvaux came from a knightly family and may have been related to the founder of the Templars. The Cistercians continued to draw their recruits from the nobility; in the twelfth century, the order seems to have had a special relationship with, and fascination for, the nobility.

The foundation of the military orders and Bernard's writing on knighthood are, however, only an extension of the monastic ideal. For evidence that the Cistercians were interested in attempting to influence the attitudes of secular knighthood, we have to look elsewhere. They were well placed to do so, as they recruited from this class, understood its mentality, and through ties of family, had continuing contact with knights and nobles to a greater extent than any other contemporary order. In the early thirteenth century, one of the leading Cistercian preachers, Caesarius of Heisterbach, wrote a *Dialogus miraculorum*, a series of sermon examples based on miracles, dreams and visions.[13] In it, there are a large number of stories, some perhaps based on oral tradition, relating to

---

[11] Forey, *The Military Orders*, p. 17.
[12] Joseph O'Callaghan, 'The Affiliation of the Order of Calatrava with the Order of Cîteaux,' *Analecta Sacri Ordinis Cisterciensis*, XV (1959), 180–3 [161–93].
[13] *Caesarii Heisterbachensis. Dialogus miraculorum*, ed. Joseph Strange (Cologne, Bonn, and Brussels, 1851).

the fate of knights who have sinned in some respect connected with their status, vivid verbal pictures which are clearly aimed at reforming the morals of the knightly class.

It is however in the *Queste del Saint Graal* that the link between Cistercianism and secular chivalry is at its most striking. To appreciate the implications of the *Queste*, we first need to look briefly at the history of the Grail romances and the concept of the Grail from which the anonymous author of the *Queste* worked.

The Grail first appears in Chrétien de Troyes' *Conte du Graal*; it is called 'a grail' when first described, but in a later passage becomes 'the Grail.' Initially, its function is as an object of mystery, in a scene which is designed to arouse the audience's curiosity, and which deliberately sets out to conceal rather than reveal. The appearance of the Grail is presented entirely from Perceval's viewpoint, and tells us what he sees; as he does not ask the crucial question, 'Whom does the Grail serve?', he is as ignorant of its purpose and meaning at the end of the scene as at the outset. The Grail passes in and out of a room in which a feast is being held, carried by a girl and accompanied by brilliant lights. In essence, it is neither religious nor symbolic at this point: it is simply a focus for Chrétien's desire to show how Perceval has taken literally Gornemans' injunction not to ask questions. It enables the author to hold the audience in suspense, to create an atmosphere of tension and expectation. As such, it fulfils its dramatic function superbly; so superbly, that it has haunted our imagination ever since.

It is only later in the romance that we learn that this dish (*gradalis* in Latin) is 'a holy thing'[14] in which a Mass wafer was served to the sick king who lay in a chamber off the hall, unseen by Perceval. Chrétien is echoing the legends of the Mass in which a single Eucharistic wafer is enough to sustain life. From this explanatory passage there evolved the legend of the 'Holy Grail.' It was given a powerful religious emphasis in the work of Robert de Boron, writing in the last decade of the twelfth century,[15] who specifically identified the Grail with the dish used by Jesus at the Last Supper, and, drawing on the apocryphal versions of the New Testament, linked it to Joseph of Arimathia, who begged Christ's body from Pilate and arranged for its burial. In creating this pre-history of the Grail, he also invented the concept of a dynasty of the Grail, whose destiny was bound up with the sacred relic. But his work, which we admittedly only have in incomplete form, has no other agenda than to link this episode of Arthurian romance with a Biblical past, and perhaps to echo some of the Eucharistic ideas of his time. There is no moral in his version from which secular knighthood might profit.

The author of the *Queste* took the physical history of the Grail as described by Robert de Boron, and turned it into a spiritual history, the history both of the Grail and of the three knights who 'achieve' the quest. In so doing, he picked up one of Chrétien's major themes, Perceval's moral and spiritual development. Furthermore, he provided a new hero, Galahad, descended not only from the

---

14 'Tant sainte chose': Chrétien de Troyes, *Le roman de Perceval, ou, le conte du Graal de Chrétien de Troyes*, ed. Keith Busby (Tübingen, 1993), line 6425.

15 Francesco Zambon, *Roberto de Boron e i segreti del Graal* (Florence, 1984), pp. 16–17.

lineage of David and of the guardians of the Grail, but from Lancelot, the peer-less secular knight. The new hero has Lancelot's baptismal name, Galaad. The name Galaad occurs in the *Song of Songs* (mount Galaad), and a Cistercian commentary says of it, 'This mountain is the head of the church.'[16] We are in a world where the haphazard excitements and adventures of the earlier romances are replaced by carefully orchestrated symbols. But why should we assume that the *Queste* is Cistercian? Any religious writer could on the face of it have reworked the romance in this symbolic vein, but there are good reasons which argue for a Cistercian author. At the most obvious level, the order itself – whose habit was white – is prominent in one respect; as the knights pursue the Grail quest and come to different abbeys, those which are identified as belonging to a specific order are always named as being houses of white monks.

More important, however, is the demonstrably Cistercian element in the theology behind the *Queste*. Etienne Gilson analysed the ideas put forward in the romance, and showed that the crucial doctrine of grace is couched in terms used by the Cistercian theologians of the period.[17] In his words, 'we acknowl-edge that the *Queste* is an abstract and systematic work, to the extent that we can hardly promise to find ten consecutive lines written simply for the pleasure of telling a tale.'[18] There are none of the gratuitous adventures found elsewhere in the romances – of which the first appearance of the Grail itself in Chrétien is a prime example. Each scene is composed as a symbol, and the whole romance is infested by hermits, whose function is to explain both to the protagonists and the reader the spiritual import of the events that unfold before them.

In Chrétien's romance, Perceval moves from untutored simpleton to some degree of self-knowledge and maturity before the text breaks off. In the *Queste*, by contrast, any odyssey is purely spiritual, and even then Galahad does not progress from innocence to a state of grace so much as lead the way for his companions, Perceval and Bohort, the two other heroes of the story. Galahad is perfect from the start, and possesses spiritual qualities which both set him apart and enable him to guide the others. The quest adventures merely set the seal on what we already know: that he is perfect, and is indeed a type of Christ himself.

But this does not mean that there is nothing to be learnt from his example. Gilson argues that the *Queste* is about approaching God through feeling (senti-ment) rather than intellectual knowledge, and that the keynote of the adventures is grace and its action on the soul. One of the innumerable hermits explains a dream, in which Lancelot attempts to drink from a spring which disappears as he kneels to slake his thirst, by saying that the spring which 'can never be emptied, no matter how much one might take from it . . . is the Holy Grail, the grace of the Holy Spirit' (*Queste*, Lacy 159). Lancelot cannot drink from it, because he has sinned.

The Cistercian doctrine of grace provides the dramatic tension of the romance because, in Bernard of Clairvaux's analysis, free will can co-exist with grace:

16 Albert Pauphilet, *Etudes sur la Queste del Saint Graal attribuée à Gautier Map* (Paris, 1980), p. 137.
17 Etienne Gilson, *Les Idées et les Lettres* (Paris, 1932), pp. 59–91.
18 Gilson, *Les Idées*, pp. 60–1.

although in a sense Galahad, Perceval and Bohort are predestined to achieve the Grail – and there are signs and symbols to remind us of this – each is ultimately a free agent, possessing free will. As another hermit tells Bohort, who has likened a man's heart to the helm of a ship, 'the helm has a master who holds and guides it . . . making it go where he wants. It is the same with a man's heart. His good deeds come from the grace and guidance of the Holy Spirit; his evil deeds are instigated by the Devil' (*Queste*, Lacy 165).

The adventures, therefore, are seen as a series of tests, in which the Grail knights must accept the action of grace if they are to succeed. The dramatic tension lies in the choice, the question of whether the hero will perform the right action. This fits well with the traditional adventures of chivalric romance, but substitutes a moral choice for the often arbitrary key to the secular versions of such episodes.

But to portray the *Queste* as a relentless sermon by example is to do it an injustice. The author is by no means rigid in his approach: a subtle theologian might detect the operation of grace in an episode such as Perceval's escape from the temptress. As he gets into bed with the lady, 'he happened to catch sight of his sword, which the servants had ungirded earlier, lying on the floor. As he stretched out his hand to grasp the sword, intending to rest it against the bed, he saw the red cross engraved on the pommel. That brought him to his senses. He crossed himself, and watched the tent fall away as smoke and fog surrounded him; it was so thick, he could see nothing, and such a strong odor emanated from everywhere that Perceval thought he was in hell' (*Queste*, Lacy 36). Equally, there is direct divine intervention, as when God prevents Bohort from fighting his brother Lionel; and we have already touched on the way in which Galahad is shown as a kind of Christ-figure. On the other side there are varying degrees of sinfulness, from Gawain's refusal to repent and Lionel's obdurate violence against his own brother, to Lancelot's efforts to free himself from Guinevere.

The author of the *Queste* is not simply using the framework of romance to put across a religious viewpoint. His grounding is in Cistercian theology, and in some ways both the weakest and strongest passages in the book stem from this: at one extreme are the sometimes laborious expositions of the meaning of the knights' adventures, and at the other the mystical vision of the scenes at Sarras when the Grail is finally achieved.

The *Queste* is carefully integrated into the cycle of romances, yet, as Malory sensed when he came to translate it, it does not confront entirely the problems that this causes, notably in the case of Lancelot. Galahad's birth is wrought by magic, and he is illegitimate; and at the end of the *Queste*, Lancelot goes back to his old sin. This makes the *Queste* seem like a journey into a different world, and the problem of the relationship of this highly religious and symbolic text to the rest of the *Lancelot-Grail Cycle* has not yet been satisfactorily analysed. The concept of using the romances to put across a theological viewpoint is not unique to the *Queste*. The *Perlesvaus* is equally concerned with theology, if of a cruder and less subtle sort: the topos here is not grace, but the role of the warrior in enforcing God's law, and bringing about the triumph of the New Law of the New Testament rather than that of the Old Law of heathendom and Judaism. The contrast between the two romances is instructive: *Perlesvaus* is the product of a baroque, violent, even grotesque imagination; the author's failure to think through his material leads to weaknesses of structure and uncertainty as to his intentions. It is a darker and wilder vision, in which the Grail plays a minor role. The disciplined world of the *Queste*, on the other hand, reflects closely both the spiritual world of the Cistercians and their links with the secular aristocracy, and enshrines the supreme vision of the Grail itself as the mystery of the Eucharist, a moment which is the spiritual climax of the Arthurian stories.

The *Estoire del Saint Graal* forms a 'prequel' to the *Queste*; it is almost certainly by another, later hand. It is often dismissed as of relatively little merit or interest and the events it recounts are hardly the stuff of romance; but, seen as an attempt by a religious writer to mold a secular form to his own ends, it has some remarkable features. The *Estoire* is full of religious echoes and images, and yet its religious milieu is not easy to establish. Stylistically it is not by the same hand as the *Queste*, but it is arguably also a work with a Cistercian background.

Its function is to provide a kind of Old Testament to the New Testament of the *Queste*, in that its narrative prefigures the events of the *Queste* in the same way that medieval theologians read the Old Testament as a foreshadowing of the New. It also provides the history of some of the objects central to the Grail quest, such as the ship of Solomon which carries the chosen heroes on their journey towards Carbonek, the Grail castle, at the end of their adventures. In terms of prefiguration, we find Josephus wounded in the thigh, like the Fisher King (*Estoire*, Lacy 49); Evalach undergoes a version of Perceval's temptation by the devil in female form (*Estoire*, Lacy 62–3); and there is a spiritual version of the love of Lancelot and Guinevere (*Estoire*, Lacy 162). The name of the Fisher King is explained (*Estoire*, Lacy 140), and we learn how Mordrain, whom Galahad releases from his pain in the *Queste*, came to be struck down with paralysis (*Estoire*, Lacy 138).

The concept of prefiguration is a commonplace of medieval theology, but there are a few other indicators. Much play is made of the virginity of Mary, and Lucian, a pagan philosopher who denies the possibility of the virgin birth, is struck dead (*Estoire*, Lacy 125). This emphasis on the role of Mary in the preaching of Joseph and his followers when they attempt to convert pagans to Christianity could arguably be due to Cistercian influence. Bernard of Clairvaux and other writers from the order (including Hélinand de Froidmont, to whom we owe the one reference to the Grail in medieval theological literature) were ardent champions of the Virgin. The vision of Josephus (*Estoire*, Lacy 23–28) might also indicate something of the author's background: it belongs to a mystic and apocalyptic tradition, and it has been argued that this is related to the writing of Joachim of Fiore, the Cistercian visionary of the late twelfth century.[19] The *Estoire* also contains an account of the first Eucharist, celebrated by Joseph of Arimathia, and the description of the service includes the ritual of 'ostentation,'

---

[19] Myrrha Lot-Borodine, 'Autour du Saint Graal,' *Romania*, 56 (1930), 526–57, examines the arguments of Eugène Anitchkof (*Romania*, 55 [1929]), who sees a strong Joachimite and Cathar influence; she admits that there are elements of Joachimite writings in the *Estoire*, but places the work in a more general Cistercian milieu. I would not go as far as she does in tentatively attributing the work to a Templar (556), given that there is very little evidence of literary activity of any sort among the religious orders of knighthood.

officially introduced by the Lateran Council in 1215, which implies some degree of special theological knowledge.

But the *Estoire* remains, despite its close relationship to the apocryphal Gospels, very much a romance. One of the most striking episodes is at the outset, when the book of the Grail, which has been given to a hermit by an angel, vanishes. The hermit sets out like a knight errant in quest of the book, guided by a strange creature, part sheep, part dog, part fox, with a lion's tail (*Estoire*, Lacy 6–9), and his adventures are typical of a knight-errant's adventures. Likewise, when Josephus is instituted as the first bishop, the text echoes the speech of the Lady of the Lake on knighthood when Lancelot is knighted, and the instruction given by Merlin to Arthur when he is crowned.

In the *Estoire* and the *Queste*, the knightly conventions of the romances are transmogrified into something as hybrid as the strange beast of the hermit's adventure; we are left wondering if we are reading the work of a monk with a lively secular imagination, or that of a devout layman wishing to adapt his favorite reading to a higher purpose. Perhaps the latter is not such a remote possibility; the mystical tradition which inspires the pages relating the culmination of the Grail quest was one in which the laity partook, and which, like the legend of the Grail, was sometimes an unofficial cult, at one remove from the official teachings of the Church. Equally, the Cistercians were the one monastic order with a special involvement in secular knighthood, and whether we are looking for a monk or a layman as author, it is to this milieu, at once chivalrous and religious, that he is most likely to have belonged.

2

The Making of the Lancelot-Grail Cycle

ELSPETH KENNEDY

The *Lancelot-Grail Cycle* as we know it was not fully planned from the start. It is generally acknowledged that the *Estoire del Saint Graal* and the *Estoire de Merlin* were later additions to the *Cycle*, carefully presented to prepare the way for later events.[1] However, the development of the romance from the account of the childhood of Lancelot, beginning 'En la marche de Gaule et de la Petite Bretaigne' (*LK* 1) [In the borderland between Gaul and Brittany],[2] to the death of Arthur has given rise to greater controversy. In contrast with some early scholars such as Brugger and Bruce who ascribed a major role to vanished cycles or interpolators,[3] Ferdinand Lot stressed the careful links made between the various branches and argued that a single author wrote the *Cycle*, apart from the *Merlin*,[4] Jean Frappier maintained that an 'architect' had planned the *Cycle* from the account of Lancelot's childhood to the death of Arthur.[5] Micha too argues for the unity of the *Cycle*.[6]

One of the remarkable features of the *Cycle* is indeed its complex interlacing structure, achieved by creating links between its various branches; but there are

1   See *L'Estoire del Saint Graal*, ed. Jean-Paul Ponceau, 2 vols. (Paris, 1997). In the introduction, pp. x–xlv, the date of this branch and its relationship with the rest of the *Lancelot-Grail Cycle* is discussed. The *Estoire de Merlin* branch of the *Cycle* consists of a prose version of Robert de Boron's *Merlin* followed by a *Merlin Continuation*. For a discussion of the Robert de Boron part of the text, see Robert de Boron, *Merlin: Roman du XIIIe siècle*, ed. Alexandre Micha (Geneva, 1980). For the whole text, see *The Vulgate Version of the Arthurian Romances*, 7 vols., ed. H. Oskar Sommer, vol. II: *L'Estoire de Merlin* (Washington, D.C., 1908–1912).
2   For the translation of the Old French texts I have based myself, where possible, on *Lancelot-Grail: The Old French Arthurian Vulgate in Translation*, ed. Norris J. Lacy, 5 vols. (New York, 1993–96). *LK*: see n. 7 below.
3   Ernst Brugger, 'L'Enserrement Merlin: Studien zur Merlinsage,' *Zeitschrift für französische Sprache und Literatur*, 29 (1906), 169–239; 31 (1907), 239–81; 33 (1908), 145–94; 34 (1909), 99–150; 35 (1910), 1–55. J. D. Bruce, 'The Composition of the Old French Prose *Lancelot*,' *Romanic Review*, 9 (1918), 241–68 and 353–95; 10 (1919), 48–66 and 97–122. J. D. Bruce, *Evolution of Arthurian Romance*, 2nd ed., 2 vols. (Göttingen and Baltimore, 1928).
4   Ferdinand Lot, *Etude sur le Lancelot en prose* (Paris, 1918).
5   Jean Frappier, *Etude sur la Mort le roi Artu*, 2nd ed. (Geneva, 1968), esp. the appendix, 'Genèse et unité de structure du *Lancelot* en prose (essai de mise en point).' Jean Frappier, 'Plaidoyer pour "l'architecte" contre une opinion d'Albert Pauphilet sur le *Lancelot en prose*,' *Romance Philology*, 8 (1954–55), 27–33. Albert Pauphilet, *Le Legs du Moyen Age* (Melun, 1950), pp. 212–27.
6   Alexandre Micha, 'L'esprit du *Lancelot-Graal*,' *Romania*, 82 (1961), 357–78; 'Sur la composition du *Lancelot en prose*,' in *Mélanges Lecoy* (Paris, 1973), pp. 417–425; *Essais sur le Lancelot-Graal* (Geneva, 1987).

problems in relation to the theory of an uninterrupted development of the story of Lancelot, with a son Galahad designed from the beginning to be the chief Grail hero. This can be clearly shown through a study of the manuscript tradition in relation to a passage to be found early in the account of Lancelot's childhood and which lists the three most beautiful women. The first was Guinevere, and the second Helene san Per, who figures in an adventure of Hector before Lancelot becomes a knight of the Round Table. In MS Paris, Bibliothèque Nationale de France, fr. 768, the third is described as follows:

> Et l'autre fu fille au roi mehaignié, ce fu li rois Pellés qui fu peres Perlesvax, a celui qui vit apertement les granz merveilles del Graal et acompli lo Siege Perilleus de la Table Reonde et mena a fin les aventures del Reiaume Perilleus Aventureus, ce fu li regnes de Logres. Cele fu sa suer, si fu de si grant biauté que nus des contes ne dit que nule qui a son tens fust se poïst de biauté a li apareillier, si avoit non Amide en sornon et an son droit non Heliabel.[7]

> [And the other was the daughter of the maimed king, that was Pelles who was father of Perlesvaus, of the man who witnessed the great wonders of the Grail and passed the test of the Perilous Seat of the Round Table and brought to an end the adventures of the danger-filled Perilous Kingdom, that was the land of Logres. She was his sister and was so beautiful that none of the tales name anyone at that time whose beauty could be compared with hers; she was called Amide, but her true name was Heliabel.]

BNF fr. 768 is not isolated here: in the majority of manuscripts it is Perceval/Perlesvaus, not Galahad, who is identified as the achiever of the Grail adventures and the Perilous Seat.[8] The allusion, which appears to be to a past event, presents a combination of elements from Chrétien's *Conte del Graal*, where Perceval seems clearly destined to be the Grail winner and has a maimed, unnamed father, and Robert de Boron's *Joseph* and *Merlin*, where there is a Perilous Seat at both the Grail Table and the Round Table.

A number of manuscripts attempt to change the reading in various ways to prepare for the *Queste*, which, of course, gives Galahad as chief Grail winner and achiever of the adventure of the Perilous Seat. This includes MS British Library, Additional 10293, the manuscript on which both the edition of Sommer and that of Micha vols. 7 and 8 are based and which reads as follows:

> Et l'autre fu fille au Roi Mahaignié, che fu li rois Pellés qui fu peires a Amite, meire Galaat, chelui qui vit apertement les grans mervelles del Graal et acompli le siege perillous de la Table Reonde et mena a fin les aventures del roialme

---

[7] *Lancelot do Lac: The non-cyclic Old French Prose Romance*, ed. Elspeth Kennedy, 2 vols. (Oxford, 1980), henceforth abbreviated to *LK* (vol. 1 unless otherwise indicated). The passage is on p. 33. The equivalent passage, but with a different reading, is at 7:59–60 in the edition of Alexandre Micha, *Lancelot: roman du XIIIe siècle*, 9 vols. (Geneva, 1978–83), henceforth abbreviated to *LM*.

[8] Twenty-two manuscripts give Perlesvaus/Perceval as seeing *apertement* the marvels of the Grail and achieving the adventure of the Perilous Seat (two of these have corrections inserted over the original reading); this reading is not confined to one or two groups of manuscripts but goes across all groupings except one, that to which MS Paris, BNF fr. 110 belongs (see n. 9 below). For details, see *LK* 2:89.

perelleus et aventureus, che fu li roialmes de Logres. Cele fu sa suer (Micha emends here to 'sa meire'), si fu de si grant biauté.

[The other was the daughter of the Maimed King, that is King Pelles, and she was Amite, the mother of Galahad; Galahad was the knight who witnessed the great wonders of the Grail and passed the test of the Perilous Seat at the Round Table and brought an end to the adventures of the danger-filled and adventurous realm that was the kingdom of Logres. The woman who was his sister was of such great beauty.]

However, it is clear from a study of the variants that Perceval/Perlesvaus was the original reading.[9]

The other Grail references within the account of Lancelot's early adventures up to the time when he was received under his own name at Arthur's court and became a Knight of the Round Table also appear to be referring to a Grail adventure already told. It is true that the name Galaaz occurs twice. Near the beginning of the romance the author explains that Lancelot is only a *sorenon* and that his baptismal name was Galaaz:

Et avoit non Lanceloz en sorenon, mais il avoit non an baptaisme Galaaz. Et ce par quoi il fu apelez Lanceloz ce devisera bien li contes ça avant, car li leus n'i est ores mies ne la raisons. (*LK* 1; *LM* 7:1)

[His baptismal name was Galahad but he was called Lancelot. Why he was called Lancelot the story will explain later on, for this is not the time or place.

The promise to explain why he is called Lancelot is fulfilled in one way during Lancelot's first adventures, in the episode in which Lancelot *discovers* his own *sorenon*, inscribed beneath the slab in the marvellous cemetery of the Dolorous Guard, and thereby earns the right to be called by it (*LK* 194; *LM* 7:332). This promise is fulfilled in a different way once the Grail Quest is explicitly incorporated within the Lancelot story.[10] The name Galaaz/Galahaz is also given to

---

9 Twelve manuscripts refer to Galaad/Galaaz/Galaaus as Grail winner, but a number of these are confused over the relationship between Pellés, Galahad, and Amide; two manuscripts have no mention of the adventure of the Perilous Seat. For details, see *LK* 2:89; to the manuscripts listed there which correct to Galahad, under various spellings, should be added an ex-Phillips manuscript, MS Amsterdam, Bibliotheca Philosophica Hermetica, 1, a member of the group to which the Bonn manuscript, University Library, 526 (82) and the Paris manuscript, BNF fr.110 belong. For a discussion of the attempts at correction to prepare for a Grail winner to come, see Kennedy, 'The Scribe as Editor,' in *Mélanges Jean Frappier*, 2 vols. (Geneva, 1970), pp. 523–31, and 'Le *Lancelot* en prose (MS 45),' in *Les manuscrits français de la bibliothèque Parker: Actes du Colloque 24–27 mars 1993*, ed. Nigel Wilkins (Cambridge, 1993), pp. 23–38. Alexandre Micha, 'La tradition manuscrite du *Lancelot en prose*,' *Romania*, 85 (1964), 297–8 [293–318], would interpret as the original reading that of the group including Bonn, 526 and BNF fr. 110, which identifies the Grail winner as Galahad (under various spellings), Pellés as his *aieul* and Amide as his mother; but this group makes a practice of correcting inconsistencies in the *Cycle*, and the Perlesvaus/Perceval reading of the majority of manuscripts is not confined to one or two groups, which provides strong evidence for its authenticity. Frappier, *Etude*, p. 454, suggests that originally the allusion was to Galahad, but that there was a scribal correction in the archetype; however, this would not fit in with the type of correction or interpolation to be found in the manuscript tradition.

10 For this less flattering explanation of Lancelot's change of name to be found in stage 2 of the

Joseph of Arimathia's son, who, like his father, is listed by the Lady of the Lake as one of the good knights of the past: 'Si an fu ses filz Galahaz, li hauz rois de Hosselice, qui puis fu apelee Gales en l'anor de lui' (*LK* 146; *LM* 7:256) [And one of those was his son Galahad, the great King of Hosselice, later called Wales in his honor]. The link with Gales is interesting as there is frequent interaction during Lancelot's childhood and first adventures with the story of Perceval as told by Chrétien de Troyes, where the hero is identified as Perceval li Galois.[11] This list of great knights contains other names linked with the Grail tradition, and note here both the reference to Perles or Pelles de Listenois in the past tense as someone no longer alive, a reference which would conflict with the role he is given in the *Queste*:

> Si an fu li rois Perles de Listenois, qui encor estoit de celui lignage li plus hauz qant il vivoit (*LK* 1:46; *LM* 7:256)

> [There was King Pelles of Listenois, who was also of that line and the greatest of them all in his lifetime]

There are other references to the Grail or to figures associated with it, and to events in Arthur's reign; these serve to link the story of Lancelot with existing twelfth- or early thirteenth-century narratives and to present it as part of a wider 'Arthurian reality.'[12]

The romance does not therefore at this stage seem to be leading up to Grail adventures, and there is indeed a group of manuscripts which brings Lancelot's story to an end without a Grail quest or a death of Arthur. BNF fr. 768 (dated by the library as early thirteenth century) is generally acknowledged to provide the best early text of the tale of Lancelot from his childhood to his installation as a Knight of the Round Table (*LK* 1–572, line 4; *LM* 7 and 8). It then gives a version of Lancelot's journey away from Arthur's court with his friend Galehot who, at Lancelot's request, had surrendered to Arthur at the moment when the king had been defeated and was preparing to make a last stand. On this journey, Galehot sees his castles crumble and has strange dreams and visions. Arthur's clerks are sent for and interpret what he has seen as foretelling his death within three years because of his love for Lancelot; they make no reference to a Grail quest to come. These events preparing the way for Galehot's death are combined with a short version of the False Guinevere episode in which the queen is accused of being an impostor and is defended against this charge by Lancelot. This version of the romance brings the story to an end with Lancelot's decision to return to Arthur's court, and with Galehot's death as the result of a false rumour of his friend's death. The last folio of BNF fr. 768 is missing, but the end of the story is to be found in two other manuscripts (Rouen, Bibliothèque municipale, 1055 (06), and

---

development of the *Cycle*, see *LM* 4:211, and Elspeth Kennedy, *Lancelot and the Grail* (Oxford, 1986), p. 279.

11 For the interaction between the story of Perceval, that of Lancelot and that of *le Bel Desconneu*, see Kennedy, *Lancelot and the Grail*, 22–26, and 'Lancelot und Perceval: Zwei junge unbekannte Helden,' *Wolfram Studien*, 9 (1985), 228–41.

12 See Kennedy, *Lancelot and the Grail*, ch. 6, and 'Etudes sur le *Lancelot* en prose, I: Les allusions au *conte Lancelot* et à d'autres contes dans le *Lancelot* en prose,' *Romania*, 105 (1984), 34–46.

Florence, Biblioteca Mediceo-Laurenziana, Laur. 89. inf. 61). These manuscripts, having described Lancelot's great grief that his friend and benefactor has 'por lui mort receue,' conclude thus:

> Ensi est remés avoc lo roi. Si tast atant li contes de lui, que plus n'en parole, car bien a a chief menees totes les avantures qi li avindrent puis qe la reine Helaine, qui sa mere fu, lo perdié par l'aventure que cist livres conta el comencement. Ne li contes ne viaut amentevoir dont il corrompist la matire. Por ce si a racontees totes les avantures q'il mena a fin jusq'a ceste ore ensi com eles furent contees en l'ostel lo roi Artu et l'estoire de ses faiz lo nos tesmoigne.[13] (*LK* 613; *LM* 3:69)

> [Thus he remained with the king. The tale now falls silent having related all the adventures he had since his mother Queen Helaine lost him as was recounted at the beginning of this book. Nor will the tale give anything which would falsify the true record. For this reason it has related all the adventures he achieved till that time as they were told in the household of King Arthur and to which the account of his deeds bears witness.]

This short pre-cyclic version of the journey to Galehot's land and the False Guinevere episode, followed by Lyonel's knighting and the death of Galehot, is given in whole or in part in fifteen manuscripts.[14]

In this first version of *le conte Lancelot*, the love between Lancelot and Guinevere is presented only in positive terms as an inspiration for Lancelot's great deeds. Lancelot, when he confesses his love to Guinevere, explains what her words 'A Deu, biaus douz amis' had meant to him as he left court on his first adventures:

> 'Ce fu li moz qui prodome me fera se gel suis. Ne onques puis ne vign an si grant meschief que de cest mot ne me manbrast. Cist moz m'a conforté an toz mes anuiz, cist moz m'a de toz mes maus garantiz et m'a gari de toz perilz; cist moz m'a saolé an totes mes fains, cist moz m'a fait riche an totes mes granz povretez.'
> (*LK* 345–46; *LM* 8:111)

> ['Those were the words that made me a worthy knight, if I am one; never have I been so badly off that I did not remember those words. They comfort me in all my troubles; they have kept me from all evil and saved me from all dangers; those words satisfied me in all my hunger, and made me rich in my great poverty.']

The Lady of the Lake admits: ' "Ne li pechié do siegle ne puent estre mené sanz folie" ' ['The sins of the world cannot be pursued without folly'], but continues, 'mais mout a grant raison de sa folie qui raison i trove et annor. Et se vos poez folie trover an voz amors, ceste folie est desor totes les autres annoree, car vos amez la seignorie et la flor de tot cest monde' (*LK* 557; *LM* 8:461) ['but he defeats his folly who finds right and honor in it. And if you can find folly in your

---

[13] 'Ne li contes ne viaut amentevoir . . . lo tesmoigne.' For a similar concluding formula, see Chrétien's *Yvain*.

[14] For details of the manuscripts giving at least part of this version, see *LK* 2:36–7 and 379–80. In addition to the manuscripts listed there, MS Amsterdam, Bibliotheca Philosophica Hermetica (see n. 9) is, for this part of the text, closely related to BL Add. 10293.

loves, this folly is to be honored above all others, for you love the lord and the flower of the whole world'].

When Guinevere hears that she has been accused of being an impostor, she is filled with grief: 'car mout a grant paor que por aucun pechié que ele ait fait ça en arrieres voille Nostres Sires que soit honie et deshonoree en terre' (LK 595; LM 3:39) [for she is very much afraid that because of some sin that she has committed in the past it is God's will that she should be shamed and dishonored in this world]. But there is no explicit reference to a particular sin.

Great care is also taken to avoid a clash of loyalties between Lancelot's love for the queen and his obligations to Arthur. From the beginning it is stressed that Lancelot's father Ban of Benoyc, a vassal of Arthur, fought hard to remain true to his lord and set off to seek help from him. Arthur, because of various troubles early in his reign, was unable to come to Ban's aid or to avenge his death. The king is reproached for his failure in a number of passages, although care is taken not to present him as such a useless king that a seat at the Round Table is devalued.[15] Thus he is contrasted favorably with Claudas; Galehot may be praised as a great prince (LK 264; LM 7:440–41), and may through Lancelot's help be on the point of victory over Arthur, but he too is later criticised for his too great ambition (LK 582; LM 3:20). Lancelot holds no land from Arthur and saves his kingdom on two occasions – from Galehot and from the Saxons. Arthur has, in a way, failed Lancelot, son of his loyal vassal, but this failure has stemmed from extreme pressure from the king's enemies early in his reign. References outwards to the chronicle tradition (LK 33, 53, 56, 180–81; LM 7:60, 96, 100–01, 308–09) link up with the heroic and active king of Geoffrey of Monmouth, Wace, and in a different way, Robert de Boron, counteracting the more passive figure evoked by other episodes (LK 296–97, 359–60, 206–207; LM 8:35–36, 134–35; 7: 351–52) recalling the inactive figure of Arthur characteristic of a number of scenes in Chrétien de Troyes.[16] Lancelot's loss of father and land is also linked to the theme of the quest for identity (another link with Chrétien, where it is a recurring theme), one which is important in the tale of Lancelot up to the revelation of his name at Arthur's court, when Gauvain reveals the name of the unknown knight to the king after Lancelot has saved Arthur and his kingdom from the Saxons. The quest-for-identity theme (already suggested by a series of parallels with Chrétien's Conte del Graal) is also picked up in a series of adventures involving Gauvain who, on a quest for Lancelot, is, as an anonymous knight, taken as an unworthy substitute for himself to defend a lady's cause and has to prove his right to his own reputation (LK 371–93; LM 8:154–90). Both identity theme and love theme are also explored in relation to Hector, young knight and lover, who has to establish his reputation in a series of adventures, here with echoes from some of Lancelot's adventures related earlier in the text (LK 221–3 and 425–32; 173 and 428; 275, 279 and 471–2; LM 7:374–7 and

[15] See Elspeth Kennedy, 'Etudes sur le Lancelot en prose, II: Le roi Arthur dans le Lancelot en prose,' Romania, 105 (1984), 46–62; also Lancelot and the Grail, 80–6 and 225–31.
[16] See Elspeth Kennedy, 'Royal Broodings and Lovers' Trances in the First Part of the Old French Prose Lancelot,' in Mélanges Jeanne Wathelet-Willem (Liège, 1978), pp. 301–14.

8:243–55; 7:296 and 8:248; 7:456–7 and 8:7 and 8:321–2) as well as from Chrétien's *Conte del Graal*.[17]

There is therefore, at this stage in Lancelot's story, no questioning of the establishment of his name as the greatest of all knights through the inspiration of his love for Arthur's queen – that is, in the account of Lancelot's adventures until he becomes a knight of the Round Table (an account common to all manuscripts), nor in the version of Lancelot's journey to the land of Galehot, the False Guinevere episode, and the death of Galehot to be found in BNF fr. 768 and the other manuscripts discussed above.

The next stage in the development of the *Cycle* is represented by the rewriting of these last mentioned episodes. This is done in terms which prepare for the incorporation of a Grail Quest with a new hero, Galahad, as well as a new prose version of the abduction of Guinevere by Meleagant and her rescue by Lancelot. There is a series of dreams and portents that foretell not only Galehot's death but also the displacement of Lancelot as the greatest knight by his son, unnamed at this point, and who will be, unlike his father, pure and virgin, and thus able to achieve the greatest adventure of all, that of the Grail. Lancelot's love for Guinevere is no longer presented in wholly positive terms – the interpretation of Galehot's visions by Arthur's learned clerks reveals this. For example, Helie explains to Galehot that in one of his dreams a leopard who is less successful than a lion is Lancelot, who will fail to achieve the greatest adventure of all, that of the Grail, because he is not virgin and chaste:

'Cist ne porroit recovrer les taiches que cil avra qui l'aventure del Graal achevera, kar il covient tot premierement qu'il soit de sa nativité jusqu'a sa mort virges et chastes si entierement qu'il n'ait amor n'a dame n'a damoisele. Et cist nel puet ore avoir, kar je sai greignor partie de son conseil que vos ne cuidiés.'

(*LM* 1:53)[18]

['He cannot regain the qualities needed by the one who will complete the adventure of the Grail. Above all, that man must be, from birth to death, so utterly virginal and chaste as never to feel love for a woman, married or not. For your companion it is too late, for I know more about what goes on in his mind than you think.']

Guinevere herself now explains the ordeal she has to go through in relation to the impostor as a punishment for her sin with Lancelot (*LM* 1:152). But in Lancelot's adventures following the False Guinevere episode and preceding Galehot's death, the quality of his love for Guinevere enables him to achieve certain adventures. For example, only Lancelot can free the knights trapped in the Val sans Retor, also called the Val as Faus Amans, because only a knight who has always been true to his *amie* in everything can put an end to the enchantments (*LM* 1:277).

---

[17] See Kennedy, *Lancelot and the Grail*, ch. 2, and pp. 231–5.
[18] The translation of 'n'a dame n'a damoisele' poses problems. The Garland translation renders it as 'a woman, married or not,' but in this period and in this romance *dame* as opposed to *damoisele* often means 'of higher rank' rather than married as opposed to unmarried status. See *LK* 2:268 and 422.

This rewriting of the events leading up to Galehot's death to be found in
LM 1, prepares the way, therefore, for the incorporation of some of the main
twelfth-century Arthurian themes within this story of Lancelot: that is the
abduction and rescue of Guinevere, a Grail quest with a new Grail winner
(Galahad, son of Lancelot). The branches of the romance which follow (*LM* 2, 4,
5, 6 [vol. 3 contains the short cyclic version of vol. 1]) both link up with the past
by picking up and sometimes reinterpreting elements in earlier adventures, and
look forward to events in the last two branches. For example, Lancelot, imprisoned by Morgain la Fee, paints earlier episodes in his career, encouraged by
Morgain, who plans to make use of them (*LM* 5:52–54 and *La Mort le roi Artu*).[19]
In the *Queste del saint Graal* which functions on an allegorical level, Lancelot's
earlier adventures are reinterpreted and his love for Guinevere is given a fully
negative force. However, it is made clear near the beginning of the *Queste* that
the meaning given to events there are valid only during the *aventures dou Saint
Graal*, for a learned monk is only willing to attribute a *senefiance* to the misfortunes of Melyant when he has been told that the Quest for the Grail has
started.[20] The *Mort Artu*, in which Lancelot's love for Guinevere has such disas-
trous consequences, was already being prepared for in the rewriting of the narrative leading up to Galehot's death. There is a reference forward to
unsuccessful attempts to cause a rift between Arthur and Lancelot (*LM* 1:171).
This prepares the way for the plotting by Gauvain's brothers to cause trouble
between Lancelot and Arthur in the *Mort Artu*, plotting which recalls that of the
barons in the twelfth-century versions of the Tristan story (those represented by
Beroul, Eilhart and Thomas). The tragic effect of the love, thrust in Arthur's face
through the jealous machinations of Gauvain's brothers, is foreshadowed by the
prophecy before the beginning of the *Queste*, where it is said of Arthur's great
love for Lancelot:

> Ne ja jor de lor vie cele grant amor ne fust departie, se ne fust Agravains
> l'orguillex et Mordrez qui par lor grant envie distrent puis au roi que Lanceloz li
> faisoit honte et deshonor de sa fame qu'il maintenoit par derriere lui (*LM* par
> delez lui).[21] Si an distrent tant que li grant parenté le roi torna a mort et a destruc-
> tion. (*LM* 6:15)

> [And that great love would never have ceased, had it not been for Agravain the
> Proud and Mordred, who, moved by great envy, later told the king that Lancelot
> had brought him shame and dishonor through his wife, with whom he was
> maintaining illicit relations behind the king's back. They said so much that the
> king's great line was brought to death and destruction.]

---

19 *La Mort le roi Artu: roman du XIIIe siècle*, ed. Jean Frappier, 3rd ed. (Geneva and Paris, 1964),
p. 61.
20 *La Queste del saint Graal, roman du XIIIe siècle*, ed. Albert Pauphilet (Paris, 1921), p. 44.
21 The meaning of Micha's reading *delez lui* in this context is not clear, so I have followed the
example of the Garland translation, 3:282, n. 13, and taken the reading given in a note to
Sommer's edition, 5:317, n. 2, *par derriere lui*, to be found in the British Library manuscripts,
Royal 20.C.VI, Royal 20.B.VIII, Harley 6342. I have also clarified the meaning given to
maintenir in this particular context, translating it as 'maintaining illicit sexual relations with'
(see Tobler-Lommatzsch, *Altfranzösisches Wörterbuch*, vol. 5, col. 843) rather than as 'keeping'
in the Garland translation.

The destructive force of the love is also emphasised through a link up with the earlier episode mentioned above in which Lancelot, in Morgain's prison, paints scenes of his past life which she, even at that time, was planning to use to make trouble. In the *Mort Artu*, she shows Lancelot's paintings to Arthur; in her commentary on them she underlines the adulterous elements and presents Lancelot's love for Guinevere as a wholly negative force. However, when Lancelot hands Guinevere back to Arthur, he reminds him of the great services he has rendered the king (true, but for Lancelot it is his love for the queen that inspired him to achieve what he did). Lancelot also denies that he is guilty of *fole amor*, of which he gives no definition – another Tristan echo.[22]

There is, therefore, in this second stage in the development of the prose romance, a careful interweaving of events from the account of Lancelot's child-hood and his adventures up to his installation as a knight of the Round Table right through to the *Mort Artu*. In the third stage, Lancelot's story is linked to the early history of the Grail by the addition of *L'Estoire*, containing elements from Robert de Boron but redesigned to link up with *Queste*, already part of the *Cycle*. The *Merlin* is also added, based closely on Robert de Boron's work but with a *Merlin Continuation* which, amongst other things, prepares the way for the wars in which Ban, father of Lancelot, loses his land and his life.[23] This development of the *Cycle* in stages, a process in which the only major rewriting of an element in the first stage is to be found in the cyclic version of the journey away from Arthur's court by Lancelot and Galehot and the False Guinevere episode, in general produces a structured narrative through the reinterpretation of earlier episodes in the light of later events.[24]

However, there are some factual inconsistencies to be found in the majority of manuscripts that later scribes have endeavoured to remove with varying success. The most obvious example of this is the Grail-winner passage referred to earlier, where a number of different scribes have striven to reconcile it with what is to come.[25] The birth of Merlin as narrated in the account of Lancelot's childhood also constitutes a problem, once the *Merlin* is added, or even in manu-scripts without a *Merlin* but which are attempting to place the Lancelot story within the framework of existing tradition in terms of Robert de Boron. In order to present the Lady of the Lake in as favourable a light as possible, given that she is to be responsible for the education of Lancelot, her magical powers are explained in terms not of knowledge inherent in a supernatural being but of

---

22 *Mort Artu*, 157–60; cf. Beroul, *Romance of Tristan*, vv. 496–502.

23 For the relative chronology of the *Estoire* and the *Merlin* in relation to the rest of the *Cycle*, see n. 1 above.

24 See Elspeth Kennedy, 'The Re-writing and Re-reading of a Text,' in *The Changing Face of Arthurian Romance: Essays on Arthurian Prose Romances in Memory of Cedric E. Pickford* (Cambridge, 1986), pp. 1–9. For the continuation of this re-writing of the *Cycle* in terms of physical presentation of the text by means of chapter divisions, rubrics, illuminations, etc., see Emmanuèle Baumgartner, 'Espace du texte, espace du manuscrit: les manuscrits du *Lancelot* en prose,' in *De l'histoire de Troyes au livre du Graal: Le temps, le récit (XIIe–XIIIe siècles)* (Orleans, 1994), pp. 379–404. See also, in more general terms, Philippe Ménard, 'La réception des romans de chevalerie à la fin du Moyen Age et au XVIe siècle,' *Bibliographical Bulletin of the International Arthurian Society*, 49 (1997), 234–73.

25 See n. 7 above on the Grail-winner passage.

acquired knowledge learned through lessons from Merlin, born as the result of a casual love affair between a girl, who does not want to marry a husband she can see, and an incubus. Merlin's diabolical nature is emphasized, but neutralized through the Lady of the Lake's imprisonment of him. A number of manuscripts containing the whole cycle replace this version with that of Robert de Boron, where Merlin is the result of a thwarted plot by the devils to repopulate Hell after the Harrowing of Hell, although such an account does not fit in well with the thematic structure of the narrative of Lancelot's childhood.[26]

Scribes and readers did indeed on occasion endeavour to smooth away inconsistencies in the *Cycle* (in doing so, often adding a different type of inconsistency) as it developed and was copied and read over the centuries, but they faced a mammoth task. The *Cycle* in its full form, starting with the early history of the Grail and ending with the *Mort Artu*, sets out to include within it the main twelfth-century Arthurian themes, apart from the Tristan story to which it refers outwards and places in the past and with which it interacts.[27] Within this *Cycle*, centered as it is on Lancelot, the Grail theme is carefully integrated. However, it would be a mistake to expect a unified structure in which, for example, the introduction of a Grail quest insisting on the need for virginity in the Grail winner has meant that the *Cycle* as a whole must, in its final version, be interpreted throughout in religious terms.[28] The reader is given no one answer and indeed the strength of this fascinating work lies in the tension between various possibilities, an interplay between literary forms (in particular, between the allegorical and the non-allegorical), between different levels of truth, and between various voices of authority, a tension built into the very structure of the work.[29]

---

[26] For details of the manuscripts which substitute for the version designed to present the Lady of the Lake's knowledge of magic in a favorable light, either a reference to the *Estoire Merlin*, or a version of Robert de Boron's account in varying lengths, see *LK* 2:12–14 and 81–2, and Kennedy, 'The Scribe as Editor.' See also Kennedy, 'The Role of the Supernatural in the First Part of the Prose *Lancelot*,' in *Studies in Medieval Literature and Languages in Memory of Frederick Whitehead* (Manchester, 1973), pp. 173–84, and Kennedy, *Lancelot and the Grail*, 111–42. BNF fr. 110 and the rest of its group regularly remove inconsistencies such as a reference to Claudas as having only one son, whereas later in the *Cycle* another son is mentioned (see *LK* 2:87). For other types of modification, see 'The Scribe as Editor.'

[27] There is, however, one manuscript, Paris, BNF fr. 113–116, which gives a complete version of the *Cycle*, but also includes Tristan adventures from the Prose *Tristan*.

[28] A number of scholars would hesitate to accept the dominance of the religious element throughout. Lot, *Etude*, p. 106, writes of 'le double esprit,' the juxtaposition of courtly and religious elements within the structural and authorial unity of the cycle. A. Micha, 'L'esprit du *Lancelot-Graal*,' *Romania*, 82 (1961), 357–79, maintains that the *Cycle* includes life in all its forms. However, Frappier argues that the profane ideal of courtly love is progressively subordinated to the mystic ideal of heavenly chivalry (*Grundriss der romanischen Literaturen des Mittelalters*, IV/1 [Heidelberg, 1978], p. 587).

[29] E. Jane Burns explores competing authorial voices in relation to rewriting within the *Cycle* in *Arthurian Fictions: Rereading the Arthurian Cycle* (Columbus, OH, 1988). Kennedy investigates the wide variety of voices of authority (dreams, visions, wise men, characters deemed to be speaking the truth) in 'Who is to be believed? Conflicting Presentations of Events in the *Lancelot-Grail Cycle*,' in *The Medieval Opus: Imitation, Rewriting and Transmission in the French Tradition*, ed. Douglas Kelly (Amsterdam and Atlanta, GA, 1996), pp. 169–80.

3

A Question of Time: Romance and History

RICHARD TRACHSLER

Stories and Histories

L'*Estoire de Lancelot*, as the epilogue of the *Mort Artu* seems to call the entire *Lancelot-Grail Cycle*, is indeed a long story.[1] From its beginnings that merge with the origins of Christianity in the Holy Land under the Roman emperor Vespasian, to its end *de vers Occident* with the passing of Arthur in the year 542 at Avalon, what we tend to see as a 'romance' shares much of its action with what medieval readers probably would have not hesitated to call 'history.' In particular the stories of Utherpendragon, the account of Arthur's youth, the Saxon and Roman wars, and the treason of Mordred have all been told by 'historians' such as Geoffrey of Monmouth and Wace. There is no doubt that the *Lancelot-Grail* draws on this historiographic model, at least in part, but it does so in order to create something entirely new.

Ostensibly historical, yet overtly *merveilleux*, the *Lancelot-Grail Cycle* shifts from story to history and combines the two modes of narration as well as the two kinds of source material. This is not unusual. In British, and especially Anglo-Norman historiography the dividing line between romance and chronicle has always been ill-defined, and the issue has not been neglected by scholars,[2] but the fact is that it involves most of the early literary narratives in the vernacular that deal with historical matters. A prime example is Benoît de Sainte-Maure's *Roman de Troie*, which draws on sources that are unimpeachably 'historical': the reports of two 'eye-witnesses' recording the Trojan war in the most trustworthy manner imaginable – in Latin (originally Greek) prose.[3]

In this particular context, it is worth remembering that the matter of Britain

---

1   Jean Frappier, ed., *La Mort le Roi Artu* (Geneva and Paris, 1964), p. 263.
2   See for example Maria Luisa Meneghetti, 'L'*Estoire des Engleis* di Geffrei Gaimar fra cronaca genealogica e romanzo cortese,' *Medioevo Romanzo*, 2 (1975), 232–46. See the chapter by Dagmar Tillmann-Bartylla, 'Versuch einer Neubestimmung des Texttyps *Volkssprachliche Reimchronistik*,' in *Grundriss der romanischen Literaturen des Mittelalters*, vol. II, part 1 (Heidelberg, 1986), pp. 341–50. The modern desire to distinguish 'chronicles' from 'romances,' 'true stories' from 'pure fiction,' stems of course from our irresistible urge to classify, but given the importance of generic systems for reception and interpretation, the issue cannot be ignored.
3   On the relation between chronicles and the first romances in French, see Michel Zink, 'Les chroniques médiévales et le modèle romanesque,' *Mesure*, I (1989), 35 [33–45]. On the sources of Benoît de Sainte-Maure's work and their manuscript tradition, see Marc-René Jung, *La légende de Troie en France au moyen âge* (Tübingen and Basel, 1995).

was not necessarily perceived as pure fiction, despite Jehan Bodel's early thirteenth-century claim that 'Li conte de Bretaigne si sont vain et plaisant/ Et cil de Ronme sage et de sens aprendant.'[4] There is no need to search for the 'historical' Arthur, when manuscript compilation offers ample evidence that the Arthurian material was considered non-fiction. For example, the *Brut* is either preceded or directly followed by texts that are indisputably 'historical,' such as Geoffrey Gaimar's *Estoire des Engleis*, the chronicles of Pierre de Langtoft or Jordan Fantosme, genealogies, annals, etc.[5] The Arthurian chronicles might therefore claim the same status as any historical text. A particularly good case in point is Paris, Bibliothèque Nationale, MS fr. 17177, an early fourteenth-century manuscript of the *Histoire Ancienne*.[6] It appears to actually 'correct' a genuine 'mistake' made by the French *cronica universalis*. Since the *Histoire Ancienne* does not contain an Arthurian section, it appeared 'incomplete' to fr. 17177's redactor or his patron. All its other manuscripts preserve the identical order: they recall the followers of Eneas, pass directly to the Assyrians 'qui de tot le monde orent la poesté et la segnorie',[7] then return to the story of Rome, but the redactor of fr. 17177 inserts the *Estoire de Brutus* before moving on to the Assyrians, thus providing what seems to be one of the very first translations into French prose of Geoffrey of Monmouth's *Historia regum Britanniae*. The manuscript clearly shows that the matter of Britain can be integrated into a compilation whose focus is essentially historical, and that it is not the *matière* that identifies a text as romance or history.[8]

When French vernacular romance emerges, then, it is not subject matter that sets it apart from historiographic texts. On the contrary, since both romancer and chronicler seem to write for the same aristocratic audience eager to learn something about the *res gestae* of the past, they both turn to the same reservoir of traditional knowledge for material. Other factors point to a kind of symbiosis between romance and historiography: in the field of vernacular literature, the two genres seem to have shared the same audiences and writers. Benoît de Sainte-Maure writes his *Roman de Troie*, then follows it up with a *Chronique des ducs de Normandie*. Wace, after finishing his *Roman de Brut*, composes a *Roman de Rou* that draws heavily on the historiographic model. We can assume that their

---

4 Annette Brasseur, ed., Jehan Bodel, *La Chanson des Saisnes*, 2 vols. (Geneva, 1989), redaction AR, 9–10. Since he is writing a *chanson de geste*, Jean Bodel is naturally concerned less with the Arthurian chronicle tradition than with the rhymed romances of the Round Table (a rival to his own literary project), which he calls 'voir chascun jour aparant'.

5 The same applies to the *Historia regum Britanniae*, which is usually compiled with 'historical' works. See Julia C. Crick, *The Historia regum Britanniae of Geoffrey of Monmouth, III: A Summary Catalogue of the Manuscripts* (Cambridge, 1989). I present the information on the manuscripts of the *Brut* in my book, *Clôtures du Cycle Arthurien: Etude et Textes* (Geneva, 1996), pp. 25–7.

6 The manuscript was first mentioned and described by Paul Meyer, 'Notice du Manuscrit fr. 17177 de la Bibliothèque Nationale,' *Bulletin de la Société des Anciens Textes Français*, 21 (1895), 80–118. The illustrations have been discussed by Doris Oltrogge, *Die Illustrationszyklen zur 'Histoire ancienne jusqu'à César' (1250–1400)* (Frankfurt, 1987), pp. 22–3 and 298.

7 Paris, BNF f. fr. 20125, fol. 177b. This 'digression' on the Assyrians is also absent from several other manuscripts. See Paul Meyer, 'Les premières compilations françaises d'histoire ancienne,' *Romania*, 14 (1885), 46 [1–81].

8 'Historical' is opposed here to 'fictional.' It is clear that medieval historiography is also moralistic.

patrons' taste evolved in a very similar milieu. The affinities between the two 'genres' may also be explained by another factor: the work of the romancer may well resemble that of the 'historian,' since both of them are involved in evaluating the multitude of sources available, identifying the most trustworthy accounts, and putting them all together, so as to create a new piece of work that is coherent, convincing and pleasing.[9]

As far as these early vernacular texts are concerned, then, modern critics rely more or less on their own intuition to differentiate historiography from fiction. It has been suggested that the term *chronique* implies a difference between the Anglo-Norman history written by Benoît and Wace's *roman*, in the sense that chronology alone might be the dominant organizing principle of a chronicle, but this is a compositional distinction that has nothing to do with authenticity. Taken together, all these factors make the story of Arthur a rather ambiguous subject, 'ne tut folie ne tut saveir', as Wace puts it,[10] located somewhere in between – or above – historiography and romance.

The *Lancelot-Grail Cycle* retains this essential ambiguity, mingling completely fictional kings, knights and ladies with genuine 'historical' characters mentioned by certified historians.[11] The desire to create an impression of authenticity is particularly visible at the beginning of the *Lancelot*, where a King *Aramon* is mentioned, a name that inevitably evokes the 'historical' Pharamon, a character unknown to the chronicle tradition but evidently necessary to the *Lancelot* author who was eager to create the most 'realistic' atmosphere possible. He therefore deliberately blended his King Aramon with the King Hoël from the chronicles in order to strengthen his text's claim to historicity.[12] Elsewhere the blending process is more uniform and consists simply of fusing an 'historical' layer, 'guaranteed' by the chronicles, with new elements introduced by the *Lancelot-Grail*. In the *Merlin* for instance, 'authentic' Saxon warlords invade the British Isles, and 'official' roman legions fight the knights of the Round Table in the *Mort Artu*.[13] In this pseudo-historical universe, where 'real' characters ride

---

9   On this topic, see Douglas Kelly, *The Art of Medieval French Romance* (Madison, WI, 1992), pp. 68–93. See the chapter 'La Documentation' in the standard study by Bernard Guenée, *Histoire et culture historique dans l'Occident médiéval* (Paris, 1980), pp. 77–128, and the articles by Robert Marichal, 'Naissance du roman,' in *Entretiens sur la Renaissance du 12e siècle*, ed. Maurice de Gandillac and Emile Jeauneau (Paris and The Hague, 1968), pp. 449–92, and Michel Zink, 'Une mutation de la conscience littéraire: Le langage romanesque à travers des exemples français du XIIe siècle,' *Cahiers de Civilisation médiévale*, 24 (1981), 3–27.

10 Emmanuèle Baumgartner and Ian Short, eds., *La Geste du roi Arthur selon le 'Roman de Brut' de Wace et l'Historia Regum Britanniae' de Geoffroy de Monmouth* (Paris, 1993), 1065.

11 For a recent account of this aspect of the *Lancelot*, see Annie Combes' chapter 'La recherche d'une complétude' in her book, *Les Voies de l'aventure: Ré-écriture et composition romanesque dans le 'Lancelot en prose'* (Paris, 2001).

12 The superposition of the two characters is obtained by means of a surname: 'Aramont . . . que les gens apeloient Hoël en sornon' (Alexandre Micha, ed., *Lancelot* [Paris and Geneva, 1980], 7:2). Cf. Ferdinand Lot, *Etude sur le Lancelot en prose* (Paris, 1918), p. 184 n. 1, and Elspeth Kennedy, *Lancelot and the Grail* (Oxford, 1990), pp. 80–1.

13 It is interesting to note that the attempt to present the new text as 'historical' is present not only in the historical branches that depend on the chronicles, but also in the passages concerning the Grail. See Elspeth Kennedy, 'The Narrative Techniques Used to Give Arthurian Romance a "Historical" Flavour,' in *Conjunctures: Medieval Studies in Honor of Douglas Kelly*, ed. Keith Busby and Norris J. Lacy (Amsterdam and Atlanta, GA, 1994), pp. 219–33.

through 'real' cities and landscapes, the author of the *Cycle* placed Lancelot and his friends – characters freely invented or taken from legendary material or simply borrowed from Chrétien de Troyes or Wace.[14]

A Question of Time

The *matière* of the *Lancelot-Grail* is indeed partly 'recycled' from other texts. In particular, Chrétien de Troyes and Wace have been major influences for, respectively, the romance and historiographic aspects of the *Cycle*. But even if the architect of the *Lancelot-Grail* drew on these authors, he also modified their legacy profoundly. The most significant change in the two models is probably in their representation of Arthurian history. Wace's *Brut* certainly supplied the *Cycle* with a virtual chronological frame leading up to Arthur and beyond Avalon, but it focused less on dates perhaps than on genealogy. According to the Anglo-Norman historian, the history of British royalty begins with the fall of Troy and Brutus' migration, and ends with the loss of British independence under King Cadvalladr in the year 689. Between these two chronological poles, the *Brut* recalls the exploits and deeds of the British kings, which includes the life of Arthur. While Arthur does occupy a proportionally large part of the *Brut*, he is just one king among many. History continues after his passing just as it had existed before him, and what the manuscript context of the *Brut* clearly shows is that history continues beyond the year 689: the *Brut* is followed by its 'sequels' that tell the story of other dynasties and other kings of Britain.[15]

The change in the conception of time and story in the *Cycle* is obvious at a glance. The origins of the romance are not Trojan but Biblical, therefore the *terminus a quo* is not the historical fact of the destruction of Troy, but the spiritual event of the 'invention' of the Holy Grail.[16] Thus, the new story ceases to be represented as an endless *register* of events leading from some starting point and heading toward an indeterminate future, but an eschatological construction with a precise goal to be reached, after which the writer can put down his pen. This main event, the adventure of adventures, is of course the conquest of the Grail. Everything else serves as mere prologue or epilogue to this glorious episode in the story of mankind. Arthur's biography is subordinated to the Grail story, yet they are linked in a way that makes Arthur's biography indispensable to the new story. The place is Arthur's realm, his reign is the time in which the conquest of the Grail will be achieved. These two choices are not accidental, but deliberate and necessary: the itinerary of the Grail follows the course of the sun, rising in the East and setting in the West – in the most westerly point of the known world, Britain and its isles. The timing is marked by the unique constellation of Merlin keeping watch over Arthur's father, Uther, and the creation of

---

[14] For an account of the *Cycle*'s geography, see Alexandre Micha, *Essais sur le cycle du Lancelot-Graal* (Geneva, 1987), pp. 265–74, and 'La géographie de la *Queste* et de la *Mort Artu*,' in *Farai chansoneta novele: Hommage à Jean-Charles Payen* (Caen, 1989), pp. 267–73.

[15] See my *Clôtures du Cycle Arthurien*, pp. 22–25.

[16] A. Michel, 'Virgile et les historiens romains,' *Mesure*, I (1989), 20–31.

the Round Table, which together lay the foundation for the next generation, the 'right' one that will see the adventures of the Grail accomplished.

So the primary filiation in the *Cycle* is not the historical bloodline of British royalty, but the spiritual genealogy of the Grail family. With their pacification of neighboring kingdoms and the 'invention' of *courtoisie*, Arthur and his knights cease to represent a value in their own right, except in so far as they provide the necessary *terrien* conditions for the rise of the Grail hero. This fundamental difference is the source of all the other differences, including the new ending imposed on the *Brut* by the *Mort Artu*. Whereas the *Brut* suggested time was a succession of dynasties following one another in an endless, unbroken line of characters who would fill a virtually never-ending Book of British Royalty, in the *Mort Artu* everything ends with the passing of Arthur's knights, the story is over, Britain has become an empty stage bereft of actors and a play to play.

It is interesting to note how this new way of linking history and fiction brings the *Cycle* closer to Chrétien de Troyes and at the same time keeps them apart. Since Chrétien locates his romances in a precise twelve-year 'gap' of peace that is not covered by any chronicle because no major political events occur in Arthur's realm during that time, he does not seem to concern himself with the historiographic tradition.[17] The fact that the action is spread over a relatively short period of time in Chrétien de Troyes' romances, 'beginning' and 'ending' at Arthur's court, also avoids a second problem: like most authors of Arthurian verse romances, he does not have to deal with what went before and what comes after, with the origin and the end of chivalry, with the passing of time and its effect on his characters and their relationships.[18] But things change as soon as Chrétien alludes to the Holy Grail. Suddenly one finds the same characteristics as in the *Cycle*, as if the mere presence of the Grail and the theme of genealogical election inherent in it necessarily suggested that the ultimate goal of chivalry might be *celestiel* and not *terrien*, and that Arthur's court and its values are nothing more than the universe the young knight must surpass after he has entered it and conformed to its ideals.

Ideology and the conception of time and story are two important criteria that set the *Cycle* apart from its romance and historiographic sources, for its difference is also defined essentially by its form and composition. Indeed, the *Cycle*'s compositional artistry is completely new. The tight interlacing of adventures is very different from what we find in Chrétien, and especially in Wace, who use a

---

17 The passage is well known: 'en cele pais que jo di/ ne sai si vus l'avez oï/ furent les merveilles provees/ e les aventures trovees/ que d'Arthur sunt [tant] recuntees/ que a fable sunt aturnees:/ [ne tut folie ne tut saveir,]/ tant unt li cuntëur cuntees/ e li fablëur tant fablees/ pur lur cuntes enbeleter,/ unt tut fait fables sembler' (*Brut*, ed. Baumgartner and Short, 1059–70).

18 Emmanuèle Baumgartner, in a now classic study, qualified the romances of Chrétien de Troyes as 'circulaires' as opposed to the prose romances in which the conception of time is linear ('Temps linéaire, temps circulaire et écriture romanesque (XIIe–XIIIe siècles),' in *Le temps et la durée dans la littérature au moyen âge et à la Renaissance: actes du colloque organisé par le Centre de Recherche sur la Littérature du Moyen Age et de la Renaissance de l'Université de Reims (Novembre 1984)*, ed. Yvonne Bellenger (Paris, 1986), pp. 7–21). The best account of the French Arthurian verse romances is still Beate Schmolke-Hasselmann, *Der arthurische Versroman von Chrestien bis Froissart: Zur Geschichte einer Gattung* (Tübingen, 1980), esp. pp. 4–6 on characterizing the genre.

more linear mode of narration that is essentially chronological.[19] Furthermore, the *Cycle*'s story that organizes all the heterogeneous ingredients into a single plot is subtly distributed among various voices that come from above or below, each one in charge of specific parts of the narrative. This technique gives the impression that the work is a genuine excerpt of a huge book, compiled from the testimony of the knights of the Round Table themselves, from Merlin's dictation to Blaise, and from other *auctoritates*.[20] It therefore has – or tries to take on – the appearance of a collection of authentic material, whereas Wace and Chrétien de Troyes have more straightforward ways of transforming their sources into the new text. The second major innovation introduced by the author of the *Cycle* concerns form. His *assemblage* is held together by a new, hermetic prose that is still rare for fiction at the beginning of the thirteenth century, but becoming the dominant form in historiography if we measure its triumph by the large number of extant manuscripts of the *Histoire Ancienne*.[21] The *Cycle*'s choice of a historiographical form for a literary text is certainly not unmotivated and requires comment.

The phenomenon of the emergence of prose, and likewise the relative chronology of the historical and romance texts written in the new form, are still very slippery ground in modern scholarship, but some preliminary observations can be made. First of all, this 'new' form admirably serves a new way of writing, as far as the Arthurian prose romances are concerned. The prose literally 'goes with' the narration, creating a *continuum* and filling in gaps where the octosyllabic couplet left fatal 'blanks': at the end of each verse and with the rhyme change.[22] It can be assumed furthermore that the choice of prose for historiographic texts was not unrelated to the problem of telling the truth and to the discredit that religious writers continued to heap on the rhymed chronicles and stories, too factitious in form to be really 'true.'[23] It is more than likely that

---

[19] Chrétien does of course use the technique of interlace in his *Conte du Graal* and in the parallel composition of his *Yvain* and *Lancelot*, as Emmanuèle Baumgartner has shown in her *Chrétien de Troyes. Yvain, Lancelot, la charrette et le lion* (Paris, 1992).

[20] The organisation of the different voices has been studied by a number of scholars, including Alexandre Leupin, 'Qui parle? Narrateurs et scripteurs dans la *Vulgate* arthurienne,' *Digraphe*, 20 (1979), 83–109; Michelle Perret, 'De l'espace romanesque à la matérialité du livre: L'espace énonciatif des premiers romans en prose,' *Poétique*, 50 (1982), 173–82; E. Jane Burns, *Arthurian Fictions: Rereading the Vulgate Cycle* (Columbus, OH, 1985), pp. 35–54 et passim; E. Baumgartner, 'Masques de l'écrivain et masques de l'écriture dans les proses du Graal,' in *Masques et déguisements*, ed. Marie-Louise Ollier (Montreal and Paris, 1988), pp. 167–75.

[21] The first part of this important compilation is edited by Mary Coker Joslin, *The Heard Word: A Moralized History. The Genesis Section of the Histoire ancienne in a Text from Saint-Jean d'Acre* (University, Miss., 1986). Further sections are now available in the edition by Marijke de Visser-van Terwisga, *Histoire ancienne jusqu'a César (Estoires Rogier)*, vols. 1–2 (Orleans, 1995–99). See the useful list of over sixty manuscripts in Jung, *Légende de Troie*, pp. 340–52.

[22] Daniel Poirion, 'Romans en vers et romans en prose,' in *Grundriss der romanischen Literaturen des Mittelalters*, IV, 1, *Le roman jusqu'à la fin du XIIIe siècle* (Heidelberg, 1978), p. 79 [74–81].

[23] Erich Köhler, 'Zur Entstehung des altfranzösischen Prosaromans,' *Wissenschaftliche Zeitschrift der Friedrich-Schiller-Universität Jena* 5 (1955–56); rpt. in E. Köhler, *Trobadorlyrik und höfischer Roman: Aufsätze zur französischen und provenzalischen Literatur des Mittelalters* (Berlin, 1962), pp. 213–23. See also Micha, *Etude sur le 'Merlin' de Robert de Boron, roman du XIIIe siècle* (Geneva, 1980), pp. 59–63.

the choice of prose as the preferred medium was initiated by an aristocracy anxious to acquire historical legitimacy by constructing for itself a new generic identity in opposition to earlier literary forms.[24] All of these factors shed a very precise light on the preference for prose manifested by the 'architect' of the *Lancelot-Grail Cycle*, who deliberately aligned his work with the historiographic model to indicate his rejection, on ideological and esthetic grounds, of the rhymed universe of Wace and Chrétien de Troyes.[25]

Retelling an Old Story

Neither the spirit nor the form of the *Cycle* are the same as in Chrétien de Troyes and Wace, yet both authors had a considerable influence on the *Lancelot-Grail*. The *Brut* in particular furnished several major elements of the plot, including the 'prehistory' of Arthur himself – the story of Utherpendragon and his wars against the invaders, which has been integrated extensively into the *Merlin*[26] – and the Arthur-Guinevere-Mordred triangle mentioned by Wace and developed extensively in the *Mort Artu*. But rather than give a list of the passages of the *Brut* which the *Lancelot-Grail Cycle* draws on, it is more interesting to compare what actually happens when one element passes from the chronicle into the *Lancelot-Grail*.

A brief survey of some of the elements borrowed from Wace and inserted into the *Cycle* will illustrate the vast range of possibilities, which can either affect the structure of the text or be more superficial. The war against the Romans, which is recalled twice in the *Cycle*, is a good example of the latter type. It is common knowledge that Wace begins the final phase of the Arthurian drama with the arrival of twelve Roman messengers demanding that King Arthur pay tribute to the emperor *Luces*. Arthur refuses and crosses the sea to fight the Roman army. Before his ship reaches land on the Continent, he has the famous dream about a dragon slaying a bear, which is interpreted by his perplexed counselors as the announcement of victory over either the Romans or a Giant. Arthur will indeed fight the Giant of Saint Michael's Mount before resuming his march against the Romans. In Burgundy, he then encounters the army of Luces and defeats his enemies in a terrible battle. Arthur is kept from continuing his campaign and conquering Rome by the news of Mordred's betrayal. He rushes back to Britain to fight his nephew's army, and the rest is history.

The *Mort Artu* draws on Wace to recall the final battle against the Romans,

---

24 Gabrielle M. Spiegel, *Romancing the Past: The Rise of Vernacular Prose Historiography in Thirteenth-Century France* (Berkeley, Los Angeles, and Oxford, 1993), pp. 2–3 et passim.

25 On the other hand, we must admit that we do not really know if the *'Petit Saint Graal'* (*Joseph–Merlin–Perceval*) predates the *Histoire Ancienne*, thus generating a reference which does not depend on historiographic models.

26 Certain details indicate that the *Lancelot-Grail Cycle* relies on Wace's *Brut* rather than on Geoffrey's *Historia Regum Britanniae*. See Micha, *Etude sur le 'Merlin,'* pp. 30–58, for the account of the story of Uther and Arthur's early years. For the *Suite-Merlin*'s debt to the *Brut*, see Micha, 'La guerre contre les Romains dans la *Vulgate* du *Merlin*,' *Romania*, 82 (1951), 310–23.

even though very few elements are retained.[27] The important point here is that the events occur at roughly the same moment in Arthur's story, which one could call the beginning of the last act: the moment when Fortune is raising the King to the peak of glory, just before casting him down to the ground. In the *Brut*, as in the *Mort Artu*, his victory over the Romans will be his last triumph before the fall.[28]

Very curiously, the Roman campaign figures in the more recent *Suite* too, in a completely different context, since Arthur's star is still in the ascendance at that point in the *Cycle*.[29] Young Arthur has defeated the rebel barons and fought the fearsome Saxons, but nothing is over yet. In fact half of the *Suite-Merlin* and the entire *Lancelot-Queste-Mort Artu* block is still to come. The fact that at this point in his plot the author of the *Suite* chooses to borrow an entire sequence from the Anglo-Norman chronicle, clearly shows that the *Brut* was seen as a sort of mine of 'genuine' Arthurian material which could be integrated into a new story and by its mere presence could authenticate the latter. So Arthur's biography could be broken down into basic elements that could be used elsewhere in an entirely different order, as the *Lancelot* had already done when it recalled the episode of Arthur's duel against Frollo, taken from the *Brut*.[30]

Freed of any obligation to respect the original plot, the authors of the *Cycle* need only obey the demands of internal coherence. When importing material from the *Brut*, they must try to avoid contradictions within the *Cycle* itself first, and then link the imported episode as firmly as possible to its new context. The need to avoid conflicting information explains, for instance, why Keu and Bedoier are simply wounded and not killed in battle: since they both appear throughout the rest of the *Cycle*, the author of the *Suite* could not make them die as his model Wace had done. The desire to link an episode to its new context accounts for the fact that several minor characters mentioned by Wace were replaced by well-known Arthurian knights with a more precise 'psychological profile.'[31]

These are not the most interesting transformations, of course. Far more representative of the technique of the *Lancelot-Grail* authors is their capacity to adapt their models to the structural needs of the new text.[32] A good example is the transformation of Mordred, who in the *Cycle* is no longer Arthur's nephew, but his incestuous son.[33] This invention is symptomatic of a general movement in

---

27 *Mort Artu*, ed. Frappier, pp. 206–09.
28 See Jean Frappier, *Etude sur la 'Mort le roi Artu'*, 3rd rev. ed. (Geneva, 1972), pp. 150–72. According to Frappier, the author of the *Mort Artu* used not only Wace, but also Geoffrey and Layamon.
29 H. Oskar Sommer, ed., *The Vulgate Version of the Arthurian Romances* (1908; rpt. New York, 1979), II, 424–41.
30 Micha, *Lancelot*, 6:161–3.
31 For a detailed list of this kind of modification see Micha, 'La guerre contre les Romains,' 313–20. On the psychological density the characters acquire in passing from the chronicles into the *Cycle*, Jean Frappier commented that in the *Brut* Guinevere, 'est tout juste un nom' (Frappier, *Etude*, p. 155).
32 I develop this aspect in my book, *Clôtures du Cycle Arthurien*, pp. 67–141.
33 There is no mention of this paternity prior to the *Cycle*, as pointed out by James Douglas Bruce, 'The Development of the *Mort Arthur* Theme in Mediaeval Romance,' *Romanic Review*,

the last part of the *Cycle*, where the real causes of the end of the Arthurian realm cease to be external and become internal to the royal family. In the *Cycle*, Arthur's fall is not the result of an unfortunate combination of circumstances whereby a coalition of infidels comes from afar to overthrow the intrepid champion of Christian civilization. The real enemies of the Arthurian world are not the Romans and Saracens but Agravain, Morgain and Mordred, Gawain's hatred and Lancelot's love. The forces causing the end of the *aetas arturiana* lay within Arthur's family, his closest friends and himself, a fact that is perhaps best illustrated by the mutual killing of father and son on the battlefield at Salisbury, an element that is absent from the chronicles and seems to be a *trouvaille* of the author of the *Mort Artu*. The mortal embrace in which Arthur suffocates his friend Lucan or Girflet who is dying of grief at the loss of his King, also shows that beyond Salisbury the dissolution of the order of the Round Table is an autonomous process, independent of external factors.

This new theme of the self-destruction of Arthurian knighthood is directly related of course to the change in the conception of time mentioned above. The introduction of the Holy Grail into the linear universe of the chronicles gives Arthurian chivalry a deadline. It is no longer possible to leave the royal sword and crown to some other young knight in order to continue the story of the 'Kings of Britain.' In the *Brut*, for example, Arthur's successor Constantine accomplishes the 'filial' duty of vengeance on Mordred's sons and carries on the Arthurian legacy for some generations to come. This way out is blocked in the *Cycle* in a way that is again totally coherent with the project of the *Lancelot-Grail*. In the *Mort Artu*, as in the *Brut*, someone is there to slay the last survivors of the traitor's clan, but the avenger is Lancelot, whose story is intimately linked to the rise and fall of Arthur, whereas Constantine is a 'fresh' character, introduced at the very moment he becomes king. As for Lancelot, without his son, without the Queen, his story is over; he is part of the Arthurian past and will never be able to play the role of young Constantine. Even if the son of Ban does virtually appear in the last pages of the *Mort Artu* as the King's sole heir and the only possible candidate for Excalibur, he cannot take the place of Arthur: in the *Lancelot-Grail* universe there is no turning back, one king cannot step in to fill the gap left by another, as happens in the chronicles. After the conquest of the Grail, chivalry, Arthurian chivalry, is doomed, and the *Mort Artu* is but an epilogue recalling what happens to all those knights who, unlike Galahad and Perceval, are not made for a *celestielle* existence. This is why the last survivors in the *Cycle* turn their backs on chivalric values and retire into their *ermitages*, while the characters of the chronicles continue to fight battles and seek out conquests after the passing of Arthur.

4 (1913), 403–71. On the same topic see Elizabeth Archibald, 'Arthur and Mordred: Variations on an Incest Theme,' *Arthurian Literature*, 8 (1989), 1–27. One can always find mythical parallels, as in M. Victoria Guérin, 'The King's Sin: The Origins of the David-Arthur Parallel,' in *The Passing of Arthur: New Essays in Arthurian Tradition*, ed. Christopher Baswell and William Sharpe (New York and London, 1988), pp. 15–30, but there are definitely no Arthurian texts or 'legendary' sources, as shown by Peter Korrel's negative results in *An Arthurian Triangle: A Study of the Origin, Development and Characterization of Arthur, Guinevere and Mordred* (Leiden, 1984).

Through the addition of the Holy Grail, the history recorded by the chronicles has definitely been transformed, and Arthur's story has become *l'Estoire de Lancelot*, the great book that combines Wace and Chrétien de Troyes, romance and history, to form the unique but true story of chivalry.

4

The Vulgate Cycle *and the* Post-Vulgate Roman du Graal

FANNI BOGDANOW

The thirteenth century was one of the most fruitful periods in the history of medieval narrative fiction. It was not only the time when the twelfth-century Arthurian and Tristan verse romances were turned into prose, but when previously unconnected themes were adapted to form parts of larger cycles. Robert de Boron who himself wrote in verse at the end of the twelfth or the beginning of the thirteenth century, and who inherited on the one hand from Geoffrey of Monmouth and Wace the stories of Merlin and Arthur's kingdom, and on the other hand from Chrétien de Troyes the theme of the Grail, was the first writer to endeavour to combine these themes into a coherent narrative. Of Robert's verse romances, conceived as a trilogy, only the first part, the early history of the Grail, known as the *Joseph* or *Le Roman de l'Estoire du Graal*, and the beginning of the second part, the *Estoire de Merlin*, have been preserved in their original verse form.[1] There is no evidence that Robert himself ever wrote a 'third' part, but shortly after the composition of the first two they were reworked in prose and in two of the prose manuscripts of the *Joseph-Merlin* the latter is followed by a third section, the so-called *Didot Perceval*, which is an account of Perceval's quest for the Grail followed by an account of Arthur's death, composed by a writer closely acquainted not only with Robert's *Joseph-Merlin*, but also with Chrétien's *Conte du Graal* and its First Continuation, as well as Geoffrey's and Wace's accounts of the final years of Arthur's reign.[2]

Although one of Chrétien's romances centres on Perceval's search for the Grail and another of his works deals with a portion of Lancelot's life (*Le Chevalier de la Charrette*), Chrétien did not attempt to combine the themes of Lancelot and Guinevere with that of the Grail; and while Robert de Boron and his anonymous continuator, the author of the *Didot Perceval*, linked the themes of the

---

[1] For bibliographical references on Robert de Boron and the various problems raised by his work, see Fanni Bogdanow, 'Robert de Boron's Vision of Arthurian History,' in *Arthurian Literature*, XIV (Woodbridge, 1996), 19–52.

[2] For bibliographical references on the *Didot Perceval* and its sources, see Bogdanow, 'La trilogie de Robert de Boron: *Le Perceval en prose*,' in *Grundriss der romanischen Literaturen des Mittelalters*, IV, parts 1 and 2, *Le Roman jusqu'à la fin du XIIIe siècle*, ed. Jean Frappier and Reinhold R. Grimm (Heidelberg, 1984), IV, 1, pp. 513–35; IV, 2, pp. 173–7; Lothar Struss, 'Le Didot Perceval,' in *Grundriss*, IV, 2, pp. 21–41; Rupert T. Pickens, '*Mais de çou ne parole pas Crestiens de Troies* . . . : A Re-examination of the *Didot-Perceval*,' *Romania*, 105 (1984), 492–510.

Grail, Merlin, and Arthur, they did not bring into their work the story of Lancelot. It was the writers of the thirteenth-century *Vulgate Cycle of Arthurian Romances* (or *Lancelot-Grail Cycle*) who for the first time assigned an important function to the Lancelot-Guinevere story in the Arthur-Merlin-Grail complex. The *Vulgate Cycle*, which grew up in stages, consisted in its final form of five branches. The first two, which were written last, are an early history of the Grail, the *Estoire del Saint Graal*, based in part on Robert de Boron's *Joseph*, and an account of the early years of Arthur's reign incorporating the prose version of Robert's *Merlin* followed by a continuation, the *Vulgate Suite* which brings the narrative down to the time of Lancelot's birth. The middle portion of the *Cycle*, no doubt written first, deals with Lancelot's youth and is followed by a prose adaptation of Chrétien's *Charrette* and a series of adventures, referred to as the *Agravain*, which serves to bring the narrative down to the time of the beginning of the Grail Quest in which Lancelot's son, Galahad, and not Perceval, is to be the main hero. The final portion, the *Mort Artu*, dealing with the destruction of Arthur's kingdom, completes the *Cycle*.[3]

Just as Lancelot plays no part in the prose adaptation of Robert's trilogy, so the story of Tristan and Yseut, though at least as important in the twelfth century as that of Lancelot and Guinevere, is totally ignored in the *Vulgate Cycle*. It was the compiler of the First Version of the *Prose Tristan*, composed shortly after the *Vulgate*, who for the first time established a link between the *Tristan* and Arthurian romances. After Tristan and Yseut's flight to Logres where they find refuge in Lancelot's castle, the *Joyeuse Garde*, Lancelot and Tristan become close friends, and just as Lancelot on account of his love for Guinevere will fail in the Grail quest, so will Tristan on account of his love for Yseut.[4]

The First Version of the *Prose Tristan*, although it makes use of *Vulgate* themes, does not in any way attempt to remodel or reinterpret the *Vulgate*. Nor does it assign a significant place to the Grail quest, concentrating instead on Tristan's exploits. The merit of producing a new Arthuriad spanning the time from the early history of the Grail down to the destruction of Arthur's kingdom, falls to the author of the *Post-Vulgate Roman du Graal*. Composing his work shortly after the *Vulgate Cycle* and the First Version of the *Prose Tristan*, but before the Second Version of the *Prose Tristan* whose compiler was in turn to make use of the

---

3 For an edition of the complete *Cycle*, see H. Oskar Sommer, *The Vulgate Version of the Arthurian Romances*, 7 vols. (1908–13; rpt. New York, 1979). For editions of individual sections, see Eugène Hucher, *Le Saint Graal, ou le Joseph d'Arimathie: première branche des romans de la Table Ronde*, 3 vols. (Le Mans, 1874–78); Jean-Paul Ponceau, ed., *L'Estoire del Saint Graal*, 2 vols. (Paris, 1997); Alexandra Micha, ed., *Lancelot: roman du XIIIe siècle*, 9 vols. (Geneva, 1978–83); Elspeth Kennedy, ed., *Lancelot do Lac: The non-cyclic Old French Prose Romance* (Oxford, 1980); Albert Pauphilet, ed., *La Queste del Saint Graal, roman du XIIIe siècle* (Paris, 1923); Jean Frappier, *La mort le roi Artu: roman du XIIIe siècle* (Paris, 1936) [with variant readings], and TLF ed. (Geneva, 1954) [without variants].

4 For an analysis of the Paris manuscripts, see Eilert Löseth, *Le roman en prose de Tristan . . . analyse critique d'après les mss de Paris*, Bibl. de l'École des Hautes Études, fasc. 82 (Paris, 1891). For an edition published under the direction of Philippe Ménard, see *Le Roman de Tristan en prose*, 9 vols. (Geneva, 1987–97), vols. VI, ed. Emmanuèle Baumgartner and Michelle Szkilnik, 1983; VII, ed. Danielle Quéruel and Monique Santucci, 1994; VIII, ed. Bernard Guidot and Jean Subrenat, 1995; IX, ed. Laurence Harf-Lancner, 1997, correspond to the sections of the *Tristan Queste* which include large portions incorporated from the *Vulgate* and *Post-Vulgate* versions.

Post-Vulgate, notably the *Queste* section, he included in his narrative significant themes adapted from the First Version of the *Prose Tristan* (*Tris. I*).[5]

Unlike the *Vulgate Cycle* and the *Prose Tristan* of which numerous manuscripts have survived, the *Post-Vulgate* has not been preserved in French in its complete form in any one manuscript, but has had to be reconstructed from fragments of varying lengths which have come to light only gradually, and Portuguese and Spanish translations, as well as the redactional indications supplied by the writer himself in various parts of the narrative. From such evidence it would appear that the original *Post-Vulgate* Arthuriad, formerly known as the 'pseudo-Robert de Boron cycle,' comprised three parts, the first two of which included an *Estoire del Saint Graal*, the prose rendering of Robert de Boron's *Merlin* and a *Suite du Merlin* partly dependent on the *Vulgate Suite*, but in most respects distinct from the latter. As for the third part, this consisted of the *P-V Queste* followed by the *P-V Mort Artu*, both based on the corresponding *Vulgate* narrative, but extensively remodelled.

The portion of the narrative from which scholars first inferred the existence of a cycle parallel to that of the *Vulgate* was the *Suite du Merlin*, known for a long time only from the early fourteenth-century Huth manuscript (MS BL Add. 38117), published by Gaston Paris in 1886,[6] the 1498 Burgos and 1535 Seville editions of the Castilian *Baladro del Sabio Merlin*,[7] and Malory's English adaptation.[8] No manuscript of the Castilian *Baladro* has so far come to light, though a small section of the Castilian *Merlin* proper has been preserved in MS 1877 of the Salamanca University Library,[9] while a fragment of a Galician-Portuguese trans-

---

5   On the *Post-Vulgate*, see Pere Bohigas Balaguer, *Los Textos españoles y gallego-portugueses de la Demanda del Santo Grial*, in *Revista de Filologia Española*, Anejo VII (Madrid, 1925); Bogdanow, 'The *Suite du Merlin* and the *Post-Vulgate Roman du Graal*,' in *Arthurian Literature in the Middle Ages: A Collaborative History*, ed. Roger Loomis (Oxford, 1959), pp. 325–35; Bogdanow, *The Romance of the Grail: A Study of the Structure and Genesis of a Thirteenth-Century Arthurian Prose Romance* (Manchester and New York, 1966), an updated Portuguese translation by Silvio de Almeida Toledo Neto is in press; *La version Post-Vulgate de la Queste del Saint Graal et de la Mort Artu, Troisième partie du Roman du Graal*, ed. Bogdanow, vols. I, II and IV,1 (Paris, 1991); vols. III (Paris, 2000), and IV,2 (Paris, 2001), contain the remainder of the text, together with an updated bibliography; Roger Lathuillère, 'Le *Roman du Graal* postérieur à la *Vulgate* (Cycle du Pseudo-Robert de Boron),' in *Grundriss*, IV,1, pp. 615–22 and IV,2, pp. 166–7; Heitor Megale, *O Jogo dos Anteparos. A Demanda do Santo Graal: a estrutura ideológica e a constução da narrativa* (São Paulo, 1992).

6   Gaston Paris and Jacob Ulrich, eds. *Merlin, roman en prose du XIIIe siècle, publié . . . d'après le manuscrit appartenant à M. Alfred H. Huth*, 2 vols. (Paris, 1886); future textual references to the prose *Merlin* will be to this edition. One of the incidents of the *Suite*, the tale of Balain, has been edited separately by M. D. Legge, with Introduction by Eugène Vinaver (Manchester, 1942). For a new edition of the *Suite*, see *La Suite du roman de Merlin*, ed. Gilles Roussineau, 2 vols. (Geneva, 1996).

7   The 1498 Burgos edition, of which G. Paris gives some extracts (*Suite* I, LXXXI–XCI), has since been edited by Bohigas Balaguer, *El Baladro del sabio Merlin segun el texto de la edicion de Burgos de 1498*, 3 vols. (Barcelona, 1957–62). The 1535 Seville edition, which contains, in addition to the *Merlin* and the *Suite du Merlin*, an abridged version of the *P-V Queste–Mort Artu* (the *Demanda do Sancto Grial*), has been reprinted by Bonilla y San Martin, *La Demanda del Sancto Grial*, vol. I: *El Baladro del sabio Merlin con sus profecias*; vol. II: *La Demanda del Sancto Grial con los maravillosos fechos de Lanzarote y de Galaz su hijo. Libros de Caballerias.* 1: *Ciclo arturico*, Nueva Biblioteca de Autores Españoles, 6 (Madrid, 1907).

8   For an edition of Malory's version of the *Suite* section, see *The Works of Sir Thomas Malory*, ed. Eugène Vinaver, 3rd rev. ed. P. J. C. Field (Oxford, 1990), I, 1–180.

9   *Spanish Grail Fragments: El Libro de Josep Abarimatia, la Estoria de Merlin, Lançarote*, ed. Karl

lation of the *Suite* was discovered in 1979 by Amadeu J. Soberanas.[10] Both the Huth manuscript and the two extant editions of the *Baladro* are incomplete at the end, the former breaking off abruptly shortly after relating the initial section of the triple adventures of Gawain, Yvain and the Morholt.[11] On the other hand, the two extant editions of the *Baladro* which deliberately omit the latter portion of the Huth manuscript, end the *Suite* with a greatly expanded account of Merlin's death.[12] That the Huth manuscript was incomplete, though already suspected by G. Paris, became evident in 1895 when a fragment covering the final portion of the Huth manuscript, but continuing the narrative beyond the point where the latter breaks off and completing the triple adventures of Gawain and his two companions, was discovered by Eduard Wechssler in a fifteenth-century compilation of Arthurian romances, MS BNF fr. 112, and published by Sommer under the title *Die Abenteuer Ywains und le Morholts mit den drei Jungfrauen*.[13] But it was not until fifty years later that another manuscript of the *Suite* came to light confirming the incomplete form of the Huth codex: in 1945 Eugène Vinaver identified a fourteenth-century manuscript (Cambridge University Library, Add. 7071), which continues the narrative beyond the Huth manuscript, though breaking off before the end of the fr. 112 fragment.[14] Finally, yet more recently, short fragments, one dating from the thirteenth century and

Pietsch, *Modern Philology Monographs of the University of Chicago*, 2 vols. (Chicago, 1924–25), I, 3–54. In addition to a fragment of the *Estoire* (fols. 252a–282a), the Salamanca codex contains the initial section of the prose rendering of the *Merlin* (fols. 282v–296r; ed. Pietsch, I, 57–81) and a small fragment of the *P–V Mort Artu* (fols. 298v–300v; ed. Pietsch, I, 85–9).

10 Amadeu J. Soberanas, 'La version galaïco-portugaise de la *Suite du Merlin*: Transcription du fragment du XIVe siècle de la Bibliothèque de Catalogne, ms 2434,' *Vox Romanica*, 38 (1979), 174–93.

11 The final colophon of the Huth MS announces that the adventures of the Grail are to follow: 'Si laisse ore a tant li contes a parler de l[a] dame et del roi et de toute la vie Merlin, et devisera d'une autre matiere qui parole dou Graal, pour chou que c'est li commenchemens de cest livre' (*Merlin*, II, 254).

12 The section omitted in the *Baladros* corresponds to the *Suite*, ed. G. Paris, II, 198–254. The two editions of the *Baladro* are collateral versions of a common original, and in addition to the modifications they share, each also omits accidentally portions of the narrative preserved by the other. It should be added that the 1535 *Baladro* ends the narrative with a series of Merlin's prophecies that are absent from the 1498 editions. See Bogdanow, 'The Spanish *Baladro* and the *Conte du Brait*,' *Romania*, 83 (1962), 383–99; Bohigas Balaguer, *El Baladro del sabio Merlin*, III, 129–94; Patricia Michon, *A la lumière du Merlin espagnol* (Geneva, 1996).

13 Published in *Beihefte zur Zeitschrift für romanische Philologie*, XLVII (1913). The fr. 112 fragment begins at a point corresponding to the *Suite*, ed. G. Paris, II, 228. On fr. 112, which consists of three volumes bound in one (*Livre II, Livre III* and *Livre IV*), see Cedric E. Pickford, *L'Évolution du roman arthurien en prose vers la fin du moyen âge d'après le manuscrit 112 du fonds français de la Bibliothèque Nationale* (Paris, 1960). The *Suite* fragment published by Sommer is incorporated in *Livre II*, fols. 17b–58b of fr. 112.

14 On the Cambridge MS, see Vinaver, 'La Genèse de la *Suite du Merlin*,' in *Mélanges de philologie romane et de littérature médiévale offerts à Ernest Hoepffner* (Paris, 1949), pp. 295–300; *The Works of Sir Thomas Malory* (1947), III, 1277–80; (2nd ed. 1967), III, 1279–82. In addition to the *Suite* (fols. 202d–343b), the Cambridge manuscript includes a copy of the *Estoire del Saint Graal* (fols. 1–158b) distinct from the Rennes manuscript, as well as the prose rendering of Robert de Boron's *Merlin* (fols. 159a–202d). The *Suite* section proper, which is preceded, like Malory's version, by an account of Arthur's wars against the rebel kings (fols. 202d–230a), breaks off at a point corresponding to Sommer, *Die Abenteuer*, p. 48. See Bogdanow, *The Romance of the Grail*, pp. 31–3.

covering a portion of the Huth and Cambridge manuscripts,[15] others dating from the fourteenth century and corresponding to certain sections of the 112 narrative, were discovered in Italian libraries, notably Imola and Bologna.[16]

The *Post-Vulgate* writer, as if he had foreseen the fate of his work, indicates specifically in the *Suite* that the third part of his *livre* begins with the *Queste (el commenchement du Graal)* and 'finished after Lancelot's death at the very point where it relates King Mark's death':[17]

> Et sacent tuit cil qui l'estoire mon signeur de Borron[18] vauront oïr come il devise son livre en trois parties,[19] l'une partie aussi grant[20] come l'autre: la premiere aussi grande come la seconde, et la seconde aussi grant coume la tierche. Et la premiere partie[21] fenist il au commenchement de ceste queste, *et la seconde el commenchement dou Graal, et la tierche fenist il apriés la mort de Lanscelot, a chelui point meisme qu'il devise de la mort le roi March.* Et cest[e] chose amentoit en la fin dou[22] premier livre, pour chou que [se][23] l'*Estoire dou Graal* estoit corrompue par auchuns translatours qui aprés lui venissent,[24] tout li sage houme qui meteroient lour entente a oïr et a escouter porroient par ceste parole savoir se elle[25] lour seroit baillie entiere out corrompue, et connisteroient bien combien il i faurrait.[26]

> [And know all those who wish to hear the story of *mon seigneur Robert de Borron* how he divides his book into three equal parts, one part as big as the other: the first part as big as the second, and the second as big as the third. And the first part ends at the beginning of this quest, *and the second at the beginning of the Grail, and the third part finishes after Lancelot's death at the very point where it relates King Mark's death,* And he told you this at the end of the first book, so that if the story of the Grail is broken up by later scribes, all the wise men who would endeavour to

---

15 For editions of the Siena fragment, see A. Micha, 'Fragment de la *Suite-Huth* du *Merlin*,' *Romania*, 78 (1957), 37–45; Bogdanow, *The Romance of the Grail*, pp. 228–41. On the relationship of the Siena fragment to the other texts of the *Suite*, see Bogdanow, 'Essai de classement des manuscrits de la *Suite du Merlin*,' *Romania*, 81 (1960), 188–98.

16 On these fragments, first identified by Monica Longobardi, see her articles, 'Frammenti di codici in antico francese dalla Bibliotheca Comunale di Imola' *Cultura Neolatina*, 47 (1987), 239–55 [223–55]: fragment corresponding to *Abenteuer*, pp. 92–8, rpt. in *Miscellanea di studi in onore di Aurelio Roncaglia* (Modena, 1989), pp. 727–59; 'Nuovi frammenti della *Post-Vulgata*: la *Suite*, la Continuazione della *Suite du Merlin*, la *Queste* e la *Mort Artu* (con l'intrusione del *Guiron*),' *Studi Mediolatini e Volgari*, XXXVIII (1992), 199–55 (fragments corresponding to *Abenteuer*, pp. 50–3, 77–80). See Bogdanow, ed., *Queste P-V*, IV, 2, pp. 572–4 and pp. 591–613 (critical edition), and Bogdanow, 'The Importance of the Bologna and Imola Fragments for the Reconstruction of the *Post-Vulgate Roman du Graal*,' *Bulletin of the John Rylands University Library of Manchester*, 80 (1998), 33–64.

17 Huth MS, fol. 123c–d (*Merlin*, I, 280); Cambridge MS, fol. 264a. The 1498 and 1535 *Baladros* both omit this passage, although they keep other references to the tripartition of the *libro del sancto Grial*.

18 Cambridge MS: 'a mon seignor Robert de Beron'.

19 Cambridge MS: 'en .iii. parties e est l'un ausi'.

20 Cambridge MS: omits 'grant'.

21 Cambridge MS: 'premiere partie se mist el commencement de la Queste du Graal e la tierce finist il'.

22 Cambridge MS: 'ceste chose rementoit il en la fine de son premier livre'.

23 Cambridge MS: 'pur ceo si l'Estoire du Graal'.

24 Cambridge MS: 'venissent e tout'.

25 Cambridge MS: 'qui lor entente i mettroient en l'oïr e en l'escouter purroient savoir par ceste parole sin l'estoire soit baillie enterine'.

26 Cambridge MS: 'e conoistroit combien il lor en faudroit'.

hear and to listen would be able to know if they have been given the story in its complete form or in a fragmentary state, and they will know how much is missing.]

The only extant version of the *Mort Artu* which ends with the death of King Arthur is the narrative that forms the final part of the Portuguese *Demanda do Santo Graal (D)*, preserved in a unique fifteenth-century codex, MS Vienna National Library 2594,[27] and the Castilian *Demanda del Sancto Grial (De)*, known only from the Toledo 1515 and Seville 1535 editions,[28] apart from a small fragment included in the Salamanca manuscript.[29] The Portuguese and Castilian *Demandas* are both translated, though not independently of each other, from the French *Post-Vulgate Queste–Mort Artu* which, like the *Suite* section, is no longer extant in its complete form,[30] but has had to be reconstructed from fragments incorporated in various manuscripts. Two of these, first identified by Wechssler in 1895, are MS BNF fr. 112 (*Livre IV*) and MS BNF fr. 343 copied in the fourteenth century by an Italian scribe.[31] The latter codex combines the first two thirds of the *Vulgate Queste* with a considerable portion of the last third of the *Post-Vulgate*,[32] while fr. 112, in addition to one of the episodes which it shares with fr. 343,[33] incorporates several others, from both earlier and later parts of the narrative.[34] Another incident derived from the *P-V Queste* was inserted between the end of the *Vulgate Mort Artu* and the beginning of the *Vulgate Queste* by the

---

27 Karl Reinhardstöttner, ed., *A historia dos cavalleiros da Mesa Redonda e da Demanda do Santo Graal* (Berlin, 1902) is an edition of fols. 1–70. The first complete edition of the *Demanda* did not appear until 1944: Augusto Magne, *A Demanda do Santo Graal*, 3 vols. (Rio de Janeiro, 1944); 2nd rev. ed.: vol. I, 1955; vol. II, 1970; *Glossário*, 1967. Other editions: Heitor Megale, *A Demanda do Santo Graal: Texto modernizado com base em cópia do século XV e nas edições Magne de 1944 e 1955–70* (1988; rpt. São Paulo, 1989); *A Demanda do Santo Graal*, ed. Joseph-Maria Piel, completed by I. Freire Nunes, intro. Ivo de Castro (Moeda, 1988); I. Nunes, *A Demanda do Santo Graal* (Moeda, 1995).

28 The 1535 edition has been reprinted by Bonilla y San Martin (see n. 7 above). The Sevilla 1515 edition has so far not been reprinted.

29 On the Salamanca MS, which has preserved a small portion of the Castilian *Mort Artu* section, see n. 9 above.

30 On the relationship of the Hispanic versions to each other and to the French *Post-Vulgate*, including references to earlier studies, see my articles: 'An Attempt to Classify the Extant Texts of the Spanish *Demanda del Sancto Grial*,' in *Studies in Honor of Tatania Fotitch* (Washington, D.C., 1972), pp. 213–26; 'Old Portuguese *seer em car teudo* and the Priority of the Portuguese *Demanda do Santo Graal*,' *Romance Philology*, 28 (1974), 48–51; 'The Relationship of the Portuguese and Spanish *Demandas*,' *Bulletin of Hispanic Studies*, LII (1975), 13–32. And Ivo Castro, 'Sobre a data da introdução na península ibérica do ciclo arturiano da Post-Vulgata,' in *Homenagem a Manuel Rodrigues Lapa, Boletim de Filologia*, XXVIII (1983), 81–98; Pickford, 'La priorité de la version portugaise de la *Demanda do Santo Graal*,' *Bulletin Hispanique*, LII (1961), 211–16; Rudolf Steiner, '*Domaa/demanda* and the Priority of the Portuguese *Demanda*,' *Modern Philology*, 74 (1966), 64–7.

31 Eduard Wechssler, *Über die verschiedenen Redaktionen des Robert von Boron zugeschriebenen Graal-Lancelot-Cyclus* (Halle, 1895), pp. 11–12 and 54–7.

32 The sections preserved in BNF fr. 343 correspond to the Portuguese *Demanda (D)*, §§ 364–303 (= 343, fols. 82b–90c); §§ 445–84 (= 343, fols. 61a–72c); §§ 510–95 [beginning] (= 343, fols. 72d–104d). See Bogdanow, *Queste P-V*, I, 112–18.

33 MS fr. 112 (*S IV*), fols. 117b–23c corresponds to MS 343, fols. 82b–90c.

34 The sections preserved in fr. 112, *Livre IV (S)* correspond to *D*, §§ 141–5 (= *S IV*, fols. 96d–97c); §§ 193–5 (= *S IV*, fols. 97d–100b); §§ 201–7 (= *S IV*, fols. 97d–100b); §§ 254–408 (= *S IV*, fols. 97c–d; 100c–128c); §§ 417–21 (= *S IV*, fols. 179d–180c); §§ 581–4 (= *S IV*, fols. 146d–147d); §§ 603–9 (= *S IV*, fols. 150c–152c). See Bogdanow, *Queste P-V*, I, 118–21.

scribe of a late fifteenth-century manuscript of the *Vulgate Cycle*, BNF fr. 116, while yet further episodes were incorporated in a manuscript of *Guiron le Courtois*, L–I–7–9 of Turin University Library,[35] as well as in certain manuscripts of Rusticien de Pise's *Roman du roi Artus et des chevaliers errans*.[36] Most importantly, extensive sections from the second half of the *P-V Queste*, combined with the first half of the *Vulgate Queste*, were incorporated into the Second Version of prose *Tristan* (*Tris. II*) and have survived in some twenty-two manuscripts of the latter, including BNF fr. 772.[37] It was not until 1984, however, that a codex, which had been in the Bodleian Library since 1755 (Rawlinson D 874), was identified as a manuscript of the *P-V Queste*, closely related to fr. 343 but continuing beyond the point where the latter breaks off.[38] Finally, as in the case of the *Suite* and most probably forming part of the same codex originally, a number of further fragments of the *P-V Queste*, some covering sections previously unknown in French, have in recent years come to light in the State Archives in Bologna.[39] Similarly, the French fragments of the *P-V Mort Artu* section have come to light only one by one. The first of these, Guinevere's death and King Mark's death and second invasion of Logres, are preserved in a manuscript of Rusticien de Pise's *Roman du Roi Artus*, BNF fr. 340,[40] and has been known but not recognized as such, since the publication of Löseth's *Analyse* in 1891.[41] A variant version of these

---

35 On this codex, see Bogdanow, 'Part 3 of the Turin Version of *Guiron le Courtois*: a hitherto unknown source of ms. B.N. fr. 112,' in *Medieval Miscellany presented to Eugène Vinaver*, ed. Frederick Whitehead, Armel H. Diverres, and F. E. Sutcliffe (Manchester, 1965), pp. 45–64; *Queste P-V*, I, 126–8.

36 Bogdanow, 'A New MS of the *Enfances Guiron* and Rusticien de Pise's *Roman du Roi Artus*,' *Romania*, 88 (1967), 323–49; Bogdanow, *Queste P-V*, I, 128–37. Löseth included in his *Analyse* a summary of most of the manuscripts of Rusticien's *Roman*, but did not realize that one of the incidents, the death of Dalides (*Analyse*, § 625), derives from the *Post-Vulgate*.

37 See Wechssler, *Über die verschiedenen Redaktionen*, pp. 16–18; Bogdanow, *Queste P-V*, I, 137–71, 175–99. Originally I suggested (*Romance of the Grail*, pp. 88–120), that there existed two versions of the *P-V Queste*, a First Version (Y) incorporated in *Tris. II*, and a Second Version (Z) on which is based the Portuguese *Demanda*. But more recently (*Queste P-V*, I, 60–97), I indicated that this theory is not tenable and that there was only one version of the *P-V Queste* as represented by the Portuguese *Demanda*. The *Queste* incorporated in *Tris. II* is in reality a combination of sections derived from the *Vulgate Queste* and the French original of the *Demanda*. See Bogdanow, 'Intertextuality and the Problem of the Relationship of the First and Second Versions of the Prose *Tristan* to the *P-V Queste del Saint Graal*, third part of the *P-V Roman du Graal*,' *Arthuriana*, 12.2 (2002), 32–68.

38 See Ceridwen Lloyd-Morgan, 'Another Manuscript of the Post-Vulgate *Queste*,' *BBIAS*, XXXVII (1985), 292–8; Bogdanow, 'A Hitherto Unknown MS of the Post-Vulgate,' *French Studies Bulletin*, 16 (1985), 4–6; 'A Newly Discovered MS of the Post-Vulgate *Queste del Saint Graal*,' in *Studia in honorem Prof. M. de Riquier* (Barcelona, 1991), pp. 347–70. In addition to the sections of the *P-V Queste* which the Rawlinson MS (fols. 136a–220a) shares with MS 343 (see n. 22 above), this codex has preserved the portions corresponding to *D* §§ 595–617 (= Rawlinson, fols. 220a–233a) lacking in MS 343. Cf. *Queste P-V*, I, 108–12.

39 See Monica Longobardi, 'Un frammento della *Queste* della Post-Vulgata nell'Archivio di Stato di Bologna,' *Studi Mediolatini e Volgari*, XXXIII (1987), 5–24; Longobardi, 'Nuovi frammenti della *Post-Vulgata* . . .,' *Studi Mediolatini e Volgari*, XXXVIII (1992), 139–43; Longobardi, 'Dall'Archivio di Stato di Bologna alla Biblioteca Comunale dell'Archiginnasio: Resti del *Tristan en prose*,' *Studi Mediolatini e Volgari*, XXXIX (1993), 57–103 [pp. 63–5 = *P-V* fragment]; Bogdanow, *Queste P-V*, I, 5–10; 101–8; IV, 2, 503, 641, 716.

40 Guinevere's death (fr. 340, fol. 205a–e) corresponds to *D*, §§ 687–9; King Mark's death (fr. 340, fols. 205e–207c) corresponds to *D*, §§ 701–6. Cf. *Queste P-V*, I, 207.

41 Löseth, *Analyse*, p. XIX; § 575a. Sommer ('The *Queste of the Holy Grail*, forming the third part of the trilogy indicated in the *Suite du Merlin*,' *Romania*, 36 [1907], 380) mentions briefly that this manuscript includes a portion of the *Mort Artu* section.

incidents, not identified until 1976, is found in a manuscript formerly belonging
to Dr. Lucien Graux and since 1957 in the Bodmer Library, Geneva (MS 105).
This codex, a copy of the three last branches of the *Vulgate Cycle*, reproduces a
complete redaction of the *Mort Artu*, combining the *Vulgate* and *Post-Vulgate*
versions. It follows the former as far as Arthur's departure for Avalon:[42] then, up
to the end of the narrative, it reproduces the *Post-Vulgate*, thus covering not only
the fr. 340 fragment, but sections of the *P-V Mort Artu* previously known only
from the *Demandas*.[43] Finally, two small strips from the same codex as the
Bologna *P-V Queste* fragments are the sole French original of a further section of
the *P-V Mort Artu*.[44]

It was Gaston Paris who, in his review of Reinhardstöttner's edition of the
first 70 folios of the Portuguese *Demanda* (D) first realized that the latter represented the third part of the tripartite *Livre* announced in the Huth *Suite du
Merlin*.[45] That this is indeed the case cannot be doubted. While neither the
Vulgate Queste nor the *Vulgate Mort Artu* has references to such subdivisions, D
and its French source, the *P-V Queste–Mort Artu* as represented by the extant
portions, refer to the tripartition of the *Livre* and mention that the *Queste* is the
'third' part:

> Et Galahaz . . . chevauche puis mainte jornee et maintes aventuires mist a fin,
> dont cil de Beron ne parole mie, car trop eust a faire se il vouxist a cestui point
> raconter toutes les merveilles del Grahal, *et la darriane partie de son livre fust trop
> grant avers les autres deus premieres.*[46]

> Todas estas cousas, que aqui convem que vos nom divis<e> compridamente,
> acha-lo-edes no *Conto do Braado*, ca me nom tremeti de divissar compridamente
> as grandes batalhas que forom antre a linhagem de rey Bam e de rey Artur, e o
> enperador de Roma e rey Artur, *por <que> seeria mais que as .iii. partes do livro.*[47]

---

[42] This corresponds to MS Bodmer 105, fol. 324a (= §193, p. 227 of Frappier's 1936 edition of the
Vulgate Mort Artu).

[43] The *Post-Vulgate* sections (Bodmer 105, fols. 324b–341b) correspond to D, §§ 682–706
(Bogdanow, *Queste P-V*, III, 473–517), but terminate with a conclusion (Bodmer,
fols. 341b–352a) that is absent from D (*Queste P-V*, III, 518–355; §§ 707–18). It is thanks to
Françoise Vielliard's description of Bodmer MS 105 (*Bibliotheca Bodmeriana: Catalogue des
manuscrits français du Moyen Age* [Geneva, 1975], pp. 67–71) that I first realized that this codex
included a section of the *Post-Vulgate*, on which see my articles, 'Another MS of a Fragment of
the Post-Vulgate *Roman du Graal*,' BBIAS, XXVIII (1976), 189–90; 'The Post-Vulgate *Mort Artu*
and the Textual Tradition of the Vulgate *Mort Artu*,' in *Estudios Romanicos dedicados al Prof.
Andres Soria Ortega* (Granada, 1985), pp. 273–90; *Queste P-V*, I, 13–22 and 203–7.

[44] See Longobardi, 'Altri recuperi d'Archivio: Le *Prophécies de Merlin*,' *Studi Mediolatini e Volgari*,
XXXV (1989), 72–139 (112–14: *P-V Mort Artu* fragment); Longobardi, 'Nuovi frammenti della
Post-Vulgata: la *Suite*, la Continuazione della *Suite du Merlin*, la *Queste* e la *Mort Artu* (con
l'intrusione del *Guiron*),' *Studi Mediolatini e Volgari*, XXXVIII (1992), 119–55 (127–43: *P-V Mort
Artu*); Bogdanow, *Queste P-V*, I, 10–13 and 200–3. These fragments correspond to D, §§ 631–3
(*Queste P-V*, III, 395–400; IV, 2, 423, 430–5, 547, 578–86).

[45] G. Paris, review of Karl von Reinhardstöttner, *Historia dos cavalleiros da Mesa Redonda e da
demanda do Santo Graal*, Romania, 16 (1887), 583–6.

[46] *Queste P-V*, III, 307, § 581 (MS Rawlinson 105, fols. 212d–213a; MS BNF fr. 343, fol. 101a). Same
reference in D (fol. 179b): 'ca sobejo averia eu que fazer, se vos contasse todalas maravilhas de
Galaaz, *e demais a postomeyra parte do meu livro ssera maior ca as duas primeyras.*'

[47] *Queste P-V*, III, 450, § 664. The corresponding reference in the Spanish *Demanda* (De 1515 and

[All the things that would be relevant here which I do not relate fully, you can find in the *Conte del Grait*, for I have refrained from relating fully the great battles between King Ban's lineage and King Arthur, and between the Emperor of Rome and King Arthur, *because the detailed account would be longer than the three parts of the book*.]

Moreover, there are in the *Suite* section references to events in the *Queste–Mort Artu* which correspond only to incidents related in the corresponding *P-V* narrative. Thus, apart from the reference to King Mark's death announced in the *Suite* and related in the *P-V Mort Artu*,[48] the *Suite* explicitly states at the point where it introduces the newly crowned Mark that he later married Yseut, 'as the story will mention in connection with an event of which the *Graaus* speaks' ('li rois Mars, qui puis ot a feme Yseut la blonde, *si comme chis contes meismes devisera apertement, pour chou que conter i couvint pour une aventure dont li Graaus parole*').[49] The *Vulgate Queste* of course does not mention King Mark, but in the *P-V Queste* Mark invades Logres in order to recover Yseut who together with Tristan had sought refuge in Joyeuse Garde.[50] Similarly the reference in the *Suite* to the *Beste Glatissant* as 'one of the adventures of the Grail'[51] is of relevance only in the *P-V Queste* where the *Beste* is finally slain and its origin is related.[52] And in reverse, in the *P-V Queste* alone, at the point where Galahad heals Pellean the Maimed King, the latter explains that it was the 'Chevalier as Deus Espees' who had caused the wound,[53] a clear reference to the scene in the *Suite* where Balain 'the Knight with the Two Swords' struck the Dolorous Stroke.[54] As for the allusions to the feud between Gawain and Pellinor's lineage in the *P-V Queste*,[55] these are of relevance in the context of the *P-V* where in the *Suite* section the writer relates the origin of this feud: in the war between Arthur and Gawain's father, King Lot, King Pellinor slew Lot, and Gawain (aged eleven) swore to avenge his father's death on Pellinor and his lineage.[56]

In the *Vulgate Cycle*, the *Queste* is preceded by the *Lancelot* proper. But what followed the end of the triple adventures of Gawain, Yvain and the Morholt (the *Abenteuer* section), long considered the end of the *P-V Suite*, in the original *P-V Cycle*? According to Wechssler,[57] whose theories were accepted with certain

1535; ed. Bonilla y San Martin, p. 325b) is even more precise: 'que fueron entre el linaje del rey Van y el rey Artur, *en tal que (De 1535 porque) las tres partes de mi libro fuessen yguales*' [so that the three parts of my book should be of equal length].

[48] See p. 37 above.

[49] *Merlin*, I, 230.

[50] *Queste P-V*, III, 82–125, §§ 445–72.

[51] *Merlin*, I, 160.

[52] *Queste P-V*, II, 111–12, 114, 127–35, 159–60, 165–8, 197, 221–3, 492, 521 (= §§ 82–3, 86, 97–9, 100–1, 121–2, 125, 128, 148, 163–5, 193–6, 369, 382); III, 133, 261, 272, 295, 307–13, 351–66 (= §§ 474, 550, 558, 571, 581–4, 603–9).

[53] *Queste P-V*, III, 321, § 590: 'Veez ci li Cop Doloreus que li Chevalier as Deus Espees me fist. Par cestui cop sunt maint mal avenu. Ce poise moi.' [This is the Dolorous Stroke that the Knight with the Two Swords dealt me. From this stroke has come much evil.]

[54] Bogdanow, *Romance of the Grail*, pp. 241–9.

[55] *Queste P-V*, II, 313 § 221; III, 257, § 548.

[56] *Merlin*, I, 261, and II, 11.

[57] Wechssler, *Über die verschiedenen Redaktionen*.

modifications by G. Paris,[58] E. Brugger[59] and E. Vettermann,[60] the original
'pseudo-Robert' cycle, which they wrongly believed predated the *Vulgate
Cycle*,[61] went through three successive redactions. The first of these, *A*, was
assumed to consist of six branches, including one corresponding to the *Lancelot*
proper; the second one, *B*, omitted the *Lancelot*, while the third one, *C*, also
omitted the *Estoire del Saint Graal*. It was argued furthermore that the compilers
of the second and third redactions shortened the remaining sections so as to
make the cycle fall into three equal parts. J. D. Bruce, while realizing that the
so-called 'pseudo-Robert' cycle was dependent on the *Vulgate*, nevertheless (like
Wechssler) regarded this cycle as having undergone two successive abridg-
ments, in the process of which some *remanieur* omitted the *Lancelot*.[62] But there is
no evidence to support any of these conjectures.[63] The problem of the form and
structure of the original *P-V Roman du Graal* can in fact only be resolved by
taking at face value the evidence provided by the extant *P-V* manuscripts.

At several points the *P-V* writer not only indicates, as mentioned above, that
he has divided his *livre* into three equal parts, but that although the substance of
the *Grant hystoire de Lanscelot* was not irrelevant to that of his work, he excluded
it from his composition because its inclusion would have made the middle part
three times as long as the other two. Thus at the point where, in the *Suite*, he
refers to the ring that the Lady of the Lake gave Lancelot, our author says:

> un anelet que li avoit doné la Dame [Huth: damoisiele] del Lac, si com la *Grant
> Estoire de Launcelot* le devise, *cele meisme estoire qui doit estre partie* [Huth: departie]
> *de mon livere*, ne mie pur ceo qu'ele n'i apartiegne [et] qu'ele n'en soit trait, mais
> pur ceo qu'il covient que les .iii. parties de mon liver soient ingeus, l'une ausi
> grant com l'autre, e si jeo ajoustasse cele grant estoire, [la moi<ene> partie de
> mon livre fust au tresble plus grant que les autres deus. *Pour chou me couvient il
> laissier celle grant ystoire*][64] *que devise* [*les oevres de Lanscelot et*][65] *la naissance* [*que*][66]
> trop i averoit a conter, mes[67] a deviser les .ix. lignes des Nasciens, tut ausi com il
> apartient a la *Haute Estoire*[68] del Saint Graal.[69]

58 G. Paris, review of *Über die verschiedenen Redaktionen, Romania*, 24 (1895), 472–3.
59 Ernst Brugger, 'L'enserrement Merlin: Studien zur Merlinsage,' *Zeitschrift für französische
    Sprache und Literatur*, XXIX (1906), 56–140; XXX (1906), 169–239; XXXI (1907), 239–81; XXXIII
    (1908), 145–94; XXXIV (1909), 99–150; XXXV (1910), 1–55.
60 Ella Vetterman, *Die Balen-Dichtungen*, Beihefte zur Zeitschrift für romanische Philologie, LX
    (1918), 85–192.
61 Pauphilet was the first scholar to realize that the so-called 'pseudo-Robert' *Queste* was a
    reworking of the *Vulgate*, in his article 'La *Queste du Saint Graal* du ms Bibl. Nat. fr. 343,'
    Romania, 36 (1907), 591–609.
62 J. Douglas Bruce, *The Evolution of Arthurian Romance from the Beginnings down to the Year 1300*,
    2nd ed. with bibliographical supplement by Alfons Hilka, 2 vols. (Göttingen and Baltimore,
    1928), I, 458–79.
63 For a detailed appraisal of the various theories, including Wechssler's and Bruce's, see
    Bogdanow, *The Romance of the Grail*, pp. 40–59.
64 Omitted in the Cambridge MS (reading of the Huth MS).
65 Reading of the Huth MS. The Cambridge MS has 'devise l'estoire de la naissance.'
66 The Cambridge MS omits *que*; the Huth MS which omits 'que trop i averoit a conter,' has 'la
    naissance, et voel deviser les neuf lignies des Nascions'.
67 The Huth MS has 'et voel deviser les neuf lignies des Nascions'.
68 Huth MS: '*Escriture*'.
69 Cambridge MS, fol. 279c; *Merlin*, II, 57. The 1535 edition of the Spanish *Baladro* has a similar

But if, as there can be no doubt, the *Lancelot* proper as such formed no part of the *Post-Vulgate*, it is equally apparent that the *Suite* cannot have ended originally with the *Abenteuer* section. Firstly there is a considerable chronological gap between the end of the *Abenteuer* and the beginning of the *P-V Queste*: the Grail knights, Galahad and Perceval, have not yet been *engenrés ne nés*,[70] while Lancelot, who will be Galahad's father, is still a small boy ('n'a pas encore deus ans d'aage').[71] And secondly, there are in the *P-V Suite* many forward references to later incidents not related before the end of the *Abenteuer* section, but to which the writer refers back in the *P-V Queste* as having taken place. Now a considerable portion of the missing narrative has in fact been preserved in two manuscripts, a thirteenth-century codex of the Prose *Tristan*, BNF fr. 12599, and *Livre III* of BNF fr. 112. This section, published in 1965 under the title *La Folie Lancelot*,[72] has made it possible to understand how the *P-V* writer was able to exclude the *Lancelot* proper and yet avoid a break in continuity: in order to provide a transition to the *P-V Queste*, he extended the *Suite* by adapting certain incidents from the *Agravain* section of the *Lancelot*, combining these with his own inventions and a number of episodes derived from the First Version of the Prose *Tristan*.[73] But the *Folie Lancelot*, which begins with an incident announced in the *Abenteuer* section, Gaheriet's slaying of his mother,[74] and is followed by such episodes as Lancelot's madness and his stay in the *Isle de Joie*, Perceval's youth, the death of two of Pellinor's sons (Lamorat and Drian) predicted in the *Suite*,[75] as well as Erec's early exploits which are concluded in the *P-V Queste*, is in itself incomplete and does not completely fill the gaps preceding and following the *Folie Lancelot*. Several, though by no means all, of the remaining lacunae can now, however, be filled by fragments preserved in libraries in Imola and Bologna.[76] Belonging originally most probably to the same codex as the

---

passage but, like the Cambridge MS, it omits the words *la moiene . . . grant ystoire* after *grande historia*: 'E aquel anillo le dio la donzella del Lago, assi como la *Historia de Lançarote* lo deuisa; *aquella historia deue ser auida e partida de mi libro*, no porque le no pertenesca e no sea dende sacada, mas porque todas partes de mi libro sean yguales, la vna tan grande como la otra, e si juntassen aquella tan grande historia que dize de los hechos de Lançarote, e de su nacencia, e de los nueuos linajes de Nacion, assi como lo deuisa la *Alta Historia del Santo Grial* . . .' (ed. Bonilla y San Martin, ch. CCXCVIII, p. 120a; omitted in the 1498 *Baladro*).

70　*Merlin*, I, 160 and 258; *Die Abenteuer*, p. 74.

71　*Merlin*, II, 66 and 143.

72　*La Folie Lancelot*, ed. F. Bogdanow, Beihefte zur Zeitschrift für romanische Philologie, 109 (Tübingen, 1965).

73　A small fragment of the *Folie Lancelot* was discovered by Keith Busby in a manuscript in Cracow; it covers pp. 11–13, lines 454–556 and pp. 18–21, lines 780–891 of my edition. See Busby, 'Quelques fragments inédits de roman en prose,' *Cultura Neolatina*, XLIV (1984), 155–63. Löseth includes in his *Analyse* (§§ 283a–291a) a summary of the *Folie Lancelot* section, based on MS 12599, without, however, identifying it.

74　*Abenteuer*, p. 93: 'Et lors dist a Gaheriet: "Tu passasses de bonté et de valeur tous les compaignons de la Table Ronde fors seulement deus, se ne fust la mort de ta mere que tu hasteras par ton pechié . . ." '

75　See *Merlin*, I, 261. This episode has been adapted from *Tris. 1*; see *Folie Lancelot*, pp. 76–80 and 241–8.

76　See Longobardi, 'Frammenti di codici in antico francese della Biblioteca Comunale di Imola,' in *Miscellanea Roncaglia* (1989), pp. 727–59 (757–9: fragment preceding the *Folie Lancelot*); Longobardi, 'Nuovi frammenti della *Post-Vulgata* . . .,' *Studi Mediolatini e Volgari*, XXXVIII (1992), 119–55 (123–6 and 134–9: fragments preceding and following the *Folie Lancelot*);

other *P-V* fragments in these libraries, this new series includes among other incidents Pellinor's death, announced in the *Suite*,[77] and Lancelot's departure from the *Isle de Joie* with Galahad (aged sixteen), adapted from the *Agravain* but interwoven with episodes that continue themes begun both in the *Suite* and the *Folie Lancelot*, such as those relating to the *Chastel Tugan* and Erec.[78] Finally, a further portion, a section of which corresponds to one of the new French fragments, has been preserved in a sixteenth-century codex of the Castilian prose *Lancelot*, MS 9611 of the Madrid National Library.[79]

As regards the first part of the *P-V* Arthuriad, this section, to judge from the redactional indications in the Huth and Cambridge manuscripts, ends at the point in the *Suite* section where Balain sets out in quest of the invisible knight.[80] In both these codices, as well as in the Castilian *Baladro*, the *Suite* is preceded by the prose rendering of Robert de Boron's *Merlin* and indeed is presented as a continuation of the latter. Further, in the Cambridge manuscript and in Malory, but neither in the Huth manuscript nor in the *Baladro*, is an account of Arthur's wars against the rebel kings, based on the *Vulgate Merlin*, inserted between the end of the *Merlin* and the beginning of the *Suite* proper.[81] It is highly probable though not absolutely certain, that as Vinaver first suggested,[82] this account of Arthur's early wars formed an integral part of the original *P-V* Arthuriad.[83] Concerning the opening section of the *P-V* Arthuriad, there can be no doubt that originally a version of the *Estoire del Saint Graal* must have preceded the *Merlin* section, and not the prose rendering of Robert's *Joseph* as in the Huth manuscript. This is evident from the fact that there is in the *P-V Queste* a specific reference to an incident related 'in the first part of our book' which figures only in the *Estoire del Saint Graal*: 'Et dedenz celui an avint il que aventure l'aporta a l'abeie ou li rois Mordrainz avoit demoré des le tens Yosep d'Arimatie dusq'a la venue de Galahaz, si plaié et si navré *com li contes l'a devisé en la primiere partie de nostre livre.*'[84]

Bogdanow, 'The Importance of the Bologna and Imola Fragments for the Reconstruction of the *Post-Vulgate Roman du Graal*,' *Bulletin of the John Rylands University Library of Manchester*, 80 (1998), 33–64; *Queste P-V*, IV, 2, pp. 511–27, 595–5, 614–40 (critical edition of these fragments: pp. 614–40).

77 *Merlin*, I, 261; *Queste P-V*, IV, 2, pp. 511–20. In the *Folie Lancelot*, the writer refers back to Pellinor's death (pp. 2.35–43; 95.584–5; 98.715–23; 127.286–128.305; 153.233).

78 See *Queste P-V*, IV, 2, pp. 527–43.

79 See Bogdanow, 'The Madrid *Tercero Libro de don Lançarote* (MS 9611) and its Relationship to the *Post-Vulgate Roman du Graal* in the light of a hitherto unknown French source of one of the incidents of the *Tercero Libro*,' *Bulletin of Hispanic Studies*, 76 (1999), 441–52; *Queste P-V*, IV, 2, pp. 724–51.

80 *Merlin*, I, 280; see n. 17 above.

81 See n. 14 above.

82 Contrary to R. H. Wilson, 'The Rebellion of the Kings in Malory and in the Cambridge *Suite du Merlin*,' *University of Texas Studies in English*, XXXI (1952), 13–26; and 'The Cambridge *Suite du Merlin* Re-examined,' *University of Texas Studies in English*, XXXVI (1957), 41–51.

83 Vinaver, *The Works of Sir Thomas Malory* (1947), III, 1277–9; Vinaver, 'Genèse de la *Suite*'; Bogdanow, 'The Rebellion of the Kings in the Cambridge MS of the *Suite du Merlin*,' *University of Texas Studies in English*, XXXIV (1955), 6–17; Bogdanow, *The Romance of the Grail*, pp. 31–9.

84 *Queste P-V*, III, 290, § 569. Although the *Vulgate Queste* relates the healing of Mordrain it does not include a reference to the *Estoire*.

The incident in question is the episode where Mordrain, on approaching too closely the ark containing the Holy Vessel, lost his sight and the use of his body, and was told that he would remain in this state until the coming of Galahad.[85]

But not only does the reference to Mordrain's fate in the *Estoire del Saint Graal* furnish conclusive evidence that the writer of the *P-V* saw the *Estoire* as an integral part of his composition. The unique codex of a Portuguese translation of the *Estoire*, the *Josep Abarimatia* of MS 643 in the Torre do Tombo, Lisbon, significantly bears the subtitle *a primeira parte da Demanda do Santo Graal*,[86] while the Salamanca codex of the Castilian *P-V* fragments places a fragment of the *Libro de Josep Abarimatia* before its *Merlin* section.[87] But to what extent did the *P-V Estoire* differ from the versions preserved by the extant *Vulgate Estoire* manuscripts?[88] Only very slightly, judging by the Portuguese *Josep*. The few divergences are, however, significant: they reveal the *P-V* writer's deliberate attempt to strengthen the links between the *Estoire* and the *P-V* versions of the *Suite du Merlin* and the *Queste*. Thus, whereas *le coup d'une seule espee* will inaugurate in Arthur's time marvels and adventures, according to the *Vulgate Estoire* manuscripts,[89] in the Portuguese *Josep* these marvels will be caused *por golpe de lança*[90] – a clear reference to Balain's Dolorous Stroke in the *P-V Suite*. Elsewhere, the reference is even more precise. In speaking of King Pellean, the Maimed King, the *Vulgate Estoire* manuscripts explain that he received his wound in a battle in Rome.[91] The Portuguese *Josep*, however, announces that it will be the *Cavaleiro das Duas Espadas* (the Knight with the Two Swords) who will strike the fatal blow with the *Lamça Vingador* and that this blow will not only maim the king, but inaugurate the adventures of Logres 'as this story will relate':

Depos el rey Lambor reinou depos ele [Pellean],[92] seu filho, que foi tolheito de ambas as coxas *de hũa lamçada que lhe deu o Cavaleiro das Duas Espadas com a Lamça*

85 Sommer, *Vulgate Version*, I, 242. This incident, it must be stressed, is not in Robert de Boron's *Joseph*.
86 See Bogdanow, *Romance of the Grail*, p. 44 n. 9. For a diplomatic transcription of the Lisbon codex, see Henry Hare Carter, *The Portuguese Book of Joseph of Arimathea* (Chapel Hill, 1967). Ivo Castro, who published the first 48 folios of the manuscript, *Livro de José de Arimateia, Estudo e ediçao do cod. antt 643* (Lisbon, 1984), is preparing a critical edition of the complete text.
87 On the Castilian fragment of the *Estoire* preserved in the Salamanca codex, see n. 9.
88 Textually the Portuguese and Castilian translations of the *Estoire* are closely related to the version preserved in Rennes, MS Bibliothèque municipale 255. But neither the Rennes codex nor the Cambridge MS contains the specific references to the Dolorous Stroke incident unique to the Portuguese *Josep*. On the relationship of the French *Estoire* manuscripts to the *Josep*, see Bogdanow, 'The Relationship of the Portuguese *Josep Abarimatia* to the Extant French MSS. of the *Estoire del Saint Graal*,' *Zeitschrift für romanische Philologie*, 76 (1960), 343–75. I am preparing an edition of the Rennes *Estoire*.
89 'Et a celui tens avendra en ceste terre *par ce coup d'une seule espee* aventures et si granz merveilles . . .' (Rennes MS 255, fol. 75a–b; Sommer, *Vulgate Version*, I, 226).
90 'Naquele tempo avera nesta terra *por golpe de lamça* tão gramdes avemturas e taão maravylhosas . . .' (Lisbon MS 643, fol. 232v). The Castilian *Josep* breaks off before reaching this point.
91 'Aprés lo roi Lambor regna Pellehan ses filz qui fu mehaigniés des dous cuisses *en une bataille de Rome*. Et pour celui mehaing qu'il prist en cele bataille, l'apelerent puis tuit cil qui le conoissoient comunalment lo Roi Mehaignié . . .' (Rennes MS 255, fol. 98c; Sommer, *Vulgate Version*, I, 290).
92 Pellean, the name of the Maimed King in the *P-V Suite-Queste* and attested by the *Vulgate Estoire* manuscripts, was omitted by the scribe of the Lisbon codex.

Vimgador, por omde as avemturas vierãom em Londres asy como depois esta estorea vos
comtara. E por aquele tolhimemto foi depois chamado [el Rei] Tolheito . . .[93]

[After King Lambor reigned his son [Pellean] who was wounded through both
the thighs by a blow which the Knight with the Two Swords struck with the Sacred Lance, as a result of which the adventures of Logres were inaugurated, as
this story will relate later. And on account of this wound he was later called the
Maimed King.]

The earliest critics not only failed to recognize the form of the *Post-Vulgate*
Roman du Graal, but condemned those of its constituent parts at their disposal as
a 'labyrinth of fantastic adventures.'[94] In reality, the *Post-Vulgate* is a creative
reinterpretation of the *Vulgate,* the work not of a *barbare maladroit* as Pauphilet
argued,[95] but of a man who attempted to produce a more homogeneous and
closely knit whole of which Arthur and the history of his kingdom, rather than
Lancelot, was the central character. The *double esprit* so characteristic of the
Vulgate – the clash between the exaltation of courtly love in large portions of the
Lancelot proper and the religious mysticism in the *Queste,* followed by a resurgence of the love theme in the *Mort Artu*[96] – is absent from the *Post-Vulgate.* Our
author not only dispensed with the greater part of the *Lancelot* proper, as we
indicated above, but radically revised both the *Queste* and the *Mort Artu*
sections. The *Vulgate Queste,* written by a man steeped in the mystical theology
of Saint Bernard,[97] is essentially a treatise on grace, with hardly a line not
intended for doctrinal exposition.[98] For the *Post-Vulgate* author, the *Queste* is part
of the history of Arthur's kingdom, hence he does not confine himself to the
adventures of the *Vulgate* Grail knights, but adds incidents relevant to the
fortunes of Logres. Moreover, to give his work a wider appeal, he omits or
shortens some of the theological disquisitions. But the *Post-Vulgate* is by no
means secular in outlook. The Grail remains a symbol of grace, and the Final
Scene at Corbenic remains the high point of the narrative. Moreover, although
the characters may not always be as assiduous in their religious practices as in
the *Vulgate,* there are many references to prayer and confession, and sin by all
standards is condemned. Lancelot not only repents of his love for Guinevere as
in the *Vulgate,* but in a passage peculiar to the *Post-Vulgate,* Count Hernoul
expresses his deep sense of guilt for not having revealed to Arthur Lancelot's

[93] Lisbon, MS 643, fol. 304v.
[94] Bruce, *The Evolution of Arthurian Romance,* I, 464. Cf. *Merlin,* I, xlviii.
[95] Pauphilet, 'La *Queste du Saint Graal* du ms Bibl. Nat. fr. 343,' *Romania,* 36 (1907), 606.
[96] See Bogdanow, 'The *double esprit* of the Prose *Lancelot,*' in *Courtly Romance: A Collection of Essays,* ed. Guy R. Mermier and Edelgard E. Du Bruck (Detroit, 1984), pp. 1–22; 'The Changing Vision of Arthur's Death,' in *Dies Illa. Death in the Middle Ages,* ed. Jane H. M. Taylor (Liverpool, 1984), pp. 107–23; 'La chute du royaume d'Arthur: Évolution du thème,' *Romania,* 107 (1986), 504–19.
[97] See Bogdanow, 'An Interpretation of the Meaning and Purpose of the Vulgate *Queste del Saint Graal* in the Light of the Mystical Theology of St. Bernard,' in *The Changing Face of Arthurian Romance: Essays on Arthurian Prose Romances in Memory of Cedric E. Pickford,* ed. Alison Adams et al., Arthurian Studies XVI (Cambridge, 1986), 23–46.
[98] See Etienne Gilson, 'La mystique de la grâce dans la *Queste del Saint Graal,*' *Romania,* 51 (1925), 321–47.

love for Guinevere which he refers to as 'folie . . . traïson . . . vilennie . . . pechié'.[99] Elsewhere too, in episodes added by our author centred on a love theme, the sinful nature of illicit love is underlined. The unrequited feelings of King Brutus' daughter for Galahad are described as *folle amour*.[100] Tristan and Yseut's relationship is belittled,[101] and while Palamedes, the Saracen and Tristan's rival for Yseut's affections, will convert and be rewarded as one of the twelve chosen knights to participate in the Final Scene at Corbenic, Tristan will not repent of his love and will be denied this honour. And although in the *P-V Mort Artu*, as in the *Vulgate*, Lancelot will relapse into his sinful ways, the anti-courtly spirit of the preceding section will continue to be reflected in the *P-V* version where our author deliberately omits most of the *Vulgate* scenes in which Lancelot and Guinevere appear alone.[102]

As for the *Suite du Merlin*, far from leading up to a *Lancelot* branch, it has the same ascetic, anti-courtly overtone as the other sections. Here too there is a constant preoccupation with sin. Tor, about to leave home, is reminded by his mother not to forget his Creator, but to guard his soul so as to render it to Him intact.[103] Gaheriet, before his fight with the giant Aupartis, does penance as a hermit had suggested,[104] Arthur, on the point of facing Lot's army, is advised by Merlin to confess all his sins because this would help him more than anything else,[105] and the author stresses that the damsels of the *Roche aux Pucelles* desist from doing too much harm by their enchantments 'pour doubtance de pechié' [for fear of sinning].[106] Above all, unlawful love is severely condemned, as in the *Queste*. Though Gaheriet is subsequently ashamed of his *mesfait* [misdeed],[107] he not only defends the murder of his mother, the Queen of Orkney, as a just punishment for a queen who *par maleureuse luxure* brought shame to her children and her whole lineage, but expresses the hope that his action 'will be a lesson for the noble ladies who commit such great disloyalties' ['et celle chose fera, se cuide je, chastier les haultes dames des grans desloyaultés qu'elles font'].[108] Similarly, Gawain's relationship with Arcade is referred to as 'pechié grant et orrible',[109] while Morgain, once beautiful, is said to have become ugly when the devil entered her heart and she was filled with *luxure*.[110] As for the episodes taken over from the *Lancelot* proper in the *Folie Lancelot* section, these in no way idealise Lancelot. Rather, they serve to explain the circumstances leading up to Galahad's conception, while stressing the pathetic and humiliating conse-

---

99 *Queste P-V*, III, 59–60, § 429.
100 *Queste P-V*, II, 142, rubric.
101 When Galahad hears Palamedes lament his unrequited love for Yseut in the presence of the sleeping Tristan, Galahad refrains from wakening the latter as he does not want him to kill Palamedes 'for such a poor reason as loving Queen Yseut' ('por si povre acheison com d'amer la reyne Yselt': *Queste P-V*, II, 494, § 370).
102 See Bogdanow, *Romance of the Grail*, pp. 146 and 214–15.
103 *Merlin*, II, 135.
104 *Die Abenteuer*, p. 121.
105 *Merlin*, I, 249.
106 *Die Abenteuer*, p. 80.
107 *Folie Lancelot*, pp. 4.162.2–4 and 5.202–6.
108 *Folie Lancelot*, p. 5.172–5.
109 Sommer, *Abenteuer*, p. 32.
110 *Merlin*, I, 166. For further examples, see Bogdanow, *Romance of the Grail*, pp. 206–14.

quences for Lancelot of his relationship with Guinevere, his madness and his exile from court.[111]

Structurally, too, the *Post-Vulgate* forms a more unified whole than the *Vulgate*. Unlike the latter which grew up in stages, the *Post-Vulgate* was conceived from the outset as a whole. The *P-V Queste* runs without a break into the *P-V Mort Artu*, and many of the discrepancies between the *Estoire del Saint Graal* and the rest of the work that mar the *Vulgate* have been avoided.[112] Above all, contrary to a long-held assumption,[113] the *P-V* writer was not content to heap up a series of disparate adventures, rather he sought to present a coherent narrative in which the principal events of Arthur's reign were skilfully motivated. And this he did, as Vinaver was the first to recognize, in a manner characteristic of thirteenth-century writers, not psychologically, but structurally, by supplying the antecedents of the incidents to be elucidated.[114] Hence the early history of Arthur's kingdom, the *Suite du Merlin* section, instead of being limited largely to a series of Arthur's wars as is the *Vulgate Suite*, is made up of long sequences of events which are completed in the later portions of the narrative. One of the most notable of these is the conception of Mordred, the opening episode of the *Suite* proper, which becomes the initial link in a chain of incidents leading up to the death of Arthur and the downfall of his kingdom.[115] Similarly, the series of episodes culminating in Balain's Dolorous Stroke and its tragic consequences, prepare for and are counterbalanced by the coming of Galahad who will end the adventures of Logres and, in the Final Scene at Corbenic, heal the Maimed King wounded by Balain's fatal stroke.[116]

But there is more to it than this. The structural unity of the *Post-Vulgate* is closely linked to the work's ascetic overtones, which are reflected in the author's conception of Arthur and his kingdom. For our writer, Arthur is the *roi aventureux*, the king of chance and mischance, and his kingdom is the *roiaume aventureux*.[117] Unintentionally, through mischance, Arthur and the knights of his kingdom are doomed to commit sinful acts which they and the whole country will subsequently have to expiate. Thus it was by chance that Balain arrived at the Grail Castle in search of the invisible knight, Garlan, who had slain his companion. It was by chance that when his sword broke in combat against Garlan's brother, King Pellean, Balain went in search of a weapon to defend himself, entered the Grail Chamber and, unaware of the sin he was committing in touching the Holy Lance, seized it and struck the Dolorous Stroke that was to bring down divine vengeance.[118] Similarly, when Arthur conceived Mordred on Lot's wife, he was unaware that she was his half-sister; although the incest was

---

[111] See Bogdanow, *Romance of the Grail*, pp. 60–87.
[112] See Bogdanow, *Romance of the Grail*, pp. 156–70 and 199.
[113] See n. 95 above.
[114] Vinaver's introduction to *Le Roman de Balain*, ed. Mary Dominica Legge (Manchester, 1942), pp. ix–xxii; Vinaver, ed. *The Works of Sir Thomas Malory* (1947), III, 1265–74; (1967), III, 1267–75; Vinaver, 'Genèse de la *Suite*'; Vinaver, 'The Dolorous Stroke,' *Medium Aevum*, XXV (1956), 175–80.
[115] See Bogdanow, *Romance of the Grail*, 144–5.
[116] See Bogdanow, *Romance of the Grail*, 129–37.
[117] *Merlin*, II, 97; *Queste P-V*, III, 469, § 679.
[118] Cf. Bogdanow, *The Romance of the Grail*, pp. 129–37.

unintentional, he and his kingdom would have to pay for this sin, as was divinely decreed and as Arthur himself recognized after the battle on Salisbury Plain, shortly before his death:

'Giflet, eu nom soo rey Artur, o que soyam chamar Rey Aventuroso polas bõas andanças que avia. Mas quem m'agora chamar per meu direyto nome, chamar-m-a mal aventurado e mizquinho. Esto me ffez ventura, que xi me tornou madrasta e enmiga. *E Nosso Senhor, <a> que praz que vi[v]a en doo e en tristeza esse pouco ey de viver, e bem mo mostra: que asi como el quis e foy poderosso de me erguer per muy fremossas aventuras e sen meu merecimento, bem assi é poderoso de me dirribar per aventuras feas e mas, per meu mericimento e per meu pecado.'*[119]

['Girflet, I am no longer the King Arthur that they used to call the *Rois Aventureux* on account of the good fortune he had. He who would now call me by my right name should call me unfortunate and wretched. Fortune did this to me; she has turned into my stepmother and Enemy. *And Our Lord whom it pleases that I should spend in grief and sadness what little of my life is left, makes me realize that just as He once desired and had the power to raise me through many beautiful adventures without my meriting it, so He now has the power to lower me again through ill adventures that I deserve on account of my sin.'*]

Nor is this the final mischance to befall Arthur and his kingdom. After the death of Arthur and the death of Lancelot, who had vanquished Mordred's two sons on his return from Gaunes (as in the *Vulgate*), King Mark invaded Logres for the second time to avenge the shame he suffered on his first invasion during the Grail Quest. And though Mark himself lost his life before the end of this second invasion, he succeeded in destroying not only Camalot, but also the symbol of Arthur's former glory, the Round Table. Yet this final tragedy could have been avoided if Mark's loyalty in his youth to Arthur had not turned to hatred through Arthur's own fault: he had allowed the adulterous Tristan and Yseut to take refuge in Logres in Lancelot's castle Joyeuse Garde, and it was in order to regain Yseut that Mark had invaded Arthur's kingdom during the *Queste*.

If, in the *Post-Vulgate*, it is not only sins committed deliberately that must be expiated, but also those committed *per ignorantiam*, this is because our author is translating into his narrative one of the Old Testament teachings that St. Bernard reaffirmed in his *Treatise on Baptism*. Contesting Abelard's assertion that one cannot sin in ignorance, St. Bernard states emphatically:

Is forsitan qui asserit non posse peccari per ignorantiam, nunquam pro suis ignorantiis deprecatur, sed potius prophetiam irrideat deprecantem et dicentem: *Delicta juventutis meae, et ignorantias meas ne memineris* (Psal. XXIV, 7) . . . Numquid no ex his satis apparet, in quantis jacet ignorantiae tenebris, qui ignorat peccari posse interdum *per ignorantiam*? ('S. Bernardi Abbatis, ad

[119] *Queste P-V*, III, 457–8, § 672. In the corresponding passage in the Vulgate *Mort Artu*, Arthur simply blames Fortune for his fate: 'Girflet, Fortune qui m'a esté mere jusque ci, et or m'est devenue marrastre, me fet user le remenant de ma vie en douleur et en corrouz et en tristesce' (ed. Frappier [Geneva, 1936], pp. 222.20–223.1).

Hugonem de Sancto Victore epistola seu tractatus, de Baptismo alliisque quaestionibus ab ipso propositis,' in *Patrologia Latina*, 182, pp. 1041–2)

[It is probable that the person who maintains that a sin committed in ignorance is not a sin, has never begged God to forgive him that sort of sin, and mocks the prophet when he hears him say: 'Do not remember the sins of my youth, nor the sins committed unwittingly' (Psalm XXIV.7) . . . All these passages, do they not indicate in what gross ignorance is he who does not know that one can sin unwittingly?]

But our author's conception of Arthur's kingdom as the *roiaume aventureux* explains not only the type of incidents that are used to prepare for the main events of Arthur's reign; it accounts also for the references to the work's tripartition. Far from being arbitrary as critics have assumed, the divisions indicated correspond to the three phases in the history of Logres. The first part, which deals with the history of Logres before the beginning of the 'adventures of the Grail,' naturally includes the early history of the Grail (the *Estoire del Saint Graal*) as well as an account of the events leading up to Arthur's reign (the prose rendering of Robert de Boron's *Merlin*). It ends logically part way through the *Suite du Merlin*, at the point where Balain sets out on the series of adventures which will lead him to the Grail Castle where he will strike the Dolorous Stroke that inaugurates the adventures of the Grail. The second part, which includes the remainder of the *Suite* sections, shows Logres labouring under the consequences of the Dolorous Stroke. The third part begins equally logically with the news of the arrival of the long-awaited deliverer, the Good Knight Galahad who is the counterpart of Balain and will end the adventures of Logres. However, as Arthur and his kingdom have yet to pay for his sin of incest, this final section includes not only the *Queste*, but also its sequel: Arthur's own death at the hands of his incestuous son, and the destruction of the kingdom.

The *Post-Vulgate* author refers to the whole of his work as the *Estoire dou Graal*,[120] or the *Haute Escriture del Saint Graal*,[121] or the *Contes del Saint Graal*,[122] a title that clearly reflects the importance of the Grail in his concept of the Arthurian world. As for the date of the *Post-Vulgate*, this can be fixed precisely. Since our author drew on both the *Vulgate Cycle* (written c. 1215–30) and the First Version of the Prose *Tristan* (written c. 1225–35),[123] the year 1235 must be considered as the *terminus a quo*. On the other hand, as the Second Version of the Prose *Tristan*, compiled probably early in the second half of the thirteenth century, in its turn made use of the *Post-Vulgate*, the latter was evidently composed before 1250. But an even more precise *terminus ad quem* is furnished by a reference in the *Palamède* to the final episode of the *Post-Vulgate*, the destruction of Camalot by King Mark:

120　*Merlin*, I, 280, II, 61, 137.
121　*Merlin*, II, 57.
122　*Folie Lancelot*, p. 21.
123　This is the date suggested by Emmanuèle Baumgartner, *Le Tristan en prose: Essai d'interprétation d'un roman médiéval* (Geneva, 1975), pp. 36–40. Vinaver thought the First Version of the Prose *Tristan* dates from 1225–30 ('The Prose *Tristan*,' in *Arthurian Literature in the Middle Ages*, p. 339).

Et pour che que li rois Artus l'ama toutes voies sour toutes autres chités, la destruit puis toute et la desoula li felons rois Marc de Cornouaille aprés [la mort] le roi Artus. (BNF fr. 350, fol. 6a)

[And because King Arthur loved all his life Camalot more than all his other cities, the treacherous King Mark of Cornwall destroyed it completely and razed it to the ground after the death of King Arthur.]

And as the *Palamède* was composed before 5 February 1240, the date of a letter from the Emperor Frederick II to one of his officials, the *secretus* of Messina, in which he mentions the *Palamède*, this means that the *Post-Vulgate* was written no later than 1235–40.

PART II

THE ART OF THE *LANCELOT-GRAIL CYCLE*

5

Interlace and the Cyclic Imagination

DOUGLAS KELLY

The recent reintroduction of the notion of cycle into critical discussion of medieval romance has not enjoyed the unanimity of definitions that characterize the use of the term interlace since Ferdinand Lot.[1] Let us turn therefore to the ancient and medieval past when cyclicity had a more precise meaning which we can use to approach the *Lancelot-Grail* as a cycle of interlacing narratives. David Staines has noted Horace's reference to cyclic poets in the *Art of Poetry* lines 131–9 and their 'tendency to diffuseness.' Although there is a 'gathering of literary creations that have the same general subject-matter, or . . . a major episode or time around which they are loosely ordered,' the 'cyclic writer has no sense of structure or proportion, and his creation is formless and disunified, finding its development only in the natural chronology of the related events.' Is the *Prose Lancelot* 'tediously and monotonously complete' because its author or authors followed 'a strict chronology and exercised no selectivity in the employment of materials'?[2]

Scholars have noted the prose romance's careful chronology. Moreover, although nineteenth-century scholars identified it as a cycle because Arthur was a central figure, they also decried its seemingly monotonous, formless, and disunified combination of disparate adventures.[3] But after Lot, this criticism declined in favor of greater appreciation of the work's careful interlace. Does interlace bring together in a coherent way the fabric of the prose romance? And if so, is it still a cycle?

Before attempting to answer these questions, let us look again briefly at Horace's references to the *scriptor cyclicus*. According to Horace, the cyclic writer's principal fault is violation of the *operis lex*, or the coherent union of parts

---

1 The proceedings of two colloquia have brought the term back into critical discussion, but without consensus on the meaning or meanings of the term – a taxonomy of cyclic writing – or, strangely enough, any real controversy about the meaning and use of the term. See *Cyclification: The Development of Narrative Cycles in the Chansons de Geste and the Arthurian Romances*, ed. Bart Besamusca et al., Koninklijke Nederlandse Akademie van Wetenschappen: Verhandelingen, Afd. Letterkunde, N.S. 159 (Amsterdam, Oxford, New York, and Tokyo, 1994), and *Transtextualities: Of Cycles and Cyclicity in Medieval French Literature*, ed. Sara Sturm-Maddox and Donald Maddox, Medieval and Renaissance Texts and Studies, 149 (Binghamton, NY, 1996).
2 'The Medieval Cycle: Mapping a Trope,' in *Transtextualities*, p. 24; Staines goes back to Greek authors, especially Aristotle, but I shall treat only the Latin authors that medieval writers might have known.
3 Cf. Staines, 'Cycle: The Misreading of a Trope,' in *Cyclification*, pp. 108–10.

in a beginning, middle, and end. This occurs when the work begins in a past so
distant that its author is unable to get to its real subject-matter and thence to a
conclusion. It also occurs when digressions become so numerous and extensive
as to be useless; the plot goes off track, finally producing a sense of endless,
monotonous byways that end in arid wastes. Although such a cycle may have a
bold, striking beginning, it quickly turns turgid or obscure. Ideally, narrative
should be coherent; in such cases, even if the beginning is obscure, the obscurity
will gradually clear up, revealing a coherent plot.

How does the *Prose Lancelot* measure up against these standards? One notes
immediately two features that distinguish it from Horace's bad cycle. First, the
romance relates a full and complete biography, that of Lancelot, from his birth at
the outset of the *Lancelot* proper to his death at the end of the *Mort Artu*. Second,
the beginning is obscure. Lancelot's name, we learn, is actually Galahad; but the
anomaly is as obscure for the uninformed reader as is the identity of the Knight
of the Cart during the first half of Chrétien's verse romance.[4]

But what about digression as a narrative device in the *Prose Lancelot*? Eugène
Vinaver likens the use of interlace in this romance to the amplificatory technique
of digression, thus implicitly linking the prose romance with a feature of cyclic
composition identified by Horace. But bringing together the notions of cycle,
digression, and interlace in the invention of prose romance, Vinaver continues,
'à la cohésion s'ajoute l'expansion, à ce que Lot appelle le "procédé de
l'entrelacement" celui, plus simple en apparence, que l'on nomme "digression." '[5]
Now, digression is usually understood in medieval theory of invention as a
source of coherence, either because it rearranges the subject-matter in order to
juxtapose more effectively matter and meaning, or by treating an extraneous
subject which may or may not be significant in the new subject-matter.[6] In this
way, digression as interlace introduces parallels, analogues, and other kinds of
additions – that is, it interlaces a cyclic structure based on 'un système intelli-
gible de relations'[7] in which 'les épisodes du roman s'organisent d'après des
lignes de force précises.'[8] The scheme is visualized early in the *Prose Lancelot* as a
tree with a clear hierarchy of narrative branches.

After naming four clerics who, in the narrative, are assigned the task of
recording the Round Table knights' reports of their adventures, the narrator
goes on to explain how the clerics arranged their memoranda:

> Si mistrent en escript lez aventures mon seignor Gauvain tout avant, por ce que
> c'estoit li commenchemens de la queste de Lancelot, et puis les Hector, por chou
> que de cel conte estoient branche, et puis lez aventures de tous lez .xviii. autres

---

4 Elspeth Kennedy, *Lancelot and the Grail: A Study of the Prose 'Lancelot'* (Oxford, 1986), pp. 47–8.
5 *A la recherche d'une poétique médiévale* (Paris, 1970), p. 133.
6 Marjorie Curry Woods, 'Poetic Digression and the Interpretation of Medieval Literary Texts,'
   in *Acta Conventus Neo-Latini Sanctandreani*, ed. I. D. McFarlane (Binghamton, NY, 1986),
   pp. 617–26.
7 Vinaver, p. 138.
8 Vinaver, p. 148. See also Emmanuèle Baumgartner, 'Les techniques narratives dans le roman
   en prose,' in *The Legacy of Chrétien de Troyes*, ed. Norris J. Lacy, Douglas Kelly, and Keith Busby
   (Amsterdam and Atlanta, 1987), 1, 167–90.

compaignons, et tout ce fu del conte Lancelot, et tout cil autre furent branche de chestui, et li contes Lancelot fu branche del Graal, si com il y fu ajoustés.[9]

[First of all they wrote down the adventures of Sir Gawain, because that was the beginning of the quest for Lancelot, and then those of Hector, because they formed a branch of that story, and then the adventures of all the other eighteen companions. All this was the story of Lancelot, and all these others were branches thereof. And the story of Lancelot formed a branch of the story of the Grail, when it was *added to* it.][10]

This crucial passage and others like it[11] illustrate the cyclic principle of a hierarchy of interlaced narratives, all of which derive from Lancelot's exploits. The narrative *conjointure* is both open-ended and coherent.[12] As Vinaver's use of the term *conjointure* suggests, the implicit multiplication of quests in Chrétien's romances produces the elaborate branching of narratives of the *Lancelot*.[13] Chrétien

invite . . . ses successeurs et ses continuateurs à entreprendre un vaste travail de renouvellement; non, certes, pour découvrir le sens 'primitif' des choses – personne à l'époque ne s'en souciait, – mais pour leur donner une signification qui puisse se recommander par la cohérence même, une *conjointure* doublement féconde, englobant à la fois les récits existants et ceux qui devaient naître à leur suite.[14]

Vinaver's words raise two issues that we must now consider in the context of cyclic romance: the meaning of *sens primitif* in cyclic invention, and the actual and potential elaboration of the subject matter over time.

Vinaver's dismissal of a *sens primitif* refers, in the context of earlier scholarship, to source studies. It is that scholarship that seeks, in R. S. Loomis's words, to recover 'the haunting undertones [in Arthurian romance] contributed by generations of story-tellers, recalling faintly the fantasies of Celtic paganism.'[15] Those faintly perceived fantasies are the core of original meaning no one, in Vinaver's opinion, cared about in the twelfth and thirteenth centuries. On the other hand, the twelfth- and thirteenth-century romancers were interested in that *sorplus de san* which Marie de France thought earlier writers intentionally buried in their writings and which subsequent generations of rewriters were

---

9   *Lancelot: Roman en prose du XIIIe siècle*, ed. Alexandre Micha, 9 vols. (Paris and Geneva, 1978–83), 8:488–9; cf. 9:200. All further references to this work (*LM*) appear in the text with volume and page.

10 Translations of the parts of the *Cycle* are from *Lancelot-Grail: The Old French Arthurian Vulgate and Post-Vulgate in Translation*, ed. Norris J. Lacy (New York and London, 1993–96), and appear in the text as *L-G* with volume and page; here at 2:238.

11 Elspeth Kennedy, ed., *Lancelot do Lac*, 2 vols. (Oxford, 1980), 2:377–8, n. 571.31, and *LM* 8:489 var. b. All further references to this work (*LK*) refer to vol. and page number; vol. 1 is the text, vol. 2 is the notes, etc.

12 See Vinaver on the evolution of the concept of *conjointure* from Chrétien's original sense to indicate larger, new and original combinations, with their own beauty (*A la recherche*, p. 124).

13 See my 'Multiple Quests in French Verse Romance: *Merveilles de Rigomer* and *Claris et Laris*,' *L'Esprit créateur*, 9 (1969), 259.

14 *A la recherche*, p. 128.

15 *Arthurian Tradition and Chrétien de Troyes* (New York and London, 1949), p. 469.

expected to elucidate. Vinaver is well aware of this kind of *sens primitif*, as the second feature of the above quote – the 'récits . . . qui devaient naître' from 'récits existants' – clearly shows.

Prose romance *conjointure*, the result of interlace and cyclic amplification, operates on two levels: on the level of *matière*, or straightforward narrative inter-lace as Ferdinand Lot describes it, and of *sens*, or the meaning of those different narratives and the way in which they harmonize or clash as a result of inter-lacing.[16] Furthermore, as the branching metaphor discussed above suggests, a real or potential hierarchy in the conception of the work contributes to the coher-ence of the whole by subordinating different narrative strands to one another. In this scheme of things, the growing tree has parts – branches – that are more important than others. This means that the Grail story is the trunk from which all other narratives branch out; furthermore, the branches themselves are of greater or less significance in the whole, depending on their connection to the trunk and to the larger branches that rise directly from the trunk (as the Lancelot branch does from the Grail trunk), and from which the smaller branches and ultimately the twigs themselves sprout. In this particular image, the Lancelot narrative's smaller branches are united as a quest for Lancelot; they are in order, beginning with the first quester, Gawain, followed by the second, Hector, and finally eighteen other questing knights. To be sure, the eighteen have a focus: they are all looking for Lancelot. But they are also subordinated to the knights whose branches have their name. Such pruning streamlined the potential for twenty interlaced quests in favor of a more coherent, tightly woven narrative.[17]

Why are only two knights named? One reason is, no doubt, aristocratic prece-dence, a common justification for inclusion in medieval romance.[18] This is illus-trated by a similar, but different branching from the Lancelot story in another quest for the Queen's lover. Agloval has one branch, but his adventures are reduced to their link with a new, major thread the author is weaving into the romance: Perceval.[19] Agloval returns by chance to his mother's dwelling and, finding his brother Perceval there, takes him away to join the Round Table (*LM* 6:182–90). The narrator suppresses almost everything else about Agloval's unsuccessful quest for Lancelot. In effect, Agloval, a withering offshoot from the Lancelot branch, is grafted onto the new Perceval branch; this branch is itself a graft directly onto the Grail trunk.

We are at this point near the end of the *Lancelot* proper. The Grail quest is approaching. As a result of their ultimate source in the Grail, adventures are proliferating. Indeed, their proliferation is so luxuriant that the text not only prunes unsuccessful quests like Agloval's, it suppresses many others, too. For example, in quests in search of Lancelot imprisoned in Morgue's castle, Agloval

---

[16] Jean Fourquet, 'Le rapport entre l'œuvre et la source et le problème des sources bretonnes,' *Romance Philology*, 9 (1956), 298–312.

[17] Contrast this with the complex, but mechanical, interlacing of up to thirty different quests in *Claris et Laris*; Kelly, 'Tout li sens du monde dans Claris et Laris,' *Romance Philology*, 36 (1983), 406–17.

[18] See my *The Art of Medieval French Romance* (Madison, Wis., and London, 1992), pp. 233–4.

[19] See Annie Combes, *Les voies de l'aventure: réécriture et composition romanesque dans le 'Lancelot' en prose*, Nouvelle Bibliothèque du Moyen Age, 59 (Paris, 2001), pp. 278–87.

and two other knights set out, 'si trouverent mainte bele aventure dont li contes se test ore, por ce que trop seroit longue l'estoire, se il devisoit tout ce' (*LM* 5:60) [and found many a fine adventure about which the story keeps silent at this point, for the story would be too long if it related all that (*L-G* 3:224)].[20] The model was already available in the non-cyclic *Lancelot* in passages adapted by the cyclic version. Banin's achievements are not related since they belong to the *contes del commun* 'general story', just as, later, Lionel's exploits are suppressed after cross-referencing his separate *conte*.[21] This reference to a vast, but only potential *conte del commun* suggests the intention to avoid the 'useless digressions'[22] that, to Horace's mind, flawed irremediably the cyclic epics he knew. The rationale for the surviving branches in the *Prose Lancelot* is a hierarchy that focuses on and favors not only high-born, even unique excellence – Lancelot above all, but also Gawain, and, later, others like Bors, Perceval, and, finally, Galahad.

We come now to a heretofore unavoidable problem in literary history, a problem which can probably never be resolved satisfactorily. How was the *Lancelot* actually written and put together? Over time, hypotheses have ranged from a version of the early *cantilène* theory of numerous short narratives brought together more or less haphazardly to Lot's argument for a single author.[23] Various compromises have also enjoyed favor. For example, Jean Frappier projected an architect supervising an atelier of scribes to whom the work had been parceled out.[24] Within this framework, the *Cycle* as we have it is not entirely consistent from beginning to end, and stages in its elaboration stand out. The distinction between the non-cyclic and cyclic version of the *Lancelot* comes to mind, as well as the later addition of the *Merlin* and the *Estoire*, the replacement of Perceval by Galahad as the supreme Grail knight, and variant scribal adaptations.[25] These occur during composition and later copying. Furthermore, there is the shimmering audience perspective, a perspective disturbed and blurred by manuscript *mouvance*.

Yet this problem of literary history is not desperate. Admitting that we cannot be sure how the romance cycle actually came into existence, we can nonetheless note the way in which the final version evolves narratively and thematically, that is, in *matière* and *sens*, for the reader who has the romance essentially as the standard lines of transmission present it and as it refers to itself in interventions like *Li contes dit* . . . That is, we may consider how, given the principle of beginning, middle, and end adumbrated in the romance as a Lancelot biography, the

---

20 Cf. *LM* 3:335, 8:261, and 5:57–8.

21 *LM* 7:243 and 1:44–5; and *LK* 1:138 lines 31–5 and 1:612 lines 12–14; cf. *LK* 2:130, 391, *LM* 8:132, and *LK* 1:358 lines 29–30.

22 Woods, p. 617.

23 For a thorough, recent review of these interpretations, see Frank Brandsma, 'De entrelacement-vertelwijze in de *Lanceloet*,' in his edition of the Middle Dutch *Lanceloet: Pars 3 (ll. 10741–16263)* (Assen and Maastricht, 1992), pp. 6–15.

24 *Etude sur La Mort le roi Artu*, 2nd rev. ed. (Geneva, 1968).

25 Like the insertion of Gawain's adventures into the *Charrette* episode in some manuscripts; see Gweneth Hutchings, ed., *Le roman en prose de Lancelot du Lac: le Conte de la charrette* (Paris, 1938), pp. 122–31. On such 'inviting gaps,' see Frank Brandsma, 'Opening Up the Narrative: The Insertion of New Episodes in Arthurian Cycles,' *Queeste*, 1 (1995), 31–9.

Lancelot story and branch is grafted onto the Grail trunk. Let us begin then at the beginning: the birth and naming of Lancelot.

Lancelot's father, Ban de Benoic, gave his son the surname Lancelot after he was christened Galahad (*LM* 7:1). The new name is already present in the non-cyclic *Lancelot* (*LK* 1:1 lines 7–8). Both versions promise to explain the change later on, justifying the tactic by an appeal to the aesthetics of the *droite voie*: 'Et che pour coi il fu apeleis Lancelos, che devisera bien li contes cha avant, car li liex n'est mie ore ne la raisons, anchois tient li contes sa droite voie.' [Why he was called Lancelot the story will explain later on, for this is not the time and place. The story moves ahead, then, *following its natural order* (*L-G* 2:3)]. Elspeth Kennedy notes that the non-cyclic version does not keep this promise, but that the cyclic version later explains the name change as the veiled announcement of Lancelot's sin and the invention of his son Galahad as supreme Grail knight (*LK* 2:67 n. 1.7–9). The two versions diverge in other ways, too. The non-cyclic narrative makes Pellés out to be Perceval's father and Perceval the supreme Grail knight (*LK* 1:33 lines 8–12) whereas the cyclic version identifies Pellés as father of Galahad's mother, Amite, and Galahad becomes the supreme Grail knight (*LM* 7:59–60). The adaptation occurs some time during the elaboration of the cyclic version (*LK* 2:89–90; cf. *LM* 7:462–76). How and why it occurs is disputed.

My purpose here is not, and cannot be, to resolve the issue. Rather, I wish to put it into the context of the cyclic coherence which Vinaver identifies in the elaboration of the *Prose Lancelot*. There are three prominent readings of these differences between the non-cyclic and the cyclic versions of the supreme Grail knight's identity. In her *Lancelot and the Grail*, Elspeth Kennedy argues that the non-cyclic version adds to the well-known Grail romances in which Perceval is the Grail knight; in this case, the Lancelot romance is an addition and an intertextual cross-reference to extant romance material. According to Alexandre Micha, the Galahad reference at the beginning of the cycle alludes obscurely to Lancelot's sin and the birth of his son, Galahad. Finally, according to Frappier, the cycle was indeed first meant to present Perceval as the supreme Grail knight; but the architect of the overall conception and his scribes hit upon a new figure, Galahad, which led them to adapt the Perceval references in order to insert a new, more perfect Grail knight.

It is important to note, I think, that all these theories postulate the coherence of the different versions and, indeed, the goal of coherence. To my mind, that is the overriding goal of all versions, although the means used to achieve it and the corresponding plots that result are different. Whether we envisage a single author modifying or gradually unfolding his plot, or an architect doing the same, or, finally, a sequence of authors making such adaptations while striving to achieve narrative and thematic coherence, the result is the same for the reader – whether that reader knows only the non-cyclic version, the *Lancelot* proper, or the whole *Lancelot-Grail Cycle*. In short, we have versions that try to make sense of Lancelot's love life, whether that life makes him an outstanding knight or a faulted knight. Their success depends on how well they bring under control what Bruckner calls the centrifugal propensity of digression, a characteristic defect of cyclic epic in Horace's criticism, so as to restore a centripetal thrust that keeps the romance on its *droite voie*.[26] This brings us to the subject of the cyclic imagination.

Imagination in the Middle Ages is the mental faculty that both fashions and identifies images.[27] The images may be true or false, depending on whether or not the author or reader accepts or rejects the model that informs and gives meaningful form to the image. The Lancelot and Grail matters inherited from Chrétien de Troyes are modified by various intermediaries on their way to the thirteenth-century prose style.[28] The Lancelot model, which was adapted from Chrétien most directly, established the Knight of the Cart as the best knight because his love for Guinevere enhanced his prowess in the achievement of his knightly obligations and challenges, confronting the reader with the challenge to accept or reject it.[29] The Grail model is different. Under the influence of Robert de Boron, Perceval became the model knight. This model implicitly corrects the Lancelot model by its greater emphasis on a Christian ethic, especially chastity. The non-cyclic *Lancelot* subordinates the Lancelot model to the Grail model in the tree image. That image makes the Grail story the trunk, implicitly suggesting that, in the clash of values represented by Lancelot's and Perceval's biographies, Perceval's ethic predominates.

However, Perceval's image is not unsullied. Chrétien shows him susceptible to love, and the Second Continuation confirms his loss of chastity and virginity and, indeed, of fidelity to Blancheflor when he makes love with the Chessboard Maiden. The Didot *Perceval* does not change matters significantly. This untidy hierarchy is corrected and smoothed out in the *Prose Lancelot*.[30] It does so by realizing a *sorplus de san*, a thematic potential in the mysterious baptismal name of Lancelot, Galahad.

The author or authors had a perfectly satisfactory explanation for Lancelot's two names: Lancelot is named after two of his ancestors, Lancelot, King of the Blanche Terre, and Galahad, son of Joseph of Arimathia and the first Christian king of 'Gales.' The names contribute to the theme of lineage that is so important in the structure and coherence of the *Prose Lancelot* by topical invention. Not only are ancestors invented for Lancelot but a progeny is, too. The change begins in the cemetery of Logres. Lancelot's achievement of this adventure permits the first topical invention: we learn that the tomb which Chrétien destined for Lancelot himself is already occupied by his baptismal ancestor, Galahad. As in Chrétien, the knight who successfully lifts the tombstone will liberate the prisoners in Gorre, including the Queen. But there is now another tomb in the cemetery. It contains the sinner Symeu, who is undergoing a kind of purgatory in

---

[26] See Matilda Tomaryn Bruckner, 'Intertextuality,' in *Legacy of Chrétien de Troyes*, 1, 223–65.

[27] See my *Medieval Imagination: Rhetoric and the Poetry of Courtly Love* (Madison, Wis., and London, 1978), ch. 3; and, more broadly, *The Arts of Poetry and Prose*, Typologie des sources du moyen âge occidental, 59 (Turnhout, 1991), pp. 64–8.

[28] Emmanuèle Baumgartner, 'From Lancelot to Galahad: The Stakes of Filiation,' in *The Lancelot-Grail Cycle: Text and Transformations*, ed. William W. Kibler (Austin, 1994), pp. 14–30; and Fanni Bogdanow, *The Romance of the Grail: A Study of the Structure and Genesis of a Thirteenth-Century Arthurian Prose Romance* (Manchester, 1966), pp. 1–22.

[29] Bruckner, 'An Interpreter's Dilemma: Why Are There So Many Interpretations of Chrétien's *Chevalier de la Charette?*' *Romance Philology*, 40 (1986), 159–80.

[30] Baumgartner, 'From Lancelot to Galahad,' pp. 18–20.

order to expiate his sins. Lancelot's effort to achieve this adventure by raising the tombstone and extinguishing the flames that punish Symeu's sin is a failure. As the narrator explains, 'cil qui la leveroit abatroit les enchantements del Roialme Aventureus et metroit fin as aventures et acompliroit le siege de la Table Reonde' (*LM* 2:32) [whoever raised it would dispel the enchantments in the Kingdom of Adventures, bring an end to the adventures, and attain the seat at the Round Table (*L-G* 2:12)]. This means that the successful knight will achieve the Grail quest, as we learn later. The as yet unborn Galahad – the third Galahad in Lancelot's line – realizes the implications of the tree image. If, literally, Galahad derives from Lancelot, allegorically he supersedes his father who himself descends from Joseph of Arimathia and, by his mother's line, from the family of Christ, Solomon, and David. All of this follows on the rewritten cemetery scene.

Now, that scene is not so tidy as my summary suggests. Symeu explains Lancelot's sin by his father's adultery, which produced Hector; his mother's virtue alone preserves her son from degeneration after his sin with Guinevere (*LM* 2:36–37).[31] Still, this evaluation comes from a sinner who has not yet atoned for his own sins. Symeu's words require further narrative elaboration and correction. Lancelot himself is still convinced that his love makes him a better knight than he would have been had he not sinned with the Queen: ' "se je ne fusse de vos si bien come je sui" ' (*LM* 5:3) ["if I had not been as favored by you as I am" (*L-G* 3:207)].

At this point the coherence of the cycle risks coming unraveled. Fortunately, however, the reader is prepared to contemplate an erroneous interpretation both by the sinners Symeu and Lancelot himself. For before either spoke, Helie de Toulouse had already pronounced Lancelot guilty (*LM* 1:53–6). His language is explicit: only a chaste virgin will achieve the Grail quest, which obviously disqualifies Lancelot. The *Queste* completes the picture and pulls the romance together as a coherent cycle. Lancelot is a truly tragic figure here. His error of judgment is sincere, if illogical. A hermit sets him straight and puts him back on the *droite voie* foreseen prior to his meeting Guinevere.[32] His explanation of Lancelot's sin and his achievements is perfectly coherent and it makes the cyclic *Lancelot* coherent as well:

> Des pechiez mortiex porte li peres son fes, et li filz le suen; ne li filz ne partira ja as iniquitez au pere, ne li peres ne partira ja as iniquitez au filz; mes chascuns selonc ce qu'il deservi recevra loier. (*Queste* 138 lines 29–32)

> [The father carries the burden of mortal sin and the son carries his. The son will never share in his father's iniquities, nor will the father share in the son's faults. Each will be compensated in accordance with his own merits (*L-G* 4:45)]

Lancelot can now atone for his sin and partially achieve the quest.

---

[31] Cf. the analogous explanation of Perceval's salvation through his mother's prayers in Chrétien's *Roman de Perceval, ou, le Conte du Graal de Chrétien de Troyes*, ed. Keith Busby (Tübingen, 1993), lines 6406–8.

[32] *La Queste del saint graal*, ed. Albert Pauphilet (Paris, 1949), p. 125 line 32.

At some point in the elaboration of the cyclic romance a major innovation fixed the moral context of the work. Whether this occurred with the invention of the name Galahad for Lancelot, as Micha suggested, or later cannot be determined, since, as we have seen, Galahad's name for Lancelot may be – as in the non-cyclic *Lancelot* – an allusion to Joseph of Arimathia's son.[33] But the allusion to Joseph and the tradition as to his place in the Grail lineage since Robert de Boron may well have inspired the rewriting of the plot that produced not only a forefather Galahad but a descendant Galahad. The further extension of the genealogy to Christ as well as to David and Solomon is sufficient to conjoin biblical history and both Grail history and Round Table history. Although changes begin earlier in the *Lancelot*,[34] the full significance of the transformation is made plain only in the *Queste* and the *Mort*.

The coherence of the *Cycle* by this invention followed two major changes. First, the Grail-Round Table moral hierarchy is firmly grounded in a biblical context, and thus a new hierarchy that include events in the Bible. To do so – and this is the second change – typology is introduced as a mode of allegorical amplification.

Typology is that kind of allegory that conjoins events according to a Providential plan; that plan in history has three great moments: the Fall, the Crucifixion, and the Last Judgment. The *Queste* introduces the first two, antecedent events in the Ship of Solomon digression,[35] by which the Grail legend becomes a branch on the biblical trunk. The Fall is shown in the apocryphal account of Adam and Eve's life after their banishment from Eden (*Queste* 210–19) and of Joseph of Arimathia's fate after Christ's death (*Queste* 134 lines 13–17). The Last Judgment is, of course, only darkly prophesied (*Queste* 149 lines 24–9; cf. 157 lines 27–9). Nonetheless, the *Queste* links the three histories – biblical, Grail, and Round Table – by the invention of Solomon's Ship, destined to sail the seas until reaching the last person in Solomon's line, Galahad himself (*Queste* 225–6).

But what of Lancelot and his love for the Queen that traditionally raised him above all other knights? The invention of the new configuration successfully integrates Lancelot as a tragic figure. Lancelot believed his love made him a better knight. But, in the context of the *Queste*, to love like Lancelot is to sin. Hence, the error of Lancelot's intention. To sin does not make one better, but worse. The *Queste* author's correction of Lancelot – he would have achieved much more, including the Grail quest, had it not been for the corruption of his virtues by love (*Queste* 126) – is dramatic and absolute. Lancelot submits and begins penance.

The disqualification of Lancelot in the *Queste* and even earlier rests on a Grail hierarchy, and specifically on continence and the crucial distinction between chastity and virginity. The five possibilities structure the narrative and provide its coherent interlace: Galahad as chaste virgin, Perceval as unchaste virgin, Bors

---

33 *LK* 1:146 line 20; see *LK* 2:134.
34 Brandsma, *Lanceloet*, ch. 3.
35 Kelly, 'L'Invention dans les romans en prose,' in *The Craft of Fiction: Essays in Medieval Poetics*, ed. Leigh A. Arrathoon (Rochester, Mich., 1984), pp. 119–24; cf. Michelle Szkilnik, *L'Archipel du graal: étude de L'Estoire del Saint Graal* (Geneva, 1991).

as chaste but not virgin, Lancelot and Gawain as neither chaste nor virgin, but the former repentant and the latter unrepentant. Almost all the other knights fall into Gawain's class in one way or the other. The distinction reserves allegorical adventures to the more or less successful and, to all the others, meaningless encounters, or *mescheances* – usually murders.

By the typological framework of redemption illustrated in history by Christ's death, the *Cycle* builds its moral authority on chastity and virginity and prepares for Galahad's own life and death. The failure of the Round Table in the great quest also prefigures the Last Judgment. On Salisbury Plain, a world and a cycle come to an end in slaughter.

6

The Gateway to the Lancelot-Grail Cycle: *L'Estoire del Saint Graal*

CAROL J. CHASE

When Chrétien de Troyes' naïve hero, Perceval, sees the Grail procession in the Fisher King's castle, he is confronted with a mystery that writers have sought to elucidate ever since. In Chrétien's text, the scene is presented as if through Perceval's eyes. A series of persons carrying various objects – a lance that bleeds, candelabra with ten candles each, a grail that gives off an extraordinary light, a silver carving dish – cross the hall where he and his host are seated, and enter another room.[1] Perceval gazes with awe at the lance and the grail, promising himself to ask about them later. Though he eventually learns the answers to some of the enigmas posed in this sequence – who is served by the grail (his maternal uncle) and what is presented in this dish (a host, on which his uncle has lived for twelve years) – a multitude of questions are left unanswered for the reader/listener. This is undoubtedly why so many thirteenth-century romances rewrite the Grail procession, transforming and amplifying it, going back in time to the origins of the Grail and forward to its ultimate destiny.[2]

The *Lancelot-Grail Cycle* elaborates all these aspects of this quintessential object, intertwining material about the Grail with the stories of Arthur, Lancelot, and Guinevere. While the five romances that compose the cycle can be read separately, they form an interlocking network, developing and rewriting the same themes and making numerous cross-references within an overall eschato-logical history that begins with the Crucifixion and ends with the fall of Arthur's kingdom. This reading of the *Estoire del Saint Graal* will therefore take into account the interrelationships among the romances.

Although there is debate over the order in which these texts were composed, critics agree that the *Lancelot* is the core around which the rest of the cycle was realized; though written later, the *Estoire* was conceived as the gateway into the

---

1   Chrétien de Troyes, *Le Conte du Graal*, ed. William Roach (Paris, 1959), lines 3191–242; the grail repeatedly passes with each course of the meal Perceval is served, lines 3290–1 and 3299–301. The first mention of the Grail in Chrétien's text refers to it with the indefinite article ('un graal', line 3220).
2   The questions Perceval wishes to ask are on a concrete, literal level; later texts transform them to reflect an inquiry into the very nature of the Grail. See Emmanuèle Baumgartner, 'Del Graal cui l'an an servoit: Variations sur un pronom,' in *The Editor and the Text*, ed. Philip E. Bennet and Graham A. Runnals (Edinburgh, 1990), pp. 137–43.

cycle and the *Mort le Roi Artu* as its closure.[3] The intent to create a coherent whole is manifest in the manuscript tradition, for the narrative is nearly always presented as continuous, with minimal demarcations between the individual works.[4] The only texts with prologues are the *Estoire* and the *Mort Artu*; the conclusions are brief and often emphasize the links between the works.[5]

The *Estoire* insists on its introductory role by preparing a number of episodes in the other romances and setting up the genealogies for the major Arthurian heroes. It is related in particular to a sort of 'twin' romance, the *Queste del Saint Graal*; together they develop the entire history of the Grail, mapping its *translatio* first from East to West – from Jerusalem to its destination at Corbenic in England – and then its return to the East before it disappears from the earth. In the *Estoire* it is Joseph of Arimathia and his son Josephus who transfer the Grail to the new Promised Land. During the course of their peregrinations, they convert the rulers of the lands they traverse. Their first urban stop is at Sarras, a mythical Eastern city, where Josephus is invested as the first bishop and the Christians celebrate their first communion. There they convert King Evalach and his brother-in-law Seraphe (who take the names Mordrain and Nascien at baptism). These two men will play an important role in the colonization of England; a long central portion of the romance is devoted to episodes in which they are transported to islands where their faith is tested. In the *Queste*, islands are also an important geographic element in the trials the knights undergo. And Sarras, not Jerusalem, is the city where the Grail is taken at the end of the romance. Finally, Corbenic is central to the *Queste*: it is there that the mysteries of the Grail are revealed to the three Grail winners, Galahad, Perceval, and Bohort, in a sequence that includes a communion scene presided by Josephus, reflecting an episode from the *Estoire*.

The *Estoire* thus shares with the *Queste* a spatial organization founded not only on the movement between East and West but also on an opposition between the inhabited, constructed space of cities and castles and the uninhabited or 'wild,' 'desert'-type space of forest, islands, sea and boats, where the Christians are tested and tempted by the devil and where they receive visits from the Lord. This structure resembles that found in the lives of saints and the Church Fathers. In early Oriental Christian works, the desert is the space where saints seek God but are also tempted by the devil; in later works written in the

---

3   While most critics follow Jean Frappier in thinking that the *Estoire* was written after the *Queste* (*Etude sur la Mort le roi Artu* [Geneva, 1972], pp. 55–9), the editor of the *Estoire*, Jean-Paul Ponceau, avers the reverse; he dates the *Estoire* in the third decade of the thirteenth century; Jean-Paul Ponceau, *L'Estoire del Saint Graal*, 2 vols. (Paris, 1997), I, xii–xiv. Michelle Szkilnik summarizes the debate up to that point in *L'Archipel du Graal: Etude de l'Estoire del Saint Graal* (Geneva, 1991), p. 1, n. 1.

4   Rubrics and illuminations often create the missing textual boundaries, especially in fourteenth- and fifteenth-century manuscripts. See Emmanuèle Baumgartner, 'Espace du texte, espace du manuscrit: les manuscrits du *Lancelot-Graal*,' *Ecritures II* (Paris, 1985), pp. 95–116.

5   The extraordinary prologue to the *Estoire* has received a certain amount of critical attention; consult in particular Alexandre Leupin, *Le Graal et la littérature* (Lausanne, 1982), pp. 23–35, and Rupert T. Pickens, 'Autobiography and History in the Vulgate *Estoire* and in the Prose *Merlin*,' in *The Lancelot-Grail Cycle: Text and Transformations*, ed. William W. Kibler (Austin, TX, 1994), pp. 98–116.

West islands, sea and forest are substituted for the desert but play the same role.[6] Both the *Estoire* and the *Queste* emphasize adventures with a religious or spiritual significance rather than those concerning courtly love – a trait that might also be compared with hagiography or spiritual literature. In the *Estoire* chivalric prowess is at the service of the Church militant, and the role women play is limited: though the conversion to Christianity of several women is part of the action, their main function is to found the families of the major Arthurian heroes.[7] In the *Queste* the focus is on the knights at the end of the lineages set forth in the *Estoire*, for whom chastity is essential in order to achieve the quest of the Grail. With the exception of Perceval's sister, women are excluded from this quest, and chivalric prowess is redefined in spiritual terms.

The two romances also have in common a number of specific elements. Both contain the same retrospective stories that recount the origins of the boat Solomon prepares for the knight at the end of his lineage (Galahad) and the marvelous bed inside, with its portico made of spindles from the Tree of Life and the sword that once belonged to David. These stories tie the cycle to the era of the Old Testament. Note that the starting point is not the Creation, the beginning of life on earth, but rather the Fall, the exile from the garden of paradise, which they rewrite. They also retell other important episodes from Old Testament history, including the audacious reworking of Solomon's lineage so that Galahad is presented as his descendant. Finally, the *Estoire* develops at length a number of stories that are resumed or referred to briefly in the *Queste*, where they appear as flashbacks about the origins or history of objects or people. Prominent in these tales are the figures Joseph of Arimathia and his son Josephus, as well as their first converts, Evalach-Mordrain and Seraphe-Nascien. These tales are situated in early Christian times, right after the Passion – with which the *Estoire* begins – rather than Christ's birth. This choice is not unmotivated, for it emphasizes the Redemption, an important theme in the romance; it also establishes a time frame based on sacred history whereby the Fall is counterpoised by the Redemption.

But the *Estoire* is also linked to the central romance, the *Lancelot*, picking up a number of threads from the retrospective tales and allusions to pre-Arthurian times in this text. It can therefore be seen as an enormous flashback recounting the origins not only of the Grail but also of the families of the major Arthurian heroes as well as of certain objects in the Arthurian landscape. This romance prepares, for example, several of the tombstone episodes that appear at regular intervals in the *Lancelot*. These sequences allow the eponymous hero to learn his identity and who his ancestors are; many of them include allusions to Joseph of Arimathia, who is presented in the *Lancelot* as the hero's paternal forebear, a genealogy that is contradicted by the *Estoire*. This essay will therefore focus on Joseph, examining his role in the *Estoire* and comparing it with his portrait in the other parts of the cycle, in particular the *Lancelot* and the *Queste* (Joseph is absent

6   Jacques LeGoff, 'Le "désert"-forêt dans l'Occident médiéval,' *L'Imaginaire médiéval* (Paris, 1985), pp. 59–75; Szkilnik, *Archipel*, pp. 19–25.
7   Carol Chase, 'La conversion des païennes dans l'*Estoire del Saint Graal*,' in *Arthurian Romance and Gender*, ed. Friedrich Wolfzettel (Amsterdam, 1995), pp. 251–64.

from the *Mort Artu;* in the *Merlin,* he is referred to only briefly). Essential to this
approach is a consideration of the technique of rewriting.

Like all the other romances of the cycle, the *Estoire* uses the technique of
rewriting,[8] but to such an extent that the romance resembles a collage or patchwork quilt. This metaphor has been chosen because, like artists who glue
different objects together to form a work of art or who sew pieces of fabric
together to make an over-all design, the anonymous author of the *Estoire* stitches
together various bits and pieces, refiguring them in a new context.[9] This process,
typical of medieval literary creation, does not rely on modern notions of text
production and originality: the medieval literary work is formed of a tissue of
relations with pre-existing texts as well as with the 'text' of the culture in which
it exists.[10] The *Estoire* author thus rewrites a number of the flashbacks from
pre-Arthurian times about Joseph of Arimathia that are scattered throughout the
Lancelot and the *Queste,* inscribing them in chronological order. Or is it the *Queste*
that rewrites the *Estoire?* A more extensive study than can be done here is
needed before resolving the debate over whether the *Estoire* was written before
or after the *Queste.* The relationship between the episodes concerning Joseph of
Arimathia in the *Estoire* and the *Lancelot* also raises questions about the order in
which at least these sequences were written.

As mentioned above, the *Estoire* author rewrites sacred history, revising Old
Testament history after the Fall. But the prose writer also rescripts events from
the New Testament and the Apocrypha, right after the Crucifixion. All four
Evangelists relate briefly how Joseph of Arimathia deposed Christ from the
Cross and buried Him in the sepulcher he had prepared for himself.
Aprocryphal stories develop Joseph's role, retold first by Robert de Boron in the
early thirteenth century, in verse and then in a prose romance attributed to
him.[11] These events are then rescripted by the *Estoire* author, who transforms
them and elaborates a much longer tale. In the *Estoire,* after the Crucifixion,
Joseph goes to the house where the Last Supper had been held, to seek an object
that belonged to Christ. There he finds the bowl from which Christ ate. He uses
this bowl to collect blood from Christ's body after taking it down from the Cross.
The first part of the *Estoire* relates Joseph's imprisonment and liberation, his

8   A number of recent studies focus on rewriting in various parts of the *Cycle.* Among the most
    important are E. Jane Burns, *Arthurian Fictions: Rereading the Vulgate Cycle* (Columbus, OH,
    1985), ch. 1; Emmanuèle Baumgartner, 'L'écriture romanesque et son modèle scripturaire:
    écriture et réécriture du Graal,' in *L'Imitation,* Colloque de l'Ecole du Louvre (Paris, 1984),
    pp. 129–43; Matilda Tomaryn Bruckner, 'Intertextuality,' in *The Legacy of Chrétien de Troyes,*
    2 vols., ed. Norris J. Lacy et al. (Amsterdam, 1987), I, 224–65; Douglas Kelly, *The Art of Medieval
    French Romance* (Madison, 1992); Paul Vincent Rockwell, *Rewriting Resemblance in Medieval
    French Romance* (New York and London, 1995).
9   The composite nature of the romance has inspired criticism from many critics. See Szkilnik,
    Archipel, pp. 6–8, who uses a number of metaphors to describe the structure before choosing
    that of an archipelago.
10 Daniel Poirion, 'Ecriture et ré-écriture au Moyen Age,' *Littérature,* 41 (1981), 107–18.
11 Richard O'Gorman, ed., *Joseph d'Arimathie: A Critical Edition of the Verse and Prose Versions*
    (Toronto, 1995). Though Robert entitles his romance the *Estoire dou Graal,* critics now refer to it
    as the *Joseph* to distinguish it from the text under study here. On the sources of the *Estoire,*
    consult Ferdinand Lot, *Etude sur le Lancelot en prose* (Paris, 1954), pp. 204–14 and Szkilnik,
    Archipel, pp. 71–3.

departure for Britain on an evangelical mission. The bowl, which later receives its name, the Grail, nourishes Joseph while he is in prison; God instructs him to take it to Britain with him and to build an ark for it. At first distinguished from the chalice used to perform the first communion celebrated at Sarras by the Christians, the Grail seems later to be confused with this object. At the beginning of the *Estoire* it is referred to systematically as an *escuelle* [bowl]; after receiving its name, it is called a vessel or the Grail. Throughout the *Estoire* it is depicted as containing God's mysteries as well as revealing His grace. It precedes the Christians as they cross the sea to Britain without boats and it provides nourishment to the elect.[12]

In Robert de Boron's works Joseph does not have any progeniture, nor does he himself travel to the West, but he is already depicted as a knight, apostle, and Grail guardian. It is the latter two functions that the *Estoire* amplifies and transforms, making him the founding father of Britain. The last third of the romance is devoted to the colonization of this land by the Christians. The *Estoire* gives Joseph two sons: Josephus, who eclipses his father as spiritual leader of the Christians, and Galahad, who becomes King of Wales and the ancestor of Yvain.[13] Joseph's relatives found the lineages of the major Arthurian heroes, with the exception of Lancelot, whose forebears are Joseph's first converts, Evalach-Mordrain's brother-in-law Seraphe-Nascien and his son Celidoine. (Note that the *Queste* delineates the same genealogy, and that both contradict the *Lancelot*.) The *Estoire* thus provides the Arthurian knights with glorious ancestors and Britain with a sacred object.[14] In order to examine how the *Estoire* develops Joseph's role, let us first consider his presentation in the *Lancelot* and the *Queste*.

In the *Lancelot* the allusions to Joseph of Arimathia are scattered throughout the romance. He is depicted as the first Christian knight, who took Christ down from the cross. He is an apostle who preaches and works miracles, but also a warrior, sent to England by God to conquer the Saracens or infidels who lived there at that time.[15] He and his descendants brought the Grail to this land. In the *Lancelot* there is no mention of Joseph's wife or of his older son, Josephus, but his younger son, Galahad, is listed as a knight by the Lady of the Lake in her discourse on chivalry. Galahad is also the occupant of one of the graves Lancelot opens; according to the inscription on the tomb, he is 'the conqueror of Sorelise, the first Christian King of Wales.' Inside the tomb lies a knight in full armor,

---

12 On the depiction of the Grail, see Myrrha Lot-Borodine, 'Le Symbolisme du Graal dans *l'Estoire del Saint Graal*,' *Neophilologus*, 34 (1950), 65–79, and Carol J. Chase, 'The Vision of the Grail in the *Estoire del Saint Graal*,' in *Philologies Old and New: Essays in Honor of Peter Florian Dembowski*, ed. Joan Tasker Grimbert and Carol J. Chase (Princeton, 2001), pp. 291–306.

13 Lot emphasizes the importance of the splitting of Joseph's role with his son Josephus, *Etude*, p. 205.

14 See Jean Frappier, 'Le Graal et la chevalerie,' in *Autour du Graal* (Geneva, 1977), pp. 89–128, and Emmanuèle Baumgartner, 'Géants et chevaliers,' in *The Spirit of the Court*, ed. Glyn S. Burgess and Robert A. Taylor (Cambridge, 1995), pp. 9–22, and 'Joseph d'Arimathie dans le *Lancelot* en prose,' in *Lancelot: Actes du Colloque des 14 et 15 janvier 1984*, ed. Danielle Buschinger (Goppingen, 1984), pp. 7–15.

15 On the depiction of Joseph of Arimathia in the *Lancelot*, see Baumgartner, 'Joseph d'Arimathie.' She provides a list of occurrences in n. 1.

emphasizing his chivalric function.[16] Readers have often interpreted this scene as presenting Galahad I as Lancelot's direct ancestor. However, there is nothing in the episode to confirm this view.[17]

The *Lancelot* does present Joseph of Arimathia as Lancelot's paternal ancestor. But there is only one clear statement of this relationship in the romance: a worthy man tells Lancelot that his grandfather was descended from this lineage and that he too fought the Saracens and helped to establish Christianity in Great Britain (*LM* 5:123). The only other passage that presents Joseph as his ancestor involves a lady telling Guerrehet that Lancelot is descended from David and Joseph of Arimathia (*LM* 4:27), but it does not indicate whether the descent is on his mother's or his father's side.

Two retrospective tales in the *Lancelot* show Joseph in an apostolic role in England. One relates the conversion of Camelot, the center of the future Arthurian kingdom; the other, the conversion of the inhabitants of the castle La Roche. The stories explain the origins of two objects – the Black Cross and the broken sword –, tracing their history to the time when England was filled with Saracens. It is striking that these tales are transcribed almost word for word in the long version of the *Lancelot* and the *Estoire*.[18] The only major difference is that in the *Estoire*, Josephus is substituted for his father in the episode of the Black Cross. The two stories follow one another directly in the *Lancelot*, at the beginning of a quest for the eponymous hero by Gauvain and his companions; they both appear in the same order in the *Estoire*, where they are part of the chronological tissue, but are separated by a sequence relating the trials of Joseph and his followers in England.

It is difficult to determine which text did the rewriting! Because scholars agree that the *Lancelot* was written before the *Estoire*, the presumption is that the writer of the latter 'lifted' these episodes and sewed them into the texture of the chronology.[19] In the *Lancelot* they seem at first glance to be a sort of hors-d'œuvre to the quest that follows, their main function being to provide links with pre-Arthurian times, creating a sense of duration in time. But the episodes also confer a feeling of coherence among the romances, for they generate echoes and repetitions in the rest of the cycle. The broken sword, for instance, reappears in the *Queste*: at Corbenic Galaad joins the two parts of the sword together, thus fulfilling the prophecy made in the accounts in the *Estoire* and the *Lancelot*. More importantly, these episodes are part of a series of allusions and stories about pagan times, some of which are *not* elaborated by the *Estoire*. For example, when Lancelot returns to the Joyous Guard to bury Galehot, he wishes to have an opulent tomb prepared. The inhabitants of the

[16] The Lady of the Lake's discourse on chivalry is in Alexandre Micha, ed., *Lancelot*, 9 vols. (Paris and Geneva, 1978–83), 7:256 (hereafter abbreviated to *LM*); the inscription on Galahad's tomb, *LM* 2:33. In order to distinguish this Galahad from Lancelot's son, who is also named Galahad, I will refer to him henceforth as Galahad I.

[17] See Annie Combes, 'From Quest to Quest: Perceval and Galahad in the Prose *Lancelot*,' *Arthuriana*, 12.3 (Fall 2002), 7–30.

[18] The relevant passages are found in *LM* 2:320–24 and 329–38, and *Estoire*, 2:479–84 and 494–501. The short version of the *Lancelot* abridges the tale of the Black Cross considerably (*LM* 3:350–1).

[19] Frappier suggests these episodes were interpolated into the *Lancelot* (*Etude*, pp. 61–2).

castle suggest that he use the cenotaph of a pagan king, Narbaduc, which was worshiped in the *mahomerie as paiens* that existed before Joseph of Arimathia came to the land (*LM* 2:253).[20] These episodes and allusions, insisting on the presence of infidels in England and on Joseph's evangelical mission, are developed by the author of the *Estoire*; they are part of a strategy to establish Joseph as the 'founding father' of Britain, replacing Brutus, who in other Arthurian texts plays this historical role.[21] But Brutus was not Christian. The *Cycle* thus rewrites Britain's early history so that its origins – and those of chivalry – are tied to Christianity. As part of this process, it transforms the giants whom Brutus fought into pagans or infidels on the one hand or into large knights on the other hand.[22]

The *Queste* likewise portrays Joseph as the knight who removed Christ from the cross, but it emphasizes his evangelical mission rather than his function as a warrior. This romance delineates Lancelot's patrilineage all the way back to early Christian times.[23] Given the information supplied in the *Lancelot*, it is surprising that Joseph of Arimathia is absent from this family tree. In the *Queste*, only Lancelot's son Galahad is connected to Joseph: when he arrives at Arthur's court, he is described as a descendant of David and a relative of Joseph of Arimathia, 'dou haut lignage le Roi David et del parenté Joseph d'Arimacie' (p. 7). While this statement echoes one made in the *Lancelot* about his father, it is vague about the exact relationship. Is this an attempt on the part of the *Queste* author to gloss over the contradictions in the family trees? Are we to assume that this connection is on Galahad's maternal grandmother's side?[24] The *Estoire* traces the same family organization as the *Queste*, elaborating the role of the founding ancestors and providing family trees for the major Arthurian heroes, all of whom are descended on the paternal side from Joseph of Arimathia or his relatives, with the exception of Lancelot.[25] The two romances thus contradict the statement in the *Lancelot* that the eponymous hero descends from Joseph, making him the direct descendant of Joseph's first converts, Seraphe-Nascien and Evalach-Mordrain instead. Otherwise the *Queste* is silent about Joseph's lineage, which the *Estoire* details, making him Yvain's direct ancestor – a surprising move, given the latter's small role in the *Cycle*. It is possible that the *Estoire* and *Queste* authors corrected the genealogy set forth in the *Lancelot*, removing Joseph from Lancelot's ancestry because of the sins that prevent Lancelot from accomplishing the Grail quest.[26] But another hypothesis is also

---

[20] *LM* 2:253. The other major episode not elaborated by the *Estoire* is the story of the Petite Aumône, *LM* 5:82–92, which Frappier also suggests may be interpolated; *Etude*, p. 55.

[21] Brutus is depicted as the founder of Britain in Geoffrey of Monmouth's Latin *The History of the Kings of Britain*, trans. Lewis Thorpe (London, 1966), ch. 1. Geoffrey attributes the conversion of Britain to the initiative of one of its kings, Lucius (pp. 124–5). See also Wace, *Le Roman de Brut*, 2 vols., ed. Ivor Arnold (Paris, 1938–40), lines 132ff and 5210ff. The *Estoire* denies the authenticity of this version and assigns the responsibility for the conversion of this king to Perron, one of Joseph's followers (II, 546).

[22] Baumgartner, 'Géants et chevaliers,' pp. 9–12.

[23] Albert Pauphilet, ed., *La Queste del Saint Graal* (Paris, 1967), pp. 134–8.

[24] In the *Lancelot*, the hero's mother is said to be descended from David, *LM* 7:23 and 192.

[25] See family trees in Chase, 'Païennes,' pp. 262–4.

[26] Chase, 'Païennes,' p. 261.

conceivable: a close study of how the *Lancelot* author provides the hero with this distinguished patrilineage reveals that he proceeds in an equivocal, vague manner. Annie Combes has detailed the contradictions and ambiguities in the prose text as Galahad is substituted for Perceval as the Grail winner and Joseph is established as his ancestor – she posits a deliberate strategy on the author's part that is intended to mask the upsetting of traditions.[27] It is only the last part of Lancelot's genealogy that is clearly traced in the *Lancelot*: Lancelot (grand-father) – Ban (father) – Lancelot – Galahad. This ancestry agrees with that of the *Estoire* and *Queste*. The rest of the family tree is referred to in vague terms throughout the *Lancelot*, with the exception of the one passage mentioned above. This obscurity suggests that the *Lancelot* author may have been creating an ancestry that was too audacious for the *Estoire* and *Queste* authors.

The *Queste* only alludes to Joseph of Arimathia's son, Galahad I, but refers often to his older son, Josephus, a character not mentioned in the *Lancelot*. Did the *Lancelot* author deliberately omit any mention of Josephus because his focus was on Joseph's other son, Galahad I? The prose writer does refer to the latter as Joseph's younger son (2, 31), implying he knew of at least one other son. Josephus is an important figure in a series of flashback tales in the *Queste* that summarize long episodes from the *Estoire*: the story of the origins of the red cross shield, the story of how Mordrain came to the abbey where he awaits Galahad, and the history of the sword Solomon prepared for Galahad. Another story of origins is only briefly mentioned – that of the broken sword, which Galahad repairs at Corbenic. All of these tales are complex; they summarize a series of episodes that appear in different sections of the *Estoire*. Which author did the rewriting? Albert Pauphilet concludes that divergences in the two texts show that the *Queste* was composed before the *Estoire*;[28] Jean-Paul Ponceau has not yet published the study in which he details the reasons why he believes the contrary. Space does not allow here an examination of the issues that would allow me to take a position in this debate.

The *Estoire* amplifies the role played by Joseph and his son Josephus in the allusions and the retrospective stories in the *Lancelot* and the *Queste*, empha-sizing their function as apostles and Grail guardians in this early Christian period. Though Joseph is called a knight and is said to have served Pilate as a soldier ('soudoiers') for seven years (1, 22 and 24), when he departs from Jeru-salem to travel to England, he is dressed like an apostle – in a robe, with bare feet – and his fight against the Saracens is solely verbal and thaumaturgic. The warrior function is assumed by the rulers who are converted to Christianity through Joseph's efforts and those of his son, Josephus. Joseph is a new Moses, leading his people out of Jerusalem to the new Promised Land. The typology is made evident by a series of actions reminiscent of those of the Old Testament leader; furthermore, God Himself makes the comparison, telling Joseph He will treat the new Christians even better than He did Moses and his people. Joseph

[27] 'From Quest to Quest.' Lot discusses the contradictions in the genealogies, pp. 218–22.
[28] A. Pauphilet, rev. of *Étude sur le 'Lancelot en Prose'*, by Ferdinand Lot, *Romania*, 45 (1918–19), 514–34; cited by Frappier, *Etude sur la Mort le Roi Artu*, pp. 46–7.

shares his evangelical role with his son Josephus, who surpasses his father, becoming the principal leader of the group of Christians. Nevertheless, both father and son preach, work miracles, convert, and baptize. They also play a role that in the *Queste* is reserved for the hermits that populate this romance: interpreting visions and dreams and revealing past and future events. They crusade verbally against the pagans or Saracens who are depicted anachronistically as inhabiting England and who are assimilated to Muslims. As in the *chanson de geste*, those who refuse to become Christians are exiled, killed, or punished – either in military actions led by the new converts or by God. The goal is to wipe out the infidel and to purify the land for Christian occupation. Thus, in each city that is converted Josephus has the idols destroyed that are falsely attributed to the Saracens, he establishes Christian churches, and invests priests and bishops.[29] The space in which these episodes take place is urban, in cities or castles. The pagans are thus associated with the constructed space of city and castle, which the Christians conquer and colonize, preparing the land for the future Arthurian kingdom. This urban topography is undoubtedly related to that of the Crusades, in which cities like Jerusalem and Constantinople play an important role.

Alternating with these episodes are sequences that relate the Christians' trials and tribulations. As we have seen, Mordrain and Nascien are transported to islands, where their faith is tested; Nascien's son Celidoine and messengers sent to seek Nascien also endure trials that take place on islands and boats, a space assimilated to that of the desert. The merit of other followers of Joseph and Josephus is also tested, in sequences devoted to their wanderings in Britain. For example, a man who dares to sit at the Grail table is immediately lifted from his seat by fiery hands and taken away. These episodes occur in the forest-desert, the space where the Christians wander – like their counterparts from the Old Testament who followed Moses into exile – and where the Grail provides nourishment for the elect, as the Lord provided manna.

Josephus' role as spiritual leader is accentuated by his celibacy, while his father is given a more terrestrial role: to engender Galahad I, who will be crowned King of Hoselice/Wales and will found one of the major lineages in the newly converted and colonized Great Britain. The other founders of lineages are all relatives of Joseph, with the exception of Lancelot's ancestors. Joseph's distinction as Grail guardian and apostle make him the ideal spiritual founder of Britain. He is thus substituted for Brutus, who is depicted in Geoffrey of Monmouth's *History of the Kings of Britain* and Wace's *Brut* as the legendary founder of Britain, but is not mentioned in the *Lancelot-Grail Cycle*. This substitution suggests that for the authors of the *Cycle*, the true origins of Britain begin with the arrival of Christianity. Furthermore, Joseph's designation as patriarch of the major Arthurian lineages provides Arthur's knights with a prestigious Christian ancestor. The major enigma remains: Why is Lancelot differentiated and why does the genealogy delineated in the *Estoire* and the *Queste* contradict that of the *Lancelot*? On the one hand, the *Estoire* and *Queste* may distance them-

---

29 Szkilnik, *Archipel*, pp. 30–31; Carol Chase, 'Des Sarrasins à Camaalot,' *Cahiers de Recherches Médiévales (XIIIe–XIVe s.)*, 5 (1998), 45–53.

selves from Lancelot because of his otherworldly upbringing in the lake and his adultery with the Queen. Though his ancestors are depicted as having colonized Britain, his realm is elsewhere: he is not tied to the same topography as Arthur.[30] On the other hand, the puzzling contradiction between the family trees may be related to the stresses and pulls of creating this important cycle – of substituting Galahad for Perceval. The *Lancelot* author is deliberately vague about Lancelot's relationship to Joseph, with one exception. Making Joseph Lancelot's direct ancestor is an audacious move, either one that flies in the face of another tradition or one that the *Estoire* and *Queste* authors refuse to recognize.

---

[30] See E. Baumgartner, 'Lancelot et le royaume,' in *La Mort du Roi Arthur ou le crépuscule de la chevalerie*, ed. Jean Dufournet (Paris, 1994), pp. 25–44.

7

The Merlin *and its* Suite

ANNIE COMBES

[Translated by Carol Dover]

The genesis of the *Merlin* is a complex romance project in the image of its eponymous character. It is a work with a history, firstly because it was fashioned from
a variety of earlier texts, and secondly because it was inserted into one cycle,
then into another. Like a polychrome print that needs several inkings before the
final printing can be made, the romance combines figures and colors from earlier
works, but the end result is a flawless landscape, a literary monument so tightly
woven and self-contained that it fits almost intact into a very different textual
environment, like a painting that serves first as the central panel of a triptych
and then as the center of a polyptych. The romance's plasticity comes from the
character of Merlin himself, whose literary representations evolved throughout
the twelfth century until they melded solidly together in our romance, in a
skillful combination of physical and moral traits, prophetic and magical powers
that had hitherto been scattered widely in the texts. In their new environment
they acquire a prodigious hierarchy and coherence, the hallmark of an
outstanding fictional achievement.

The forty-six manuscripts and eight fragments in which it has survived
suggest that the *Roman de Merlin* (written c. 1205) was a great success in the
Middle Ages.[1] But the character of Merlin himself, under the name of Myrddin,
was already a glorious figure from the Celtic legends that must have circulated
before the twelfth century. Merlin's Celtic ancestry has not always been obvious
to critics, but today we accept it and acknowledge the importance of Celtic folk-
lore in his makeup, even though so little remains from a literature that was
primarily oral.[2] Six Welsh poems found in manuscripts ranging from the twelfth
to the fifteenth century portray Myrddin as a warrior chief.[3] Whether they give

---

1   See Alexandre Micha, 'Les manuscrits du *Merlin* en prose de Robert de Boron,' *Romania*, 79
    (1958), 78–94 and 145–74. The edition I use is Robert de Boron, *Merlin: Roman du XIIIe siècle*, ed.
    A. Micha (Geneva, 1980); chapter and line numbers of this work appear in the text. The essen-
    tial critical literature on the *Merlin* includes: Paul Zumthor, *Merlin le prophète: un thème de la
    littérature polémique, de l'historiographie et des romans* (1943; rpt. Geneva, 1973); A. Micha, *Etude
    sur le 'Merlin' de Robert de Boron, roman du XIIIe siècle* (Geneva, 1980); Richard Trachsler, *Merlin
    l'enchanteur: étude sur le 'Merlin' de Robert de Boron* (Paris, 2000); Emmanuèle Baumgartner and
    Nelly Andrieux-Reix, *Le Merlin en prose* (Paris, 2001).
2   See Trachsler, *Merlin l'enchanteur*, pp. 17–25.
3   See J. K. Bollard, 'Myrddin in Early Welsh Tradition,' in *The Romance of Merlin: An Anthology*,
    ed. P. Goodrich (New York, 1990), pp. 13–54.

him the status of king or great lord, in all of them he goes mad after the battle of Arferdydd, where he witnesses the death of his lord and nephews. He flees civilization and lives in the woods in harmony with nature. In other sources he has the gift of prophecy, which he exercises from time to time in enigmatic language. Thus, the solitary figure we can glimpse in silhouette already combines the attributes of the wild man with those of the seer.

We find the same characteristics in the *Vita Merlini*, composed by Geoffrey of Monmouth c. 1148.[4] Geoffrey's Merlinus is King of the Demetes, a people living in the south of Wales. After losing his companions in combat, he goes mad and lives in the woods like a wild animal. He is found however, brought back to court, and kept in chains. It is at this point that he reveals his gift of second sight: when the King tenderly removes a leaf from his wife's hair, Merlin alone knows the leaf is a sign of her adultery. The madman reveals what is secret or concealed, and with each revelation his laughter expresses the joy of the clairvoyant who can savor the irony of fate. At the end of his life he lives in a luxurious woodland palace where he devotes himself to prophecy and learning: his encyclopedic knowledge enables him to describe the world and interpret it.

So Geoffrey's narrative brings together several faces of Merlin: that of the warrior, the man of the woods, the seer, and the scholar. These are the colors that will reappear throughout the prose *Merlin*, sometimes more subdued, sometimes more vivid in tone, but Geoffrey is also responsible for adding new shades to the Merlin character. In his Latin chronicle of the history of the Britons, *Historia Regum Britanniae* (c. 1138), he clearly associates Merlin with the reign of King Uther, the father of Arthur. The association will bring the seer a measure of historicity and veracity. Merlin enters the narrative during the reign of Vortigern [Vertigier], a seneschal who has seized the throne and is following his clerics' advice to find a 'fatherless child.' When his messengers discover the child, the mother admits to carnal relations with a supernatural being. Merlin joins Vortigern and prophesies at length, using the obscure, enigmatic style typical of phatic discourse. After Uther's accession to the throne Merlin is off-stage, with two exceptions. The first is when he moves the Circle of Giants from Ireland to Great Britain in memory of the dead British warriors (thus he 'raises' the site of Stonehenge). The second and highly significant intervention is when he leads King Uther to the Duchess Igerne's bed after changing the King's appearance. During this night of deception Arthur is conceived. Then Merlin disappears from the narrative. When Wace transposes Geoffrey's Latin prose into Anglo-Norman verse to make his *Brut*, he leaves Merlin's biography and functions intact, choosing to omit only his prophecies.

These are the changing – and at times contradictory – faces of Merlin before the thirteenth century. The author of the prose *Merlin* will likewise connect Merlin with the reigns of Vortigern and Utherpendragon, but he will leave the figure of the wild man, the seer, and the sage (in the sense of 'scholar') intact and add the function of master shape-shifter. His crucial innovation will be to

---

4 Geoffrey of Monmouth, *Life of Merlin: Vita Merlini*, ed. and trans. Basil Clarke (Cardiff, 1973).

arrange the colors of his palette under two great chromatic dominants: one belonging to God, the other to the Devil.

To make sense of this radical change, we need to consider the *Merlin*'s original environment and remember that it was a romance written as a sequel to another romance. Metaphorically speaking, we could say that the works mentioned above deposited their fossilized layers in the *Merlin*. While these sedimentary deposits explain its geological formation, the *Merlin*'s landscape can be understood only in relation to its adjoining lands whose physiognomy was not immune to change.

A *Roman de l'Estoire dou Graal* (also known as the *Joseph d'Arimathie*) was written in prose c. 1205. This is the narrative that precedes the *Merlin* and is followed by a *Perceval* in two of the manuscripts.[5] Together they form a mini-cycle, a prose trilogy attributed to Robert de Boron. The first of the three romances narrates the life of Joseph of Arimathia, a soldier of Pontius Pilate who was present at the death of Christ and collected His blood in a *veissel*. The voice of God gives this precious bowl the name of 'Graal.' Joseph is the leader of a small community of Christians and at the end of the narrative several of his companions set out for Great Britain with the precious relic. So the *Joseph* romance relates the origin of the Grail by linking it to Christ's Passion. Its theological perspective is identical to the one we find at the beginning of the *Merlin*, which has been enlarged with the addition of a struggle between God and the Devil. This romance (to which I shall return) tells the story of the seer's birth, the aid Merlin brings to the Breton kings, and describes his role in the conception of Arthur. The narrative ends with Arthur's accession to the throne; then the *Perceval* tells the story of a knight whose trajectory recalls that of Chrétien's hero in the *Conte du Graal*, who succeeds in the Grail quest and becomes the last guardian of the holy relic.

That is the triptych. The polyptych, composed c. 1220–35, inserts a slightly modified version of the first *Merlin* between the *Estoire del Saint Graal* (theological in its coloring) and the *Lancelot*.[6] To connect the *Merlin* of 1210 harmoniously to the *Lancelot* of approximately 1220, a long bridging narrative is added that we call the *Suite-Merlin*.

If the *Merlin* is moved from one cycle to another, this is because it gives a historical and religious foundation to the Arthurian world, and simultaneously defines a new ideology. From the literary standpoint, the *Merlin* is not exactly 'Arthurian' if we judge it by the usual criteria of quests, marvels, adventures, all absent here, but its purpose is to inscribe the Arthurian world in an eschatological perspective that is vast and ambitious.

Our romance is as colorful as its hero, so I will limit myself to selected aspects

---

5 Robert de Boron is the author of a *Joseph* in verse. It has survived in a single manuscript, where it is followed by 500 verses that are the model for the beginning of our *Merlin*. On these texts and the verse/prose shift, see Micha, *Etude*, pp. 59–72; L. Evdokimova, 'Vers et prose au début du XIIIe siècle: le *Joseph* de Robert de Boron,' *Romania*, 117 (1999), 448–73; Trachsler, *Merlin l'enchanteur*, pp. 40–8.

6 The *Merlin* of the triptych (small cycle) is called the 'alpha' version, the *Lancelot-Graal*'s version is 'beta.' Micha's edition gives the alpha version, but the beta version can be reconstituted from the footnotes.

of this polyphonic work. Returning to my earlier metaphor, I will describe first
the colors we find at the opening of the story, which are more demonic than
evangelical in tone. Then I will look at the lighting, both divine and diabolical,
that haloes the figure of a seer adept at shape-shifting, a *saige hom*, the prime
counselor of kings and the founder of the Round Table. With his many faces,
Merlin gives the romance its momentum and even seems to manage the transformation of history into romance. It is this colorful mix that I will focus on, a
multi-colored patchwork caused by the diversity of the earlier texts and linked
to Merlin's profound duality.

'Duality' is the operative word, for the lengthy account of the circumstances
surrounding Merlin's conception clearly makes him a son of the Devil and a son
of God. The subtlety of the author's craft is quite remarkable, for he has painted
in words a diabolical imitation of one of the greatest Christian mysteries, the
conception of Christ by the Holy Spirit. The romance opens with a council of
devils deploring the fact that their dwellings are deserted. This is because Christ
has descended into Hell and delivered all the Just and taken them to Paradise.
Furthermore, He has established new sacraments – baptism and confession –
that allow men to be cleansed of their sins from birth to death. The devils react to
this critical situation by deciding to create a being endowed, like them, with the
ability to know the past. With this power he will win men's trust, then lead them
to their ruin . . . and to Hell. If this ambitious plan succeeds, it will diminish the
effects of the Redemption by creating a veritable Antichrist. A devil is therefore
sent to earth to make preparations for the sexual union of an incubus and a
woman. The scenario is a carbon copy of the conception of Christ: the selected
victim is a virtuous young virgin, which complicates the task. It takes two years
of maneuvering to bring about the 'maculate conception,' as Francis Dubost so
aptly calls it:[7] the girl falls asleep without making the sign of the cross because
she is angry, the incubus works fast and she loses her virginity as she sleeps.
However, she has not committed the sin of fornication, and the priest she immediately goes to see hears her confession, accepts her contrition, and orders
penance. In this way she is absolved of a sin she did not commit willingly, and
the devils' plot is foiled by the very sacrament that they abhor: confession.

What might appear to be an ironic outcome is really the result of divine intervention. The circumstances of this conception are in fact part of God's plan. He
knew of the devils' plan and allowed it to proceed, for He wished such a creature to be conceived. At the birth of the child He adds to the devils' special gifts
(knowledge of 'things done and said' [1, 75])[8] another form of knowledge: 'the
ability to know things to come' (10, 25). Thus, Merlin's knowledge is symmetrically configured with a dual orientation to the past and the future: in him are
conjoined the knowledge of beginnings and of final ends. From the perspective
of the *Cycle* it means that he knows the origin of the Grail on the one hand, and
the future of Breton chivalry on the other.[9] He is a strange creature that the

7   *Aspects fantastiques de la littérature narrative médiévale (XIIe–XIIIe siècles): l'Autre, l'Ailleurs,*
    l'Autrefois, 2 vols. (Paris, 1992), II, 712.
8   The figures refer to paragraph and line in Micha's edition.
9   This knowledge is a veritable *mise en abyme* of the organization of the first cycle. See Larry S.

author builds carefully and coherently in order to make him the king-pin of the narrative. But will Merlin be on the side of God or the Devil?

The child is born with a fearfully hairy appearance; however his hairiness seems to be forgotten, and does not prevent him from being baptized. Most importantly, his good disposition clearly shows in the way he intervenes to save his mother, who has been condemned to death for giving birth to a child out of wedlock. At the tender age of two, Merlin brilliantly produces proof that the judge himself was the product of an adulterous union, and that it is therefore the judge's own mother who should be condemned. The incident demonstrates the child's goodness as well as his incomparable gifts that come from his 'spiritual' parents: he knows the past (the judge's conception) and the future (he predicts that the judge's true father, a priest, will commit suicide when he learns that his secret is out). His judicious words promptly earn him the label *saige*. A long conversation with his mother's confessor, Blaise, confirms his exceptional knowledge and his desire to act in God's name.

On his journey to Great Britain with King Vortigern's messengers, two more scenes prove the child's gifts, in a comic mode. In the first scene, a commoner buys some leather to make shoes for himself, but Merlin knows that the man will die first. In the second scene, a father weeps at his son's burial, not knowing that his son's real father is the priest leading the funeral procession. As in the *Vita Merlini*, Merlin laughs at man's blindness, and wins the absolute trust of the messengers, who will introduce him to their king as 'the wisest man and the finest seer ever, apart from God' (26, 32–3).

All the same, the Devil's share is not erased from the narrative, and we can see it in three kinds of marvels. First of all, Merlin is capable of shape-shifting, like the Devil in the Bible (this is a power specific to devils, never to saints or prophets).[10] Merlin has this troubling gift, which he uses to win the joyful hearts of the two young kings, Pendragon and Uther: one moment he has the appearance of a youth, the next moment (in the same place) there is no one but a respectable lord. Elsewhere, he is a hideous woodcutter. Beyond the entertainment-value of these instances of shape-shifting we can sense that they have a preparatory function: they anticipate the shape-shifting that will lead to the conception of Arthur, when Merlin will change his own appearance as well as that of the King and his companion Ulfin in order to deceive the Duchess of Tintagel. This particular power has contributed much to the glory and posterity of the character we often call the 'enchanter.' Although the word itself does not appear in the medieval text, it is there by implication when Uther, astounded by his companion's various *semblances*, exclaims ' "je suis touz enchantez" ' (38, 11).

According to Saint Augustine, 'The nature of demons is such that, because their body is made from an airy substance, they move infinitely faster than men and animals, and even faster than birds in flight.'[11] This is the second of Merlin's

Crist, 'Les livres de Merlin,' in *Mélanges de langue et de littérature françaises du Moyen Age offerts à Pierre Jonin* (Paris, 1979), p. 204, and Annie Combes, 'La science de Merlin,' *Op. Cit.*, 15 (2000), 11–19.

10 See Francis Dubost, *Aspects fantastiques*, I, 723–30.

11 *De Divinatione Daemonum* (III, 7), Corpus Scriptorum Ecclesiastorum Latinorum., vol. 41, 5, 3 (Prague and Vienna, 1900).

diabolical attributes. No sooner does a king express the desire to meet him, than
he appears on the spot: for him, space has no extension. His last diabolical
attribute, in keeping with medieval belief in devils, is the power to move objects.
When Pendragon dies, Merlin brings to Salisbury some Irish megaliths that no
one could lift. The populace is dumbfounded, for 'no one had seen it or knew of
it' (47, 66). This, it seems, was how Stonehenge was built, and Uther's remark is
there to mitigate the diabolical dimension of the event: ' "No one except God
could do this, unless you did" ' (47, 69).

We can in fact still detect God's share in Merlin's actions. Is he not God's creature, after all? The seer's great missions are the creation of the Round Table
(never called by this name) and the conception of Arthur. First of all, Merlin
wishes to have a table at Carduel that will seat Utherpendragon's barons. After
mentioning to the King the table of the Last Supper and the Grail Table (at which
Joseph and his companions gathered), he declares: ' "And if you have confidence in me, we will establish the third one in the name of the Trinity" ' (48, 75).
Merlin has the ability to imagine this project that conjoins past and future and
will ensure the prosperity of the King and his successor, Arthur. Fifty knights sit
down at the table and have no desire to ever leave the court: ' "Now we love one
another as much as or more than a son should love his father and never shall we
be separated till death us do part" ' (49, 63–5). Thus chivalry's elite come
together around the King. Never in literature had the Round Table been given
an origin so complex and so significant: this etiological narrative alone justifies
the *Merlin* being inserted into the *Lancelot-Graal*.

Merlin's other great mission concerns the conception of Arthur. The author
had to make do with the event as told by his predecessors, which involved
shape-shifting. But he positions the scene skillfully within the work's internal
structure so that it corresponds to the conception of Merlin and that of Christ.[12]
In all three cases a woman is visited by a supernatural being – Holy Ghost, evil
spirit, or the more human form of a shape-shifter. It is an amazing invention that
basks in the glory of the Trinity and promises an illustrious destiny for the child
of the Duchess.

This is how the Devil's share and God's share combine in the composition of
Merlin. The alchemy is bold and risky, yet it does not scoff at Church doctrine
because Merlin, with a nature that is not completely pure and not really impure,
is the manager of a grandiose plan whose ultimate director is God. What the
romance author has done is exploit the rich variety of his character. The seer's
dual origin thus allows him to carry out dubious schemes: Merlin, the instigator
of an act of royal adultery, reveals the dark side of Breton history and at the same
time builds a monument to its glory.

There is, then, a political dimension to the role Merlin plays. On a broader
front, the sovereignty issue subtends the entire romance, except for the hero's
childhood. Beginning with § 17, the romance takes on a decidedly historical
coloring, using a narrative line inspired directly by the *Historia* and the *Brut*.
King Constantine has three sons, Monk, Pendragon and Uther. When he dies he

[12] Trachsler demonstrates this in *Merlin l'enchanteur*, pp. 132–5.

is succeeded by his eldest son, who is a mere child and 'was not as courageous or as knowlegeable as he needed to be' (17, 26). These are serious weaknesses that hasten his downfall when Vortigern the seneschal decides to seize the throne and insidiously has Monk killed. The illegitimate King is soon hated for his deceit, and his reliance on Saxon aid makes a bad situation worse. Enter Merlin, who announces the return of the two brothers from exile. From this point on, the monarchy improves constantly with the succession of three kings – Pendragon, Uther, and Arthur – and the manner in which they are appointed. The first two demonstrate that a good king is courageous in combat and governs in consultation with his counselors. Uther has all the qualities of his older brother (emblematized in the name Utherpendragon that he assumes on the death of his brother), but what is more, in Merlin's care he enters the realm of godliness with the founding of the Third Table. However, it is Arthur who provides the finest incarnation of kingship, because of his personal qualities and because he does not accede to the throne by *heritage* but by an effect of divine election.[13]

At birth, the duchess's child was given by Merlin to a vavassor, and grew up in modest surroundings, ignorant of his own identity. Thus, Utherpendragon dies without a known heir. The lords do not know what to do next about the empty throne, but Merlin asks them to wait for a sign from God. The following Christmas, the people and the nobility discover a sword that is stuck in an anvil encased in a block of marble. An inscription on the blade says that he who removes the sword from the anvil must be king. All the lords, from the highest to the lowest, fail the test, but one day young Arthur draws the sword effortlessly. He will still have to overcome the barons' refusal to accept as their king an obscure young man who is not even a knight, and they put him through tests that reveal his wisdom and generosity. So Arthur combines a sign of election from above with the foresight expected of a king. The sword destined for him also suggests that he will not be lacking in courage. This is the exemplary man who is anointed king, and this is the lesson of equity and wisdom that the romance develops. The reader knows, of course, that Arthur *is* Uther's son, but his concealed identity allows for a lengthy exposition of the qualities that make a perfect king and a perfect knight.

Over and above these magical and political interventions, Merlin is assigned one final function: that of author. He actually dictates to Blaise the subject matter of a book that is, it seems, the one that we are reading.[14] So we discover in the romance how the fiction generates itself. The authorial trait has been grafted onto the wild-man trait inherited from the earlier texts. As Merlin explains it, his *nature* urges him to withdraw far from the world (39, 46). However, the seer no longer needs solitude; instead he joins Blaise, his mother's former confessor, somewhere in Northumberland. From his childhood days Merlin has appointed him as his scribe, dictating to this simple cleric what ' "no man could tell you, save God and myself" ' (16, 38). His words are then summarized by the narrator

13 See the comments of Daniel Boutet, *Charlemagne et Arthur, ou le roi imaginaire* (Paris, 1992).
14 This aspect has been discussed by Anne Berthelot, *Figures et fonction de l'écrivain au XIIIe siècle* (Montreal and Paris, 1991), pp. 414–18; Mireille Séguy, 'Le point aveugle: la fabrique du récit fictionnel dans le *Merlin*,' *Op. Cit.*, 5 (2000), 27–35.

and the reader is amazed to find Merlin recounting the relationship between Joseph of Arimathia and Christ, recalling the lineage of the Guardians of the Grail that has come to Britain and then the devils' plot that led to his birth – in other words, the content of Robert de Boron's *Joseph* and the *Merlin*'s events up to the moment he begins his dictation to Blaise. In a second session with Blaise he gives an account of what has happened since the first session. Thus, the narrative is repeated by Merlin's discourse, which corresponds in the smallest detail with what the reader has read – and is about to read. Moreover, Merlin explains to his scribe that their collaboration will produce the *livre dou Graal* (23, 63). So Merlin the omniscient character casts himself in the role of literary architect, directing not only 'present' events but also the narratives which will someday record them.

If Merlin's words beget the narrative, by the same token they confirm the story's claim to be true. The source of the book, Merlin's voice, is indeed reliable: *Voirement dist voir Merlins*, as the King's subjects say. Merlin speaks the truth, therefore what he narrates to Blaise is true, and what we are reading is also true. Even if Merlin explains to Blaise that his book cannot be *en auctorité* (16, 98) because its redactor (Blaise), unlike the apostles, has not witnessed in person what he is re-transcribing, the whole mechanism he has set up tends to prove the contrary, for it gives this restriction the appearance of a negation of a negation. Meanwhile, this locking in of truth creates a formidable problem of narratorial coherence. The real author, who has managed to build a unified character out of a polymorphous one, is less successful when it comes to controlling the enunciation of his own narrative. The result is that the *je* that appears throughout the text lacks unity at the level of representation.

We start off with an omniscient narrator who oversees the fiction. He punctuates the dealings of the demon (who has now arrived on earth) with edifying commentary intended to instruct his readers and put them on their guard against devils. Thanks to the narrator's learned voice, the narrative resembles an exemplum: 'And in this way you can tell that a devil is very foolish and we should be furious if we are tricked by such a foolish thing' (1, 91). But the child Merlin overturns the coloration as well as the control of the narrative. As soon as he is old enough to speak, he is the one who directs events and analyses them. The narrator no longer intervenes to give history lessons: Merlin takes over. Even more remarkable is the fact that the narrator ceases to direct the narrative in his way. There are times when he has to keep quiet, as if he had to wait for Merlin to deal with an event before he could have the right to speak of it: 'I must speak of these two children no more until the text takes me back to them' (18, 46–7). The seer has to arrive in Britain and announce the return of the two children before the narrative can return to them. This narrator, once omniscient and now restricted in his narrative choices, lacks stability and becomes a highly unreliable enunciator.[15] His position is all the more fragile because the romance is made largely from direct speech – essentially spoken by Merlin!

---

[15] His weakness is not repaired by the false name he acquires (in two manuscripts only): 'Einsi dist mes sires Roberz de Borron qui cest conte retrait que il se redouble' (16, 115–16; also 91 and 59, at the end of the romance).

So one character rules the fiction with his own words, while the narrator is deprived of his primary functions, tendentiously dispossessed of what was his by right: the responsibility for the narrative. This is confirmed by the recurring sentences that suffice to indicate Merlin's retreats and the writing of the book, after the first two lengthy writing sessions. For example: 'Et ainsis s'en ala [Merlins] en Norhumbellande a Blaises et li conta les choses, et Blaises le mist en son livre et par son livre le resavons nos encore' (31, 11–13). Here the narrator recalls all the readers who, like him, have read Blaise's *livre*; significantly, they are on the reception side rather than the production side of his work.

We have seen that in the *Merlin* the real author invents a dangerous type of narrative, according to which the discourse of one character orients and manages the diegesis, controls the narrative flow, traps it in the net of his predictions and his retrospectives – leaving the narrator with a subsidiary role, a role constrained by the control the hero exercises over the story and the narrative. Thus, Merlin appears as the artisan of one of medieval literature's most extraordinary experiments.

The *Suite du Merlin*, also known as the *Vulgate Suite*, is the last component to be added to the *Lancelot-Grail Cycle*.[16] In the manuscripts it is placed on principle between the *Merlin* and the *Lancelot*, where it fulfills its most obvious function of linking the two works and bringing the *Cycle* to completion. It is a lengthy narrative that owes its existence to the fact that the *Merlin* and the *Lancelot* were composed roughly ten years apart, before the idea of a cyclic ensemble required the connection. Around 1235 an unknown author takes on this difficult task. To make it succeed, he draws on all the other works in the *Cycle*. He is particularly fond of using forwards and backwards references: he clearly has the advantage in predicting facts that are already in the *Lancelot*, the *Queste*, or the *Mort Artu*, whereas allusions to the past recall circumstances or characters already mentioned in the *Estoire del Saint Graal* and the *Merlin*.

The author's main goal is to fill a chronological gap and achieve coherence among the characters in the *Cycle*. At the end of the *Merlin*, Arthur is only fifteen years old, a mere silhouette but full of promise. As for Merlin, he has proven his exceptional talents and accomplished a prestigious mission. When we reach the opening pages of the *Lancelot*, Merlin and Arthur are fallen characters, the first demonized and dead, the second a weary, middle-aged man who is powerless to come to the aid of his vassals. However, the *Lancelot* puts forward two kings of great merit, Ban (Lancelot's father) and Bohort, who were completely unknown to the *Merlin*. This massive split in the diegesis sets the agenda of the *Suite*: to continue the *Merlin* and prepare the way for the *Lancelot* by creating links

16 H. Oskar Sommer ed., *The Vulgate Version of the Arthurian Romances*, 7 vols. (Washington, D.C., 1908–13; rpt. New York, 1979) vol. II. Also in the Pléiade edition based on MS Bonn, University Library, 526 (82): *Le Livre du Graal*, vol. I: *Les premiers Faits du roi Arthur*, ed. Irène Freire-Nunes, intro. Philippe Walter, trans. and notes Anne Berthelot and Philippe Walter (Paris, 2001), pp. 807–1662. Micha has written a series of articles on the *Suite*: 'La guerre contre les Romains dans la *Vulgate* du *Merlin*,' *Romania*, 72 (1951), 310–23; 'Les sources de la *Vulgate* du *Merlin*,' *Le Moyen Age*, 57 (1952), 299–346; 'La composition de la *Vulgate* du *Merlin*,' *Romania*, 74 (1953), 200–20; 'La *Suite-Vulgate* du *Merlin*, étude littéraire,' *Zeitschrift für romanische Philologie*, 71 (1955), 33–59. Cf. Eugene Vinaver, 'La genèse de la suite du *Merlin*,' in *Mélanges de philologie romane et de littérature médiévale offerts à Ernest Hoepffner* (Paris, 1949), pp. 295–300.

between narratives and characters that are largely unconnected, thus filling an intervening period that allows Arthur and Merlin to age and King Ban and King Bohort to demonstrate their prowess.

This plan is accomplished thanks to a theme of constant bellicosity that shows off Arthur's excellence as a warrior. The British King is in fact the true hero of the narrative. Nowhere else in the *Cycle* is he magnified so greatly: an excellent warrior, a clever strategist who heeds Merlin's advice, a generous king to his vassals, a fervent supporter of Christianity.[17]

The young king begins by tackling the hostility of the Bretons, who have done an about-face and refuse to accept him as their sovereign lord, first on the grounds of his low birth, and second, once they learn of his filiation, on the grounds of his bastardy. Arthur wins, and in the process he wins the support of his young subjects such as Gauvain. After this the Saxons will take on their role of fearsome invaders, and the Britons will unite to conquer them. Next there will be a new, lengthy depiction of the traditional enmity between Britons and Romans.[18] The entire narrative has an undeniably epic coloring that makes it special within the *Cycle*. In the *Suite* Merlin delights in assuming the figure of enchanter, changing shape with great charm, and building a fairy palace for the young Viviane, with whom he is in love. But he continues as the strategist from the *Merlin*, and when he acts as standard bearer in combat against the Saxons, for example, he even fights alongside the Bretons and comes close to the warrior status he had in the *Vita Merlini*. It is Merlin who advises Arthur to appeal for help from the two kings of Brittany, Ban and Bohort:

> "Et d'autre part en la petite Bretagne a .II. rois qui sont frere & ont a feme .II. serors germaines ... & por ce quil sont si preudome & si loial voldroie ie bien que tu les mandasses si lor manderas que tu les veus veoir ... si te feront hommage moult volentiers." (97, 4–16)

> ["And moreover in Brittany there are two kings who are brothers married to two sisters ... and because they are so worthy and so loyal I would like you to send them a message telling them you want to see them ... and they will gladly do homage to you."]

Merlin keeps his role as reporter of events to Blaise, but more discreetly than in the *Merlin*. It turns out that Arthur rises to glory, while the prophet follows the opposite trajectory: in love with Viviane, who deceives him, he ends up imprisoned in the forest of Broceliande because of a spell that he himself had taught her. This is where the *Suite* sets up the future power of the Lady of the Lake and the downfall of the seer, who is dead and irrelevant at the beginning of the *Lancelot*. The scenes with Viviane bring variety to unrelieved narrative matter. Certain episodes are like windows on other romance forms; for example, the story of Grisandole (in which a young woman disguises herself as a man),

---

[17] For this reason, the linkage with the figure of Arthur at the beginning of the *Lancelot* will be problematic.

[18] As Micha shows in his series of articles, the author has relied heavily on the *Brut*.

the story of the cat from Lausanne (a monster that Arthur fights), and the misadventure of Gauvain who changes into a dwarf.

After the varied coloring of the *Merlin*, the *Suite* (the last of the *Cycle*'s compositions) offers a more subdued and more restricted range of colors. The two works are next to each another in the manuscripts and they are the only ones that represent Merlin, yet they turn out to be very different from one another. One is prolific, exuberant, surprising; the other relies on effects of recurrence and similarity. The *Merlin* provides the Arthurian romance world with its prestigious foundation; the *Suite* seizes on the Arthurian world at the point where it is about to soar, but the work constantly refuses to anticipate the adventures and marvels that bejewel the *Lancelot*, so the Arthurian romance world is frozen in a repetition of similar actions that translate, by their incessant accumulation, a time passing that is oppressive, weighed down with the threat of war and death. It is as if the author of the *Suite,* knowing the end of the *Cycle* and the outcome of the murderous battles that will take place in the *Mort Artu*, has decided to balance their effect with endless victories whose success relies on the alliance of a flamboyant king and a seer henceforth grown wise.

8

The Book of Lancelot

CAROL DOVER

The anonymous *Lancelot*, probably composed between 1215 and 1220, is acknowledged as the oldest member of the *Lancelot-Grail Cycle*.[1] We may never know the identity of its author(s) beyond Lot's suggestion that he was a cleric of aristocratic background in service at court,[2] whose work combined a Grail story with a courtly story, apparently to make good on what Chrétien had attempted in his Grail story. Although each of the members of the *Cycle* has its particular perspective and texture, Jean Frappier's concept of the entire *Cycle* being planned and directed by a single mind that he calls the 'architect,' is still convincing.[3] We may never know more about the actual production of the *Lancelot* than the text itself can actually reveal: did it exist first as a 'non-cyclic' work, or was it planned from the start as a cyclic work? On the one hand Elspeth Kennedy argues that the *Lancelot* existed initially as a small prose romance, courtly in tone and independent of the cyclic intent, before being appropriated as the basis of a large cyclic composition and elaborated to three times its original size to form the cyclic *Lancelot*.[4] Alexandre Micha, on the other hand, believes that the end of the non-cyclic *Lancelot* is a truncation of the cyclic version and that the cyclic intent was present from the beginning of the work.[5] The debate has been recently re-opened on Micha's side by Annie Combes, who

---

1 Ferdinand Lot, *Etude sur le Lancelot en prose* (Paris, 1918), pp. 150ff. For a discussion of the medieval notion of 'cycle' see David Staines, 'The Medieval Cycle: Mapping a Trope,' in *Transtextualities: Of Cycles and Cyclicity in Medieval French Literature*, ed. Sara Sturm-Maddox and Donald Maddox (Binghamton, NY, 1996), pp. 15–37.
2 Lot, *Etude*, pp. 152–9.
3 'Plaidoyer pour l'"Architecte" contre une opinion d'Albert Pauphilet sur le *Lancelot en prose*,' *Romance Philology*, 8 (1954–5), 27–33.
4 See her articles, 'The Two Versions of the False Guinevere Episode in the Old French Prose *Lancelot*,' *Romania*, 77 (1956), 94–104; 'The Scribe as Editor,' in *Mélanges Jean Frappier* (Geneva, 1970), I, 523–31. She backs up her theory with a list of non-cyclic manuscripts and a critical edition of the non-cyclic version of the text, *Lancelot do Lac* (Oxford, 1980). The issue is developed in greater detail in *Lancelot and the Grail: A Study of the Prose* Lancelot (Oxford, 1986).
5 'Les épisodes du Voyage en Sorelois et de la Fausse Guenièvre,' *Romania*, 76 (1955), 334–41; reprinted in Micha, *De la chanson de geste au roman* (Geneva, 1976), pp. 313–16. 'Tradition manuscrite et versions du *Lancelot en prose*,' *BBSIA*, XIV (1962), 99–106; 'La tradition manuscrite du *Lancelot en prose*: les deux versions du *Lancelot en prose*,' *Romania*, 87 (1966), 194–233; 'Le départ en Sorelois: réflexions sur deux versions,' in *Mélanges Maurice Delbouille* (Paris, 1964), II, 495–507; 'Sur la composition du *Lancelot en prose*,' in *Mélanges Felix Lecoy* (Paris, 1973), pp. 417–25, reprinted in A. Micha, *De la chanson de geste au roman*, pp. 233–4.

presents the non-cyclic textual evidence as the effect of important narrative strat-
egies devised to create mystery and to introduce a revised Grail tradition.[6]

Whether we accept the theory of an initially independent narrative or not, the
Lancelot exists today in a cyclic environment that is really a dual one: in the
Lancelot–Queste–Mort Artu trilogy (or *Prose Lancelot*) which is by far the
commonest grouping in the extant cyclic manuscripts and probably its earliest
cyclic environment, and in the five-part *Cycle* formed with the addition of the
Estoire and *Merlin-Suite*. In the trilogy, the *Lancelot* is the foundation of the
edifice: a romance chronicle of the state of Arthurian chivalry and the realm. In
the *Cycle*, the *Lancelot* is at the center of the new edifice, flanked symmetrically
on either side by a Grail narrative and an Arthurian narrative.[7] Three times
larger than the *Queste* and *Mort Artu*, larger than the *Estoire*, *Merlin*, *Queste*, and
Mort Artu combined, the *Lancelot* is indeed the *Cycle*'s huge centerpiece which,
as it joins and separates the diegetic past (*Estoire* and *Merlin-Suite*) and future
(*Queste* and *Mort Artu*), centers its storytelling unmistakably on Lancelot.[8] The
central position it occupies – structurally and metaphorically – within the *Cycle*,
literally repeats like a mirror-image within the work itself, which is traditionally
divided into three parts with the 'Conte de la Charrette' (the prose retelling of
Chrétien's Lancelot romance) at its heart.

Whether we read the new story of Lancelot in a non-cyclic or cyclic environment, he is offered by name as Chrétien's paradoxical Knight of the Cart whose
service to King Arthur was inspired by his love for Arthur's Queen, and we are
obliged to read him against that intertextual background.[9] But the prose author
transplants him in an environment at once similar to and different from that of
the verse romance.[10] Chrétien's Lancelot exists in a timeless space which,
through its characters, geography, and thematic concerns, clearly evokes the
time of Arthurian chivalry but is so vague as to invest the hero with a mythical
aura that exists out of time. In contrast, the prose author reduces the mythical
timelessness by placing him on a panoramic stage with a historical location in
time and space, defined at the beginning of the work by Arthur's continental
lands in Brittany and his mainland kingdom during the period of the continental

6   See Combes, 'From Quest to Quest: Perceval and Galahad in the Prose *Lancelot*,' *Arthuriana*,
    12.3 (Winter 2002), 7–31. Baumgartner, 'Sainte(s) Hélène(s),' in *Femmes-Mariages – Lignages
    XIIe–XIVe siècles. Mélanges afferts à Georges Duby* (Brussels, 1992), pp. 43–53.
7   Jean Frappier likened the configuration to the west facade of the great Gothic cathedrals, with
    their large central portal flanked on either side by two smaller portals; see his 'Genèse et unité
    de structure du *Lancelot en prose*,' printed as an appendix in his *Etude sur la Mort le roi Artu*
    (Geneva and Paris, 1961), pp. 440–55.
8   See Jean Frappier, 'Le cycle de la *Vulgate* (*Lancelot en prose* et *Lancelot-Graal*),' in *Grundriss der
    romanischen Literaturen des Mittelalters*, IV,1, ed. Jean Frappier and Reinhold R. Grimm
    (Heidelberg, 1978), p. 536.
9   See Matilda T. Bruckner, *Shaping Romance: Interpretation, Truth, and Closure in Twelfth-Century
    French Fictions* (Philadelphia, 1993), ch. 3, for a remarkable exploration of Chrétien's Lancelot
    in the Pomeleslgais tournament episode, esp. the intertextual reading at pp. 90–108. Frappier
    lists some of the intertextual romance material in 'Cycle de la Vulgate,' pp. 549–50.
10 Emmanuèle Baumgartner discusses the time-space of Chrétien's romances in 'Temps linéaire,
    temps circulaire et écriture romanesque (XIIe–XIIIe siècles),' in *Le Temps et la durée dans la
    littérature du Moyen Age à la Renaissance*, ed. Yvonne Bellenger (Paris, 1984), pp. 7–21, esp.:
    'Tout se passe . . . comme si les récits de Chrétien suspendaient le temps arthurien . . . Un
    temps toujours présent, "présentifié", qui n'a ni début ni fin, ni passé ni futur' (p. 11).

invasions, when Arthur's rule was well established and his power was on the wane. Within this panorama, where Lancelot will be one in a hierarchy of many, the prose author subtly lays the foundations of two contrasting concepts of chivalry and their mission in the world: an earthly chivalry embodying the ideals of Arthurian knighthood, and a spiritual one reflecting an ideal of service to the Church. To counter the panoramic spread of the narrative, the author creates an entire biography of his hero from birth to manhood, ending with his death in the *Mort Artu*. From the opening lines of the romance the prose author re-motivates the mystery surrounding the familiar name 'Lancelot' and links it to a past and a future, to a mysterious genealogy, and eventually to a messianic vision of history through the creation of a son. Time is of the essence, but the prose author's tactic is to fill significant gaps in the reader's knowledge so that we discover what we did and did not know about Lancelot from Chrétien's poem, so that we see what I have called elsewhere 'a former self revised.'[11] The thematic constants of the poem's Lancelot are retained: his unfailing love for Arthur's Queen on which his service to Arthur depends, and the mystery in which the author cloaks him. Not only does the prose romance tell a much longer and denser story than the *Charrette*, it also requires a much more complex reading strategy because it commands from its readers intertextual as well as extensive intratextual interaction with the text.[12] Moreover, while the use of prose may well give the overall impression of an authorial desire to tell the truth,[13] the *Lancelot*'s interlace device complicates the prose narrative to an extraordinary degree because it not only serializes but also obfuscates. Each shift from one segment to the next refocuses the narrative on a specific character or group within a vast panoramic action, but the ritualistic opening and closing of each narrative segment – 'Ci dist li contes' / 'Or laisse li contes' – also conjoins fragments which are thematically unrelated, with the result that related segments can be separated by hundreds of pages of our reading. The end-product is a vast and intricate narrative that conceals in its fragmentation as much as it reveals.

The sheer size of the *Lancelot*, coupled with the intricacy of its composition, raises the key question of how readers could keep track of the action across large expanses of storytelling and also interpret as they went along. How did they make sense of it all and find it compelling enough to come back for more and more, as we know they did? Did they find a structure that for them would facilitate recall?

The *Lancelot* is today an object of scholarly investigation, but it was composed for unscholarly aristocratic audiences for whom it was popular literature of the

---

11 Carol R. Dover, 'From Non-Cyclic to Cyclic *Lancelot*: Recycling the Heart,' in *Transtextualities*, ed. Maddox and Maddox, p. 56 [53–70].

12 The audience could, of course, have ignored such textual richness and read through without the benefits of them, but the resulting comprehension would have been much diminished (reading for the storyline rather than for the plot).

13 Vernacular prose came into its own in the late twelfth and early thirteenth centuries as the medium for historiography, chronicles, the *Faits des Romains*, legal documents, charters, religious writings, translations of the Bible and sermons. See Daniel Poirion, 'La naissance et l'évolution du roman arthurien en prose,' *Grundriss der romanischen Literaturen des Mittelalters*, IV/1, 504–5 [503–12].

highest order. Dante conjures up for us the delight they took in its storytelling, when Francesca says, not without moral ambiguity, that she and Paolo were reading of Lancelot and the Queen 'per diletto' [for pleasure].[14] It was a book they loved, which had moreover been skillfully crafted to be loved, but unfortunately they did not read far enough.[15] Despite this vivid example of the power of its storytelling, modern scholarly criticism has struggled to explain the powerful impact it had on its medieval audiences, who probably heard the book of Lancelot read aloud in a group setting or might also have read it themselves as Paolo and Francesca did.[16]

Eugène Vinaver, who was the first to give a positive sense of the pleasure the prose romances must have afforded their audiences, suggested that thematic patterning was a significant structuring element in the interlace.[17] Since then, Elspeth Kennedy's groundbreaking work has carefully traced the structural interweaving of themes in the first part of the *Lancelot*, with emphasis on the process.[18] E. Jane Burns has identified a system of 'allomorphs,' motif-like objects and places, e.g., prison, tower, cemetery, that provide linkage and cohesion at the semantic level across the whole *Lancelot-Grail Cycle* but have allegorical significance.[19] Charles Méla's study of *conjointure* in the romances of Chrétien de Troyes and the *Lancelot*, examines the prose romance's complex interlacing of Biblical and romance themes through its various mystification tactics.[20] His conclusion retains the paradoxical nature attributed to Chrétien's hero by countless critics, while retaining Vinaver's seemingly paradoxical description of the *Lancelot* as 'an eminently *acentric* composition, with as much internal cohesion as one would find in any centralized pattern.'[21] Jean-René Valette's recent study discovers two attitudes towards the marvelous in the *Lancelot*, one that lacks critical distance and one that is 'objective,' but he studiously eschews reception.[22] How then, we may ask again, did the *Lancelot*'s medieval audiences keep track of the action across large expanses of storytelling and also interpret such a complex composition as they went along?

Eugène Vinaver linked the demanding nature of the *Lancelot*'s composition to

---

14 *Inferno* V.127–38.
15 Mary J. Carruthers, *The Book of Memory: A Study of Memory in Medieval Culture* (Cambridge, Eng., and New York, 1990), p. 187.
16 The reading vs. hearing debate has generally been framed as a question of literacy vs. illiteracy in parallel with orality vs. ocular reading, but Robert Hanning argues judiciously for the contrary in 'Arthurian Evangelists: The Language of Truth in Thirteenth-Century French Romances,' *Philological Quarterly*, 64 (1985), 347–65. Most recently, Joyce Coleman's *Public Reading and the Reading Public in Late Medieval England and France* (Cambridge, 1996) demonstrates that, even in the late fourteenth and the fifteenth centuries, the social value of French romances in France meant that they were still public reading (read aloud by a reader to a group), with discussion following and the possibility of a private reading from the manuscript later.
17 See *The Rise of Romance* (Oxford, 1971) and *A la recherche d'une poétique médiévale* (Paris, 1970).
18 *Lancelot and the Grail*, where the repeated appearance of the same or similar objects is noted as they appear.
19 *Arthurian Fictions: Rereading the Vulgate Cycle* (Columbus, OH, 1985).
20 *La reine et le Graal: la conjointure dans les romans du Graal de Chrétien de Troyes au Livre de Lancelot* (Paris, 1984), part III.
21 *Form and Meaning in Medieval Romance* (Cambridge, Eng., 1966), p. 10.
22 *La Poétique du merveilleux dans le Lancelot en prose* (Paris, 1998).

the pleasure of the text: 'The assumption is not only that the reader's memory is infallible, but that the exercise of that memory is in itself a pleasurable pursuit which carries with it its own reward.'[23] This raises important questions about reception. How did memory and pleasure interact for the *Lancelot*'s audiences of romance connoisseurs? Was it memory that made the reading pleasurable, or pleasure that made the reading memorable? How did memory and pleasure interact to make the reading such a pleasurable pursuit and an instructive one over such a vast expanse of text, especially if its audiences also comprehended it with reference to other romances? When we ask such questions, we are really asking how the author crafted his narrative for reception. Since its reception was not scholarly, the effort of memory required of romance audiences was not that of the cleric's trained, 'technological' memory, but rather a 'romance memory' that had not been trained by book learning, but by their own cultural identity and 'education' in the sense of previous experiences of hearing romances read over and over. Such a memory would be stocked with many similar and differentiated memories of topics relevant to its owner's experience and imagination, all of them engraved large in memory by the sheer delight of hearing romances read time and time again.[24] In other words, to be effective the presentation had to also be affective.

I have described elsewhere the rhetorical basis of the affective aspect of the romance memory, which is fundamental to the interaction of text and audience, but one visible trace of the *Lancelot* author's efforts to reach out to his audience's memory is that, while preserving the mystery and suspense that are essential to romance composition, he has created a structure consisting of a series of images. I call them 'landmark images' because they are a set of crucial signposts to meaning along a dense and shifting trail. They are placed strategically at important turning points in the narrative, where the pictorial quality of the images and their compelling appeal to the reader's imagination make them powerful kernels of reflection and interpretation in the search for truth in this vast romance. Planted one by one in the readers' memory, they stretch across the interlace like a beaded thread, as each image reflects back to its predecessor and forward to its successor. In this way they constitute a string of memory hooks the audience can use in order to grasp distant points in the narrative and interrelate them.

The *Lancelot*'s images are descriptions whose vivid use of figurative language literally invites the audience to picture the object/place/thing they describe. But if we understood description merely as a rhetorical device that retards the forward movement of the narrative, we would miss what medieval writers understood by the term and what medieval romance audiences expected and enjoyed from it. Because its vividness often included hyperbole, it could be perceived as overstatement and exaggeration, when in fact its purpose was not to deceive but to exalt the thing/person/place being described, by making it an

---

23 *A la recherche*, p. 136.
24 This notion of a 'romance memory' finds support in the notion that medieval compilers regarded Chrétien de Troyes' romance corpus as an evolving series.

object of wonder, marvelous to behold.[25] In this guise, *descriptio*'s narrative function was to 'speak out' from the text, implying that it had something important to say that could not be expressed otherwise.

To capture the audience's attention, *descriptio* had to appear credible,[26] but more importantly for our purposes, it had to enable the audience to literally picture the description.[27] Hence Matthew of Vendôme's advice on how such *descriptio* should strike its audience – 'Listeners should concentrate, not on what is said, but on the manner in which it is said'[28] – points to the author's artistry in depicting artistry, which was the work of the medieval imagination, the making of poetic pictures to 'make the invisible visible.'[29] Each of the *Lancelot*'s landmark images is indeed credible insofar as it describes an object or place or person occurring within the diegesis, not as an excrescence on the storytelling. This means we could take the descriptions at face value and be unaware of their special status, as some medieval readers no doubt did because they were not alert to the ingenuity of the detail.[30] Indeed we could still reach the end of the tale without availing ourselves of the landmark images' special powers of revelation, but our understanding of the tale would suffer from discontinuities, significant blind spots, and it would be superficial, for the essential function of these images is to 'make visible what is invisible.' In short, we would be depriving ourselves of the hidden depths of its story.

The *Lancelot*'s author spread his landmark images along the thematic thread of the hero's identity. Identity is a major theme of twelfth-century Arthurian romance, indeed the hero's identity quest is what traditionally gives verse romance its linear structure. Issues crystallize around his efforts to realize his noble potential through prowess and love, the twin poles of aristocratic identity.[31] In the present of romance narrative, he reshapes his existing chivalric identity through the experience of love. Ideally, love completes identity, perfecting it for a productive, shared adult life. Chrétien's Lancelot, however, is an identity mystery for other characters as well as for readers in the first half of the story, an anonymous knight with no family, no father, no past; the sustained anonymity reflects the secrecy he must have in order to safeguard a hidden truth: his chivalric quest is really a secret love quest. This relationship between

---

25 Douglas Kelly, *The Art of Medieval French Romance* (Madison, WI, 1992), p. 50, with reference to Matthew of Vendôme.

26 Matthew of Vendôme, *Ars versificatoria*, I.73. I use Aubrey Galyon's translation, *The Art of Versification* (Ames, IA, 1980).

27 See, for example, Richard de Fournival's emphasis on the role of description in 'making things present again' (*Li bestiaires d'amour di Maistre Richart de Fornival*, ed. Cesare Segre [Milan, 1957], p. 5).

28 *Ars versificatoria*, I.60, p. 45.

29 See Kelly, *Medieval Imagination: Rhetoric and the Poetry of Courtly Love* (Madison, WI, 1978), pp. 30–1; the same process is used in neoplatonic poetics.

30 I think the *Lancelot* author envisages not one, homogeneous audience in general, but different ones.

31 As Bruckner points out in *Narrative Invention in Twelfth-Century French Romance: The Convention of Hospitality (1160–1200)* (Lexington, KY, 1980), p. 159, with very useful discussion throughout ch. IV. See also Robert Hanning, 'The Social Significance of Twelfth-Century Chivalric Romance', *Medievalia et Humanistica*, 3 (1972), 3–29, and *The Individual in Twelfth-Century French Romance* (New Haven and London, 1977). Also Kelly, *The Art of Medieval French Romance*, pp. 200, 231, 233, 262, 291, 320.

love and prowess creates a nexus of apparent contradictions that all overlap and intersect, but Chrétien left them unresolved. As Matilda Bruckner has so cogently argued, Chrétien's Lancelot is able to dissolve apparent dichotomies because of the special way in which love and prowess are entwined in his heart, making him 'a touchstone who reveals the paradoxical and contradictory norms of his society.'[32]

The author of the *Roman de Lancelot*, as some manuscripts call the *Lancelot*, was clearly intrigued by the ambiguities surrounding Chrétien's paradoxical hero. He goes back to a new beginning and makes his prose hero's identity a mystery as colossal and as complex as the romance itself.[33] From the first few lines of the tale, it is signaled as an object of curiosity for the audience and given powerful genealogical underpinnings that weave a hidden chronological chain behind events. In the *Lancelot*, identity is the tale's primary object of mystery for the hero as well as audience, since his true identity is a secret even he does not know. In the fragmentation of the interlace, form here mirrors not meaning, but the difficulty of finding meaning. The fragmentation whose complexity keeps us wondering, pondering, and guessing, also mirrors the situation of the hero himself as he tries to accumulate and piece together the fragments of his self, his world, and his place in it, to see in its scattered and imperfect fragments a continuity in time. In other words, the interlace mirrors – as through a glass darkly – the process of the hero's discovery of his own identity.

At watershed points that signal new aspects of his identity, the landmark images pull these fragments into focus to throw light on the inner man. What, they ask, can we know about how this hero measures up to knightly ideals in light of our existing knowledge of him? What does he know? What can we know that he does or does not know? What do the signs suggest? Are their sources reliable? Where are they leading to? The questions bring only partial answers, leaving ambiguities, puzzles for the audience, and projecting new questions that demand more reading in order to fulfill the tale's promise of seemingly endless romance.

The landmark images project across the *Lancelot* a simple steel structure, strong enough to counteract the centrifugal tendencies of the work's panoramic stage, yet crafted to articulate finely the work's romance matter and meaning. For the romance audience alert to the attraction and rewards of the landmark images, they figure an inside story that is in itself a book: the transformation of a hero from the Knight of the Cart into the Knight of the Heart, whether he be found in the trilogy or the full *Lancelot-Grail Cycle*.

---

32 *Shaping Romance*, p. 7.
33 Charles Méla notes wryly that 'Ce roman . . . est, en son fond, l'élucidation d'un nom propre' (*La reine et le Graal*, p. 350).

9

Redefining the Center: Verse and Prose Charrette

MATILDA TOMARYN BRUCKNER

A knight paradoxically associated with a shameful cart rescues the Queen, liberates the captives, and becomes Guinevere's lover. In its barest outline, that is the plot of Chrétien de Troyes's *Chevalier de la Charrete*, the romance that catapulted Lancelot into fame and forever changed the course of Arthurian history. What existed before Chrétien remains uncertain, but there is no doubt that his version became the starting point for all subsequent tales of Lancelot as the knight whose extraordinary prowess is inextricably linked to his love for Arthur's Queen. Identity and love, the two great themes of the *Charrete*, set the agenda for the prose *Lancelot*, where they were amplified, redeployed, and ultimately redefined.[1] Across the large canvas of the *Lancelot-Grail Cycle*, the Cart episode remains at the center of Lancelot's story, even as it marks an important shift in Lancelot as hero, still the best of Arthurian chivalry but not 'the good knight' who will achieve the Grail.

The manner in which the prose author exploits Chrétien's model is as idiosyncratic as Lancelot himself for subsequent romance tradition. In Myrrha Lot-Borodine's words, the prose *Lancelot* literally incorporates *Le Chevalier de la Charrete*.[2] Fully digested, Chrétien's text reappears as 'li contes de la Charete.'[3] The reference is a tribute to the fame of Chrétien's romance, but the loss of authorial connection corroborates the extent to which the episode has lost its separate boundaries within the interlaced space of the prose narrative. How does the prose romancer both recapitulate and transform Chrétien's romance? Comparison of their opening passages will give a detailed sense of what the global change in context entails on the levels of style and narrative shape. That analysis will lead in turn to a better understanding of the thematic consequences observable with particular clarity in two sets of episodes, the eponymous cart and the marvelous tomb adventures.

---

1 See Elspeth Kennedy, *Lancelot and the Grail: A Study of the Prose* Lancelot (Oxford, 1986), pp. 10–78.
2 'L'épisode de la *Charrette* dans le *Lancelot* en prose et dans le poème de Chrétien de Troyes,' in Ferdinand Lot, *Etude sur le Lancelot en prose* (Paris, 1954), p. 384. Cf. my discussion of 'centripetal' intertextuality in *The Legacy of Chrétien de Troyes*, ed. Norris J. Lacy, Douglas Kelly, and Keith Busby (Amsterdam, 1987), I, 225–6 and 237–50.
3 *Lancelot: roman en prose du XIIIe siècle*, ed. Alexandre Micha (Geneva, 1978). Volume and page numbers identify the quotations, here at 2:2; the translations of *Lancelot* and the *Charrete* are mine.

Chrétien's romance opens with a prologue, which places author, story, and public in a triangular dialogue:

> Puis que ma dame de Chanpaigne
> vialt que romans a feire anpraigne,
> je l'anprendrai molt volontiers
> come cil qui est suens antiers . . .
> Del Chevalier de la Charrete
> comance Crestïens son livre;
> matiere et san li done et livre
> la contesse, et il s'antremet
> de panser, que gueres n'i met
> fors sa painne et s'antancïon.   (lines 1–4 and 24–9)[4]

[Since my lady of Champagne wants me to undertake the writing of a romance, I will do so most willingly, as one who is completely hers . . . Chrétien begins his book on the *Knight of the Cart*. The countess furnishes him the story matter and the orientation/meaning, and he takes charge of arranging, for he scarcely adds anything but his hard work and concentration.]

These verses clearly demarcate not only a beginning for the story but for the act and occasion of telling it. They establish the tone and character of the narrative, along with an implicit warning: the artistic shaping of the author will filter everything recounted. His narrating voice, a heady mix of provocation, irony, and rhetorical dazzle, frequently introduces more questions than clarifications. Here the puzzle constituted by the mysterious title is compounded by the mysteries attending the author-patron relationship. What *matiere* and *sen* did the countess give him? How should we read Marie's praise in the passage between the verses quoted? The accumulation of conventional hyperboles and superlatives describing her are disavowed, only to be acknowledged as true in spite of himself, as Chrétien effaces his own contribution to highlight his patron's. The ironical game of saying and unsaying is clearly present; less clear are the boundaries and effects of its application. Chrétien's octosyllables give fitting expression to his wit; they set up a lively rhythm across regular spaces, even when the poet plays against the divisions established by rhyme (e.g. lines 26–7 and 27–8) and rhyming couplets (e.g. lines 23–9). His verses are at once readily perceptible wholes, neatly aligned on the manuscript page, and fragments of syntax, whose rhythmic accumulation provides continuity even where his narrative leaves plenty of holes to fuel curiosity.

As soon as we move into the world of the prose romance, the tone and pace of the narrative reveal the extent to which Chrétien's Cart episode has been thoroughly re-conceptualized. The story, like Lancelot, can no longer emerge surprisingly as if from a black hole. Not only is the story itself well-known but many of its threads have been woven extensively through the preceding pages, as they will be similarly extended across those that follow. In some sense, Chrétien's arrangement of the story takes inspiration from the *ordo artificialis*

4   *Les romans de Chrétien de Troyes, III Le Chevalier de la Charrete*, ed. Mario Roques (Paris, 1967).

recommended by rhetorical treatises and classical precedents – his opening starts in the middle and implies a beginning not (yet) related. The prose romancer prefers the *ordo naturalis*, the chronological order of events according to which everything can be prepared and explained. Following the death of Galehot, the story returns to Lancelot, briefly summarizes an episode of madness cured by the Dame du Lac and prepares the transition to the story of the Cart:

> Ne onques de la mort Galehout ne sot riens tant com il fu avec sa dame: kar ele li cela et fist celer a son pooir. Ensi demora avec sa dame jusqu'al quinzime jor devant l'Acension. Et lors ala a la cort le roi Artu. Et sa dame li ot appareillié cheval et armes, si li dist: 'Lancelot, or vient li tens que tu recoverras quanque tu as perdu, se tu vels; et sachies qu'il te covient estre le jor de l'Acension ains none a Camaalot; et se tu a cele ore n'i estoies, tu ameroies miels ta mort que ta vie. – Ha, dame, fet il, or me dites donc por quoi. – Por ce, fet ele, que la roine en sera a force menee; et se tu ies la, tu la secorras, et de la ou nus ne fu onques rescos. – Et je vos jur, fet il, que je i serai ou soit a cheval ou soit a pié.' Si le fet movoir .XV. jors devant l'Acension, si qu'il vint a droite ore de miedi a Camaalot en la place ou Kex li seneschals fu abatus et navrés por la roine qu'il conduisoit, si com li contes de la Charete le devise. (*LM* 2:1–2)

> [As long as he was with his lady he knew nothing of Galehot's death, for she hid it and had it hidden from him as much as possible. He stayed thus with his lady until two weeks before Ascension Day, then he went to King Arthur's court. And his lady, who had prepared horse and arms for him, told him: 'Lancelot, now comes the time when you will regain all you lost, if you wish. Know that you should be at Camaalot before noon on the day of the Ascension. And if you aren't there then, you'd rather be dead than alive,' 'Ah, lady,' says Lancelot, 'tell me why.' 'Because,' she says, 'the queen will be led away by force and, if you're there you'll rescue her from the place where no one has ever been rescued.' 'I swear to you,' says he, 'that I'll be there on horseback or on foot.' And so she sends him off two weeks before Ascension Day, so that he came to Camaalot at precisely noon at the place where Kay the seneschal was unhorsed and wounded for the queen he was escorting, just as the tale of the Cart tells it.]

Anyone who has tried to skim through this passage quickly can appreciate how much the prose romance resists speed reading, as sentences meander back and forth through clauses and repetitions, with no easily recognizable pattern to guide their reception.[5] The narrating voice recedes behind the story, as if it could tell itself without any mediating agent, while the complexities of the prose seek to totalize knowledge through temporal and explanatory continuities that leave no space unfilled.[6] Whereas Chrétien's wit foregrounds his role in delivering the tale and creates a fast-moving narrative we can rapidly take in (and then find ourselves endlessly trying to solve the mysteries left lurking in the interstices), the prose romancer slows down the process of reception, forces us to parse each

---

5   Modern editors give a good deal more help than the manuscripts: Emmanuèle Baumgartner, 'Remarques sur la prose du *Lancelot*,' *Romania*, 105 (1984), 3–5.
6   Daniel Poirion, 'Romans en vers et romans en prose,' in *Grundriss der romanischen Literaturen des Mittelalters*, IV,1, ed. Jean Frappier and Reinhold R. Grimm (Heidelberg, 1978), p. 79.

sentence, move like the characters step by step, as if to promise that, once this initial difficulty is overcome, all will be explained through the sober and painstaking process of accumulation.

In appreciating the thickness of such narrative art, we should not lose sight of the prose romancer's ability to streamline Chrétien's romance. In comparison with the 7,000 plus verses of Chrétien's *Charrete*, the episode of the Cart occupies a fairly short segment of *Lancelot* (109 pages in Micha's nine-volume edition). Matching corresponding passages in the verse and prose romances would illustrate how well-trained in the techniques of medieval composition this anonymous author must have been, as he expands and contracts in inverse proportion to Chrétien's narrator. The passage quoted above shows some of the ways in which the prose author has used both abbreviation and amplification to elaborate Lancelot's story within and beyond the confines of the Cart episode. From the seed of one short passage in the *Charrete* comes the Dame du Lac: a fairy who raised Lancelot and gave him a magic ring, who continues to help him wherever he may find himself (2335–50), provides the barest outline but an excellent job description for the Dame du Lac as she is pictured at length in the prose romance. Her appearance in the transition between Galehot's death and the Cart episode encapsulates her instrumental role not only in rescuing Lancelot but in preparing him to be the knight whose greatness is so directly tied to his capacity to love and be loved. His devoted friend Galehot does not appear in Chrétien, yet news of his death, withheld and then finally revealed, weaves like a leitmotif throughout the Cart episode (*LM* 2:2, 19, 62, 76, 99, 108). Significantly, the Queen herself informs Lancelot during the highly condensed description of their secret night of love in Gorre, when the joy of their reunion prevents the full expression of Lancelot's grief (*LM* 2:76).

That night furnishes one of the most famous scenes in Chrétien's romance, the first consummation of their love precipitated by misunderstandings, suicide attempts, amd much soul-searching. But long before the Cart episode, the prose romancer has used amplification and displacement to follow step by step the lovers' first meeting, their first kiss, and the consummation of their love. Not only has the anonymous author reorganized the distribution of narrative material, he has significantly modified the means of representing Lancelot and Guinevere's love. Gone are their extended monologues, the minute explorations of feeling, disquisitions on appropriate conduct in love, in which Chrétien displays all his rhetorical skills in the style of the troubadours.[7] Where Chrétien's lovers express their emotions in monologue, their counterparts in prose prefer love translated into narrative acts and occasionally dialogue in direct discourse that gives clear and simple expression to the force of their passion. This can be glimpsed in the exchange between Lancelot and the Dame du Lac quoted above, where the lady's words connect Lancelot's love to the difference between life and death, just as his response immediately transforms love into prowess unquestioningly sworn. Completely focused on action to be performed, his statement nevertheless gives direct expression to his love and

---

[7] Cf. Lot-Borodine, 'L'épisode de la *Charrette*,' pp. 405–17.

typifies the prose romancer's achievements in representing not only the depths of Lancelot's passion but his tenderness, perhaps in great measure because the ironic play of Chrétien's narrating voice (with its potential for undercutting and distancing) has been eliminated from the prose transposition. The soberness of the prose style, which in some contexts may seem flat by comparison with Chrétien's dazzling command of poetry, turns out paradoxically to be the perfect instrument for expressing the sweet, unswerving loyalty of Lancelot's devotion.

If the Queen's love for Lancelot has also deepened in the prose representation, it still retains the uneven ebb and flow of her emotions, as suggested in Chrétien when she refuses to thank Lancelot for his extraordinary feats on her behalf. Only much later does she explain her cold reception, motivated by Lancelot's two steps of hesitation before entering the shameful cart in order to continue his pursuit. In the prose version, the Queen's anger has been completely re-motivated and tied to events that precede the Cart episode: Lancelot's departure without her leave and his failure to guard the ring she gave him (*LM* 2:74). While the future of their relationship remains uncertain at the end of the *Charrete*, across the long duration represented in the *Cycle*, Lancelot and Guinevere's love will be played out against the external events of Arthurian history; internally they will be shaped by the shifting moods of the Queen, as her love gives rise to recurrent bouts of anger and jealousy, despite the constancy of Lancelot's passion, periodically tipped into madness.

As one might expect in a romance whose title catches the paradox of this (un)knightly adventure, Lancelot's ride in the cart is a defining moment in Chrétien and remains so in the prose *Lancelot*. The episode is highlighted in *Le Chevalier de la Charrete* not only by the number of verses, but by the length and character of the narrator's interventions calling attention to it. In one of the rare instances of extended commentary (lines 321–44), the narrator explains the custom attached to carts 'in those days' (line 325): a man who rides in the cart reserved for thieves, murderers, and knights vanquished in judicial combats has forever lost all honor and can expect scorn in every court.[8] This information dramatizes the dialogue between the unknown knight and a most discourteous dwarf who promises to give the desired information about the Queen only if the knight climbs aboard his cart. He hesitates as Reason and Love debate, or rather Reason argues but Love, enclosed in his heart, simply commands and he obeys (lines 360–77). Even before reporting the inner monologue as an allegorized psychomachia,[9] the narrator hints that Lancelot will regret his shame and hesitation (lines 362–4). Foreshadowing conceals as much as it reveals and thus begins a chain of events that will reverberate throughout the first part of the romance, as rumor flies and the knight of the cart is vilified by all who meet him. The

---

8   On the problematic character of the description, see David Shirt, 'Chrétien de Troyes and the Cart,' in *Studies in Medieval Language and Literature in Memory of F. Whitehead*, ed. W. Rothwell et al. (Manchester, 1973), pp. 279–301.

9   Charles Muscatine, 'The Emergence of Psychological Allegory in Old French Romance,' *PMLA*, 73 (1957–58), 1160–82. Peter Haidu's *Lion-Queue Coupée: l'écart symbolique chez Chrétien de Troyes* (Geneva, 1972), examines how Chrétien's romances flirt with, but ultimately refuse, allegorical readings.

romance repeatedly sets up a clash of expectations between the unknown's superlative performance and the shameful associations of the cart ride, until the Queen identifies him as 'Lancelot du Lac' during the first combat with Meleagant. Accusations against the cartrider then disappear from the public arena, despite the claim of permanent damage to the knight's reputation, and only reappear for the final, but important twist in the private dimension of Lancelot's relationship with the Queen.

The prose romancer's initial approach to relating the adventure is radical condensation: the whole scene with Lancelot seeing the cart, interrogating the dwarf and climbing aboard is told in a paragraph, with the description of the custom reduced to four lines (*LM* 2:11–12). This is•characteristic of the prose transposition's tendency to minimize where Chrétien maximizes. In a sense, the prose version does not have to give the scene much play precisely because it has already gained instant recognition with the public. Like his crossing of the Swordbridge, Lancelot seated in the cart has become a kind of signature image for this hero and no other.[10] Where Chrétien's narrator develops the psychological dimension of a character who willingly risks dishonor and places love as the highest value, the prose rendition eliminates all hesitation and moves on quickly with the action. Lancelot is no longer an unknown knight; there can be no paradoxical and suspenseful build up to the revelation of his heroic identity, at least not in this part of the romance. The issue of identity will be addressed more pointedly in the tomb episode to be examined shortly.

Having thus briefly summarized Lancelot's cartride, the prose romancer reserves his narrative talents for a replay of the scene introduced into the narrative between the discovery of Lancelot's disappearance and his reappearance at the tournament (*LM* 2:86–95). Through displacement and doubling the prose author demonstrates not only how well he has read and digested Chrétien but how boldly he can reinvent Lancelot's signature image. A dispirited Arthur holds court at Pentecost, when he sees a cart approach. The horse's ears and tail have been clipped; the driver is a short, fat dwarf with full beard and graying hair. Hands and feet tied, the knight who rides in the cart wears a dirty 'chemise' (*LM* 2:87),[11] though shield, hauberk, helmet and horse, all attached to the cart, are dazzlingly white. The detailed description immediately prepares a number of connections with Chrétien and earlier episodes in prose. Over and over again the links are explicitly signaled in the ensuing dialogue, first when Arthur asks what the knight did wrong: ' "Altant, fet il, comme li autre" ' (*LM* 2:87). Arthur fails to understand, as he will repeatedly fail to act appropriately throughout the episode. On the contrary, Gawain, who arrives at court while the cartrider is taunted through the city, remembers Lancelot's adventure and defends the cartrider, for which Arthur declares his seat at the Round Table forfeit.

The unknown knight returns fully armed, challenges anyone who blames

---

10 Bruckner, 'Reinventing Arthurian History: Lancelot and the Vulgate Cycle,' in *Memory and the Middle Ages*, ed. Nancy Netzer and Virginia Reinburg (Boston College Museum of Art, 1995), pp. 57–77.

11 See E. Jane Burns, 'Ladies Don't Wear *Braies*: Underwear and Outerwear in the French *Prose Lancelot*,' in *The Lancelot-Grail Cycle: Text and Transformations*, ed. William W. Kibler (Austin, TX, 1994), pp. 155–8, on the difficulty of translating *chemise*.

Gawain, and takes away the King's best horse while insulting him as 'li plus faillis et li plus recreans qui onques fust' (*LM* 2:89). To a replay of the unknown knight riding in a cart (this time unknown to readers, as well as participants, just as in Chrétien), the prose romance adds a variation on Meleagant's challenge to Arthur in the opening scene. A series of combats follow in which the unknown knight defeats Saigremor, Lucan, Bedoier, Girflet and Keu, adding five more horses to his collection – and simultaneously echoing similar events from other romances by Chrétien, in which Erec and Perceval, unrecognized, defeat Arthurian knights. Criticism of Arthur's kingship, which remains implicit in Chrétien's romances, has already appeared in the prose *Lancelot*. It will be developed further when the cart returns and only Gawain is willing to aid the lady riding in it by taking her place. She identifies the knight who rode in the cart for love of Lancelot as his newly knighted cousin (*LM* 2:93). Her words make explicit the recall of Lancelot's own arrival at Arthur's court, all dressed in white and accompanied by the Dame du Lac, a young unknown who demanded to be knighted the following day. As soon as the Queen learns that this lady is the Dame du Lac, she chases off after the cart and mounts on board, as does the King, and then all his knights in turn. Never again in Arthur's lifetime will the cart function as a sign of shame.[12]

While many of the elements reinvented in this episode thus work toward removing any taint of shame left over by Lancelot's ride in the cart, others work just as effectively to criticize the failures of Arthur and his knights to live up to their ideals. When the second cartrider identifies himself as 'Bohort the exiled' (*LM* 2:93), his epithet encapsulates one of Arthur's most egregious failings, his failure to defend his vassals, the fathers of Lancelot, Lionel and Bohort, the critical opening event upon which the entire structure of *Lancelot* rests. The failure to defend his own was already one of the crucial problems signaled by Chrétien's representation of Arthur as a king unable to defend the Queen from Meleagant. But, as is so often the case, what remains a troubling undercurrent in Chrétien's romance is played out in the open over the long duration of the prose cycle, once Lancelot's story has been joined to the story of the Grail. The episode of the Cart plays a pivotal role in that conjoining, and it is the Dame du Lac herself who announces it to Arthur's court, when she chastises him with the warning that ' "ta cors aproche de delivrer, si prendront fin les aventures" ' (*LM* 2:92) ['your court will soon be delivered and the adventures will come to an end']. This phrase will be taken up later in the opening scenes of the *Queste del saint Graal*, but it already echoes an earlier announcement made to the readers and Lancelot himself in the course of his doubled tomb adventures (*LM* 2:32, 36). In the prose *translatio*, the limits of Lancelot's own future achievements in the Grail quest have been inscribed in the very adventure used by Chrétien to forecast the cartrider's success in liberating the Queen and rescuing the captives held in Gorre.

This episode plays a crucial role in defining Lancelot's identity and marks one of the dramatic high points in both the *Chevalier de la Charrete* and *Lancelot*.

---

[12] And yet paradoxically, as if to underline the shift in values, the cart will reappear as an instrument of shame marking Gawain's failure to recognize the Grail at Corbenic (*LM* 2:385–86).

Contrary to his usual tendency to summarize Chrétien's major scenes, the prose romancer here echoes his model's elaborate treatment (lines 1837–2010; *LM* 2:31–8, 41–2). Perhaps better than any other, this example demonstrates how much the prose author has penetrated and redefined the essence of Lancelot's complex identity as given in the *Charrete*. A key to grasping this profound change appears in the contrast between Chrétien's marvelous cemetery, where Arthurian heroes *will* lie at rest in the future, and the prose romance's two tombs already fully occupied in the 'Saint Cimentiere' (*LM* 2:32). If both cemeteries remain oriented toward the future, the mysteries they reveal and conceal differ significantly, just as the process of discovery itself unfolds according to the specific character of each version.

In Chrétien's *Charrete*, action and information emerge out of Lancelot's own initiative; his point of view largely determines what will or will not be described. When he passes by a church on his way to the Sword Bridge and wants to learn what lies behind the wall next to it, we readers are still almost as much in the dark as the characters about who he is. Though the characters seek an answer to that question in terms of the knight's name, the episode itself will offer only actions – and the evaluations generated by them. Our desire to know is abundantly thematized by the monk at the cemetery, the damsel accompanying him, and the father and son who follow them. Their questions set up a frame within which to highlight the cartrider's marvelous adventure behind the closed walls of the cemetery.

Lancelot observes the tombstones and reads their inscriptions; he notices one tomb whose workmanship places it above all the others. This leads him to ask about the tombs' function: ' "de coi servent? . . . – Et de cele plus grant/ me dites de qu'ele sert" ' (lines 876 and 1881–2). These may seem like strange questions, until we focus on the strangeness of the inscriptions themselves, phrased in the future, naming live Arthurian heroes, thus setting an open challenge. The monk describes the special tomb lavishly, while at the same time expressing doubt that this knight will see the inside, since seven men could hardly lift the stone, yet only the one who can do so will enter the land from which no one has returned and allow the captives to go home. Once the monk 'rereads' the ten-line inscription, Lancelot goes over to the stone and lifts it easily. His extraordinary strength, which both narrator and monk designate as a marvel (lines 1917 and 1968), remains unexplained but corresponds mysteriously to the adventures destiny sets before him. As in the Cart episode, while some explanation precedes the hero's action, once that action is accomplished, we realize how much more is necessary to understand and identify this knight. In Chrétien, information tends to generate further mystery.

Although he refuses to give his name, Lancelot himself asks one more question. ' "An cele tonbe qui girra?" ' (line 1933). It will belong to the liberator of the prisoners, says the monk. Why does Lancelot ask this particular question now? First, it forces by comparison a return to the earlier inscriptions, where the future occupant is clearly designated. This is one of the rare moments in Chrétien's romances when we catch a glimpse of the Arthurian future, foreseen and yet concealed in this marvelous rather than historical space in and out of time. Secondly, Lancelot's question emphatically recalls the distinction in quality and kind between the tombstones and, therefore, between the knights who will be buried under them. Finally, it indicates that Lancelot's name is not found on his tombstone either inside or out. For his name, we have to substitute the superlatives supplied by the characters themselves: ' "il n'a tel chevalier vivant/ tant con vantent les quatre vant" ' (lines 1953–4), says the damsel to the monk, choosing a phrase that recalls the author's praise of Marie de Champagne (lines 10–13). Hyperboles for Lancelot run no risk of sounding like empty praise; they are solidly based on extraordinary actions performed before our very eyes or guaranteed to follow shortly.

If this knight is to be identified primarily in terms of what he can do, and if (as the Cart episode demonstrates) what he can do is motivated primarily by love, then we may well ask what more can a name add to his identity? Of course, the very desire for that absent name, which reverberates so insistently in the entire first half of the romance, implies that the name itself supplies an indispensable key to the knight's identity. Not surprisingly, the prose *Lancelot* has responded to that dramatic cue by connecting the revelation of Lancelot's name, in fact Lancelot's two names, to not one but two tomb episodes. Lancelot discovered his name for the first time during his first great exploits as a new knight, when he raised the tombstone in the cemetery at the Dolerouse Garde. Lancelot himself recalls his adventure there as soon as he sees the tombs at the Saint Cimentiere (*LM* 2:33). The prose author has transposed to that earlier episode and the preceding description of his childhood much of the mystery surrounding Lancelot's incognito. Where Chrétien was content to let enigmas proliferate, the prose author guarantees the worth of Lancelot's identity not only in terms of his accomplishments but through the lines of inheritance, the maternal and paternal lineages of a king's son.

That leaves open the tomb adventure in the Cart episode for a different kind of discovery regarding Lancelot's identity. Doubling the tombs located at the church allows the prose author to demonstrate not only the magnitude of Lancelot's success, as modeled by Chrétien, but the limits of the hero's greatness, as shown by his failure to achieve the second adventure. Lancelot's extraordinary prowess motivated by love for the Queen explains both success and failure in the 'double spirit' of the *Cycle*.[13] Two sets of explanations seek to clarify and prepare this turning point in Lancelot's career. As soon as Lancelot arrives at the church (*LM* 2:31–2), before he is invited the next morning to try 'li premiers assaus' (*LM* 2:33) awaiting the Queen's rescuer, the narrator announces that the first tomb belongs to Galahad, the first Christian king of the country named 'Gales' in his honor. As the voice of Symeu, the occupant of the second tomb explains, Lancelot's baptismal name was Galahad (the connection goes through his maternal lineage), but his father preferred to call him Lancelot in honor of his paternal grandfather (*LM* 2:36). This information takes us back to the *Lancelot*'s opening paragraph, where the narrator enigmatically revealed the name switch, promising an explanation in due time (*LM* 7:1). We have now arrived at the long anticipated moment.

[13] Lot-Borodine, 'L'épisode de la *Charrette*,' pp. 443–56.

Although the prose romancer has retained the lifting of the tombstone as the sign of Lancelot's successful rescue of the Queen, he has otherwise radically redesigned how and what these tombs signify. Lancelot's own sense of shame and his place in a lineage extending before and after him are the two most significant threads added to Lancelot's identity by the doubled adventure. Once Galahad's body has been taken away, noise and smoke issuing from the cave where Symeu's tomb is located catch Lancelot's attention. This time he asks about what lies hidden, as in Chrétien, and insists on trying the adventure even though told he cannot be the one to achieve it (*LM* 2:35–6 and 37). He inadvertently initiates a dialogue with the voice in the tomb by exclaiming, ' "Ha, Diex, com grant damage!" ' (*LM* 2:35). Asked to explain why, Lancelot reveals his shameful drawing back with fear, temporarily overwhelmed by the hideous noise from the tomb. The shame mistakenly attached to and then removed from the cartrider has been redefined here by Lancelot's own internalization of it. Yet Symeu corrects Lancelot's exclamation: he is the best now, the best among 'home corrumpu' (*LM* 2:36–7). The man who will pull him out of the flames has not yet been born but will be born from Lancelot's line.

The mystery surrounding Lancelot's name and identity, magnified in Chrétien's tomb adventure, reappears in the prose version but concerns the future Galahad, Lancelot's son whose character and accomplishments are here established in the readers' expectation, his name and father only indirectly announced for those who can read back from the future *Queste*. This is still a cemetery connected to the future but not the future imagined in Chrétien's *Charrete*. Lancelot's identity within a lineage and history that go back to the New Testament and forward to the Grail quest and the end of Arthurian knighthood is already firmly in place in this pivotal episode. While Lancelot's good qualities are specifically connected to his mother, according to Symeu, his failure because of sin is just as specifically connected to his father. Lancelot would have achieved the feat that now only his *parens* 'relative' will, if it had not been for his father's one infidelity.[14] The term *luxure*, which the *Queste* will later use to characterize Lancelot's love for Guinevere, cannot appear in the episode of the Cart, where Lancelot's greatness is still tied precisely to the greatness of his love for the Queen. But its place in Lancelot's double identity has already been carved out by opposition to the 'vertuoses teches' (*LM* 2:37) of the good knight whose own sinlessness has the power to end Symeu's purgatorial suffering, liberate him from this world and spare him the next one's torment (*LM* 2:36). In that future of the prose cycle, the messianic overtones inscribed in Chrétien's *Charrete* will be shifted to a new mode: the Christlike elements of Lancelot liberating the prisoners will be transmuted into Galahad as a figure for Christ in the *Queste*.

What happens in that process to the overall picture of Lancelot du Lac? The Lancelot who emerges from the paradoxical adventures of cart and tombstone is himself a hero caught in the structure of paradox. Chrétien takes advantage of

---

[14] The general term 'relative' (*LM* 2:37) masks the father-son connection. The father's sin as an exculpating factor appears in the α family of manuscripts not in the β group: Gweneth Hutchings, *Le roman en prose de Lancelot du Lac: le Conte de la Charrette* (Paris, 1938), pp. xlix, 49–50.

the power of fiction to hold together the contradictions as a potential, a meditation on the unresolvable. As the best of Arthur's knights precisely because he is the Queen's lover, Lancelot alone reconciles contradictory demands, reveals the lines of tension operating within the search for an ideal.[15] In a romance that foregrounds the best of Lancelot, without completely hiding the conflicts embedded in his complex character, as in the society he heroically serves, Chrétien offers a view of the human condition that leaves room for aspiration toward the ideal, even as it limns what makes it impossible to realize within the contradictions of human existence. This is a kind of magical realism *avant la lettre* where fiction and the marvelous allow both distance from and confrontation with the co-text of history, where there is a space for experimentation and rethinking, which may ultimately reshape reality.

In the prose romance, Lancelot remains a heroic figure based on a complex view of human nature. But what is held in tension in Chrétien is played out as an opposition that cannot be suspended forever over the long duration of the cycle. Lancelot's two names become two separate figures, their twin identities polarized by a son who escapes the human mix of vice and virtue. The tomb adventure doubled in the episode of the Cart still affirms Lancelot's greatness within the realm of fallen men. But his marvelous potential within the uncharted spaces of Chrétien's romance has been circumscribed and redefined over the course of Arthurian history. His success and failure are openly placed back to back in the 'contes de la Charete.' If much more will be disclosed once Galahad arrives on the scene to put an end to the adventures of Arthur's 'Adventurous Kingdom' (*LM* 2:32), the seeds have already been carefully planted in the heart of Lancelot's doubled identity.

Within *Lancelot*'s tripartite structure, the Cart episode clearly plays a pivotal role.[16] While it no longer furnishes one of the most intense moments in Lancelot and Guinevere's unfolding love story, it remains crucial to the evolution of his identity as hero. If the prose author invites readers familiar with Chrétien's romance to admire a reading that powerfully fills in the spaces of his model in order to elucidate and surpass it, the vast panoply of the prose cycle eventually catches up the episode of the Cart within its own system of intratextual reference. It becomes one of many stories named in the course of the narrative and told within its branches, like 'the story of the Queen of Great Sorrow' (*LM* 7:29) or 'the great story of the Grail' (*LM* 2:32). While those of us who read Chrétien can continue to enjoy the play of point and counterpoint, within the *Cycle* the prose *Lancelot*'s integration and total absorption of *Le Chevalier de la Charrete* is complete and stands on its own merits as 'li contes de la Charete,' a compelling turning point in the elaboration of Lancelot's double identity as the greatest knight of the Round Table – except for his son Galahad.

---

15 See my argument for reading the romance as 'case' in *Shaping Romance: Interpretation, Truth, and Closure in Twelfth-Century French Fictions* (Philadelphia, 1995), pp. 101–8.
16 The manuscript titles identify the three parts as *Galehaut*, the *Charrette*, and *Agravain* (Lot, *Etude*, p. 13).

10

The Queste del saint Graal: *from* semblance *to* veraie semblance

EMMANUÈLE BAUMGARTNER

[Translated by Carol Dover]

The *Queste del saint Graal*, composed c. 1225–1230, survives in a large number of manuscripts – currently forty-three complete manuscripts – which contain either the entire *Lancelot-Grail Cycle* or the *Lancelot–Queste–Mort Artu* trilogy. In the epilogue, the name 'Mestre Gautier Map' purports to be the one who, 'pour l'amour du roi Henri son seigneur,' transposed from Latin into French this *estoire* that has been kept since the days of Arthur in the *armoire* [library] at Salesbieres [Salisbury]. The attribution of the narrative to Gautier Map, a cleric who lived at the court of Henry II and composed works in Latin, is of course a literary hoax. The hoax testifies nevertheless to the anonymous author's desire to inscribe the genesis and the trajectory of this disconcerting text in a space-time that goes from the fictional world of Arthur to the Norman kingdom of England at the end of the twelfth century, the time and the place in which the Arthurian legend did in fact come into its own, no doubt promoted by the Plantagenets.[1]

One more fact seems certain. Even though the origin of the *Lancelot-Grail* still eludes us, the *Queste*, a narrative whose real title is given in the epilogue as *Les Aventures del seint Graal* (280),[2] presents itself as the expected and programmed continuation of the *Lancelot* and, given the reduction of the normal resources of the narrative it entails, it announces *La Mort le roi Artu* as the text that will conclude the *Cycle*. There may have been, as Elspeth Kennedy believes, a non-cyclic *Lancelot* that focused on the heroic and amorous adventures of the titular hero and located the quest for the Holy Grail and its hero, Perceval, in a time long past.[3] The *Lancelot* has nonetheless come down to us as a narrative whose hero was given the 'droit nom' of Galaad, which his son will eventually bear; a narrative in which the quest for the holy Grail is defined as the quest for

---

1 For an in-depth study see Pauphilet, *Etudes sur la Queste del saint Graal attribuée à Gautier Map* (Paris, 1921); Pauline Matarasso, *The Redemption of Chivalry: A Study of the Queste del saint Graal* (Geneva, 1979); Emmanuèle Baumgartner, *L'Arbre et le pain* (Paris, 1981).
2 I use the edition by Albert Pauphilet, *La Queste del saint Graal, roman du XIIIe siècle* (Paris, 1921). References to this work appear in the text. On the narrative's real title, see *L'Arbre et le pain*, pp. 49–52.
3 Kennedy, *Lancelot and the Grail: A Study of the Prose Lancelot* (Oxford, 1986).

the *grans repostailles*,[4] the secrets of Our Lord, and is projected into the future; a narrative which announces several times that the quest will be completed by Galahad because Lancelot's sin of adultery will disqualify him from being the Elect. In the *Agravain*, the last part of the *Lancelot*, knights such as Gawain, Lancelot, and particularly Bohort, have already found their way to Corbenic, the Fisher King's Palace, and have already glimpsed some of the strange marvels of the Grail.[5] We should therefore read the *Queste* and evaluate what is at stake in it not as an autonomous narrative, but in relation to the *Lancelot* and more widely to the entire Arthurian tradition written down at that time, regardless of the fact that this relatively short narrative, through its mode of writing and the anti-courtly morality that it reactivates, conflicts with the text and with the tradition it intends to complete and 'finish off.' The *Queste* explicitly sets itself up as the end of the adventures that, in the *Lancelot*, formed the basis of Arthurian chivalry's existence and justified its mission in the world. This is achieved by displacing meaning and exhausting the resources of the narrative. Though unable to fulfill the Holy Scriptures as Christ did in the medieval reading of the New Testament as a fulfillment of the Old, Lancelot's son Galahad, the virgin hero (who will have no issue) wastes no time in 'accomplishing' the earlier 'scriptures,' the adventures, predictions, prophecies left suspended in the *Lancelot*. This explains the numerous episodes in which Galahad cuts off narrative threads going back to the reign of Arthur, to the heroic days of Joseph of Arimathia and the first Christian kings of Great Britain, and in some cases as far back as what the author sees as the dawn of time. Throughout his text the author uses the technique of retrospective narration to go back to the origins (more or less) of Christian time, recalling the fall of Adam and Eve, the (revised and corrected) legend of the Tree of Life and the building of the ship of Solomon, a narrative that joins across the centuries the time of Christian myth and Arthurian time (210–26).

Elsewhere in the text the time-span filled in is slightly shorter. Examples include the episode in which Galahad finds in an abbey the white shield with the red cross (the blood is still fresh on the shield) that was destined for him by Josephé (Joseph of Arimathia's son in the *Queste*); the episode in which he completes the circle of the Round Table by sitting first in the *Siege perilleux*, reserved by Merlin for the Elect and founded in 'semblance' and 'remembrance' of Christ's seat at the Table of the Last Supper, and then in the *Sieges redoutez* occupied by Joseph of Arimathia at the Table of the Holy Grail; the episode in which he cools the water of a 'fountain' that had been boiling since the murder of Lancelot's ancestor (also a Lancelot), and when he delivers Symeu from the tourment that Lancelot had been unable to end (26–35, 75–7, 263–5). As for the achievement of the ultimate adventure, the vision finally granted to Galahad of God's secrets concealed in a Holy Grail gradually 'uncovered,'[6] it is the moment

---

[4] See, for example, Alexandre Micha, ed., *Lancelot: roman en prose du XIIIe siècle*, 9 vols. (Geneva and Paris, 1978–83), 7:25.

[5] See *L'Arbre et le pain*, pp. 51–2, Jean-René Valette, *La Poétique du merveilleux dans le Lancelot en prose* (Paris, 1998), pp. 339–47, and Mireille Séguy, *Les Romans du Graal, ou le signe imaginé* (Paris, 2001).

[6] The dish Perceval sees in *Le Conte du Graal* is 'trestot descovert' [uncovered completely]

that brings narrative, temporal, and spatial closure all in one. The narrative ends with Galahad's death as he 'crosses beyond' at the very instant of vision, taking with him the secret of the revelation. The Holy Grail and the Lance return to the East whence they came, before a mysterious hand transports them into the beyond. Perceval dies too and Bohort, who occupies third place in the trinity of the Elect, no doubt returns to Arthur's court for the express purpose of ensuring that the adventures he has witnessed are recorded accurately in his own words.

This representation of the fulfillment of time is circular, while the quest motif – a motif that has already proved its worth in the Arthurian text – adds the straight line needed for the successful unfolding of the diegesis. In principle, the text should use the *Lancelot*'s interlace technique and follow the adventures of the fifty knights who have left court with Gawain. But the selection is very quick, made as a function not of the questers' prowess but of their moral and spiritual value, which will govern henceforth their right to 'find' adventures and thereby to make narrative. So the interlace gradually gives way to linear narrative. The quantity, duration, and nature of the adventures, or even, in the case of Lancelot and Perceval, the length of their *compagnonnage* [comradeship] with Galahad, are in direct proportion to the spiritual merit of the selected questers. As for the hardened sinners, they are ejected from the narrative space, either killed or dismissed without ceremony, so that the actual development of the text illustrates the word of the Gospels (Matt. 22.14): 'for many are called, but few are chosen.'

The new adventures, which in the hermits' official terminology are nothing less than *demostrances* (the manifestations of the Holy Grail destined for the Arthurian knights [160, lines 33ff]), do not fit neatly into the customary scenarios or, when they do, give them new direction. For example, in the dark forests, in the enigmatic universe traveled by knights who must rid themselves of their old habits, a tournament is not a 'real' tournament but a struggle between 'earthly' knights (in black) and 'celestial' knights (in white) (140–5), as Lancelot learns to his detriment. Delivering maidens detained by force at the *Chastel des Puceles* has little to do with Yvain's apparently similar exploit at the Castle of Pesme Aventure in the *Chevalier au Lion*. In fact the deliverer – only Galahad can succeed in the adventure – must free the 'bones ames qui a tort i estoient enserrees devant la Pasion Jhesucrist' (55) [good souls wrongfully held before the Passion of Jesus Christ], and the knights who bar the castle are in fact incarnations of the seven deadly sins. More often than not, however, the diverse list of adventures consists of temptations of the flesh, apparitions, dreams and visions, random boat trips, etc.

In contrast, the appearances of the Holy Grail and the para-liturgical scenes that reveal with increasing clarity the great mysteries of the faith located in the Holy Vessel, are reserved specifically for Lancelot and the three Elect knights. At Corbenic, for example, Lancelot attends a mass served by angels at which the Holy Grail is used for the consecration of the Host [bread and wine] and the 'demonstration' of the mystery of the Holy Trinity (255). The Elect, on the other

whereas the *Queste*'s Grail is 'covers d'un samit blanc' (p. 15, line 20) [covered with a white silk cloth] when it appears for the first time at Arthur's court.

hand, attend (again at Corbenic) a liturgy that offers in the union of the blood from the Holy Lance and the wafer present in the Grail, the mysteries of the Eucharist and the Incarnation as well as the bleeding body of the Crucified Christ: the celebration of the mass unfolds in concrete terms the entire Christian economy of salvation, from the Incarnation of the God to his bloody sacrifice (269–70). Finally, the ultimate vision, at Sarras in the context of 'la messe de la glorieuse Mere Dieu' [the Mass of the glorious Mother of God], exalts the ulti-mate desire of the Elect Knight who says that he sees ' "l'acomençaille des granz hardemenz et l'achoison des proeces . . . les merveilles de totes autres merveilles" ' (277) ["the source of great deeds and the cause of all prowess . . ., the marvels that surpass all marvels"], and can do no more than ask God to transport him instantly from the earthly world at the very moment of his vision (278).

A constant of these *demostrances* is their initial incomprehensibility to the knight-heroes, who cannot decipher them at once (though the meaning is trans-parently clear to a minimally experienced reader), but question with laudable persistence those who will bring out the *senefiance* for them. Whatever its general drift of meaning might be, the adventure calls for elucidation, a gloss given to the responsive knight (Gawain is the sole exception) by a man of God, frequently a hermit, who provides one and often several levels of explanation, thereby inscribing in the text an interpretive commentary whose authority must prevail. This creates the strange impression of a blurring of genres in the *Queste*,[7] a 'romance' that draws the essentials of its narrative material from earlier Arthurian texts even as it systematically weighs down this fictional material, which provides the 'literal' sense of the text, with a 'figurative' meaning. At this period, writing based on the concordance of literal and figurative senses is rare in fiction. It does occur, albeit discreetly, in the prose *Merlin* and more frequently in the *Lancelot*, where its purpose is limited to passages of moral or didactic intent. As, for example, in the Lady of the Lake's speech to Lancelot on the mission of the knight and the 'symbolic' value of his arms and mount.

The *Queste* author's innovation, or audacity, is to systematize this procedure and impose figurative meaning on any and every motif from the Arthurian pre-text, while allowing himself to borrow from other kinds of texts when neces-sary. He draws on the *Bestiaries*, for example, but even more surprising is his use of key passages from the Scriptures, which he uses as pre-texts. When the Holy Grail appears to Arthur's court on Whitsunday, the circumstances of its arrival replay (as Etienne Gilson showed long ago) the narrative of the coming of the Holy Spirit as told in Acts 2.1–3.[8] A more secular example is the arrival of Galahad at Arthur's court and his success in specific tests (he sits in the Perilous Seat and fulfills the adventure of the Sword in the Stone); these episodes weave a tight network of correspondences with the prose *Merlin* episode in which Arthur's identity as king is revealed by the test of the Sword in the Stone, and

7 See Nancy Freeman-Regalado, 'La chevalerie celestiel: Spiritual Transformations of Secular Romance in *La Queste del Saint Graal*,' in *Romance: Generic Transformations from Chrétien de Troyes to Cervantes*, ed. Kevin Brownlee and Marina Scordilis Brownlee (Hanover, NH, and London, 1985), pp. 91–113.
8 See his article, 'La mystique de la grâce dans la *Queste del Saint Graal*,' *Romania*, 51 (1925), 321–47.

especially with the *Lancelot* episode of the arrival and knighting of Lancelot at Arthur's court. But whereas in the *Lancelot* the knighting of Guinevere's lover is placed under the dual sign of faerie and love for the Queen, and takes place on Saint John the Baptist's day, the feast day of Christ's prophetic precursor, the knighting of Galahad (by Lancelot nonetheless) takes place in an abbey of nuns and the date selected for his arrival at court – Pentecost – singles him out as a new *semblance* of the Messiah foretold by Saint John, and puts Lancelot retrospectively in the role of the prophet.[9]

The *demostrances* (the adventures of the Holy Grail) are very varied in terms of 'sources' and content, but we can also differentiate them from one another according to the type of gloss they support. The majority of them occur in the forest – the realm of matter and *errance* – and tend to elicit first-level elucidation, according to the 'moral sense,' which denounces, through the brief adventures of Melyant, Gawain's occasional adventures, and Lancelot's much longer series of trials, the worst vices of chivalry: pride, vainglory, covetousness, and above all lust, the supreme sin in the world of the *Queste*. Severely reprimanded for his guilty love for the Queen, Lancelot gradually realizes through confession that his love, which at the beginning of the narrative he still sees as the sole source of his prowess, is in fact the cause of his repeated failures, and he finally repents and renounces the Queen. Despite his firm resolution to sin no more, at Corbenic he cannot approach the Holy Grail and lies paralyzed for twenty-four days, which correspond to his twenty-four years of living in sin (254–5).

The failure that Lancelot accepts with humility, signifies of course the condemnation of the very values upon which Arthur's world was founded; it constitutes a failure of heroic action based solely on the inspiration of carnal desire. All the same, the *Queste* author could not or would not push his condemnation to its logical conclusion. Evalach-Mordrain's dream that reveals Lancelot's origin when elucidated for him by a hermit, leaves no doubt that Galahad the winged lion surpasses Lancelot and the line of kings from which father and son are born. But it is to this same origin that the Elect Grail Knight owes his superiority: only the best knight in the earthly (*terrien*) world (a world incarnated, in the literal sense of the word, by the Arthurian world), could engender the best knight in the *celestiel* world. Just as the prose *Lancelot* and its hero 'engender' the *Queste* and its Elect, so the conjugated resources of human love and chivalric prowess can alone 'engender' a sublime form of prowess consecrated entirely to the service and love of God.

The text's relentlessness in denouncing chivalric conduct and human passions, the hermits' insistence on preaching chastity, penance, the ascetic life, and glorifying virginity to the Arthurian knights, probably express the anonymous author's desire to compose what others have called a new Gospel for chivalry, a Gospel that would give chivalry the means of achieving its own salvation by moralizing its way of life, by transferring warrior combat to the spiritual sphere, in the endless struggle against evil in its many forms. As early as the first half of the twelfth century Saint Bernard, in his treatise *In Praise of the New Knighthood*, had been a force for the creation and propagation of the image of the

---

[9] See *LM* 7:260–8.

miles Christi, the soldier in the service of God, by which he meant the Templars, the monk-knights who played such an important role during the Crusades in the twelfth and thirteenth centuries. The *Queste* translates his expression literally when it exhorts the knight to become the *serjant Jesu Crist*, to achieve his salvation while fulfilling his mission in the world. We can certainly imagine that in the early thirteenth century the crusading spirit was still powerful enough to inspire such a resurgence of Saint Bernard's preaching and convictions. In fact Pauphilet drew a 'picture of Christian life' from the *Queste*, to show just how important the author's borrowings from the ideas, customs, and writings of the Cistercian Order were for giving the reader 'une représentation de la vie chrétienne telle qu'on la voyait à Cîteaux' [a portrait of Christian life at Cîteaux] and an 'apologie de Cîteaux' [a defense of Cîteaux] in the text.[10] This may be so, but it is not in a Cistercian house that the *Queste*'s author, whoever he might be, read so assiduously the works of Chrétien and especially the newly completed *Lancelot*, as his borrowings from them prove. Furthermore, is it likely that the *Queste* was a commissioned work inspired by the Cistercian Order? There is no reason to think that the Church ever saw the 'holy' Grail as a genuine relic of the Passion or that it ever encouraged the daring symbolic apparatus that was supported by this relic tied so specifically to the chivalric class, an apparatus that tends to reserve the revelation of the divine mysteries for this 'order,' in the absence of clergy.[11]

The almost sacrilegious ambition of the *Queste*'s author does not stop at giving a somewhat conventional moral content to the 'adventures of the Holy Grail' or guiding the knights in their fight against the forces of evil. His ambition goes further to make this relic, invented in the likeness of the holy Bowl used by Joseph of Arimathia to catch Christ's blood, the center of a text that openly declares its literary intent: writing in the *semblance* of the sacred text that would support reading according to the four levels of meaning, through which medieval theology read the Old and New Testaments. A mode of writing, moreover, that Dante himself will use overtly almost a century later when he lays out in his Letter to Can Grande the plan underpinning the *Divine Comedy*.

A whole string of *demostrances* are designed to weave, on the model of the 'concordances' established by Christian exegesis between the Old Testament and the New, a tissue of interrelationships between the Arthurian material (conceived as an 'old testament' and a support for the allegoresis) and the new text. Thus Perceval's vision, which takes the struggle between the lion and the serpent from the *Chevalier au Lion* and transforms it into a *demostrance* of the combat between the Old Law (the Synagogue) and the New Law (the Church). Hence the numerous investiture tests (the Perilous Seat, the Sword in the Stone, Josephé's sword, etc.) that identify Galahad as the *Chevalier desirré* and make him the new (and final?) Messiah long awaited by the Arthurian world. But the most important adventures, essentially reserved (as we have seen) for Galahad, Perceval (and his sister), and Bohort, are interpreted at the highest level of

[10] *Etudes sur la Queste*, pp. 53–84.

[11] On the Grail's attachment to the chivalric class see Jean Frappier, 'Le Graal et la chevalerie,' in *Autour du Graal* (Geneva, 1977), pp. 89–128.

exegesis – the 'mystical meaning' – and they gradually initiate the Elect into the divine secrets.

In *Le Conte du Graal*, the founding text for the motif of the grail and its quest, the hero's mission was to ask the Fisher King who the recipient of the grail was and why the lance bleeds. At the time the *Queste* author was writing, the motif of the questions made no sense because the answers had lost their mystery. The prose author's masterstroke (but we should also examine the new approach to the motif used at the same point in time by the author of the *Perlesvaus*) was to enlarge the motif of the questions to be asked, so as to give it the dimensions of a myth, the myth of knowledge itself. For Galahad it is no longer a question of possessing the grail and lance and becoming king of the castle where they are jealously guarded by the lineage of the Fisher Kings, rather it is a matter of seeing what their 'earthly' form still conceals from sight. To quest for the Holy Grail – a grail moreover that constantly 'ventures forth' and shows itself in the Arthurian domain – means henceforth to see clearly the mysteries that dwell therein. What the various liturgies emanating from the Grail offer with increasing clarity to the eyes of the Elect knights are of course the mysteries that found the Christian faith and they give the text its indisputably religious coloring. But in these early years of the thirteenth century is there any other way for a medieval cleric to examine knowledge, the mystery of beginnings and ultimate ends, any other way to gain access to the *senefiance* of the world than by framing his questions within the grid offered by the dogma of the Incarnation, the dogma of the Trinity, the mystery of the Eucharist, the sacrifice of the Passion, the signifying chain woven from God's *aombrement* [Incarnation] in the bosom of matter itself to His bloody death and triumphal Resurrection?

This perspective helps us better understand the episode of the Ship of Solomon, which functions in many ways as a *mise en abyme* of the narrative and consecrates Galahad as the master of an age, of a universe finally possessed, if only in dreams, in its perfect circularity. The story of the branch taken by Eve from the Tree of Life, of the fruitfulness in time of this branch, initially one, in the triple form of the white, green, and red trees, is an image of the diachronic unfolding of Christian time, the time of the Father, then that of the Son finding fulfillment in the time of Galahad (time of the Holy Spirit?), the last Messiah. Galahad sleeping the sleep of the initiate in the Ship, beneath the cross formed by the three *fuseaux* [spindles], white, green, red, signifies moreover that these three times are joined and fused in him, just as the three persons of the Trinity are joined as one. And with the return to Sarras, the end of the text enunciates the moment when the *semblance* possessed in a dream is finally succeeded by the *veraie semblance*, the unclouded vision, the instant when the gaze plunging into the crucible of the Grail permits and dies at the sight of the ultimate secret: namely, how the Tree of Knowledge and the Tree of Life, equally forbidden but finally stripped for the Chosen One of their dark bark, are truly one.

We might believe that this narrative, which tries so hard to exhaust the source of the Arthurian adventures by 'completing' them or fixing a single meaning for them in God, was written out of hatred for romance, to stigmatize the vacuousness, the derisory, pernicious character of the 'fables' that the Round Table had been spreading since the twelfth century. We might also see at work in the prose story the (diabolical) ambition of a writer bent on demonstrating the princely dignity of profane writing, of the Arthurian fable, of its ability to represent the conditions, the stages, and the endpoint of the quest for knowledge, to ask questions about the *senefiance* of the world. An ambition that will be taken up again even more clearly at the end of the thirteenth century by the 'Romance' of Jean de Meun, when he substitutes for the mystical unveiling of the Grail the amorous plucking of the Rose in the garden of knowledge.

[Translator's note: I would like to thank Matilda Tomaryn Bruckner for her useful suggestions which I have incorporated into the translation.]

11

The Sense of an Ending: La Mort le Roi Artu

NORRIS J. LACY

The reader approaching the end of the *Queste del saint Graal* learns that only Bors, Perceval, and Galahad are able, though to differing degrees, to achieve visions of the Holy Grail. We read of the death of Galahad, after which the Grail is taken up into heaven. Soon Perceval dies as well, leaving only Bors to tell the full story of the quest. He returns to Camelot, where the adventures he recounts are recorded in writing. And with that, we are told, 'si se test a tant li contes, que plus n'en dist des Aventures del Seint Graal' [the story falls silent and has nothing more to say about the adventures of the Holy Grail].[1] No conclusion could be more decisive.

But that is the conclusion to the *Queste*, not to the *Lancelot-Grail Cycle*. An entire, if comparatively brief, romance remains. The *Mort le Roi Artu*, rather than the *Queste*, is the *Cycle*'s ultimate conclusion, but its author's task is complicated by the apparent finality of the Grail quest.[2] The *Mort Artu* is in effect a second conclusion and thus, almost by definition, an anti-climax, recounting events that follow the tribulations, triumphs, and tragedies of the Grail quest. It is in fact, as Pauphilet suggests, the *Cycle*'s epilogue.[3]

The fundamental promise of the *Cycle*, a promise made repeatedly in its early romances, has been kept: the Grail knight has come and has accomplished his quest. But the Arthurian court survives the quest, if only as a pale reflection of its formerly glorious presence. Many of the best knights are dead. Two of the greatest – Lancelot and Gawain – have survived, but their mutual antagonism will be one of the pivots on which the remaining story will turn and one of the principal keys to the terrible catastrophe that is to befall Arthur and his realm.

The text of this romance and, indeed, that of the preceding one offer abundant portents of that catastrophe. At the beginning of the *Queste*, Gawain and

---

1   Albert Pauphilet, ed., *La Queste del saint Graal, roman du XIIIe siècle* (Paris, 1921), p. 280. Accompanying translations of both the *Queste* and the *Mort Artu* are taken from vol. IV of Norris J. Lacy, ed., *Lancelot-Grail: The Old French Arthurian Vulgate and Post-Vulgate in Translation*, 5 vols. (New York, 1993–96).

2   Portions of the present essay overlap my earlier discussion of the *Mort Artu* in 'The *Mort Artu* and Cyclic Closure,' in *The Lancelot-Grail Cycle: Text and Transformations*, ed. William W. Kibler (Austin, 1994), pp. 85–97. Matters treated in both essays include the 'end of adventures' and the Wheel of Fortune. For another discussion of the way the author draws the *Lancelot-Grail Cycle* to an end, see E. Jane Burns's essential *Arthurian Fictions: Rereading the Vulgate Cycle* (Columbus, OH, 1985), pp. 151–67.

3   *Queste*, p. iii.

then all the other knights vow that they will set out in search of the Grail and will continue the quest 'un an et un jor et encor plus se mestiers est' (16) [a year and a day and even longer if need be]. Whereas Arthur might be expected to praise either the intrinsic nobility of the quest or, at least, his knights' resolve, his reaction is neither joy at the prospect nor increased admiration of his knights. Instead of celebrating the quest as an initiative to unite the Round Table in a concerted search for perfection, Arthur is 'molt a malese: car bien set qu'il nes porra pas retorner de ceste emprise' (*Queste* 16) [very distressed, knowing he could not dissuade them from this undertaking], and he blames Gawain above the others:

> 'vos m'avez mort par le veu que vos avez fet, car vos m'avez ci tolue la plus bele compaignie et la plus loial que je onques trovasse, et ce est la compaignie de la Table Reonde. Car quant il departiront de moi, de quele ore que ce soit, je sai bien qu'il ne revendront ja mes tuit arriere, ainz demorront li plusor en ceste Queste, qui ne faudra pas si tost com vos cuidiez. Si ne m'en poise pas petit.' (*Queste* 17)

> ['Your vow will be the end of me, for it will deprive me of the best and most loyal retinue I ever have known: the knights of the Round Table. Once they depart, whenever that might be, I know they won't all return. Most will remain on the Quest, which will last longer than you think. This is no small concern for me.']

The king begins to weep, saying to Gawain, ' "trop ai grant doute que mi ami charnel n'en reviegnent ja" ' (*Queste* 17) ['I fear greatly that my dear friends will never return']; then he repeats, this time to Lancelot, his concern that once the knights of the Round Table leave, they will never again be assembled at his table.

Thus, the very genesis of the Grail quest also prefigures, indeed overtly announces, the destruction of the Round Table and the ultimate ruin of the Arthurian fellowship. Readers of the *Lancelot*, noting the praise of chivalry in that romance, might expect the Grail quest to be the highest expression of chivalric endeavor. If by that we mean chivalry as espoused and practiced at Camelot, the truth is exactly opposite: the Holy Grail and the Round Table incarnate radically incompatible ideals.

The narrator of the *Mort Artu* wastes neither time nor words in deepening the sense of foreboding generated by Arthur's reaction to the initiation of the quest. This final romance begins by announcing the ominous title of the work we are about to read – *La Mort le Roi Artu*, the death of King Arthur – and explains what it will recount: 'conment li rois Artus fu navrez en la bataille de Salebieres et conment il se parti de Girflet qui si longuement li fist compaignie que aprés lui ne fu nus hom qui le veïst vivant' (*Mort* 1) [how King Arthur was wounded in the battle at Salisbury and how he was separated from Girflet, who stayed with him so long that he was the last one to see Arthur alive].[4]

Bors's task, at the beginning of the *Mort Artu*, is to relate the events of the quest, beginning with the deaths of Galahad and of Perceval (1). Arthur then requests a census of those who have died in the quest, and the number runs to

---

4 Citations are from Jean Frappier, ed., *La Mort le Roi Artu*, 3rd ed. (Geneva, 1964).

thirty-two. Moreover, all of those were 'morz par armes' (2), a fact that puts into question the validity of chivalric endeavor, even when chivalry aims to serve a higher, spiritual purpose.

Arthur, having heard that Gawain himself had killed several of the knights, asks the number. Gawain admits to having killed eighteen (2), but his explanation is telling: he killed them

'non pas pour ce que je fusse mieudres chevaliers que nus autres, mes la mescheance se torna plus vers moi que vers nul de mes compaignons. Et si sachiez bien que ce n'a pas esté par ma chevalerie, mes par mon pechié; si m'avez fet dire ma honte.' (2)

['not because I was a better knight than any other, but because misfortune afflicted me more than any of my companions. And you may be assured that it was not a feat of prowess, but rather the consequence of my sin. Now you have made me confess my shame.']

In these few words Gawain, one of Arthur's finest knights, not only declares his shame but acknowledges yet again the insufficiency, already explicitly established in the *Queste*, of traditional ('earthly' or secular) chivalry.[5] The motive forces in the preceding romance had been, as Gawain attests, sin and misfortune, the former engendering the latter. In the *Mort Artu*, only the latter remains: chivalry is vain and morality is a matter of slight concern.[6]

Having learned of the chivalric and personal tragedies that had accompanied the Grail triumph, Arthur understands that 'les aventures del roiaume de Logres estoient si menees a fin qu'il n'en avenoit mes nule se petit non' (3) [the adventures of the kingdom of Logres had been brought to a close, so that scarcely anything more could occur]. Consequently, as he will do more than once, he has a tournament announced, 'por ce qu'il ne vouloit pas toutevoies que si compaignon lessassent a porter armes' (3) [because he did not want his companions to give up bearing arms]. This single sentence conveys clearly the futility, almost the absurdity, of what is to come. The absence of adventures in a chivalric romance is virtually a contradiction in terms: adventures are the life-blood of such narratives. Now adventures are finished, and the activity provided by tournaments is an end in itself; it is no more than pretense or, at best, sport.

In other circumstances, *mescheance*, the word that characterizes Gawain's killing of eighteen knights, might indicate nothing more than poor luck, but in this text the word (like its translation as 'misfortune') must be seen as a reference

---

5 Since the *Queste* had insisted that chivalry should be remade into 'celestial chivalry' (143–44), which is a rigorous moral code and religious ideal, it may be tempting to see in that romance a simple repudiation of chivalric endeavor in its traditional form. That is however an oversimplification, and even Galahad distinguishes himself in battle. The narrator's contention appears instead to be that the conventional skills of chivalry are useless only when they serve no higher purpose.

6 This contention may appear questionable, considering the emphasis placed, throughout the *Cycle*, on the love affair of Lancelot and Guinevere. However, in the final romance, that affair is the subject less of moral condemnation than of personal jealousy and political intrigue, by Agravain and others.

to fate or Fortune (see below), an inexorable force working through and behind events. The impression that cataclysmic forces long held in check have now been unleashed is confirmed by the first reference to Lancelot and Guinevere, occurring just after Gawain's confession and the announcement of the tournament. In the *Queste*, Lancelot renounced Guinevere and swore to remain chaste. Such, at least temporarily, was the ennobling influence of the quest: even the Round Table's most prominent sinner can be inspired, albeit briefly, to reform. Such, also, is the *tragedy* of the quest: its inspirational power is transitory, and even the knight whose efforts are most sincere is doomed to fail – unless he happens to be Galahad.

Despite his vow, within a month of his return to court, Lancelot 'fu autresi espris et alumez come il avoit onques esté plus nul jor, si qu'il rencheï el pechié de la reïne autresi comme il avoit fet autrefoiz' (3) [was as enamored and inflamed as he had ever been before, so that he again lapsed into sin with the Queen just as he had done formerly]. For him in particular, the influence and moral force of the quest endure only until that quest is ended; then baser or, at least, 'more human' urges and secular influences reassert themselves. And, perhaps curiously, they exert greater power than before: now Lancelot is not even concerned to conduct his 'sinful passion' with ordinary discretion and prudence. As a result, Gawain's brother Agravain is soon certain that the love of Lancelot and Guinevere goes far beyond the proper relationship between a knight and his Queen, and he begins to plot their betrayal.

It is customary to trace the destruction of the Arthurian world to the illicit love of Lancelot and Guinevere or, at least, to the dual influence of that love and of the treason committed by Mordred. In fact, although both of those causes are crucial, they are only two links in a much longer chain of causality. A fuller accounting for Camelot's ruin may be made most easily and clearly by working backward from the cataclysm to its genesis. Arthur is mortally wounded by Mordred in a battle provoked by the latter's effort to usurp the throne (and marry Guinevere). Yet, Mordred would not have had the opportunity for treason had Arthur not decided to march against Lancelot; nor would the king, presumably, have made the decision to pursue Lancelot had not Gawain urged him to do so: 'et toute ceste chose estoit par l'esmuete monseignor Gauvain' (164) [and it was Gawain who had provoked all this]. Gawain's enmity, in turn, had been incited by the deaths of his brothers at the hands of Lancelot and Bors, in a battle undertaken when Lancelot returned to rescue Guinevere. And the Queen had been condemned to death when she and Lancelot, failing to exercise discretion, were discovered *in flagrante delicto* by Agravain.

What is so remarkable about this interlocking sequence of events, held together in a chain of causes and effects, is that Agravain's action is one of the few, in this sequence or indeed in the romance, that are the result of choice – if indeed his jealousy of and hatred for Lancelot really left him any choice in the matter. Once he acts, other events occur much in the manner of falling dominos, each one toppling the next, until Camelot itself is ultimately destroyed.

We can easily enough identify situations in which decisive action or even prudence by one or another character could in theory have altered the course of events. But, in fact, the text leaves no doubt that inclination, passion, and accident, as well as notions of duty, destiny, and family honor, have deprived the characters of the normal range of behaviors and have determined that they must act precisely as they do.

For example, although we may not be surprised that Lancelot and Guinevere resume their affair at the beginning of the romance, we must be struck by the brevity and casualness with which that momentous event is related to us (see above). Lancelot's conversion and vow in the *Queste* should at very least lead us to expect him to agonize over the resumption of their illicit relationship, but there is no indication that he does so. Nor is there an indication even that the lovers actually *make* a decision; the matter-of-fact presentation of this development implies its inevitability. It is something that just happens, without deliberation and, so far as we know, without anguish. The lovers cannot consider an alternative to their actions simply because, for them, no alternative exists.

Later, Lancelot is informed that Arthur knows about him and the Queen (114), but even then the couple might well have avoided detection had they separated briefly or simply conducted themselves more discreetly. That, however, is an impossibility, for one of the unspoken but obvious premises of the *Mort Artu* is that their love is inevitable and uncontrollable. Thus, although it is correct, in principle, to contend that discretion on their part would have averted the tragedy, it is no less true that such discretion is simply not a behavior that is available to them.

Just as characters cannot avoid precipitating catastrophic events, they are similarly unable to intercede to alter the effects of their (or others') actions. Once begun, the events leading to the death of Arthur and the destruction of the Round Table cannot be stopped. Even Arthur himself is increasingly powerless, constrained by the demands of his system of justice, by the often conflicting demands of chivalry and lineage (which, for example, set Gawain against Lancelot through the death of the former's brothers), and, as we shall see, by the king's own decline.

All these events leading to disaster are causes or, at least, provocations, but more accurately, they are simply the inevitable steps toward a conclusion implied long before. The love of Lancelot and Guinevere, a love that the *Lancelot* may have glorified but that was roundly condemned in the stricter moral climate of the *Queste del saint Graal*, is a decidedly destructive force that can finally have no effect other than the division of the court and the setting of friend against friend and vassal against king.

In the *Mort Artu*, Fortune assumes the central role, and the characters, with remarkably few exceptions, are simply swept along by the force of events. In part, the same comment could be made about the *Queste del saint Graal*, in that the quest was foreordained and long predicted; moreover, the Grail knight, Galahad, was chosen, whereas other questers were predestined to fail, the degree of their failure determined by the flaws in their character and their past behavior. But in the *Queste*, events were shaped not only by historical forces but also by divine plan. In the *Mort Artu*, on the other hand, the narrative force is not divinity but Fortune (presented most often as a personified figure). More precisely, it is instead *mis*fortune, for in this romance Fortune's wheel is seen only in its inexorable downward turn, bringing Arthur from glory to death.

Here, disasters are routinely attributed to Fortune. Apostrophizing Gawain's corpse, Arthur laments:

'comment pot soufrir Fortune vostre destruiement si let et si vilain, qui vos avoit garni de toutes bontez? Ja vos seut ele estre si douce et si amiable et vos avoit levé en sa plus mestre roe. Biaus frere, ce a ele fet por moi ocire et por ce que ge muire de duel de vos.' (131)

['how could Fortune, who endowed you with all good qualities, permit your awful and vile destruction? She was so kind and generous to you and raised you up on her great wheel. Dear brother, she did that to kill me, because she knew I would die of grief.']

Moreover, one of the key scenes in the entire *Mort Artu*, occurring just before the fateful battle on Salisbury Plain, is a dream in which Arthur sees the Wheel of Fortune and learns of the disaster that awaits him. It is a passage worth quoting *in extenso*:

Quant il fu endormiz, il li fu avis que une dame venoit devant lui, la plus bele qu'il eüst onques mes veüe el monde, qui le levoit de terre et l'enportoit en la plus haute montaigne qu'il onques veïst; illuec l'asseoit seur une roe. En cele roe avoit sieges dont li un montoient et li autre avaloient; le rois regardoit en quel leu de la roe il estoit assis et voit que ses sieges estoit li plus hauz. La dame li demandoit: 'Artus, ou ies tu? – Dame, fet il, ge sui en une haute roe, mes ge ne sei quele ele est. – C'est, fet ele, la roe de Fortune.' Lors li demandoit: 'Artus, que voiz tu? – Dame, il me semble que ge voie tout le monde. – Voire, fet ele, tu le voiz, n'il n'i a granmnet chose dont tu n'aies esté sires jusques ci, et de toute la circuitude que tu voiz as tu esté li plus puissanz rois qui i fust. Mes tel sont li orgueil terrien qu'il n'i a nul si haut assiz qu'il ne le coviegne cheoir de la poesté del monde.' Et lors le prenoit et le trebuschoit a terre si felenessement que au cheoir estoit avis au roi Artu qu'il estoit touz debrisiez et qu'il perdoit tout le pooir del cors et des menbres. Einsi vit li rois Artus les mescheances qui li estoient a avenir. (226–7)

[When he (Arthur) had fallen asleep, it seemed to him that the most beautiful lady in the world appeared before him and lifted him up from the earth and took him up onto the highest mountain he had ever seen; and there she set him upon a wheel. The wheel had seats, some of which rose as others sank. The King saw that his seat was in the highest position. The lady asked him, 'Arthur, where are you?'
'Lady,' he said, 'I'm on a large wheel, but I don't know what wheel it is.'
She said, 'It's the Wheel of Fortune.' Then she asked him, 'Arthur, what do you see?'
'Lady, it seems to me that I see the whole world.'
'Indeed,' she said, 'you do see it, and in it there is little that you have not been lord of until now, and of all you see, you have been the most powerful king who ever was. But such are the effects of earthly pride that no one is so highly placed that he can avoid falling from worldly power.' And then she took him and dashed him to the earth so cruelly that it seemed to King Arthur that he was crushed and that he lost all the strength of his body and its members.
Thus did King Arthur see the misfortunes that were to befall him.]

Even when a character occasionally blames God for a terrible event, someone else will quickly correct the misperception: God was not responsible for it –

Fortune was. Thus, when Mordred kills Yvain, Arthur wonders why God would permit such an act. To that, Sagremor replies, ' "Sire, ce sont li geu de Fortune; or poez veoir qu'ele vos vent chierement les granz biens et les granz honors que vos avez eü pieça, qu'ele vos tolt de voz meilleurs amis" ' (243) ['Sir, these are Fortune's games; now you can see that she is making you pay dearly for the great benefits and honors you've enjoyed before, by taking away your best friends'].

The emphasis on Fortune means, again, that events are effectively removed from the agency of human control. As a result, a good many incidents appear to be random occurrences: with powerful forces unleashed both by the love affair and by the end of adventures, things often seem just to happen, ostensibly by accident. We are told, for example (76), that a knight who wishes to kill Gawain gives poisoned fruit to the Queen, expecting her to offer it first to Gawain. Instead – and the narrator is entirely unconcerned with the reason – she offers it to Gaheris of Carahew, who eats it and immediately dies. Guinevere is arrested and accused of murder. What interests the narrator is neither the cause of the Queen's action nor the relative wrong it involves – the death of Gawain would certainly have been a greater tragedy – but instead its narrative consequences: the dead man's brother demands vengeance and offers to fight any knight who might take her side. That knight will of course be Lancelot, and thus the lovers are brought together again, in preparation for the next link in this narrative chain.

In reality, what appear to be narrative accidents in this text are of course an illusion created in large part by the inability of characters to determine the direction of events. Apparently unmotivated occurrences – accidents – are a specialized expression of the force of fate or Fortune, whose turning wheel links events so as to propel the text toward its predictably catastrophic ending.

Yet, despite the impression that each event provokes the next, or that the illicit love of Lancelot and the Queen propels them all and topples the realm, the reader never loses sight of the fact that there is another – ultimate and overarching – cause of Camelot's fall: the futility and vanity of Arthurian chivalry, which has simply outlived its time. Degeneration and decay are broadly symptomatic of this world. With the Grail quest completed, there are no more adventures to seek and no more challenges to face, except the challenge of somehow keeping Camelot alive, if only by artificial means such as serial tournaments. Arthur's ideal is a largely useless relic of the past; his is a culture whose glory, whose time, is gone.

As with most developments in the *Cycle*, events are prepared long before their exposition is presented explicitly to us. Paul Rockwell has pointed out that the decline of Arthur and of his court (and his ethic) is in fact gradual.[7] In the earlier parts of the *Cycle* Arthur is able to meet challenges and make decisions that become increasingly difficult and are, by the end, beyond his capabilities. The *Mort Artu* is thus a continuation of a development begun long before, but it

---

7 In ' "Je ne suiz mie soffisanz": Insufficiency and Cyclicity in the Lancelot-Grail Cycle,' in Sara Sturm-Maddox and Donald Maddox, eds., *Transtextualities: Of Cycles and Cyclicity in Medieval French Literature* (Binghamton, 1996), pp. 71–91, esp. 72.

is a most dramatic continuation, which takes this change in Arthur's character and his court's efficacy to its logical conclusion: moral paralysis and physical destruction. The king is still able to lead an army to victory against the Romans, but within his own realm, he is an increasingly impotent monarch. His power is now martial but not moral. He can defeat external enemies but cannot hold his own kingdom together.

Arthur himself is the saddest representative of this new world, not merely because, by definition, the mighty fall from the greatest heights, but because his bland passivity contrasts dramatically with the passion of Gawain, Lancelot, even Agravain. The characters in this romance, though unable to act other than as they do, are nonetheless capable of fervor, and the narrator maintains the appearance, the fiction, of decisive action. Although readers know that Lancelot cannot fail to return to rescue Guinevere when she is condemned to death, his doing so is presented as a matter of bold resolve. Gawain rages against Lancelot and provokes a war to avenge his own brothers' deaths. Mordred plots systematically against the King. In contrast to all of these is Arthur, an aging symbol of a past era,[8] a man who appears to have surrendered to his destiny, even leaving to others the decisions that should be his. He now responds to the changes in his world in ways that involve pathos, sadness, and resignation, with no attempt to rebel against the forces of fate, that is, of Fortune.

Arthur's aging and ineffectiveness are dramatic, and there comes a time when he is virtually helpless. When Gawain contends that Arthur wants Lancelot to leave the land and never return, Lancelot asks the king for confirmation of that desire. Arthur's feeble reply is, ' "Puis que Gauvains le velt, . . . il me plest bien" ' (158) ["Since Gawain wishes it, so do I"]. And when Lancelot then asks Arthur whether he can expect peace or war with the king, the latter offers no response, standing by in silence as Gawain threatens Lancelot and promises a terrible war.

Once the tide of events has engulfed Arthur, leading him to do battle with Lancelot's army and eventually with Mordred's, he dies, with no promise or hope of return.[9] At that point, readers might expect the romance to end. Indeed, the prediction of the beginning (and indeed of the title) has been realized. Yet Arthur is survived by Lancelot and Guinevere, as well as by Bors and others. The major action following the king's death is a war between Lancelot and the sons of Mordred, who attempt to overrun the land. This war is not only a matter of justice or revenge, nor is it simply the narrative 'loose end' it may appear to be. It is in fact a crucial thematic development, serving in particular as a partial vindication of Lancelot. Though transformed by events into Arthur's enemy, he

---

[8] The narrative leaves little doubt that Arthur's inability to assert his will or even make a choice is not in fact the cause, but rather the effect, or simply a symptom, of his world's disintegration.

[9] In keeping with the doleful atmosphere of this romance, the familiar story of Arthur's departure for Avalon, where his wounds will be tended and from where he will return in the hour of Britain's greatest need, is not part of the *Mort Artu*. His body is taken away on a boat by Morgan and other women, but then it is brought back and placed in a tomb. In this romance, the 'once and future king' has no future.

is shown to be still a devoted knight and faithful subject, serving his country and his king even after the latter's death.

Guinevere, having entered a convent, dies, and the news of her death reaches Lancelot on the very day he is to march against Mordred's sons. After his victory over them – a symbolic victory as well over their father, the traitor – Lancelot lives on for some time, and after his death he is buried at his castle of Joyous Guard.

With those events, the story reaches its end.[10] The narrator of the 'death of Arthur,' insisting that nothing can be added to the *Estoire de Lancelot* (263), indicates thereby that the *Mort Artu* is in fact merely the last chapter in the Lancelot romance. The point is important, and it surely implies that even the *Queste* was to a considerable degree Lancelot's story. Transformed from a central character in the *Lancelot* into a secondary (and ultimately disqualified) one in the *Queste* and then into an enemy of King Arthur in the final romance, Lancelot as knight, as father of Galahad, as lover of the Queen remains the conceptual pivot of the *Cycle*.[11] The influence of his illicit love, of his unsurpassed chivalric skills, of his devotion to Arthur – in short, the influence of his laudable qualities and his flaws alike – molds the *Cycle* from beginning to end, and although we have come to know the *Cycle* by a number of titles,[12] the text itself, in its very last sentence, calls it simply 'Lancelot's story.'

That story is now finished, and the narrator insists that 'n'en porroit nus riens conter qui n'en mentist de toutes choses' (263): anything else that might be added would be a complete lie. The Arthurian world is no more.

---

[10] However, Bors, Blioberis, and the Archbishop have survived and will spend the rest of their lives together 'por l'amour de Nostre Seigneur' (263). It is with their deaths that the Arthurian realm will entirely disappear. Incidentally, Bors has in a sense been the unofficial chronicler of the Arthurian era: emerging gradually as a major character, he is one of the three witnesses to the final Grail vision, and he returns to court to recount the quest, serving thus as a direct and authoritative link between the *Queste* and the *Mort Artu*.

[11] Although he is disqualified from the Grail quest, he plays a prominent role in the *Queste*. He dubs Galahad at the beginning; later, in a long sequence, he converts and abjures his past sins, and he makes other appearances in the romance. It is only very near the end of the quest that he is injured while trying to approach the Grail. Disheartened, he returns to court as Bors, Perceval, and Galahad proceed to Corbenic Castle for the final vision.

[12] Of those various titles (Vulgate Cycle, *Lancelot-Grail*, etc.), the one that most accurately reflects the author's (or authors') apparent intent is *Lancelot en prose* (*Prose Lancelot*). However, that title has fallen largely into disuse, owing to its possible confusion with the title of the central romance.

12

'Mise en page' in the French Lancelot-Grail: the First 150 Years of the Illustrative Tradition

ALISON STONES

If the number of surviving manuscripts is a reliable guide to what was read in the Middle Ages, the five-part *Lancelot-Grail Cycle* (or *Vulgate Cycle*) and its derivatives and followers ranked with Geoffrey of Monmouth's *Historia regum Britanniae* and the Pseudo-Turpin Chronicle of Charlemagne's exploits in Spain as one of the most popular vernacular texts.[1] Surviving in over a hundred manu-scripts, most of which are densely illustrated, it provides a formidable and

---

This essay was first given as a paper at the Oxford 'History of the Book' Conference in 1992. I thank Linda Brownrigg for helpful comments.

At the end of this chapter, Appendix 1 is a list of the abbreviations used for manuscripts and Appendix 2 summarizes information about the manuscripts.

[1] The manuscripts of the *Lancelot-Grail Cycle* are listed in Brian Woledge, *Bibliographie des romans et nouvelles en prose française antérieurs à 1500* (Geneva, 1954), nos. 93, 96, 114, and idem, *Supplément 1954–1973* (Geneva, 1975), nos. 93, 96, 114; Alexandre Micha, 'Les manuscrits du *Lancelot* en prose,' *Romania*, 84 (1963), 28–60, 478–99, and 'La tradition manuscrite du *Lancelot* en prose,' *Romania*, 85 (1964), 293–318, 478–517; all the above emended by Alison Stones, 'The Earliest Illustrated Prose *Lancelot* Manuscript?' *Reading Medieval Studies*, 3 (1977), 3–44, and 'Aspects of Arthur's Death in Medieval Illumination,' in *The Passing of Arthur: New Essays in Arthurian Tradition*, ed. Christopher Baswell and William Sharpe (New York, 1988), pp. 52–101. The text editions, in order of publication, are: F. J. Furnivall, ed., *Seynt Graal or the sank Ryal*, 2 vols. (London, 1861–63), based on Royal 14.E.III (see Appendix 1 for a list of abbre-viations); Gaston Paris and Jacob Ulrich, eds., *Merlin: roman en prose du XIIIe siècle*, 2 vols. (Paris, 1886), based on Add. 38117; Eugène Hucher, ed., *Le saint Graal*, 3 vols. (Le Mans, 1877–78; rpt. Geneva, 1967), based on Le Mans 354; H. Oskar Sommer, *The Vulgate Version of the Arthurian Romances, edited from manuscripts in the British Museum*, 8 vols. (Washington, D.C., 1909–16), based on Add. 10292–4; J. Douglas Bruce, ed., *Mort Artu: An Old French Prose Romance of the XIIIth Century, being the last division of Lancelot du Lac* (Halle, 1910), based on BNF fr. 342; Albert Pauphilet, ed., *La queste del saint Graal* (Paris, 1921), based on Lyon, Bibliothèque municipale Palais des Arts 77; William Albert Nitze and T. Atkinson Jenkins, *Le haut livre du Graal: Perlesvaus*, 2 vols. (Chicago, 1932–37); Jean Frappier, ed., *La mort le roi Artu: roman du XIIIe siècle* (Paris, 1936), based on Ars. 3347; Gweneth Hutchings, ed., *Le roman en prose de Lancelot du Lac: le Conte de la charette* (Paris, 1938), based on CCC 45 and Rawl. Q.b.6; William Roach, ed. *The Didot Perceval, according to the manuscripts of Modena and Paris* (Phila-delphia, 1941), based on Modena E 39 and Paris, Bibliothèque nationale de France MS nouvelles acquisitions françaises 4166; Elspeth Kennedy, ed. *Lancelot do Lac: The non-cyclic Old French Prose Romance*, 2 vols. (Oxford, 1980), based on BNF fr. 768; Alexandre Micha, ed., *Lancelot: roman du XIIIe siècle*, 9 vols. (Geneva, 1978–83), based on CCC 45, and A. Micha, *Merlin, roman du XIIIe siècle* (Geneva, 1980), based on BNF fr. 747; Fanni Bogdanow, ed., *La Version Post-Vulgate de la Queste del Saint Graal et de la Mort Artu, troisième partie du Roman du Graal*, 3 vols. (Paris, 1991), based on a series of manuscripts; Richard O'Gorman, ed., *Robert de Boron, Joseph d'Arimathie* (Toronto, 1995), based on Tours 951; Jean-Paul Ponceau, ed., *L'Estoire del saint Graal*, 2 vols. (Paris, 1997), based on Amsterdam and Rennes 255.

somewhat unwieldy corpus from which to explore questions about the format and layout of text and illustration in the period between the composition of the texts c. 1220 and the decline of interest in vernacular manuscripts towards the end of the fifteenth century. This is the period that witnesses the origin and development of the illustration of vernacular texts in France, to which the *Lancelot-Grail* in its various forms, both non-cyclic and cyclic, is a significant contributor. I survey here what patterns of textual and pictorial layout the manuscripts of the first 150 years of the *Lancelot-Grail* present. I focus on the appearance of the illustrated page: how its text is laid out and what format is used for the illustrations.

The kinds of questions I ask are these: What kinds of variation occur in the layout of text and picture? Do changes in text layout and picture formats vary together? How important are regional preferences? Is there a chronological progression? How close can we come, in this period of sparse documentation, to determining who made the choices, and on what basis? The attributions I propose for dating and placing these manuscripts are based on a study of the style of their illustrations; it is on this basis, too, that I reconstruct 'groups' of related manuscripts (to use a more neutral term than 'atelier' or 'workshop'). Almost all the *Lancelot-Grail* manuscripts can be shown to have been made by teams of craftsmen whose activities were not limited to the production of romances, but included liturgical and devotional works as well as those made for knowledge or for pleasure. Nor are these books necessarily of inferior artistic quality to their more expensive relatives, although there are instances where qualitative distinctions exist. In most cases I have argued the justification of the stylistic and chronological sequence in more detail elsewhere, and further collaborative work on these questions is in progress.[2]

The present investigation is limited to those books, made before 1350, which contain one or more branches of the *Cycle* and whose pictorial decoration is substantial, consisting of more than a single opening illustration for each branch of the *Cycle*. There are approximately fifty such manuscripts or sets of volumes. The others, which either have decoration or are unillustrated, I reserve for separate treatment at another time. I also exclude from consideration here the several manuscripts that were made in England and Italy.[3]

Findings

The patterns of layout in thirteenth- and early fourteenth-century *Lancelot-Grail* manuscripts are far from straightforward. There is no chronological progression from one kind of layout to another, nor is one format preferred in any one

2   A collaborative project of analysis is underway with the participation of text scholars, art historians, and specialists in codicology and information science. See http://vrlab.pitt.edu/stones-www/lance.html

3   For the fifteenth-century manuscripts, see Susan A. Blackman, 'The Manuscripts and Patronage of Jacques d'Armagnac,' Diss. Pittsburgh 1993. The charts are also reproduced in Blackman, 'A Pictorial Synopsis of Arthurian Episodes for Jacques d'Armagnac, Duke of Nemours,' in *Word and Image in Arthurian Romance*, ed. Keith Busby (New York, 1996), pp. 3–57.

region. Patterns that match on one dimension, such as the number of columns of text, may differ on another, such as the format of the miniatures or historiated initials. I summarize, under headings, some of the relationships that have emerged.

Overall format

These books are not uniform and it is not clear whether it was the rule or the exception for all five branches of the *Cycle* to be copied as a complete *Lancelot-Grail Cycle*. Several more or less complete sets are preserved: Bonn 526 (Amiens and Thérouanne or Cambrai, 1286, fig. 4); BNF fr. 110 (same provenance about a decade later); probably BNF fr. 95 and Yale 229 (Thérouanne or its region in the 1290s); BNF fr. 344 (Lorraine soon after 1300); Add. 10292–4 (Flanders or Artois, 1317); Amsterdam/Rylands/Douce 215 (same approximate date and provenance); BNF fr. 105, or more likely BNF 9123, and Ars. 3481 (fig. 6) with a lost third volume (Paris, second quarter of the fourteenth century). Only three of the surviving complete sets (Bonn 526, BNF fr. 110, BNF fr. 344) are still bound as a single volume. Those three, as we shall see, do not have the same text layout, or choice of format for illumination. We do not know whether the others were originally bound in single volumes, for I know of no *Lancelot-Grail* manuscript that preserves an original binding. The other manuscripts all include one or more branches of the *Cycle* and it is unusual for other texts to be included in the same volume: the manuscripts that do so are Modena E 39 (second quarter of the thirteenth century, of uncertain provenance); BNF fr. 95; UCB 106 (c. 1250, Paris?); UCB 107 (c. 1250, Paris?); BNF fr. 770 (Douai, c. 1285); Add. 5474 (same artists as BNF fr. 110); Geneva, Bod. 147 (c. 1300, of uncertain provenance). Of these, Modena E 39, UCB 106 and 107, BNF fr. 95, and BNF fr. 770 are books in which the additional texts occur in separate quires that, although contemporary and in some cases (BNF fr. 95, BNF fr. 770) certainly by the same scribes and painters, need not originally have interfered with the textual structure of a set of *Lancelot-Grail* volumes. Perhaps they were purchased in the same lot and stayed together. They might have been originally bound together too, for Add. 5474 and Geneva, Bod. 147 show that other material could even be interpolated into or excised from *Lancelot-Grail* text. Whether these last two books were originally part of complete *Lancelot-Grail* cycles, we do not know.

The few mentions of *Lancelot-Grail* manuscripts in the contemporary inventories suggest that an owner might have a copy of one of the branches without the others: at the death in 1304 of Jean d'Avesnes, count of Hainaut, the item at the top of his inventory was 'uns grans roumans a rouges couvertures, ki parolle de Nasciien de Mellin et de Lancelot dou Lach.'[4] Extant manuscripts containing these branches and made before 1304 are: Rennes 255 (fig. 1); UCB 106; Tours

---

4 Chanoine Chrétien Dehaisnes, *Documents et extraits divers concernant l'histoire de l'art dans la Flandre, l'Artois et le Hainaut avant le XVe siècle*, 2 vols. (Lille, 1886), I, 156. I have commented upon this reference in Alison Stones, 'The Illustrations in the Prose *Lancelot*, New Haven, Yale University, Beinecke MS 229 and Paris, BN fr. 95, Prolegomena to a Comparative Study,' in *Word and Image in Arthurian Romance*, pp. 206–83, n. 144.

951 (assuming the presence of the *Lancelot* announced on the last folio but now lost); BNF fr. 748/754 (assuming they were originally bound as one volume). The inventory made at the death of Robert de Béthune, count of Flanders from 1305 to1322, listed 'un livre de Merlin,' as did the 1303 will of Jean Cole, bourgeois of Tournai.[5] None of the extant copies has *Merlin* alone, but if the documented volumes actually included *Estoire* or *Joseph* as well, then BL Add. 38117 might have belonged to Robert of Béthune. It is probably a little too late in date to be considered as Jean Cole's book. In the manuscripts themselves, however, there is no positive evidence of ownership. The list of ten 'roumans qui sont monseignieur' – written by a thirteenth- or early fourteenth-century hand on the back flyleaf (fol. 269) of BNF fr. 12569 (*Chevalier au Cygne* and *Chanson d'Antioche*) – includes a 'Lancelot du Lac.' We do not know who 'monseigneur' was, or whether one of the extant copies of *Lancelot* is meant, but the wording makes it clear that someone on the staff of the household was in charge of the books and kept records.[6]

Text columns

It is known from numerous manuscripts whose pictures were never finished that in the process of making the book, the copying of the text preceded the drawing and painting. Spaces for pictures had to be anticipated at appropriate places on the written page and left blank by the scribe. Considerable attention has focused recently on the various intermediaries that were used in this process: notes, sketches, lists, and combinations of all three.[7] Just how this worked is still a question on which there is much research to be done, including the placement of the minor initials in the unillustrated books. Two aspects of the problem of direct concern here are: the number of columns in which the text is written and whether this correlates with the format selected for the illumination. Another dimension of the question of text/picture relationships is that of the rubrics, which I touch on briefly below.

Of the fifty or so manuscripts under consideration here, thirteen are written in three columns, one manuscript alone in one column, and the rest in two columns. There are no manuscripts in four columns.[8] Those in three columns are: Rennes 255 (Paris, c. 1220, fig. 1); BNF fr. 770 (Douai, c. 1285); Bonn 526 (Amiens and Thérouanne or Cambrai, 1286 [fig. 4]); BNF fr. 110 (Thérouanne or Cambrai, c. 1295); Morgan M 805–6 (Amiens or Laon, c. 1312); Royal 14.E.III

---

5   For Robert de Béthune see Stones, 'Yale 229 and fr. 95,' p. 240; for Jean Cole see A. de la Grange, 'Choix de testaments tournaisiens antérieurs au XVIe siècle,' *Annales de la Société historique et archéologique de Tournai*, ii (1897), 38 [1–365], and Stones, 'Yale 229 and fr. 95,' nn. 143 and 147.
6   The manuscript is described in Suzanne Duparc-Quioc, ed., *La Chanson d'Antioche*, 2 vols. (Paris, 1976–78), pp. 60–6, and ascribed to Arras c. 1300. See also Stones, 'Yale 229 and fr. 95,' n. 144.
7   The most comprehensive survey is by Jonathan J. G. Alexander, *Medieval Illuminators and their Methods of Work* (New Haven and London, 1992).
8   This layout is rarely used for texts in prose, but exceptions include parts of the verse and prose compilation from Saint-Omer, Ars. 3516, which can be dated by its computus table to 1268 and localized by its calendar. BNF fr. 1553, a comparable miscellany of verse and prose texts composed soon after 1284, is smaller in format and has all its texts in two columns.

(Flanders or Artois, c. 1315); Add. 10292–4 (Flanders or Artois, 1317); and the Parisian-made books of the 1320s–40s: BNF fr. 105, BNF fr. 9123, Ars. 3481 (fig. 6), BNF fr. 333, Ars. 3482, and BNF fr. 16999.

Parisian products account for six of the thirteen copies; they represent a wide chronological range, from the earliest, Rennes 255, c. 1220 (fig. 1),[9] to the cluster of five books made at the end of our period, between c. 1320 and 1340, for and perhaps by, the *libraires* Thomas de Maubeuge, Geoffroy de Saint-Ligier, and Richard de Monbaston.[10] Generally, the three-column text layout is common in books made by this team (fig. 6) in the second quarter of the fourteenth century, for the styles in the books they made show clear evidence of collaboration, yet it is not the only layout used for Parisian *Lancelots* of this period: Douce 199 (unique among *Lancelot-Grail* manuscripts) is written in one column, and Rawl. Q.b.6 and SSL Fr.F.v.XV.5 are in two columns. Parisian *Lancelot-Grail* manuscripts of the mid-thirteenth century do not continue the three-column layout, the preference is for two columns, a format which can already be found perhaps in the second quarter of the century (?) in Modena E 39 (of uncertain provenance). The sparsely illustrated manuscript BNF fr. 768, the base manuscript of Kennedy's edition,[11] which contains a single historiated initial, is another early example of a *Lancelot* manuscript written in two columns, and there are unillustrated early examples.

The other six three-column *Lancelot-Grail* manuscripts include two pairs associated with the diocese of Thérouanne: Bonn 526 (fig. 4) and BNF fr. 110 (c. 1285–95), and a second pair, Royal 14.E.III and Add. 10292–4 (made a generation later, c. 1315–25). But both groups also include a third *Lancelot-Grail* manuscript, or part of one, written in two columns: Amsterdam/Rylands/Douce in the latter case and Add. 5474 in the former. The two-column text layout was also the rule in the earlier Thérouanne products, BNF fr. 748/754, and the pair of *Estoire/Merlin* manuscripts, BNF fr. 19162 and BNF fr. 24394.

Of the remaining books with a three-column text layout, BNF fr. 770 was made in Douai c. 1275 and associated with three two-column *Lancelot-Grail* manuscripts: BNF fr. 342, written in 1274; Le Mans 354 (fig. 3), and Digby 223.[12] No other *Lancelot-Grail* manuscripts can be connected at the moment with

9 For the date and provenance, see Stones, 'The Earliest Illustrated Prose *Lancelot* Manuscript?'
10 Their roles in the Paris book trade have recently been addressed in several of the articles in *Fauvel Studies*, ed. Margaret Bent and Andrew Wathey (Oxford, 1998). See also R. H. Rouse and M. A. Rouse, *Illiterati at uxorati, Manuscripts and their Makers: Commercial Book Producers in Medieval Paris, 1200–1500* (London, 2000), chs. 7, 8, and 9.
11 Cited in n. 1. The artistic context of the manuscript is discussed by Patricia Stirnemann, 'Some Champenois Vernacular Manuscripts and the Manerius Style of Illumination,' in *Les manuscrits de Chrétien de Troyes*, ed. Keith Busby et al., 2 vols. (Amsterdam, 1993), pp. 195–226 (p. 207) and fig. 24.
12 The localization is based on Valenciennes, Bibliothèque municipale 838, a martyrology of Notre-Dame des Prés (O. Cist.), Douai, and the psalter-hours Brussels, Bibliothèque Royale 9391, of the use of Saint-Amé (O.S.A.), Douai. Le Mans 354 was written by Walterus de Kayo who, as Terry Nixon has noted, wrote another manuscript in 1285, see Alison Stones, 'The Illustrated Chrétien Manuscripts and their Artistic Context,' in *Manuscrits de Chrétien de Troyes*, pp. 252–3 [227–323].

Morgan M 805–6 (made in Amiens or Laon c. 1315), nor do any of its associates have a three-column layout.[13]

Overall, the three-column books tend to be larger – approximately 400x300mm – than those written in two columns and the one written in one column, but there are exceptions. Several two-column volumes are comparable in size: BNF fr. 95/Yale 229 is 470x330/40mm, Amsterdam/Rylands/Douce is 405/411x290/292mm, Rawl. Q.b.6 is 412x262mm; BNF fr. 122 is 408x305mm, and some of the three-column volumes are smaller: BNF fr. 770 is only 318x232mm; Morgan M 805–6 (admittedly heavily cropped) is 346x254mm and BNF fr. 333 is 380x280mm.

Format of the illustrations

The range of format used to enclose the narrative scenes covers historiated initials, miniatures in one, two, or three text-columns, and multiple images consisting of a single large miniature across several columns or single miniatures juxtaposed on the same page. Most manuscripts include borders with figures, hybrids, or animals, particularly on opening pages. Superficially, they seem rarely to fulfill a function intrinsic to the narrative, and appear to reflect designs invented by workshops or individuals for other contexts. Only in the Ars. 5218 *Queste* manuscript, written, illuminated, and bound by Pierart dou Thielt in 1351, do the marginal figures support the kind of parallel action that can be said to present a coherently understandable commentary on the main illumination.[14] Further work on the other manuscripts may yield different results, particularly for BNF fr. 95 and Yale 229 which have more marginalia within the body of the manuscript than is usual.

Opening illustrations

Most manuscripts adopt one format for the main body of the illumination and another for the opening pages of the five major branches, as Emmanuèle Baumgartner has observed for *Tristan* manuscripts,[15] and Lori Walters for those of Chrétien de Troyes.[16] Although the *Suite Vulgate* and subdivisions of *Lancelot* are not usually singled out for special openings, the opening of *Joseph* is given special treatment when it follows an illuminated *Estoire*. What that special treatment consists of depends partly on what is used for the illustrations throughout:

---

13 For the related material, see Alison Stones, 'L'atelier artistique du Maître de la Vie de sainte Benoîte: nouvelles considérations,' *Bulletin de la Société nationale des antiquaires de France* (no volume number) (1990), 378–400 and S. Castronovo, *La Biblioteca dei conti di Savoia e la pittura in area savoianda (1285–1343)* (Turin et al., 2002), 55–69, 195–206, pl. VI–XI, figs. 21–39, for Turin, BN L.II.14, a literary miscellany.

14 Analysis and references are in Lori Walters, 'Wonders and Illuminations, Pierart dou Tielt and the *Queste del saint Graal*,' in *Word and Image in Arthurian Romance*, pp. 339–72.

15 Emmanuèle Baumgartner, 'La "première page" dans les manuscrits du *Tristan* en prose,' in *La présentation du livre, Actes du Colloque de Paris X-Nanterre*, ed. Emmanuèle Baumgartner and Nicole Boulestreau, *Littérales*, 2 (Paris, 1987), pp. 51–63.

16 Lori Walters, 'Paris, BN, fr. 1433: The Creation of a "Super Romance,"' *The Arthurian Yearbook*, 1 (1991), 3–25, and Walters, 'The Use of Multi-Compartment Opening Miniatures in the Illustrated Manuscripts of Chrétien de Troyes,' in *Les Manuscrits de Chrétien de Troyes*, pp. 331–50.

so if historiated initials are the rule, the opening one is bigger, with a more emphatic border (Rennes 255; BNF fr. 748/754), or a miniature (BR 9627–8 [fig. 2]; Tours 951; Rawl. Q.b.6; Add. 38117; BNF fr. 1422–4); or a cluster of miniatures (BNF fr. 344, Yale 227). If miniatures are the rule, then the opening illustration may be a historiated initial (BNF fr. 95/Yale 229; BNF fr. 122 for *Mort Artu*). More usual, however, is a cluster of miniatures or a large subdivided miniature to mark the opening (BNF fr. 342; Le Mans 354; BNF fr. 770; BNF fr. 19162; Bonn 526 [fig. 4]; BNF fr. 110; Geneva, Bod. 147; BNF fr. 749; Morgan M 805–6; Amsterdam/Rylands/Douce; Royal 14.E.III; Add. 10292–4; SSL Fr.F.v.XV.5; BNF fr. 105; BNF fr. 9123; Ars. 3481 [fig. 6]; Douce 199; Ars. 3482). This is the largest sub-group, comprising eighteen manuscripts. Some simply include a larger miniature at the opening: BNF fr. 333; or a large miniature at the opening and others sporadically in the text: UCB 107; Ash. 828; BL Royal 20.D.IV; Ars. 5218. The opening pages are given no special treatment in Modena E 39; BNF fr. 339, BNF fr. 24394; Add. 5474; BNF fr. 12573; BNF fr. 12582.

What precisely were the criteria that guided the selection of subjects to form part of the opening miniature or initial? This is an area that needs more work. I have shown elsewhere that the selection of the subject in *Mort Artu* manuscripts can have important implications for how the ending of the story was interpreted, and the formal treatment of the subject selected can also play a key role in determining a subject's effect.[17] At other times the format, and even the selection of the subjects, may be more a matter of workshop practice, particularly in the environment of mass-production that characterizes Parisian output in the second quarter of the fourteenth century.

Historiated initials

Historiated initials are the standard format for illustrations at the beginning of the *Lancelot-Grail* illustrative tradition (Rennes 255 [fig.1], Modena E 39, BNF fr. 339), as also in the earliest illustrated verse romances in Latin, for example the Virgil, BNF lat. 7936 of c. 1200,[18] or in French, the *Roman de Troie*, Ars. 3340, written in 1237.[19] At the end of our period historiated initials are still current, if no longer exclusive (BNF fr. 1422–4, c. 1320–40),[20] but their use no longer correlates with the three-column text format: if Rennes 255 has three columns (fig. 1),

17 Alison Stones, 'Some Aspects of Arthur's Death in Medieval Art,' in *The Passing of Arthur: New Essays in Arthurian Tradition*, ed. Christopher Baswell and William Sharpe (New York, 1988), pp. 52–101.

18 François Avril, 'Un manuscrit d'auteurs classiques et ses illustrations,' in *The Year 1200: A Symposium* (New York, 1975), pp. 261–82.

19 It is reproduced in Charles Samaran and Robert Marichal, *Catalogue des manuscrits en écriture latine portant des indications de date, de lieu ou de copiste*, 7 vols. (Paris, 1959–89), I, 159, pl. 12, but is still neglected in the literature because it was omitted by Hugo Buchthal, *Historia Troiana: Studies in the History of Mediaeval Secular Illustration* (London and Leiden, 1971).

20 Its illuminator also collaborated with Pierart dou Thielt in part of the French verse *Alexander*, Oxford, Bodl., Bod. 264 (facsimile by M. R. James, *The Romance of Alexander: a collotype facsimile of ms. Bodley 264* [Oxford, 1933]) and he can be traced in several other manuscripts, including a Pontifical of Tournai in Wrocław. For a summary, with previous literature, see Alison Stones, 'The Artistic Context of the *Roman de Fauvel*, with a Note on *Fauvain*,' in *Fauvel Studies*, pp. 563–4 [529–67]. Another unnoticed manuscript that can be added to the oeuvre of Pierart dou Thielt is Chartres, BM 549, a photograph of which is in the Fonds Porcher at the BNF.

Modena E 39 and Paris, BNF fr. 1422–4 have two. The use of historiated initials does however appear to be related to geographical distribution, for they are the rule rather than the exception in Parisian products of the thirteenth century (Rennes 255 [fig. 1], BNF fr. 339, UCB 106, Tours 951, Oxford Bod. Rawl. Q.b.6), no doubt under the impetus of the small, illuminated academic study-Bibles that dominated the Paris book trade.[21] But other Parisian-made books, such as the law books in Latin,[22] and William of Tyre's *Outremer* in French, prefer single-column miniatures.[23] Perhaps UCB 107, a Parisian *Lancelot* with miniatures, was made under their influence. By c. 1310 (SSL Fr.F.v.XV.5) the extensively illustrated *Lancelot-Grail* has also come to be produced in Paris with single-column miniatures.[24] With the mass-production enterprises associated with the Maubeuge/Saint-Ligier/Monbaston *libraires* in the 1320s–40s,[25] the change to miniatures in one or two columns has become decisive; it will become the dominant format for the fifteenth century. Yet the thirteenth-century Parisian preference for historiated initials was not limited to Paris. They are also the exclusive or primary format for the illustration of manuscripts made in Flanders, Artois, and Lorraine: BNF fr. 748/754 is probably from Thérouanne,[26] BNF fr. 344 and its twin, Sotheby's 1.7.46 (ex-Phillipps 1047), are from Lorraine, probably Metz (the former including some miniatures as well [fig. 5]);[27] and BL Additional 38117 (Huth Merlin) is probably from Arras,[28] and BNF fr. 1422–4 from Tournai. It is worth noting that the Tournai manuscript can be considered a lesser product from an artistic environment where the major products had full-page miniatures.[29]

Miniatures

The most visually impressive *Lancelot-Grail* manuscripts are the ones illustrated predominantly with miniatures. Even one-column miniatures are bigger on average than historiated initials, which normally occupy less than the width of a text column. The miniature format allows more picture space, and the multiple-column miniature increases it. No doubt the cost factor rose proportionately as well, a question I have discussed elsewhere.[30]

---

[21] Numerous examples are reproduced in Robert Branner, *Manuscript Painting in Paris during the Reign of Saint Louis* (Berkeley and Los Angeles, 1977).

[22] See Anthony Melnikas, *The Corpus of the Miniatures in the Manuscripts of Decretum Gratiani*, 3 vols. (Rome and Columbus, OH, 1975).

[23] See Jaroslav Folda, *Crusader Manuscript Illumination at Saint-Jean d'Acre, 1275–1291* (Princeton, 1975).

[24] Alexandre de Laborde, *Les principaux manuscrits à peintures conservés dans l'ancienne Bibliothèque impériale publique de Saint-Pétersbourg*, 2 vols. (Paris, 1936–38), I, 7, no. 6, and I, 31, no. 27.

[25] See Stones, 'The Artistic Content,' and Rouse and Rouse, *Manuscripts and Makers*.

[26] My attribution, based on similarities with Ars. 3516, the literary miscellany having a calendar of Saint-Omer (diocese of Thérouanne).

[27] BNF fr. 344 was mentioned by Georg von Vitzthum, *Die Pariser Miniaturmalerei zur Zeit des heiligen Ludwigs* (Leipzig, 1907), p. 123.

[28] Localization based on linguistic analysis by Antonij Dees, *Atlas des formes linguistiques des textes littéraires de l'ancien français* (Tübingen, 1987), p. 522: 'Pas-de-Calais, sud-est.'

[29] The major example is the *Roman d'Alexandre*, Oxford, Bodl. Bod. 264.

[30] Stones, 'Yale 229 and fr. 95,' pp. 80–3.

On the whole, miniatures, rather than historiated initials, are the preferred format for *Lancelot-Grail* manuscripts made in the northern provinces.[31] Again, there are several exceptions – the occasional Parisian book with miniatures (UCB 107 and the fourteenth-century ones), books with mainly historiated initials but with miniatures for the openings of branches, as noted above. This might suggest that, in a scale of relative hierarchies, the miniature was more highly regarded, but evidence to the contrary comes from the books (cited above) that are predominantly illustrated with miniatures but open with a historiated initial. Further evidence comes from manuscripts in which substantial numbers of both miniatures and historiated initials are scattered throughout the book: Le Mans 354 (4 miniatures [fig. 3], 11 historiated initials); BNF fr. 770 (102 miniatures, 52 historiated initials), Yale 229 (77 large miniatures, 51 small miniatures, 36 historiated initials – but note the different proportions in BNF fr. 95, which has 99 miniatures, 28 small miniatures, 9 historiated initials), Morgan M 805 (38 miniatures, 157 historiated initials). Then there are the instances where the illumination is predominantly miniatures, but the occasional historiated initial appears: Bonn 526; Geneva, Bod. 147; Add. 10292–4; Amsterdam/Rylands/ Douce.

Most striking among the manuscripts with miniatures are the multiple-column pictures that spread horizontally across the page, allowing sequential episodes to be represented or simply more supporting landscape or architectural elements to be included than in the single-column miniature or historiated initial. To what extent do the subjects change when these long miniatures are used instead of the compressed space of the historiated initial or single-column miniature? This is another area where much is still to be done.

Of the books written in three columns, only New York, M 805–6 exploits the full width of the page, with three-column miniatures scattered throughout the book as well as on opening pages. In contrast, BNF fr. 770, although written in three columns, limits the width of its large miniatures to two columns – was this because it is related to BNF fr. 342, which has text and miniatures in two columns? Yet a third *Lancelot-Grail* manuscript, Le Mans 354, which is related to both, has a two-column text with only single-column miniatures or historiated initials (apart from the opening miniature [fig. 3]). The rectangular miniature spanning the full width of the written space seems not to have occurred in *Lancelot-Grail* manuscripts produced in Paris. While the possibility of a lost example should not be discounted because there are numerous parallels in other texts, the multiple-column miniatures are generally found on opening pages rather than in the body of the illustration.[32] By c. 1320–40 the three-column

---

31 The possibility of influences coming to this region from the Empire might be a factor in the preference for miniatures over historiated initials: the Heisterbach Bible, for instance, attributed by Swarzenski to 'Cologne?' in the mid-thirteenth century, presents some striking formal and iconographical parallels with Bonn 526. See Hanns Swarzenski, *Lateinischen illuminierten Handschriften des XIII. Jahrhunderts in den Ländern am Rhein, Main und Donau* (Berlin, 1936), pp. 91–5, no. 10.
32 Several examples are reproduced in the exhibition catalogue *Les Rois maudits, Philippe le Bel et ses fils*, ed. François Avril (Paris, 1998).

books BNF fr. 105, Ars. 3481, and BNF fr. 333 have miniatures in two columns (apart from openings [fig. 6]), while BNF fr. 9123 and Ars. 3482 are also written in three columns but have miniatures in a single column (apart from openings). The lack of uniformity is all the more striking because the stylistic links between BNF fr. 9123 (main hand), BNF fr. 105 and Ars. 3481 are so close that they must be by the same painter (Geoffroi de Saint-Ligier?).[33] Both BNF fr. 342 and Morgan M 805–6 are from the north, if not from the same place (most likely Douai and Amiens or Laon, respectively). The three other books with two-column miniatures across the width of the page are Royal 20.D.IV, BNF fr. 122 (written in 1344), and Ars. 5218 (written, illuminated and bound by Pierart dou Thielt in 1351). There is no doubt that Ars. 5218 was made at Tournai, and the other two books were probably produced there too: both Royal 20.D.IV and BNF fr. 122 have a two-column miniature illustrating the same subject (Lancelot and the enchanted dance) at the same place in the text, and textual lacunae account for the absence of correlation between the others.[34] Yet even here it is worth noting the close textual relationship between Royal 20.D.IV and BNF fr. 1422–4, probably also from Tournai a decade or so later, and the corresponding absence of links in the format of the illustrations: BNF fr. 1422–4, as mentioned above, has historiated initials.

The absence of full-page miniatures in *Lancelot-Grail* manuscripts is probably the most surprising gap in this complex web of possible choices that producers, patrons, and illustrators faced. Even in the manuscripts with multiple miniatures, whether these occur in isolation or clustered in their columns on opening pages, the pictures always have lines of text beneath them, and usually a good half-page of it. In the manuscripts under consideration here, there is no extant parallel (and perhaps none ever existed) for the full-page scenes found in the *Roman de Troie*, BNF fr. 1610 or the *Chevalier au Cygne* and *Chanson d'Antioche* manuscripts BNF fr. 12558 and BNF fr. 12569. Crusading tales, with their obvious parallels in the iconography of the Bible (the Old Testament Picture Bible, Morgan M 638, is the most likely source, particularly for BNF fr. 12558), are not alone in preserving full-page miniatures. If the *Roman de la Poire*, BNF fr. 2186, is something of a special case whose circumstances are still not altogether clear,[35] there are also the groups of full-page miniatures in the French prose

---

[33] See Stones, 'The Artistic Content.' There is a numbered rubric-table at the beginning of BNF fr. 9123 which omits one of the miniatures, and the miniatures in the manuscript are numbered. The number next to the miniature that is missed in the rubric-table repeats the previous figure: so the rubric-list and the numbers followed the miniatures and rubrics present in the text, not vice-versa. The rubric-list and the rubrics themselves repeat verbatim. The presence of a similar list in Ars. 3481 but not in BNF fr. 105, another copy of *Estoire*, suggests that BNF fr. 9123 and Ars. 3481 were the first two parts of a three-part set (of which the last has not survived). See now Rouse and Rouse, *Manuscripts and Makers*, p. 197, where Ars. 3481 and BNF fr. 105 are considered parts of the same set.

[34] See Stones, 'Yale 229 and fr. 95.'

[35] Its illustrations are fully reproduced in Christiane Marchello-Nizia, ed., *Le Roman de la Poire, par Tibaut* (Paris, 1984). For a date c. 1270–80 for BNF fr. 2186, see Hans-Erich Keller, 'La structure du *Roman de la Poire*,' in *Conjunctures: Medieval Studies in Honor of Douglas Kelly*, ed. Keith Busby and Norris J. Lacy (Amsterdam, 1994), pp. 205–17.

Alexanders of c. 1300,[36] and the *Yvain/Atre périlleux* in BNF fr. 1433, perhaps made in Tournai c. 1320–30.[37]

There are also numerous examples of the painters of *Lancelot-Grail* manuscripts working on another book that does have full-page pictures: the best example is Morgan M 805–6. Its main artist also painted the *Vie de Sainte Benoîte*, Berlin, MS Dahlem Museum, Kupferstichkabinett 78.B.16, two detached leaves from a Missal in the Vienna Kunstgewerbemuseum, and the medical treatise BL Sloane 1977, all with full-page miniatures that are highly idiosyncratic in treatment.[38] That painter was clearly fully capable of handling the full-page format if required.

Finally, there is the question of the density of the illumination, whatever the format. Textual lacunae account for some of the differences in numbers of illustrations, and full tabulation of the distribution of illustrations in each branch would be required to determine exactly where the differences occur. The numbers listed in the Appendix show the overall totals of illustrations for each manuscript. Among those that preserve the complete *Lancelot-Grail Cycle*, for example, there are densities of illumination that range from 325 pictures in BNF fr. 95/Yale 229 (lacking the first two parts of *Lancelot*, which might add another 100–120 images) to 346 in BNF fr. 344 (though *Queste* and *Mort Artu* are incomplete), to 349 in Bonn 526, to 748 in Add. 10292–4. Was the sheer number of pictures a factor in determining the format? One could argue that, for speed of production, the single-column miniature can be made most quickly as there is no need to waste time deciding which initial letter is required (though guide letters usually indicate it), whereas multiple-column miniatures would clearly take longer to paint. Bonn 526 and Add. 10292–4 do indeed have single-column miniatures.

If one conclusion emerges from this survey, it is that the choices were not altogether governed by the easily detected criteria of type of text, date, or regional preference. If inherited tradition and workshop practice were to some extent significant factors, the results were neither predictable nor uniform. More comparative work on the iconography of these lengthy cycles would help clarify what the dependency patterns are and establish more clearly which aspects of the texts were considered most important through pictorial emphasis. Overall, the matrix of determinants is a highly complex one that must include substantial unknowns and missing links.

---

36 Alison Stones, 'Notes on Three Illustrated Alexander Manuscripts,' in *The Medieval Alexander Legend and Romance Epic: Essays in Honour of D. J. A. Ross*, ed. Peter Noble, Lucie Polak, and Claire Isoz (Millwood, NY, 1982), pp. 193–254. See also A. Stones and † D. J. A. Ross, 'The *Roman d'Alexandre* in French Prose: Another Illustrated Manuscript from Champagne or Flanders c. 1300,' *Scriptorium*, 56 (2002), 151–62.

37 See Walters, 'Super Romance.'

38 See Stones, 'Vie de sainte Benoîte' and Castronovo, cited in n. 13. The Turin manuscript is written in 2 columns and does not have full-page miniatures.

*Appendix 1. List of Abbreviations used for Manuscripts
and Manuscript Collections*

Add.	London, British Library, Additional collection
Amsterdam	(Amsterdam/Rylands/Douce) Amsterdam, Bibliotheca Philosophica Hermetica MS 1
Ars.	Paris, Bibliothèque de l'Arsenal
Ash. 828	Oxford, Bodleian Library, Ashmole MS 828
BL	British Library
BNF fr.	Paris, Bibliothèque nationale de France, fonds français
Bodl.	Bodleian Library, Oxford
Bonn 526	Bonn, Universitätsbibliothek MS 526
BR 9627–8	Brussels, Bibliothèque Royale MS 9627–8
CCC 45	Cambridge, Corpus Christi College MS 45
Digby 223	Oxford, Bodleian Library MS Digby 223
Douce	Oxford, Bodleian Library, Douce collection (see also Amsterdam)
The Hague, KB	The Hague, Koninklijke Bibliotheek
Geneva, Bod. 147	Geneva-Coligny, Bodmer 147
Le Mans 354	Le Mans, Médiathèque Louis Aragon MS 354
Modena E 39	Modena, Biblioteca Estense MS E 39
Morgan M 805–6	New York, Pierpont Morgan Library MS M 805–6
Rawl. Q.b.6	Oxford, Bodleian Library MS Rawlinson Q.b.6
Rennes 255	Rennes, Bibliothèque municipale MS 255
Royal	London, British Library, Royal collection
Rylands	Manchester, The John Rylands University Library (see also Amsterdam)
SSL Fr.F.v.XV.5	St. Petersburg, Saltykov-Chtchredine State Library, MS Fr.F.v.XV.5
Tours 951	Tours, Bibliothèque municipale MS 951
UCB	Berkeley, University of California at Berkeley
Yale	New Haven, Yale University, Beinecke collection

*Appendix 2. Working List of Manuscripts with Cycles of Illustrations
made in France before 1360*

Manuscripts are listed in alphabetical order of place. The four tabulated columns give the following information about the manuscripts, in order: their textual components (E=*Estoire*, J=*Joseph*, M=*Merlin*, L=*Lancelot* or part of *Lancelot*, Q=*Queste*, MA=*Mort Artu*); date; provenance; the approximate number of illustrations included.

Amsterdam, Bibliotheca Philosophica Hermetica1 (ex-Phillipps 1045/7[sic], 3630)/
Oxford, Bodl. Douce 215/ Manchester, Rylands fr. 1

EMLQMA	c. 1315	Flanders or Artois	189

Berkeley, UCB 106 (ex-Phillipps 3643)

EM	c. 1250?	Paris?	21

Berkeley, UCB 107 (ex-Phillips 1279)

L	c. 1250?	Paris?	5

Bologna, Archivio di Stato b.1. bis, n. g			
E, fragment	c. 1300	Thérouanne?	1
Bonn, Universitätsbibliothek 526			
EMLQMA	1286	Amiens and Thérouanne or Cambrai	346
Brussels, Bibliothèque Royale 9627–8			
QMA	c. 1250	Paris?	37
Chicago, Newberry f21Ry.34 12261			
L	c. 1250?	Paris?	3
Florence, Biblioteca Mediceo-Laurenziana, Ashburnham 48 (121)			
Q	dated 1319	Avignon	62
Geneva-Coligny, Bodmer 147 (ex-Phillips 1046)			
EMLQMA	c. 1290	?	167
Le Mans, Médiathèque Louis Aragon 354			
E	c. 1285	Douai	17
London, BL Add. 5474			
Tristan, L	c. 1290	Thérouanne or Cambrai	23
London, BL Add. 10292–4			
EMLQMA	1317	Flanders or Artois	748 [sic]
London, BL Add. 38117			
Huth EJM	c. 1310?	Arras?	67
London, BL Royal 14.E.III			
EQMA	c. 1315	Flanders or Artois	116
London, BL Royal 20.D.IV			
L	c. 1315	Tournai?	12
[Manchester, see Amsterdam]			
Modena, Bibliotheca Estense E 39			
Didot version	c. 1220?	?	15
New Haven, Yale, Beinecke 227			
EM	1357	Flanders or Hainaut	164
New Haven, Yale, Beinecke 229			
LQMA	c. 1295	Thérouanne	166
New York, Morgan M 805–6			
L	c. 1315	Amiens? Laon?	175
Oxford, Bodl. Ash. 828			
L	c. 1300?	Thérouanne?	40
Oxford, Bodl. Digby 223			
LQMA	c. 1280?	Douai	12
Oxford, Bodl. Douce 199			
LQ	c. 1320?	Paris?	32
[Oxford, Bodl. Douce 215, see Amsterdam]			
Oxford, Bodl. Rawl. Q.b.6			
LQMA	c. 1310	Paris	212
Paris, Ars. 3481 (cf. BNF fr. 9123 or 105)			
L	c. 1330	Paris	78
Paris, Ars. 3482			
MLQMA	c. 1330	Paris	136
Paris, Ars. 5218			
Q	1351	Tournai	3
Paris, BNF fr. 95			
EM, Sept sages, Pénitence Adam	c. 1295	Thérouanne	163
Paris, BNF fr. 105 (cf. Ars. 3481)			
EM	c. 1330	Paris	127

Paris, BNF fr. 110			
EMLQMA	c. 1295	Thérouanne or Cambrai	99
Paris, BNF fr. 122			
LQMA	1344	Tournai?	120
Paris, BNF fr. 123			
LQMA	c. 1275–1280	England	90
Paris, BNF fr. 333			
L(Agravain)	c. 1320	Paris	36
Paris, BNF fr. 339			
LQMA	c. 1250	Paris	120
Paris, BNF fr. 342			
LQMA	1274	Arras or Douai?	92
Paris, BNF fr. 344			
EMLQMA	c. 1290–1300	Metz or Verdun	344 [sic]
Paris, BNF fr. 748 (cf. fr. 754)			
JM	c. 1230?	Thérouanne?	15
Paris, BNF fr. 749			
EM	c. 1300	Thérouanne?	126
Paris, BNF fr. 754 (cf. fr. 748)			
L	c. 1230?	Thérouanne	27
Paris, BNF fr. 769			
E	c. 1340?	Paris	5, rest unfinished
Paris, BNF fr. 770			
EM, Prise de Jerusalem	c. 1285	Douai	140
Paris, BNF fr. 1422–4			
LQMA	c. 1320	Tournai	73
Paris, BNF fr. 9123 (cf. Ars. 3481)			
EM	c. 1330	Paris	167
Paris, BNF fr. 12573			
LQMA	c. 1310?	Arras?	78
Paris, BNF fr. 12582			
E	c. 1300?	Metz?	?
Paris, BNF fr. 16999			
L	c. 1350	Paris	?
Paris, BNF fr 19162			
EM	c. 1280	Thérouanne or Cambrai	83
Paris, BNF fr. 24394			
EM	c. 1280	Thérouanne or Cambrai	71
Rennes, Bibliothèque municipale 255			
EML	c. 1220	Paris	64
St Petersburg, Saltykov-Chtchredine State Library Fr. F.v.X.V.5			
EJ	c. 1310	Paris	43
Tours, Bibliothèque municipale 951			
EJM	c. 1290	Acre, Cyprus?	133
Turin, Biblioteca Nazionale L.III.12			
M	c.1300	Thérouanne?	20
Private Collection ex Phillipps 1047			
EM	c. 1290–1300	Metz or Verdun	129

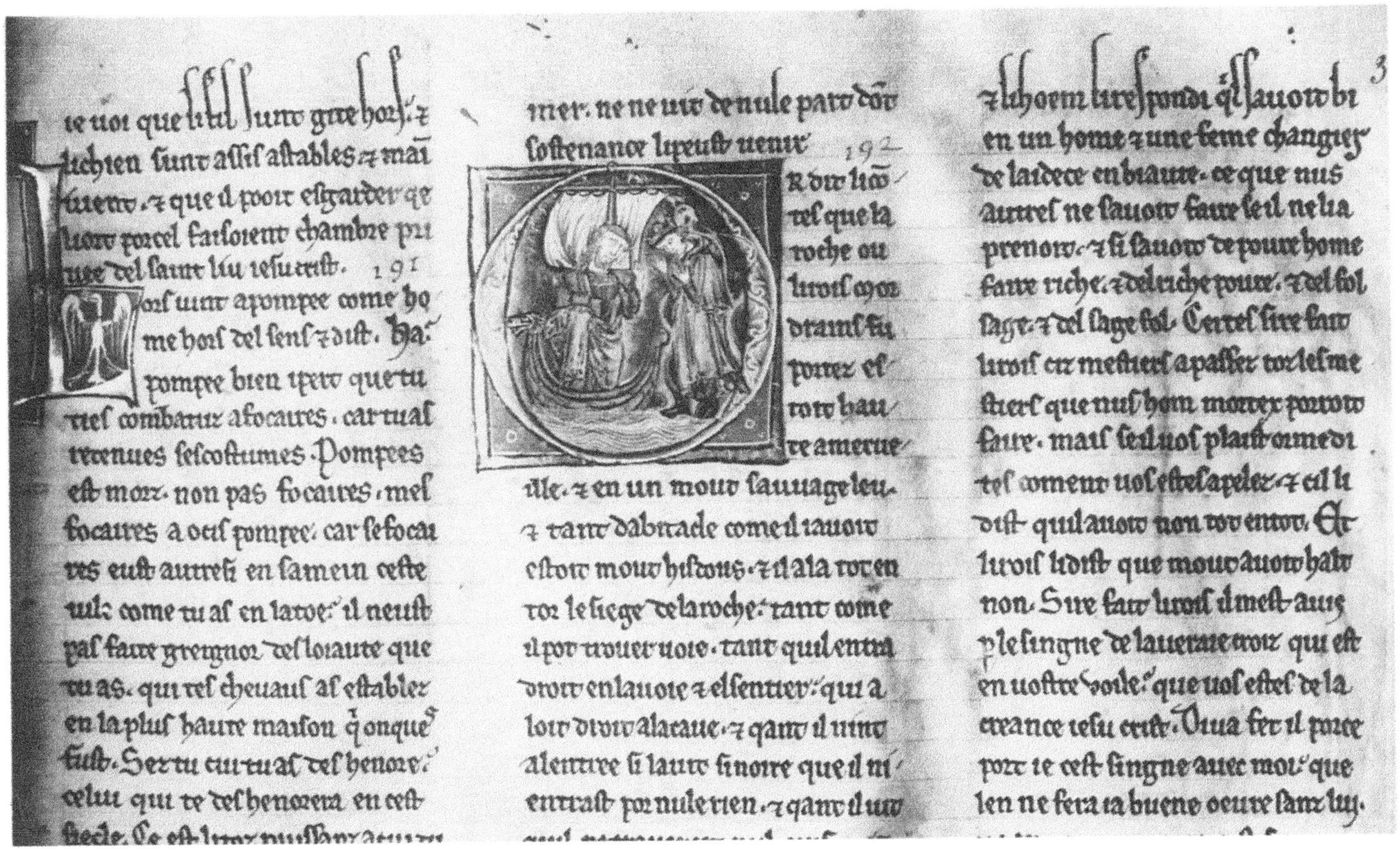

Fig. 1. Rennes, BM 255 (148), fol. 32 (*Estoire del saint Graal*). By permission of the Bibliothèque municipale, Rennes

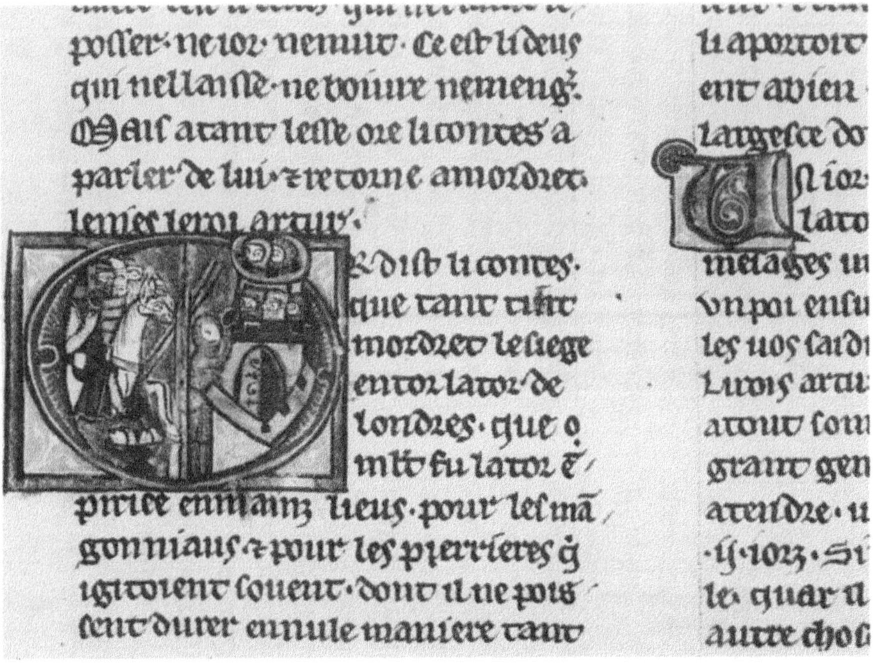

Fig. 2. Brussels, BR 9627–8, fol. 139v (*Mort Artu*). By permission of the Bibliothèque royale Albert 1er, Brussels

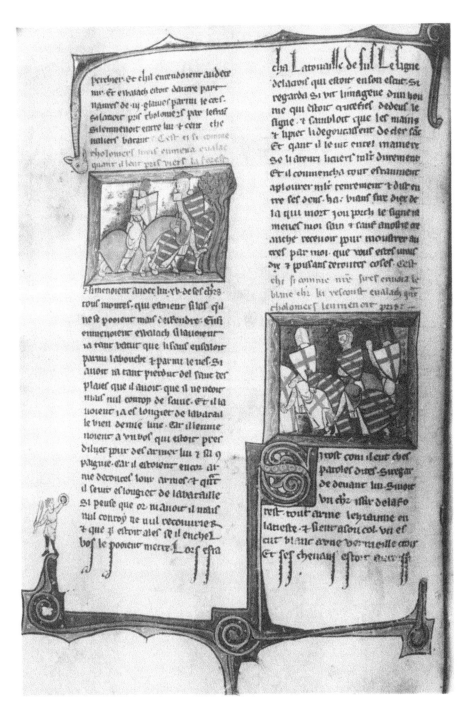

Fig. 3. Le Mans, MM 354, fol. 49v (*Estoire del saint Graal*). By permission of the Médiathèque municipale Louis Aragon, Le Mans

Fig. 4. Bonn, UB 526, fol. 455v (*Mort Artu*). By permission of the Universitäts und Landsbibliothek, Bonn

Fig. 5. Paris, BNF fr. 344, fol. 184 (beginning of the *Lancelot*). By permission of the Bibliothèque nationale de France, Paris

Fig. 6. Paris, Ars. 3481, fol. 3 (beginning of the *Lancelot*). By permission of the Bibliothèque de l'Arsenal, Paris

PART III

POSTERITY

13

The Lancelot-Grail Cycle *in England: Malory and his Predecessors*

HELEN COOPER

Sir Thomas Malory's *Morte Darthur*, completed in 1469–70 and printed by William Caxton in 1485, is England's Arthuriad, and as such it is the closest English equivalent to the *Lancelot-Grail Cycle*.[1] Equivalence in scope, however, does not imply mere translation or adaptation. Malory's work is the fullest single representative of the *Lancelot-Grail* in English, but he was neither the only, nor by any means the most faithful, English adapter of *Cycle* material.[2] His version is indeed strikingly innovative: he both alters his *Cycle* material and combines it with different sources in French and English to design (to use Chrétien de Troyes' famous terms) a *conjointure* for the resulting work from which he can draw out a *sens* radically different from that of the *Lancelot-Grail*.

Malory's distinctiveness is best approached through the history of Arthurian romance in English, for the kind of emphasis he gives his work often accords with this much better than with its French developments. 'English' here means Middle English language; insular culture is a much broader term, as the likely Anglo-Norman origins of both the Thomas of the *Tristan* and Marie de France indicate. If the author of the *Lancelot-Grail* had indeed been Walter Map, as it claimed, then the *Cycle* itself would have been English in that broader cultural sense. The lack of distinction between French and Anglo-Norman culture in the late twelfth and early thirteenth centuries is indeed indicated by the fact that Map could so happily have been regarded as its author: there was clearly nothing felt to be implausible about the attribution. Early English-language Arthurian material, however, looks very different from that in French. The stress

---

1 The edition cited is that of Eugène Vinaver, *The Works of Sir Thomas Malory,* 3rd ed. rev. P. J. C. Field (Oxford and New York, 1990), as this contains substantial notes on sources not contained in his more widely available one-volume student edition; both are based primarily on the manuscript of the work discovered in Winchester College in 1934, now MS London, British Library Add. 59678. For ease of reference to other editions, including those of Caxton's print, Caxton's book and chapter numbers are also provided; see also *Caxton's Malory,* ed. James W. Spisak (Berkeley, 1983). Modern-spelling versions usually give the Caxton text; the exception is *Sir Thomas Malory: Le Morte Darthur, The Winchester Manuscript,* ed. and abridged Helen Cooper (Oxford and New York, 1998).

2 For an account of Arthurian romances in English, see *The Arthur of the English: The Arthurian Legend in Medieval Life and Literature,* ed. W. R. J. Barron (Cardiff, 1999); and for a summary, see Helaine Newstead, 'Arthurian Legends,' in J. Burke Severs, gen. ed., *A Manual of the Writings in Middle English 1050–1350, I: Romances* (New Haven, 1967), pp. 38–53, 72–5.

fell strongly on the life and death of Arthur, and its sources lay in Geoffrey of Monmouth's *History of the Kings of Britain* and its numerous chronicle derivatives rather than French romance; this legendary, historical version is the ultimate source of works from Layamon's *Brut* (c. 1200) to the alliterative *Morte Arthure* (c. 1400). That difference of content, combined with the change of language, makes the history of Middle English Arthurian romance decisively different from the history of the genre in French, even after the *Cycle* material comes to dominate English Arthurian writing in the fifteenth century.

The divergence of the two histories can be summed up as the interrelated effects of changes of historical moment, language, social focus, and national interests. The chronological slippage is immediately striking: there are few Middle English romances surviving from before 1300, and the great age of romance composition was the fourteenth and fifteenth centuries. Many Middle English romances had French or Anglo-Norman originals, but the time difference between them is generally much greater than is required for the process of translation alone. The fullest English version of any of Chrétien's romances, *Ywain and Gawain*, dates from over a century after the original was composed; and the *Cycle* translations spread from a century after the composition of the original to 250 years later. The receiving English culture was therefore very different from that in which the *Lancelot-Grail* had been conceived. This difference was compounded by the contrasting audiences implied by the different languages. Many barons, administrators, merchants and lawyers were bilingual; but the comments contained in some of the English Arthurian romances make it clear that they were designed to be read by those who could not speak French, not, or not primarily, by those who were fluent in both languages and cultures. The target audience therefore does not exclude the noble and the cosmopolitan, but it is primarily focused on the level below that (gentry, franklins, townsmen and so on) rather than great households or the court. The audience is also typically conceived as predominantly male, in marked contrast to the reading of French romance in England being associated with women.[3] The shift away from courtliness and ideological and sexual fantasies is reflected in the different social and ethical priorities contained in much Middle English romance. Adultery is rare; genealogy and the sense of a plausible history of Britain are given a higher profile; ideals are more practical, in terms of homosocial relations, courtship leading to marriage, and a piety characterized by devotional duty rather than mysticism; and adventures tend at least to be grounded in a sense of the possible. A final but important difference is that of form. Verse, whether rhymed or alliterative, remained the expected medium for narrative fiction in English until well into the fifteenth century. The great majority of the English redactions of the *Cycle* therefore translate it into verse. Malory is not quite the first person

---

3   See Carol M. Meale, '. . . alle the bokes that I haue of latyn, englisch and frensch: Laywomen and their Books in Late Medieval England,' in *Women and Literature in Britain 1150–1500*, ed. C. Meale (Cambridge, 1993), pp. 128–58; see also *Canterbury Tales*, VII.3212–13, in *The Riverside Chaucer*, gen. ed. Larry D. Benson (Boston, Mass., 1987; Oxford, 1988), where Chaucer's Nun's Priest refers to his story as being as true 'As is the book of Launcelot de Lake, / That wommen holde in ful greet reverence.'

to translate any of it into prose, but he and most of his readers may well have thought that he was.

The earliest adaptations of the *Cycle* material into English indicate singularly little interest in the romance elements of the Arthurian stories. The sections of the *Cycle* most frequently called on are the *Estoire del Saint Graal* and the *Merlin*. These two parts of the *Cycle* between them account for five Middle English works, composed between the early fourteenth century and the mid fifteenth. Their popularity may have something to do with the fact that both could be taken as being concerned with the foundations and history of Britain rather than with the knights of the Round Table – who indeed rarely get a mention. By the beginning of the fourteenth century, the legend that Joseph of Arimathia had been the apostle to the English appears to have become established as a historical possibility in English chronicles, especially those connected with Glastonbury. John of Glastonbury indeed cites the book 'qui Sanctum Graal appellatur,' the *Estoire*, as his source for his version of the origins of Christianity in Britain.[4] The beginning of the *Merlin* (on the conception and birth of Merlin and Arthur) and the end (on Arthur's campaigns against the Roman Emperor) themselves draw closely on Geoffrey of Monmouth's history of Arthur, and so, as Layamon bears witness, translations of the text again accord with the agenda of recording the British past.

The first appearance of *Lancelot-Grail Cycle* material in English was *Of Arthour and of Merlin*, a version of the early part of the *Merlin* translated into octosyllabics (or its English equivalent, four-stress lines rhyming in couplets; the form is typical of the French verse romances, including Chrétien's, and of many French-derived Middle English romances).[5] It was composed in the London area some time before 1330, that being the approximate date of the Auchinleck manuscript in which it is preserved, and it runs to almost 10,000 lines. The poem summarizes the account found in the *Merlin* (and much of it also in Geoffrey of Monmouth) of King Constance (father of Uther Pendragon), the birth and childhood of Merlin, Vortigern's attempt to build a castle, the foundation of the Round Table, the conception and birth of Arthur, the sword in the stone, and his establishment of his rule down to his war against King Rion and his betrothal to Guinevere. One of the most striking features of the poem is its opening, in which the poet declares his reasons for making the translation: those who know French and Latin, he says, have a cultural and religious advantage, and therefore he will write in the language that is known to all those who were born in England:

> Riȝt is þat Inglische vnderstond
> Þat was born in Inglond.
> Freynsche vse þis gentil man
> Ac euerich Inglische Inglische can.   (lines 21–4)

---

4 John of Glastonbury, *The Chronicle of Glastonbury Abbey*, ed. James P. Carley, trans. David Townsend (1985; rpt. Woodbridge, 2001), p. 48; and see Aelred Watkin, 'The Glastonbury Legends,' *Arthurian Literature*, XV (1997), 89–90 [77–91]. The further legend that Joseph brought the Holy Grail to Glastonbury is a later, post-medieval invention.

5 *Of Arthour and of Merlin*, ed. O. D. Macrae-Gibson, Early English Text Society, 268, 279 (London and New York, 1973).

This, coupled with the stress of the narrative on the legendary-historical tradition of Arthur rather than courtly romance, suggests an agenda of reclaiming him for the English such as is repeated with greater force in Caxton's preface to Malory: 'the moost renomed Crysten kyng, fyrst and chyef of the thre best Crysten, and worthy, kyng Arthur, whyche ought moost to be remembred emonge us Englysshemen tofore al other Crysten kynges.'[6] The reclaiming goes so far as some judicious censorship: the work omits any mention of the incestuous birth of Mordred. It thus brings the *Cycle's Merlin* into line with Geoffrey's account, to the point where anyone not thoroughly familiar with the *History of the Kings of Britain* would probably believe themselves to be reading an English version of Geoffrey. It was to be another century before that slur on the character of Arthur made its way across the language barrier.

A variant text of *Of Arthour and of Merlin*, better described as *The Birth of Merlin*, appeared a century or so later, which cut the story still shorter. In its fifteenth-century manuscripts, it stops with the death of Vortigern; a longer version is preserved in an early print and in the mid-seventeenth century Percy Folio manuscript, which take the story as far as the accession of Uther.[7] The number of surviving manuscripts and its dissemination in print indicate that it was widely known – probably the best-known, and the longest-known example of *Lancelot-Grail Cycle* material in English apart from Malory's. It is all the more ironic, therefore, that it never mentions Arthur at all.

The next work after *Of Arthour and of Merlin* to base itself on the *Cycle* was the alliterative *Joseph of Arimathie*, preserved in the Vernon manuscript of the late fourteenth century, a collection of pious and devotional works possibly compiled for use in a convent.[8] This is a fragment of some 700 lines that summarizes an early part of the story of Joseph from the *Estoire del Saint Graal*, from his release from prison by Vespasian to Evelak's baptism under the name of Mordreins. Its manuscript context strongly suggests that it was valued as a religious work rather than for any Arthurian connections it might have; it includes the heavily didactic section in which Joseph expounds Christian doctrine to the King of Sarras. Arthur does not get a mention in the whole work, and the Grail is never named: it does appear as an object, but only in a single line, when Joseph and his son see a vision of an altar on which lie the lance and nails of the Crucifixion, 'And vppon þat oþer ende   þe disch wiþ þe blode' (line 297). Apart from a predictive reference in one line of *Of Arthour and of Merlin*, there is no mention of the 'grail' in English until a full two centuries after the composition of the *Lancelot-Grail*.

Any sense that the *Estoire* and the *Merlin* might lead into the larger story of

---

6 Ed. Vinaver, p. cxliii. The three Christian worthies are Arthur himself, Charlemagne, and Godfrey of Bulloigne.

7 *Here begynneth a lytel treatyse of ye byrth and prophecye of Marlyn*, printed by Wynkyn de Worde c. 1510 (there is also a fragment of a later edition surviving of c. 1529); *Merline*, in *Bishop Percy's Folio Manuscript: Ballads and Romances*, ed. John W. Hales and Frederick J. Furnivall (London, 1867), I.417–96.

8 *Joseph of Arimathie*, ed. W. W. Skeat, Early English Text Society, O.S. 44 (1871). The leaf containing the opening of the poem is missing; Skeat estimates that around 100 lines have been lost.

Arthur had to wait until the fifteenth century. That was in many ways the great age of romance in England, with abundant recopyings of earlier works and the composition of new ones,[9] and the *Lancelot-Graal* received a corresponding concentration of attention. Around 1425, Henry Lovelich, a member of one of the great London trade guilds, the Company of Skinners, produced huge translations of the *Estoire del Saint Graal* and the *Merlin* for a fellow member, Harry Barton, who was twice Lord Mayor of London.[10] Lovelich's vast and unwieldy redactions, in rhyming couplets of somewhat indeterminate metrical form, survive in a single manuscript, and there is no evidence of their wider readership or influence. The *Merlin* was translated again, this time into prose – one of the earliest English prose romances on any subject and Malory's only Arthurian precursor in the medium – around 1450.[11]

The things that are most obviously missing from this run of romances are the ones that give the *Lancelot-Grail Cycle* its modern name: Lancelot, and the Grail quest itself. There were numerous English romances concerning Gawain, and occasionally of other Round Table knights, but none of these were derived from the *Cycle*. English interest in Lancelot, and with him the *Cycle* version of Arthur's downfall, is barely traceable in English before 1400. The one allusion to his affair with Guinevere appears as an interpolation in one redaction of the *Anonymous Metrical Chronicle* (in the Auchinleck Manuscript, the same manuscript that contains the earliest text of *Of Arthour and of Merlin*), and there it is recast as a foundation legend for the caves under Nottingham Castle – excavated by Lancelot after he had abducted the Queen, the passage informs us, to hide her in should Arthur come looking for her.[12] The lines were clearly inspired by the arrest of another queen's lover, Roger Mortimer, late in 1330, by captors who made their way into the castle by way of the caves through the rock. There is no further mention of their love until the stanzaic *Morte Arthur*, composed probably around 1400 – the same period as the Geoffrey-derived alliterative *Morte* – and surviving in a single manuscript of the late fifteenth century.[13] This is a redaction of the *Cycle*'s *Mort Artu*, translated into an understated, almost ballad-style register in 8-line stanzas rhyming abababab, a form that seems to have had some associations with historical material or rhymed chronicles.[14] Although its material is drawn entirely from the *Lancelot-Grail*, the tone and ethos of the poem are both very different from the French, even in episodes such as the final battle where one might most expect similarity. Its quality can be indi-

---

9 Derek Pearsall, 'The English Romance in the Fifteenth Century,' *Essays and Studies*, N.S. 29 (1976), 56–83.

10 *The History of the Holy Grail by Henry Lovelich*, ed. F. J. Furnivall, Early English Text Society, E.S. 20, 24, 28, 30, 95 (1874–78, 1905); *Merlin by Herry Lovelich*, ed. Ernst A. Kock, Early English Text Society, E.S. 93, 112 (1904, 1913). On Lovelich, see also Robert W. Ackerman, 'Herry Lovelich's "Merlin," ' *PMLA*, 67 (1952), 473–84.

11 *Merlin*, ed. H. B. Wheatley, Early English Text Society, O.S. 10, 21, 36, 112 (1865–99).

12 *An Anonymous Short English Metrical Chronicle*, ed. Ewald Zettl, Early English Text Society, O.S. 196 (1935), Auchinleck additions lines 1071–90 (pp. 70–1).

13 Both the stanzaic *Morte Arthur* and the non-Vulgate alliterative *Morte Arthure* are edited by Larry D. Benson, *King Arthur's Death* (Indianapolis, 1974; Exeter, 1986).

14 See Helen Cooper, 'Romance after 1400,' in the *Cambridge History of Medieval English Literature*, ed. David Wallace (Cambridge, 1999), pp. 709–11.

cated by its account of that battle, which is reduced from the ten pages it occupies in Frappier's edition of the French[15] to a single forceful stanza:

> There was many a spere sprent,
>   And many a thro word they spake;
> Many a brand was bowed and bent,
>   And many a knightes helm they brake;
> Riche helmes they rove and rente;
>   The riche routes gan togeder raike,
> An hundreth thousand upon the bente;
>   The boldest ere even was made right meek.   (lines 3368–75)

The poem differs from its French source in a number of interesting ways besides its conciseness and chosen form. For the first time in English, the incestuous birth of Mordred gets a mention, though in the context of his pursuit of his father's wife: the poet devotes all his opprobrium to Mordred's own incestuous desires, not Arthur's unwitting act in begetting him. Also for the first time in English romance, Lancelot and Guinevere are presented as lovers. None the less, the separation of the story from the Grail quest means that the element of sexual sin and the contrast of earthly and heavenly chivalry are much less emphasised than in the French. Little is made of the adultery beyond what the narrative demands, and some episodes of the French that lay emphasis on it, such as Arthur's discovery of Lancelot's paintings, are omitted. The poem does, however, include the famous episode – famous not least from its reappearance in Malory – of Lancelot's encounter with Guinevere in the nunnery, which does not form a part of the received text of the *Cycle*.[16] Guinevere's refusal of a final kiss to Lancelot is the poet's own addition.

The poem seems to have been little known; Malory is the only subsequent author to make any use of it, and he was able to supplement his knowledge of the traditions of Mordred's incestuous birth and the adultery of Lancelot from earlier sections of the *Lancelot-Grail*. Even in the second half of the fifteenth century, those parts of the Arthurian story seem not to have been widely known, or else rejected as incompatible with the historical Arthur. A prose *Brut* of c. 1479, which incorporates a number of stories not found in Geoffrey (such as the stories of Constance and, from more recent history, Thomas Becket), makes a number of additions to its Arthurian material that indicate an indirect knowledge of the *Lancelot-Grail* version: a little about Longinus (original wielder of the bleeding lance) and Joseph of Arimathia; a *Merlin*-influenced account of the birth and childhood of Merlin; and a story of 'King Arthur and the Wildcats' which has an analogue in the *Merlin* story of Arthur's killing of the Demon Cat of Lausanne – all of them, as the editor of these interpolations notes, 'felines of decidedly anti-social and homicidal character.'[17] Neither Lancelot nor the Grail

---

[15] *La Mort le Roi Artu: roman du XIIIe siècle*, ed. Jean Frappier (Geneva, 1964), pp. 231–40.

[16] It survives in only a single manuscript, MS Palatinus Latinus 1967 (in Frappier's edition of *La Mort le Roi Artu*, pp. 264–6); translated by Norris J. Lacy in *Lancelot-Grail: The Old French Vulgate in Translation*, ed. Norris J. Lacy, 5 vols. (New York and London, 1993–96), IV, 158.

[17] Lister M. Matheson, 'The Arthurian Stories of Lambeth Palace Library MS 84,' *Arthurian Literature*, V (Cambridge, 1985), 86 [70–91].

is among the borrowings. They were eventually included in a chronicle version of British history by the Arthurian enthusiast John Harding, who wrote a verse chronicle of the history of Britain from Brut to his own times in the 1460s, but they underwent considerable metamorphosis in the process. As a historian, he used Geoffrey of Monmouth's account as the basis of his work, but he was keen to promote the greatest British king further through selective supplementation from the rival romance tradition. His interest in Arthur may indeed be one reason why he writes in verse, the medium still standard for Arthurian narrative, rather than the prose typical of chronicle. He does, however, choose the most serious and courtly form of verse available, rhyme royal – the verse form of Chaucer's *Troilus*. He certainly intended his work to be serious and courtly: he designed it for presentation to the King (or to the successive kings of the Wars of the Roses, first Henry VI, then Edward IV), and his inclusion of the Round Table and its knights, Lancelot among them, helps to shift the balance of the work towards courtly interests. He wrote it, however, at least in part as propaganda in support of the English claim to the throne of Scotland: King Lot, or Loth, the eponymous founder of the kingdom of Lothian, is accordingly the first person to pay homage to Arthur. This purpose also means that Harding is anxious to avoid anything that might denigrate the English, and he accordingly avoids anything morally dubious. Mordred is therefore Arthur's nephew, as in Geoffrey, not his son; and there is no affair between Lancelot and Guinevere. He includes a summary of the Grail quest, since it represented the summit of glory of the Arthurian age, but his Lancelot is married to Elaine, and begets Galahad 'in very clene spousage.'[18] This must have come as something of a surprise to readers familiar with the French versions of the stories; it is perhaps an indication of how many of Harding's English-speaking readers were not familiar with them. We need to consider very seriously a late-medieval population of England for the vast majority of whom Arthur was a great king supported by Gawain as his leading knight and overthrown by a usurping nephew; for whom Lancelot, if they had heard of him at all, was merely one of the minor knights; and to whom any ideas of Arthur's incest and Lancelot's adultery with Guinevere were either unknown, or else regarded as slanderous French fictions – as indeed they were.

For anything resembling an account of the early stages of Lancelot's love for Guinevere, anglophone readers had to wait until the very end of the century, since not even Malory gives the story. The Scottish *Lancelot of the Laik* is the last medieval work to be derived from the *Lancelot-Grail*, and the only work apart from Malory's *Morte Darthur* to draw on the prose *Lancelot*.[19] Although its composition may well post-date Caxton's publication of the *Morte* in 1485, the author shows no signs of knowing it. He was however strongly influenced by

---

18 *The Chronicle of Iohn Harding*, ed. Henry Ellis (London, 1812), ch. 76.
19 This has been most recently edited by Alan Lupack, *Lancelot of the Laik and Sir Tristrem* (Kalamazoo, 1994). There are also editions by W. W. Skeat (Early English Text Society, O.S. 6 [1865]), and by Margaret Muriel Gray (Scottish Text Society, N.S. 2 [1912]). Bertram Vogel, 'Secular Politics and the Date of *Lancelot of the Laik*,' *Studies in Philology*, 40 (1943), 1–13, suggested a date of 1482–1500 on the grounds that its lengthy section of political advice may have been directed at James III, but the advice is so generalized as to make a sure dating impossible.

Chaucer: he uses riding-rhyme, the Chaucerian ancestor of the pentameter couplet, and draws generously on the *Legend of Good Women*, the *General Prologue* and the *Knight's Tale*. He claims, in a prologue, to be writing in order to attract the love of his lady, in a rare predication of female readership for an English Arthurian work; but the contents of the poem accord rather ill with such an agenda, as love plays singularly little part in the work. It draws on only a small portion of the prose *Lancelot*, describing Arthur's war against Galiot (Galehot) from its inception to the renewal of the war a year later; Lancelot himself gets comparatively little mention, and most of that has to do with his prowess in battle. His birth, upbringing and early adventures are described in a massive rhetorical *occupatio* in the prologue (eighty lines of 'nor think I not to tell . . .'), but even there his decision to love Guinevere is allotted only one couplet; and in the main narrative, apart from a rather fine lyric lament in Book I, his role as lover is similarly secondary. Instead, the emphasis of the poem, and almost the whole of its lengthy second book, is devoted to an elaboration of the section of the prose *Lancelot* in which Arthur is instructed in good kingship by a wise clerk. It is true that the loss of leaves from the single surviving manuscript must have made some difference to the poem as we now read it: a summary in the prologue announces that it will cover not only the reconciliation between Arthur and Galiot brought about by Lancelot – the desirability of peace being an established element of mirror-for-princes literature – but also apparently the first admission of love between Lancelot and Guinevere:

> . . . How he (Lancelot) by the wais of fourtoune
> Tuex the two princis makith the accorde
> Of al there mortall weris to concorde;
> And how that Venus, siting hie abuf,
> Reuardith hyme of travell into love
> And makith hyme his ladice grace to have,
> And thankfully his service to resave.[20]

This 'reward' is of course the famous first kiss brokered by Galehot and the Dame de Malehot, which caused the downfall of Dante's Paolo and Francesca – 'Galeotto fu il libro, e chi lo scrisse' (*Inferno* V.137) ['the book was our Galehot, and whoever wrote it']. It is a section of the prose *Lancelot* that Malory either did not have or did not use;[21] in the absence of those final leaves of the poem, there is no Middle English account of how Lancelot and Guinevere fell in love. Even if the work had survived complete, however, one suspects that it would have retained its heavy weighting towards political advice. Dante's account of the kiss takes for granted the adultery that follows, but there is no evidence that the Scots *Lancelot* ever included that; there are too few leaves missing to take the

---

[20] Ed. Lupack, lines 306–12. The events recounted in the poem correspond to *Lancelot: roman en prose du XIIIe siècle*, ed. Alexandre Micha, 8 vols. (Geneva, 1978–82), 7:434–8:72; if completed, it would presumably have continued to 8:128.

[21] Probably, that he did not use: he shows some familiarity with the early parts of the *Lancelot* in Lancelot's account of Guinevere's assistance at the time of his being made knight, and although the story is not quite the same as in the prose *Lancelot*, the variants may well be Malory's own (ed. Vinaver, p. 1058; Caxton, XVIII.7).

story so far. Stopping short with the kiss would accord with its concern with the fashioning of the wise king, the deep British disquiet with adultery, and also the author's proclaimed purpose of winning his lady's heart: continuing into the affair would have warned her rather to lock her door against him.

Sir Thomas Malory's contribution to the history of the *Lancelot-Grail Cycle* in England is therefore unique, by virtue not only of its range, but its comprehensiveness across all the available Arthurian traditions. He combined the historical account of Arthur deriving from Geoffrey of Monmouth with the *Lancelot-Graal* version into a single plausible history; a history that, like Harding's, includes the Grail quest, but, unlike Harding, also comprehends the incestuous birth of Mordred and the love of Lancelot and Guinevere as a catalyst for the downfall. Those choices were unique for a writer working with the historical tradition; but their nature as *choices* must be emphasized. Malory had both the historical and the *Cycle* traditions available to him, and where they were at odds he made his own, unparalleled selection, to produce a unique redaction of Arthurian material. His continuing strong historical interests show not only in his use of the Geoffrey-derived alliterative *Morte Arthure* as one of his sources, but in his historicizing of the *Cycle* material. There is an insistent location in contemporary English topography of many of the exotic place-names of the original: Camelot is identified with Winchester, no doubt because of the presence in the Great Hall there of the Round Table; Joyous Guard becomes Bambrough, the mighty castle that commands the Northumberland coast. Action dominates over feeling; magic or supernatural elements are reduced; and the style in which he writes leans strongly towards the chronicle.[22] His selection of material is almost exactly complementary to the later versions of *The Birth of Merlin*, which stop just before Uther's affair with Igraine. Malory designs his own work to cover Arthur's life, from the circumstances of his begetting to his disappearance with Morgan in the barge, with only a short coda beyond that to bring Guinevere and Lancelot to their own deaths. He is not therefore interested in the early history of the Grail: he recounts a version of those parts of the story that are retold in the course of the Grail quest, but he either did not have, or did not use, a copy of the *Estoire*. Similarly, he is not interested in the early life of Merlin, or perhaps believes it to be sufficiently covered by *The Birth of Merlin*.

A summary of the sources of his work will indicate both the extent of his use of the *Lancelot-Grail*, and some of the puzzles associated with his selection of material. Copies of parts of the *Lancelot-Grail* are known to have been available in England – it seems rarely or never to have circulated complete, even in France – and Malory would probably not have needed to go to France to find his source romances.[23] It is still open to question, however, how much material he had beyond his principal sources: whether, for instance, he had significant access to the *Cycle*'s *Merlin*, to the whole of the *Lancelot*, or to the *Tristan* version of the

---

22 See in particular the studies by P. J. C. Field, *Romance and Chronicle: A Study of Malory's Prose Style* (Bloomington, IN, and London, 1971); Mark Lambert, *Malory: Style and Vision in* Le Morte Darthur (New Haven, 1975); Andrew Lynch, *Malory's Book of Arms: The Narrative of Combat in* Le Morte Darthur (Cambridge, 1997).

23 Carol M. Meale, 'Manuscripts, Readers and Patrons in Fifteenth-Century England: Sir Thomas Malory and Arthurian Romance,' *Arthurian Literature*, IV (1985), 93–126.

Grail quest.[24] The titles of the individual sections of the work given below are those used by Eugène Vinaver, many of them being based on the incipits or colophons appearing in the manuscript; Vinaver's further claim that the tales represent eight separate works has however been greeted with considerable resistance, and is not implied here.[25] Caxton's book numbers are given for ease of cross-reference.

The Tale of King Arthur (Caxton I–IV): from the post-Vulgate *Suite du Merlin*

Malory's redaction starts part-way through the text, with the begetting and birth of Arthur and his drawing the sword from the stone: this material is common to the original *Merlin* and to the post-Vulgate *Suite*. The *Suite* provides the stories of his consolidation of his kingdom, of Balin and Balan, of his marriage to Guinevere, of Accolon, and of Pelleas (though his final falling in love with the Lady of the Lake is Malory's own invention: in the French, he is reconciled to Ettarde). The later adventures of Marhalt and Uwain also appear to be original to Malory. The logic of the narrative indicates that the omission of the early stages of the story before the begetting of Arthur must be deliberate, rather than because the copy of the *Suite* from which he was working had lost its opening leaves; that would certainly be true if the manuscript he used is the one surviving in the Cambridge University Library, which was in English ownership in the fifteenth century and which contains an annotation from c. 1500 noting where Malory's own version starts.[26] His choice of the post-Vulgate *Suite* rather than the *Merlin* proper to start his work may similarly have been deliberate, and not simply due to the unavailability of the *Cycle* text: see the discussion in the next section.

The Tale of the Noble King Arthur that was Emperor himself through dignity of his hands (Caxton V): from the late fourteenth-century Middle English alliterative *Morte Arthure*

Stylistically very different from the rest of the work on account of its retention of many of the northernisms and the alliterative structure of its original, this section raises both major textual problems (the versions in the manuscript and in Caxton's print are substantially different, and there is considerable debate as to whether the revision was carried out by Caxton, by Malory himself, or some

---

[24] James I. Wimsatt suggests that Malory had access to the whole of the *Lancelot-Grail Cycle*, the Post-Vulgate Cycle (including the *Suite du Merlin* and the *Roman du Graal*) and the *Tristan* ('The Idea of a Cycle: Malory, the *Lancelot-Grail*, and the *Prose Tristan*,' in *The Lancelot-Grail Cycle: Texts and Transformations*, ed. William W. Kibler [Austin, TX, 1994], pp. 206–18); but from what we know about manuscript circulation, such extensive knowledge would be highly unlikely.

[25] Various critics have suggested anything from four to eleven parts, or denied that there is any significant division at all. For a recent discussion, see Carol M. Meale, ' "The Hoole Book": Editing and the Creation of Meaning in Malory's Text,' in *A Companion to Malory*, ed. Elizabeth Archibald and A. S. G. Edwards (Cambridge, 1996), pp. 3–18.

[26] CUL, MS Add. 7071; the annotation is found at the top of fol. 189r. Vinaver (*Works of Sir Thomas Malory*, pp. 1280–1) declares that the manuscript is not Malory's source, but he does not give any decisive evidence, i.e. of material common to Malory and other manuscripts of the *Suite* but not found in Add. 7071.

unknown third party),[27] and also the question of whether Malory did indeed have knowledge of the *Cycle*'s *Merlin*. Geoffrey of Monmouth had placed a nine-year space between Arthur's great conquests in Europe and the war against Rome from which he was recalled to Britain by Mordred's usurpation; these nine years allowed a space in which the adventures of Arthur's knights could be located. The *Cycle*'s *Merlin*, however, conflates the two wars, and gives them the same placing as in Malory, after Arthur's pacification of his kingdom. The *Mort Artu* also gives the Roman wars a brief mention, but after Arthur's campaign against Lancelot, just before his return to fight against Mordred; and a second source almost certainly known to Malory, the fifteenth-century rhymed *Chronicle* of John Harding, likewise places them at the end, after its account of the Grail quest, which Harding locates immediately before the arrival of the Roman ambassadors.[28] Whether Malory was adapting the chronicle tradition in re-inserting the space for adventure after Arthur's exploits on the continent, or whether he was following the *Cycle*'s *Merlin*, is not finally resolvable.[29]

The Most Noble Tale of Sir Launcelot du Lake (Caxton VI): principally from the prose *Lancelot*[30]

Malory's choice of episodes is very selective indeed. He adopts three stories, together constituting only about 2.5% of the original, all from the second half of the *Lancelot* and two from close to the end: those of Lancelot's abduction by four queens (three sorceresses in the French), his rescue of Lionel and other knights from Sir Tarquin, and his riding disguised in Kay's armor.[31] These episodes are supplemented by his adventure at the Chapel Perilous, which has its closest analogue, probably its source, in the *Perlesvaus*. The most surprising thing about the Tale is how much Malory leaves out: there is nothing on Lancelot's birth or upbringing (an alternative version has received a mention in his *Suite du Merlin* material), and his love for the Queen is raised only in order for him to reject both marriage and all love *paramours* as ways of life for knights errant: 'who that usyth paramours shall be unhappy, and all thynge unhappy that is aboute them' (ed. Vinaver, p. 271; Caxton, VI.10). The other major episode of the *Lancelot* that

---

27 Vinaver's view that Caxton had carried out the revision was first contested by William Matthews in a lecture in 1975; the whole summer issue of *Arthuriana*, 5.2 (1995) is devoted to the debate, and Matthews' own work is posthumously printed as 'A Question of Texts,' *Arthuriana*, 7 (1997), 93–133. The debate is reprinted and reviewed in *The Malory Debate: Essays on the Texts of Le Morte Darthur*, ed. Bonnie Wheeler, Robert L. Kindrick, and Michael N. Salda (Cambridge, 2000).

28 *The Chronicle of Iohn Harding*, caps. 77–83 (pp. 133–46).

29 The fullest discussion is by Ad Putter, 'Finding Time for Romance: Mediaeval Arthurian Literary History,' *Medium Ævum*, 63.1 (1994), 1–16. Contrary to scholars such as Matthews ('A Question of Texts,' 101–13, in which he also points out some correspondences of detail) and Wimsatt, 'The Idea of a Cycle,' Putter comes down against Malory's knowledge of the Vulgate *Merlin*.

30 See P. J. C. Field, 'Malory and the French Prose *Lancelot*,' reprinted in his *Malory: Texts and Sources* (Cambridge, 1998), pp. 199–233, for a discussion as to what kind of manuscript Malory may have used.

31 *LM* 4:165–95, 5:26–45, 281–92 (*Lancelot-Grail in Translation* (ed. Lacy), trans. William W. Kibler, III, 153–61; trans. Carleton W. Carroll, III, 274–7). The begetting of Galahad follows immediately after the first of these sections in the *Lancelot*; Malory delays that until the end of his *Tristram*, which also serves as his source for the episode.

Malory uses, the 'Knight of the Cart' story in which Lancelot is shown sleeping with Guinevere, comes much later in his version despite its early placing in the French: see 'The Book of Sir Launcelot and Queen Guinevere' below.

The Tale of Sir Gareth of Orkney (Caxton VII): probably original to Malory

Analogous stories are those of La Cote Male Tayle, which Malory adapts in his *Tristram*, and the stories of Le Bel Inconnu and Ipomedon, both of which existed in English metrical versions. Malory makes the 'good knight' Gareth one of his principal characters after Lancelot and Arthur himself; his creation of such a role indeed constitutes forceful evidence of his having conceived of the *Morte Darthur* as in some sense a single work. His Gareth is the youngest son of King Lot, and therefore corresponds with the Guerrehet of the *Suite du Merlin* but with the Gaheriet of the *Merlin*. The respect accorded him for his chivalry and his place in the events leading to Arthur's downfall correspond to the *Cycle*'s Gaheriet; but Malory transfers Gaheriet's less attractive exploits (such as his murder of his mother, recounted in both the prose *Lancelot* and the *Tristram*) to the third son, whom he names Gaheris.

The Book of Sir Tristram de Lyones (Caxton VIII–XII): from the Prose *Tristan*

Malory brings the *Tristan* down to about one-sixth of its length in the French original, but it still constitutes just about a third of his own book. As such, it fulfils one of the major roles of the *Cycle*'s *Lancelot*, of supplying an account of the central part of Arthur's reign, after he has established himself against the warring kings and before the breaking of the Round Table fellowship in the Grail quest and the downfall. Malory takes over from the *Tristan* some episodes that also occur in the *Lancelot*, in particular those that relate to the feud between the sons of Lot and Pellinore (including Gaheriet-Gaheris's killing of his mother) or that look forward to the Grail quest itself – the conception and birth of Galahad, Lancelot's madness, and the curing of Bors and Percival by the Grail. His statement at the end, that 'Here ys no rehersall of the thirde booke' of the *Tristan*, may indicate either that he did not have a copy, or that he preferred to switch to the *Lancelot-Grail* version for his account of the Grail quest.

The Tale of the Sankgreal (Caxton XIII–XVII): from the *Cycle*'s *Queste del Saint Graal*

This is the section of his work in which Malory adheres most closely to his source, with some abbreviation; but that closeness does not prevent him from making striking alterations to the significance and meaning of the narrative. Lancelot has a strong claim to being the hero of the story, despite, or because of, his failure; and although divine principles are recognized as being stronger than the world's, God does not steal the show. To quote the conclusion of Sandra Ness Ihle's detailed study of the two versions, 'From a completely allegorical work whose adventures are a means to a partial discovery of a higher truth, [Malory] has fashioned a tale whose final goal becomes an excuse for the discovery, through adventure, of the good to which man can attain on earth.'[32]

---

[32] Sandra Ness Ihle, *Malory's Grail Quest: Invention and Adaptation in Medieval Prose Romance* (Madison, WI, 1983), p. 164.

The Book of Sir Launcelot and Queen Guinevere (Caxton XVIII–XIX):
from the *Mort Artu*, the English stanzaic *Morte Arthur*,
some version of *Lancelot*, and original invention

Malory largely follows the selection of events from the *Mort Artu* already made
by its English adaptation, the stanzaic *Morte Arthur*, and accordingly omits
Arthur's seeing Lancelot's paintings of his love for Guinevere: the English
Arthur never has direct evidence of the couple's adultery. The principal episodes
Malory takes from the French and the stanzaic poem are those of the poisoned
apple, and the maid of Ascolat; he also includes Lancelot's wounding by a
hunter (who in his version becomes a huntress), an episode not included in the
English poem. In his greatest single textual intervention in the entire work,
Malory inserts at this point the story of the Knight of the Cart, which the prose
Lancelot places earlier than any of his other borrowings from the romance.
Malory's version does, however, differ significantly from that in the *Lancelot*,
whether because he was working from a different source or because he was
making alterations beyond what his own story required. One small but telling
difference from the prose *Lancelot*, for instance, occurs when Lancelot recalls the
incident from his knighting when Arthur failed to gird on his sword, not elsewhere described by Malory; but the account differs from that in the *Lancelot*,
with Lancelot himself mislaying his sword 'thorow my hastynes . . . and my
lady, youre quene, founde hit, and lapped hit in her trayne, and gave me my
swerde whan I had nede thereto; and ells had I bene shamed.'[33] What is beyond
question is that by inserting the 'Knight of the Cart' episode at this point in his
Arthuriad, Malory introduces an extraordinary, and entirely original, climax to
his work, in which Lancelot rescues Guinevere three times (the third occurs in
the next Tale) but with an increasing presumption of guilt on each occasion.
Between the last two, however – that is, immediately following the 'Knight of
the Cart' episode, and closing this Tale – Lancelot performs the miracle of the
healing of Sir Urry, an episode which appears to be Malory's own invention.

The most piteous Tale of the Morte Arthur saunz Guerdon
(Caxton XX–XXI): the English stanzaic *Morte Arthur*,
supplemented for some small details by the *Mort Artu*

Malory's direct dependence on the English poem is abundantly attested by
numerous verbal parallels; it is hard to find any points in this section where the
Mort Artu is not transmitted through the English. His spare account of the last
battle, for instance, shows the closeness of his adherence: 'ever they fought
stylle tylle hit was nere nyght, and by than was there an hondred thousand
leyde dede upon the downe.'[34] He was also ready to make significant additions
of his own, including Lancelot's great speech of defense and justification to

---

33 Ed. Vinaver, p. 1058; Caxton, XVIII.7. In the prose *Lancelot*, Arthur fails to gird on Lancelot's
    sword because the young knight is distracted by other adventures, and he chooses to have it
    girded on him by the Queen herself (*LM* 7:261–87); trans. Samuel N. Rosenberg, *Lancelot-Grail
    in Translation*, ed. Lacy, II, 61–8.
34 Ed. Vinaver, p. 1236; Caxton, XI.4; the manuscript reads 'uppon the erthe.' Compare the
    quotation on p. 152 above.

Arthur when he brings Guinevere back to the King. Malory retains from the poem, almost verbatim, the episode in which Lancelot finds Guinevere in a nunnery and she makes her final rejection of him, including her refusal of a last kiss.

It should be clear from this outline that Malory's 'whole book of King Arthur,' to use the least tendentious of the various possible titles,[35] is very far from being the *Lancelot-Grail* in English. He omitted vast tracts; he ranged far outside it for alternative sources both between and within narrative episodes; he was ready to invent; and the resulting emphasis of his redaction is very different. He made as new and coherent a work out of his various sources as Shakespeare made out of Chaucer and Ovid and fairy-stories when he wrote *A Midsummer Night's Dream*. Even when he is working most closely to his sources, as in the Grail quest, he will give his *matière* an entirely new *sens* (*sentence* in Middle English), as a result of a series of small but consistent changes made across the whole work – not only within his *Tale of the Sankgreall* but over the rest of his Arthuriad too. Critics have often delighted in pointing out inconsistencies in the work; Vinaver used them in support of his argument that Malory wrote not one single work but eight separate ones. Much less commented on is the consistency that he intro-duces. Knights who appear in the sources only for the early parts of his work are brought in again at the end; those who figure in his sources for the end are often given pre-histories. The result is a sense of a hinterland of adventures for the entire fellowship, so that the work becomes not only a 'life and death of Arthur' but a life and death of the whole of the Round Table. Nor are the two separate. It is sometimes held against Malory that King Arthur is weak, or offstage, for much of the work; but by contrast with the *Lancelot-Grail*, Malory keeps him notably central. The Round Table and its fellowship are always presented in their association with Arthur, and the adventures of the individual knights always keep that as their focus – even Tristram, whose great desire is to be asso-ciated with the Round Table, and even more Lancelot himself. In the *Lancelot-Grail*, Lancelot spends much of his career operating in effect as a free-lance; in Malory, he is shown repeatedly at court, or in relation to the knights of the fellowship, or sending defeated opponents back to the Queen. His beloved friend in the French, Galehot, is effectively written out of Malory's version, and his relationship with Arthur is enlarged to fill a comparable thematic space.

Malory never forgets, or allows his readers to forget, the participation of his knights in the fellowship focused on the King. The knights' oath of chivalry, based by Malory on the oath taken at the ceremonial of the Order of the Bath and inserted into his *Suite du Merlin* material,[36] becomes a measure of chivalry that underlies the whole work. His knights offer something of a taxonomy of

---

[35] Vinaver claimed that the title given the work by Caxton, *Le Morte Darthur*, properly referred to the last section alone, and was a misunderstanding on his part; William Matthews mounts a spirited, and almost certainly correct, defence of the title having been Malory's own for the whole book: 'The Besieged Printer,' *Arthuriana*, 7.1 (1997), 85–8.

[36] Viscount Dillon, 'A Manuscript Collection of Ordinances of Chivalry of the Fifteenth Century,' *Archaeologia*, 57.1 (1900), 67–8 [27–70]; ed. Vinaver, p. 120; Caxton, III.15.

chivalry, not just by virtue of the supremacy of the Grail knights, but within the secular world too. Lancelot is the peak, and is presented markedly differently from in the prose *Lancelot*. He is extremely reluctant to kill his opponents; he is never seen languishing for love; the overtly sexual nature of his love for Guinevere is played down (only once, in the 'Knight of the Cart' episode, does he explicitly sleep with her, though the magic that twice lands him in bed with Elaine the daughter of Pelles acknowledges that the affair exists); and he is given much more sympathetic treatment in the Grail quest, including a final message of greeting from Galahad. Lancelot is backed by a group of other 'good knights,' in Malory's phrase: chief among them being Tristram, who is defined in terms of his relationship with Lancelot,[37] and Gareth, Malory's reworking of Gaheriet-Guerrehet, who is now given a largely original biography that spans much of the work, and which leaves all the chivalrically dubious actions with Gaheris. Gawain is a much less sympathetic character in Malory than he is in either the prose *Lancelot* or elsewhere in the English tradition: the *Suite du Merlin*, the *Cycle*'s *Grail Quest* and the Prose *Tristan* all make him less than admirable, and Malory seems contented to follow suit. He does, however, treat Gawain with notable respect through Agravain's accusation of Lancelot and the rescuing of the Queen from the fire, a respect that is essential if the tragic irony of Gawain's feud with Lancelot over the death of Gareth – the brother that both of them have most loved – is to carry its full weight.

This emphasis on the whole fellowship, and on earthly chivalry, in turn makes for a very different kind of meaning carried by the whole book from that found in the *Lancelot-Grail*. Individual hermits on the Grail quest may condemn earthly chivalry and earthly love – and Malory seems entirely content that they should do so: that is what hermits are for – but he gives singularly little sign of endorsing such a moral for the whole work. What Malory shows as going wrong in his Arthurian world, and what he shows as good, do not belong to different moral schemata. His intensification of both human tragedy and of God's approval of earthly knighthood is demonstrated by his greatest single departure from the broad outline of the *Lancelot-Grail* structure: his relocation of the 'Knight of the Cart' episode into the course of the *Mort Artu*. This is the one incident in the whole of his work in which Lancelot explicitly makes love to the Queen; Malory places it as the central one of three increasingly incriminating accusations of Guinevere – of the poisoned apple, of sleeping with the wounded knights (or with Kay, in the prose *Lancelot* version of the 'Cart' episode), and of adultery with Lancelot when she is surprised with him in her chamber: a series that follows a progression from her innocence, to her innocence on a technicality, to a presumption of guilt.[38] Malory also, however, encloses his Knight of the Cart interpolation within two passages apparently of his own invention. It is preceded by his own encomium of 'the olde love' used in King Arthur's days, a

---

[37] See Helen Cooper, 'The Book of Sir Tristram de Lyones,' in Archibald and Edwards, *Companion to Malory*, pp. 183–202.

[38] Malory refuses to endorse their guilt within the narrative, however: 'Whether they were abed other at other maner of disportis, me lyste nat thereof make no mencion, for love that tyme was nat as love ys nowadayes' (ed. Vinaver, p. 1165; Caxton, XX.3).

passage that ends with praise of Guinevere, 'that whyle she lyved she was a trew lover, and therefor she had a good ende' (ed. Vinaver, p. 1120; Caxton, XVIII.25) – a formula of good death that effectively insists that God's approval of faithful love far outweighs His disapproval of adultery. Following the episode, Malory inserts the healing of Sir Urry, in which God goes still further, in allowing Lancelot his own personal miracle. When Malory speaks in his own narrative voice to allot blame for the downfall of Arthur, he points the finger at Agravain and Mordred and their hatred of Lancelot, not at Lancelot and the Queen. In the *Mort Artu*, God's displeasure is explicit in the final battle between Arthur and Mordred, but Malory makes the operative principle destiny rather than divine judgement. When God re-enters his narrative, it is for Guinevere's repentance in the nunnery – she blames herself, as the narrative never does – and for her final rejection of Lancelot. Malory never tells of the famous first kiss, the one that speeds Paolo and Francesca to hell; but the kiss that never happens is one of the greatest moments of Arthurian narrative in any language. Lancelot tells her,

> 'But sythen I fynde you thus desposed, I ensure you faythfully, I wyl ever take me to penaunce and praye whyle my lyf lasteth, yf that I may fynde ony heremyte, other graye or whyte, that wyl receyve me. Wherfore, madame, I praye you kysse me, and never no more.'
> 'Nay,' sayd the quene, 'that shal I never do, but absteyne you from suche werkes.'
> And they departed.   (ed. Vinaver, p. 1253; Caxton, XXI.10)

Lancelot proceeds to die, not only being heaved up into heaven by angels, but in the odour of sanctity. A final addition of Malory's gives the strong implication that this is due to his excellence not as a penitent, but as a knight. Ector's threnody over his corpse, probably inspired by the laments over Gawain in the alliterative *Morte Arthure*, doubles as a threnody for all earthly chivalry:

> 'And now I dare say,' sayd sir Ector, 'thou sir Launcelot, there thou lyest, that thou were never matched of erthely knyghtes hande. And thou were the curtest knyght that ever bare shelde! And thou were the truest frende to thy lovar that ever bestrade hors, and thou were the trewest lover, of a synful man, that ever loved woman, and thou were the kyndest man that ever strake wyth swerde.'
> (ed. Vinaver, p. 1259; Caxton, XXI.13)

It is impossible to imagine a *Lancelot-Grail* that would finish with such regret for a lost world of knightliness and love.

14

Lancelot in Italy

DONALD L. HOFFMAN

The most perceptive student of the Lancelot tradition in Italy may well be Francesca da Rimini. The well-read adulteress provides important evidence that, although no medieval Italian text of the prose *Lancelot* exists,[1] the story was familiar, at least to the noble and educated, in fourteenth-century Italy.[2] Almost too well known to merit repetition, her discussion of the *Lancelot* nevertheless raises too many relevant issues not to require yet another look.

> 'Ma s'a conoscer la prima radice
>   del nostro amor tu hai cotanto affetto.
>   dirò come colui che piange e dice.
> Noi leggiavamo un giorno per diletto
>   di Lancialotto come amor lo strinse;
>   soli eravamo e sanza alcuno sospetto.
> Per più fiate li occhi ci sospinse
>   quella lettura, e scolorocci il viso;
>   ma solo un punto fu quel che vinse.
> Quando leggemmo il disïato riso
>   esser basciato da cotanto amante,
>   questi, che mai da me non fia diviso,
> la bocca mi basciò tutto tremante.
>   Galeotto fu 'l libro e chi lo scrisse:
>   quel giorno più non vi leggemmo avante.'   (*Inf.* V.124–38)

['But if you have such great desire to know the first root of our love, I will tell you as one who weeps and tells. One day, for pastime, we read of Lancelot, how love constrained him; we were alone, suspecting nothing. Several times that reading urged our eyes to meet and took the color from our faces, but one moment alone it was that

---

[1] The sixteenth century does seem to display a rise in interest in Lancelot, as evidenced, for example, by a Venetian text: *L'illustre, et famosa historia di Lancialotto del lago, che fu al tempo del Re Artù, nellaquale si fu fa mentione dei gran fatti & alta sua caualleria & di molti altri ualorosi cauallieri suoi compagni della tauola ritonda* (Venice, 1558–59). Selections from this printing were edited in the nineteenth century by Francesco Zambrini (Bologna, 1862).

[2] Her learning shows, for example, in the Vergilian allusion with which she opens her *Lancelot* recollection: ' "Nessun maggior dolore/ che ricordarsi del tempo felice/ ne la miseria" ' (*Inf.* V.121–23) ['There is no greater sorrow than to recall, in wretchedness, the happy time']. The edition I use is Dante Alighieri, *The Divine Comedy*, trans. Charles S. Singleton, *Inferno*, vol. 1: *Italian Text and Translation* (Princeton, 1970). Translations of other works in this essay are my own unless otherwise indicated.

> overcame us. When we read how the longed-for smile was kissed by
> so great a lover, this one, who never shall be parted from me, kissed
> my mouth all trembling. A Gallehaut was the book and he who wrote
> it; that day we read no farther in it.']

This *abbreviatio* of a crucial moment in the adultery of Lancelot and Guinevere
(itself a 'cover' for a crucial moment in the adultery of Paolo and Francesca)
indicates Dante's (and Francesca's) knowledge of the story but, as many have
noted,[3] it provides no clue as to what version of the *Lancelot-Grail* might have
been available to either the poet of Florence or the lady of Rimini.

This irrecoverable source is analogous to Francesca's attempt to achieve an
infinite recession of blame (i.e. 'it was the book's fault,' *but* there is no book), and
an ever increasing procession of complicity. Francesca's crime includes the book,
the author, the art of reading, and Dante himself, since he elicits her narration.
The concentric circles of implication expand, however, to include some lines that
precede her specific recollection of the *Lancelot-Grail*:

> 'Amor, ch'al cor gentil ratto s'apprende,
>   prese costui de la bella persona
>   che mi fu tolta; e 'l modo ancor m'offende.
> Amor, ch'a nullo amato amar perdona,
>   me prese del costui piacer sì forte,
>   che, come vedi, ancor non m'abbandona.
> Amor, condusse noi ad una morte.'   (*Inf.* V.100–106)

> ['Love, which is quickly kindled in a gentle heart, seized this one for
> the fair form that was taken from me – and the way of it afflicts me
> still. Love, which absolves no loved one from loving, seized me so
> strongly with delight in him, that, as you see, it does not leave me
> even now. Love brought us to one death.']

In these lines, Francesca adopts the elegant poetics of the *dolce stil nuovo* and
echoes as well the *cortesìa* of the courtly poets of France and their early Italian
imitators at the court of Frederick II in Palermo. The language of *amour courtois*
crashes to a halt, however, in the third invocation of Amor that leads to a single
death. The combination of courtliness and love inextricably entwined with
death inevitably evokes the legend of Tristan and Isolde. For Francesca, and
perhaps for all who recollect Lancelot and Guinevere, their association with
Tristan and Isolde is all but automatic. Francesca's rhetorical glide from Tristan
to Lancelot represents, however, a kind of metonym for the history of Lancelot
in Italy.

In France, the verse narratives of Tristan and Lancelot are as distinct as the
careers and *oeuvres* of Thomas and Chrétien de Troyes. But in the prose tradition,
the *Lancelot-Grail Cycle* precedes the prose *Tristan* and the latter cycle attempts to
include much of the *Lancelot* material. In Italy the influence of the *Tristan* is
pervasive, whereas the influence of the *Lancelot* is elusive, perhaps because the

---

3   Most recently, Daniela Delcorno Branca, 'Dante and the *Roman de Lancelot*,' in *Text and Intertext
    in Medieval Arthurian Literature*, ed. Norris J. Lacy (New York, 1996), p. 134 [133–45].

Tristan is considered more 'correct' because it is more inclusive. As Francesca suggests, even when a *raconteuse* chooses to tell a story about Lancelot, she almost automatically frames it with the themes and ambience of *Tristan*. In Italy, Tristan inevitably takes precedence over Lancelot.[4]

This does not mean, however, that the prose *Lancelot* was unknown or without influence. Before Dante, casual allusions occur with some frequency. Several of these refer to Lancelot and Tristan together as patterns of chivalry, as in Brunetto Latini's dedication of the *Tesoretto* to the *valente signore* whom he compares to Tristan and Lancelot and, for good measure, to Hector and Achilles as well.[5] Lancelot does, however, stand on his own on many occasions. In the thirteenth century, Guittone d'Arezzo's Sonnet 62 recognizes him as the model of knighthood: 'Siccome a Lancellotto omo simiglia/ un prode cavalier, simil se face/ a lei, di fere donna a maraviglia'[6] [Even as a man compares a valiant knight to Lancelot, so a wondrously austere lady is likened to her (Gardner, p. 27)]. Folgore di San Gimignano also refers to Lancelot in a poem addressed to a Sienese spendthrift club:

> Prodi e cortesi più che Lancialotto;
> se bisognasse, con le lance in mano,
> farian torneamenti a Camelotto.[7]

> [Valiant and courteous more than Lancelot, if need were, with lance in hand, they would make tournaments at Camelot (Gardner, p. 42)]

More important and more precise than these is Lapuccio Belfradelli's canzone, 'Donna senza pietanza,' which records for the first time in Italian, Galeotto's love for Lancelotto:

> Pensate a Galeotto,
> di ciò c'a Lancelotto
> promise in sua vogliena,
> che no volle mentire:
> poi ch'ebe dato il botto
> ad Artu re d'a'motto
> li si diede in servenza.[8]

> [Think of Galehaut, of what he promised Lancelot at his will, which he would not gainsay; after he had overthrown King Arthur, at a word he yielded to him in allegiance. (Gardner, p. 33)]

---

4 The same is not true, however, of Lancelot's lover. The rescue of 'Winloge' (usually, if not universally, assumed to be Guinevere) graces the famous Modena archivolt more than a century before any literary mention of Lancelot in Italy.
5 Edmund G. Gardner, *The Arthurian Legend in Italian Literature* (London, 1930), p. 32.
6 Guittone d'Arezzo, *Le Rime di Fra Guittone d'Arezzo*, ed. Francesco Pellegrini (Bologna, 1901), p. 93. The feminine model in this comparison is Guittone's lady, not Guinevere.
7 Aldo Francesco Massèra, ed., *Sonnetti burleschi e realistici dei primi due secoli*, 2 vols. (Bari, 1920), I, 105.
8 From Codex Vaticanus 3793, no. 296; cited in Gardner, p. 33. An earlier poem in the manuscript, no. 290, refers to Lancelot's fidelity to Guinevere when he had been imprisoned by Morgan.

Similarly, Guinevere is usually linked with Isolde, as in Dante's list of courtly
lovers and Maestro Torrigiano's praise of *la compiuta donzella di Firenze* as being
greater than either Guinevere or Isolde, because of her great skill in the poetic
arts.[9]

While Francesca reflects the Italian subordination of Lancelot to Tristan, the
most important medieval Italian Arthurian romance, the *Tavola Ritonda*, demonstrates the process with unusual clarity.[10] The *Tavola* is an imaginative
re-working of the prose Tristan, including a Grail narrative that develops a
contrast between Tristan and Lancelot as lovers, as has recently been noted.[11]
While it energetically celebrates the love that transcends death and virtually
canonizes Tristan as a tragic saint of Eros, it has unusually little sympathy with
Lancelot's tragic situation. The text recognizes the traditional 'conflict of love
and honor' that afflicts Tristan,[12] but is less understanding of Lancelot's tortured
conflict between earthly and spiritual chivalry. The complex triad of Lancelot's
loves, Arthur, Guinevere and God (which, properly ordered, reflect the affective
hierarchy defined by the commentaries on the three Greek words for love –
philia, *erôs*, and *agapê*), are reduced to a mere problem of instability.

For the author of the *Tavola*, love of God is hardly of greater significance than
Dante's love for the screen lady at the beginning of the *Vita Nuova* or the *donna
gentile* who appears at the window before he returns to his love of Beatrice. Like
these ladies, God is little more than a distraction and a temptation to infidelity.
In the *Tavola* Lancelot is not praised for his desire for the Grail or honored for his
love of God; rather, he is merely excused for his weakness in allowing himself to
be converted from the path of true love, and pardoned for his lapse in fidelity to
his lady Guinevere. His brief flirtation with the Grail demotes him to second
place behind Tristan, whom the *Tavola* author, like Francesca, recognizes as the
pattern of the lover faithful unto death.

The crucial separation of Tristan and Lancelot occurs in Chapter CXV:

Ed essendo in fra due confini, Tristano si diparte da Lancialotto, e Lancialotto da
Tristano; imperò che Tristano lascia la'mprese del Sangradale, per ritornare a
vedere la bella reina Isotta la bionda. E sie si diparte sanza commiato, imperò che
non era allicenziato; chè men era tanto degno, cioè fermo, che, per ricevere la
grazia, lasciasse il pensiere del peccato; ed era assai più desideroso de veder la

---

9   Gardner, p. 34; Ernesto Monaci, ed., *Crestomazi Italiana dei Primi Secoli* (Città di Castello, 1912),
    p. 281.
10 *La Tavola Ritonda*, ed. Filippo-Luigi Polidori, 2 vols. (Bologna, 1864–65). This is probably the
    most studied of the Italian prose romances. It is likely to receive even greater recognition
    among English-speaking scholars since it is the only one of these works currently available in
    English in Anne Shaver's accessible and readable translation, which I use here: *Tristan and the
    Round Table: A Translation of 'La Tavola Ritonda,'* trans. Ann Shaver (Binghamton, NY, 1983).
11 Donald L. Hoffman, '*Radix Amoris*: The *Tavola Ritonda* and its Response to Dante's Paolo and
    Francesca,' in *Tristan and Isolde: A Casebook*, ed. Joan Tasker Grimbert (New York, 1995),
    pp. 207–22; Joan Grimbert, 'Translating Tristan-Love from the *Prose Tristan* to the *Tavola
    Ritonda*,' *Romance Languages Annual*, 6 (1995), 92–7.
12 The phrase is fairly traditional, but is also the title of an important contribution by Joan
    Ferrante which includes one of the earliest careful readings of the *Tavola* by a scholar writing
    in English (excluding of course the discussion in Gardner, whose ground-breaking work on
    the Italian Arthurian tradition has been refined, but not surpassed). See Ferrante, *The Conflict
    of Love and Honor: The Medieval Tristan Legend in France, Germany, and Italy* (The Hague, 1973).

reina Isotta, che di sedere alla santa Tavola, sì come sedeano i dodici cavalieri ch'erano sanza pensiere di peccato carnale, e sanza odio nè superbia; chè peccato d'avarizia non regnava in quel tempo. . . . [I]l pensiere e la volontà de vedere Isotta, tolsa a Tristano la grazia di non vedere e di non sentire; e se non ciò fosse stato, sarebbe stato, pella sua leanza e cortesia, degli primi a vedere e a gustare la grazia del santo Vasello. (*Tavola Ritonda* 453–4)[13]

[Coming to two boundary posts, Tristano and Lancilotto took leave of each other, because Tristano was leaving the quest for the Sangradale to go back to the beautiful Queen Isotta the Blonde. And if he departed without leave – for he was not dismissed – it was because he was not worthy, that is, chosen to receive grace, that he might leave behind all thought of sin. He was more desirous of seeing Queen Isotta than of sitting at the Holy Table where the twelve knights would be who had no thought of carnal sin, or hate, or pride – for there was no avarice in those days. . . . [H]is desire to see Queen Isotta, robbed Tristano of the grace not to see or feel such thoughts, and if this had not been so he would have been of the first to see and taste from the Holy Vessel because of his courtesy and loyalty.
(Shaver, p. 290)]

The argument that Tristan has been robbed of grace which had been made available to Lancelot (and, of course, to his son Galahad/Galasso) may imply that Tristan is, after all, secondary. But the primacy of the spiritual chivalry represented by the Grail is not particularly privileged in this text. Tristan may be deprived of grace, but he does not as a consequence feel particularly deprived. Indeed, the judgment most explicitly encouraged by the text is not to condemn Tristan the sinner, but to wonder at his excellence and realize that were it not for this arbitrary and irrelevant quality called grace, Tristan would surely have surpassed Lancelot in this quest as well.

By the end of the *Tavola*, Tristan's lack of grace is more than compensated for by his erotic sanctification, a process by which he becomes the patron saint of lovers and the grape vines over his and Isotta's grave provide the wine for a lovers' Eucharist.[14] Lancelot survives Tristan, but only so that he may lead the obsequies and avenge Tristan's death.

In works subsequent to the *Tavola*, the dependency of Lancelot on Tristan remains in both the popular and the courtly traditions. The two *cantari* that feature Lancelot do so, as one might expect, by relating him to Tristan. *La Vendetta* narrates Lancelot's vengeance on Mark for the murder of Tristan. Lancelot may be the hero of the piece, but he is heroic essentially through his service to the memory of Tristan.[15] The *Cantare di Tristano e Lancialotto quando combattettero al petrone di Merlino* gives almost equal weight to the two heroes but (like the *Vendetta*) is derived from episodes in the prose *Tristan*, episodes which

13 Denunciations of avarice, particularly as a translation of Augustine's primal sin, *cupiditas*, are by no means uncommon in the Middle Ages, but its appearance here, signaling as it does a particular paradigm shift between Arthurian and contemporary sins, may reflect the decline of the nobility in northern Italy and the rise of a pre-capitalist economy, most notably in the great banking families of Florence.

14 A point more fully argued in Hoffman, '*Radix Amoris*.'

15 *La vendetta che fe messer Lanzelloto de la morte de Miser Tristano*, cited in Gardner, p. 263, from Biblioteca Ambrosiana, cod. 95 sup., fols. 255–64. Also printed as an appendix in *Tavola Ritonda*, ed. Polidori. See 'Qui se comenza la morte de mess: Tristano dal Codice Ambrosiano N. 95, par. sup. 1,' II, 275–84.

were created to support the claim that the new hero, Tristan, is the equal of his literary predecessor, Lancelot.[16] For the Italian audience, this point is assumed, and the narratives are merely further evidence of the popularity of Tristan as hero.

On the other hand, Lancelot does not share the stage with Tristan in the fifteenth-century *ottava rima* narrative, *Li Chantari di Lancellotto della Struzione della Tavola Ritonda*.[17] For students of Sir Thomas Malory, this Italian text is of particular interest because it adapts episodes from the *Mort Artu* that are also related in the Middle English *Stanzaic Morte Arthur*, which is the primary source for Malory's Books XVIII, XX, XXI, crucial episodes in 'The Book of Lancelot and Guinevere' and 'The Dolorous Death and Departing.' *Li Chantari* covers this material with a condensed rapidity that would astonish even Malory, the master of *abbreviatio*.

The first section ('Il Primo Chantare') recounts the Tournament at Winchester with the episode of Lancelot's wound. The fast-moving second *chantare* tells of the arrival of the Fair Maid of Astolat's ship at the port of Camelot and the letter she carries with her. This is followed by the story of Mador de la Porte and the Poisoned Apple (reversing the order of these episodes in Malory) and concludes (after a few missing connecting stanzas) with Mordred and his brothers ambushing Lancelot in Guinevere's chamber. The third *chantare* deals with Guinevere's condemnation, her rescue by Lancelot, and Gawain's lament for the death of his brothers (primarily Gaheris/Ghueriesse, not Gareth as in Malory). The fourth *chantare* deals with the siege of Joyous Guard, a brief episode (absent in Malory) in the Valley of False Lovers ('La Valle de Fallaci Amanti'), the Queen's return to Arthur, and Lancelot's retreat to Benwick, *suo diritto patrimonio anticho*. In the fifth *chantare*, Gawain pleads his case for Arthur's pursuit of Lancelot across the Channel into Benwick in order to avenge the death of Gaheris. The sixth *chantare* records Mordred's treachery and, intriguingly, takes note of the blame placed on Lancelot by the people of Camelot: 'piangeva e ricordava Chamellotto,/ e maladice sempre Lancelotto' (*Chantari* 44, lines 3551–2) [They were weeping and remembering Camelot, and cursed Lancelot continually]. In the last moments of Arthur's reign, it is Gilfrette il Biondo who is asked to return Excalibur to the Lady of the Lake. Arthur's body is taken into a ship, and his possible return is mentioned, although the Queen's is not:

> Che po' che morti son si torna in vita,
> benchè ssi disse po' ch'en una chiesa
> trovossi morto dopo suo finita,
> dal sì al no io non vi fo chontesa,
> se non ch'al certo mai non fè redita.   (*Chantari* 53, lines 417–21)

> [(It was said) that after his death, he would return to life, although they later said that he was found dead in a church after his end, whether true or not I cannot say, for not everything is true that has been told.]

---

[16] Pio Rajna, ed., *Il Cantari di Carduini giuntovi quello di Tristano e Lanciolotto quand combattetterro al Petrone de Merlino* (Bologna, 1873).

[17] *Li chantari di Lancellotto*, ed. E. T. Griffiths (Oxford, 1924).

In the final *chantare* Lancelot quashes the revolt of Mordred's sons and the death of the last knights of the Round Table is recounted.

Whereas audiences for the *Chantari* were popular and probably urban, the last era of significant Italian interest in Arthuriana engages a quite different milieu: the illustrious court of the Este dynasty in Ferrara, and their celebrated poet, Boiardo, who simultaneously celebrates Lancelot in his intricate epic *Orlando Innamorato* and continues to pair him with (or even subordinate him to) Tristan, as his less learned predecessors had done:

> Dame legiadre a cavallier pregiate,
> Che onorati la corte e gentilezza,
> Tiratevi davanti ede ascoltati
> Delli antiqui baron l'alta prodezza,
> Che seran sempre in terra nominati:
> Tristano e Isotta della bionda trezza,
> Genevra e Lancilotto del re Bando;
> Ma sopra tutti il franco conte Orlando.   (*Orlando Innamorato* II.viii.2)[18]

> [Fair ladies and prized cavaliers
> Who grace this court's nobility,
> Draw nearer so that you may hear
> The prowess of the knights of old,
> Whose names on earth always will revere.
> Tristan and blond Isolde, King Ban's
> Son Lancelot and Guinevere,
> But most of all, bold Count Orlando.   (Ross, p. 473)]

Much as the prose *Tristan* encompassed the prose *Lancelot*, so Boiardo (to be followed by Ariosto) encompasses and subordinates the Matter of Britain to the Matter of France. Boiardo however, unlike the prose *Tristan*, has no interest in retelling oft-told tales. He assumes his audience is familiar with Tristan and Lancelot, and feels no need to refresh their memories of the details of the ancient plots as he goes on to invent more and more amazing and fantastic stories about his pseudo-Carolingian heroes. The Este, whose library contained Italian translations of the Lancillotto, Merlino, Galeotto, Morte del Re Artú, and Il Santo Gradale,[19] were described by Pio Rajna as 'quasi piú francese che italiana' [almost more French than Italian].[20] Boiardo's monument to this nearly French Italian dynasty was, according to Mazzocco, intended as 'a wake-up call to the fiction-obsessed Ferrarese.'[21] Whether they woke from their dream of Lancelot

---

18 The edition is Matteo Maria Boiardo, *Orlando Innamorato*, ed. Aldo Scaglione, trans. Charles Stanley Ross (Berkeley, 1989). Boiardo later makes an almost identical point, but in a structure that recalls Francesca (II.xxvi.2–3, lines 9–20). Like Francesca, Boiardo privileges Tristan over Lancelot and focuses on the specific moment of the lovers' conjoined deaths.

19 Elizabeth H. D. Mazzocco, 'An Italian Reaction to the French Prose Lancelot-Grail Cycle: Matteo Maria Boiardo and the Knight's Quest for Identity,' in *The Lancelot-Grail Cycle: Text and Transformations*, ed. William W. Kibler (Austin, 1994), pp. 191–205.

20 Pio Rajna, 'Ricordi di codici francesi posseduti dagli Estense nel secolo XV,' *Romania*, 2 (1873), 58.

21 Mazzocco, 'An Italian Reaction,' 202.

or not, the heroes of Camelot and the love of Lancelot and Guinevere fade, if not from memory, certainly from prominence in the Italian literary tradition.

Between the *cantari* and the romance-epics of Boiardo and Ariosto, the *Lancelot-Grail* appears in either a fragmentary or derivative state. Dante himself provides four additional allusions. He famously refers in the *De Vulgari Eloquentia* to the 'Arturi regis ambages pulcerrime' (I.X.2) and, speaking of the Fourth Age of Man in the *Convivio*, approvingly cites Lancelot as one of those who 'lower their sails' as they reach the end of life;[22] ironically, Lancelot is praised along with Guido da Montefeltro, who will be found in Hell along with Ulysses whose sea voyage may be read as a commentary on the *Convivio*'s metaphor. Both of these references suggest a far more positive and certainly a far more complete understanding of the *Lancelot* than Francesca offers. Once more in the *Inferno* and again in the *Paradiso*, Dante alludes to episodes in the *Lancelot*. In the ninth circle (Caina), Camision dei Pazzi refers to the death of Mordred in the *Mort Artu* ("cui fu rotto il petto e l'ombra/ con esso un colpo per la man d'Artù" [*Inf.* XXXII.61–2]). As if to redeem Francesca's reading of the *Lancelot* in Hell, Dante recalls Galeotto's mistress as he enters the sphere of Mars, and compares Beatrice to the Lady of Malehot:

> Dal 'voi' che prima a Roma s'offerie,
> in che la sua famiglia men persevra,
> ricominciaron le parole mie;
>   onde Beatrice, ch'era un poco scevra.
> ridendo, parve quella che tossio
> al primo fallo scritto di Ginevra.   (*Par.* XVI.10–15)[23]

> [With that *You* which was first used in Rome and in which her family least perseveres, my words began again; at which, Beatrice, who was a little withdrawn, smiled and seemed to me like her who coughed at the first fault that is written of Guinevere.]

In revisiting the scene of seduction, Dante shifts from Galehot who brought the lovers together to the Lady of Malehot, whose cough warns the lovers before they go too far, while the past participle (*scritto*) and past perfect (Francesca's *scrisse*) of the verb *scrivere* remind us that the scene of seduction is also a scene of writing. The celestial revision of the episode tinges Paradise with *courtoisie* and heightens the value (literary and moral) of the *Lancelot*, which read *in bono* or *in malo* can reveal lessons equally suitable for Hell or Heaven. The specific cause of Beatrice's warning – Dante's lapse into family pride as he enters the sphere of Mars where he is about to meet his ancestor, Cacciaguida – signals his *fallo* and courteously dissuades him from excess, as it also softens the martial atmosphere quite gracefully with an ambience of *amour courtois*. While Francesca's narrative is Dante's most powerful evocation of the *Lancelot*, its celestial echo remains an elegant and sensitive redemption of the text as 'Galeotto.'

The great 'Galeotto' of Italian literature, however, is Boccaccio's *Decameron*,

---

[22] *Il Convivio*, ed. Maria Simonelli (Bologna, 1966), IV.28.7–8.
[23] The edition is *The Divine Comedy*, trans. Charles S. Singleton, *Paradiso*, vol. 1: *Italian Text and Translation* (Princeton, 1970).

subtitled the *Galeotto*. While Boccaccio seems to define his audience primarily as the readily seduceable ladies like Francesca, who are the acknowledged readers of romances, the two Dantean references suggest the wider scope of his book, which includes agreeably moral narratives as well as the more entertaining immoral ones.

The thirteenth-century collection of stories and anecdotes known as *Il Novellino* is earlier than both Dante and Boccaccio, and includes two brief Lancelot narratives from the prose *Lancelot* and the *Mort Artu*.[24] No. 45, 'Come Lancialotto si combattè a una fontana,' tells of a combat between Lancelot and Alibano. When during a pause, Lancelot lets Alibano know whom he is fighting, the minor hero replies that his name is scarier than his prowess. Like some of Boccaccio's briefer tales, the point of the anecdote is the snappy rejoinder rather than any narrative complication. Of somewhat greater complexity is no. 82, 'Qui conta come la damigella di Scalot morì per amore di Lancialotto del Lac.' Although briefly told, the tale conveys the poignant demise of the damsel infatuated *oltre misura* and her careful, spectacular funeral plans. When her little boat is at last discovered on the banks of Camelot, her dying declaration is proclaimed to the court:

> "A tutti i cavallieri della Tavola Ritonda manda salute questa damigella di Scalot, siccome alla migliore gente del mondo. E se voi volete sapere perch'io a mia fine sono venuta, sì è per lo migliore cavaliere del mondo e per lo più villano, cioè monsignore messere Lancialotto di Lac, che già nol seppi tanto pregare d'amore, ch'elli avesse di me mercede. E così, lassa!, sono morta per ben amare, come voi potete vedere."[25]

> ["To all the knights of the Round Table this damsel of Escalot sends greeting, as to the greatest people of this world. And if you want to know why I have come to my end, it is because of the best knight in the world and the most villainous, that is My Lord Sir Lancelot of the Lake, for I did not know how to beg him enough for love, so that he would have pity on me. And so, alas, I am dead because of loving well, as you can see."]

While the Fair Maid of Escalot invariably inspires pity, here the issue of Lancelot's blame seems almost irrelevant, since the reader is invited to share the damsel's assessment of Lancelot as both the best and the most villainous knight in the world. Because *Il Novellino*'s treatment of Tristan (no. 45) is only a brief recounting of the episode of Mark spying on the lovers from the pine tree, it is difficult to have a secure sense of the author's intended contrast between the two heroes. It seems, however, that by presenting Tristan as victim, the text shares the general Italian approbation of the Cornish lover. The presence of two Lancelot episodes seems to acknowledge his undeniable prominence as a hero, but it is also intriguing that neither of the two episodes portray him at his best. In a context of chivalry that praises knights as fighters and lovers, it seems significant that the first episode in *Il Novellino* scorns his abilities as a fighter, while the second questions his virtues as a lover. As if in anticipation of the

---

24 In *Prosatori del Duecento: Trattati Morali e Allegorici Novelle*, ed. Cesare Segre (Turin, 1976), p. 99.
25 *Prosatori*, pp. 132–3.

Tavola, the thirteenth-century anthology of anecdotes and narratives already establishes the Italian preference for Tristan, the eternally faithful lover victimized by a contemptible court, over Lancelot, the lesser hero in both arms and amours.

There are, however, other treatments of Lancelot that convey an alternative view. There are a few stray references in the works of lyric poets ranging from Stoppa de' Bostichi, who praises the valor of Lancelot and the beauty of Guinevere,[26] to Petrarch, whose reference to Lancelot, Tristan and 'la coppia d'Arimino che 'nseme/ vanno facendo dolorosi pianti' [the couple from Rimini who go together making dolorous laments] is clearly derived from Dante.[27]

There are also a few *cantari* derived from the *Lancelot* with a more positive view of Lancelot. *La Struzione della Tavola Ritonda* contains several that deal with the heroic adventures of Lancelot derived from the *Mort Artu*. He also features in the thirteenth-century *Conto di Brunor*, and the fifteenth-century *Battaglia di Tristano*. Finally, trickling into the sixteenth century, the *Lancialotto del Lago* (1558–59) marks the sunset of Italian texts directly derived from the *Lancelot*.

This impression of Lancelot in Italy as both a minor and an inferior figure in contrast to Tristan may, however, be subject to change. The recent discovery of an Italian *Queste* independent of the prose *Tristan* may open the door to future discoveries. The research of Marco Infurna may signal the possibility that Lancelot is a little less secondary than he at present appears to be.[28]

---

26 Lori J. Walters, ed., *Lancelot and Guinevere: A Casebook* (New York, 1996), p. xxxv.
27 Triumphus Cupidinis, III, lines 83–4; cited in Gardner, p. 232. See Petrarch, *The Triumphs of Petrarch*, trans. Ernest Hatch Wilkins (Chicago, 1962), pp. 5–34; note esp. p. 23:
    Here too are those who fill our books with dreams:
    Lancelot, Tristram, Guinevere and Isolt, among the rest;
    The twain of Rimini, who together go,
    Forever uttering their sad laments.
    (Note how quickly Paolo and Francesca are elevated to the pantheon of courtly lovers.) On its relationship to Dante, see Daniela Delcorno Branca, 'Dante and the *Roman de Lancelot*,' p. 142.
28 'La Queste del Saint Graal in Italia e il manoscritto udinese,' in *La grant queste del saint graal: la grande ricerca del santo Graal. Versione inedita della fine del XIII secolo del ms. Udine, Biblioteca Arciescovile, 177*, ed. and trans. Aldo Rosellini (Tricesimo [Udine], 1990), pp. 49–57.

15

Lancelot in Germany

HANS-HUGO STEINHOFF

[Translated by Carol Dover and Astrid Weigert]

The importance of the *Lancelot-Grail Cycle* was recognized early in Germany – too early perhaps, for the reception of the work is highly fragmented, like a broken line of stops and starts. The long process of appropriation began before the mid-thirteenth century and reached its peak in the second half of the fifteenth century. Even so, a complete German translation of the *Lancelot–Queste–Mort Artu* trilogy did not appear for another hundred years, and the sole surviving manuscript, dated 1576, also marks the end of the history of the *Cycle*.[1] Neither of the translations was printed, and we have no illuminated luxury codices that might have sustained an interest in the *Cycle* after the end of the Middle Ages. So the first – and for a long time the only – German prose romance was practically unknown, even after the discovery of its two oldest fragments which date back to the High Middle Ages.[2] Scholarly interest in the prose romance revived with the publication of the first volume of a critical edition, in 1948.[3] The (limited) popularity of the *Cycle* in recent years – Tankred Dorst's play *Merlin oder Das wüste Land* (1981) and Christoph Hein's *Die Ritter der Tafelrunde* (1989), for example – owe more to Malory/Caxton, T. H. White, and Hollywood's Grail films than to research.

I

Shortly after the completion of the *Lancelot-Grail Cycle*, efforts were made to adapt it into German. The oldest extant fragment (M) dates from the mid-thirteenth century. Its language points to the Mosel region. Fragment A, in contrast, was made twenty years later and comes from the Main-Franconian

1 Only these three parts of the *Cycle* (referred to hereafter as the *Prosa-Lancelot* or simply *Lancelot*) were translated. The translation of the *Estoire del Saint Graal* and the *Merlin* was a Westphalian transcription of a Dutch verse adaptation by Jacob van Maerlant and Lodewijk van Velthem, and has nothing to do with the Middle German and Upper German reception of the *Lancelot*.
2 Edward Schröder, 'Der deutsche *Lanzelot* in Prosa, ein Werk aus dem Anfang (!) des 13. Jahrhunderts,' *Zeitschrift für deutsches Altertum*, 60 (1923), 148–51.
3 *Lancelot*, ed. Reinhold Kluge, vols. I–III (Berlin, 1948–74); vol. IV: *Namen- und Figurenregister* (Berlin, 1997).

area, so we know that initial interest in the *Cycle* was not limited to territory west of the Rhine. The German *Prosa-Lancelot* is as anonymous as its French counterpart. Who the translators were and who they worked for is a mystery, and the hypothesis that they were Cistercians is a mere assumption based on the romance's so-called Cistercian patterns of thought.[4] Cistercians did begin to write religious prose in the vernacular in the mid-thirteenth century,[5] but none of the extant manuscripts indicates a connection with a monastery or religious order. We can safely assume that the translators were related to the secular nobility. Support for this comes from the high calligraphic quality of the early fragments, one of which is remarkably similar to fragments of an illuminated manuscript of Wolfram's *Willehalm* and another of Hartmann's *Erec*.[6] However, this does not point to a specific court such as the Hessian landgrave's court in Marburg:[7] 'linguistically and generically, the text is like a foundling without a home in the literary landscape of thirteenth-century Germany.'[8]

The translation is probably not based on the French original but passes through a Netherlandish intermediary. This conclusion is based on linguistic peculiarities that survive in part even in the latest manuscripts.[9] The three Netherlandish compilations of the *Cycle* undoubtedly use different redactions from the MHG *Lancelot*, so there must somehow have been another, much earlier translation in the Netherlands which has not survived. Here we run into chronological problems, for the MHG *Lancelot* text follows a version of the *Cycle* that is itself a revision which cannot have been produced much before 1235. This leaves precious little time for an intermediary. However, there would be no need to assume an intermediary if the author of the Mosel-Franconian *Lancelot* was from the Netherlands.[10]

If the precise circumstances surrounding the origin of the text are uncertain, so is its subsequent history. Early attention to the text seems to have been short-lived. There is no trace of its reception, and scant evidence of texts. From the fourteenth century we have only two incomplete manuscripts (m, c. 1350; w, c. 1400), both of the last part of the *Cycle*, and both from the Rheno-Franconian area. Not until the second half of the fifteenth century – at roughly the same time as Thomas Malory was composing his *Morte Darthur* in England – did the prose romance come to light, and then in the form of a large, lavishly decorated manuscript (P). It was produced in a Middle Rhine workshop for the Count Palatine

---

4   Hans Fromm is skeptical (regarding Myrrha Lot-Borodine), 'Lancelot und die Einsiedler' (1984), in his *Arbeiten zur deutschen Literatur des Mittelalters* (Tübingen, 1989), pp. 232ff [219–34].

5   Joachim Heinzle, 'Zur Stellung des *Prosa-Lancelot* in der deutschen Literatur des 13. Jahrhunderts,' in *Artusrittertum im späten Mittelalter*, ed. Friedrich Wolfzettel (Giessen, 1984), pp. 104–13.

6   Karin Schneider, *Gotische Schriften in deutscher Sprache*, vol. I (Wiesbaden, 1987), p. 199.

7   Volker Mertens, *Der deutsche Artusroman* (Stuttgart, 1998), p. 150.

8   Hartmut Beckers, 'Die mittelfränkischen Rheinlande als literarische Landschaft von 1150 bis 1450,' *Zeitschrift für deutsche Philologie*, Special Issue, 108 (1989), 30 [19–49].

9   Pentti Tilvis, *Prosa-Lancelot-Studien* (Helsinki, 1957); Thomas Klein, 'Zur Sprache des Münchener *Prosa-Lancelot*-Fragments,' *Amsterdamer Beiträge zur älteren Germanistik*, 38/39 (1994), 223–40.

10 See Fritz Peter Knapp, rev. of *Lancelot und Ginover*, *Literaturwissenschaftliches Jahrbuch*, N.F. 38 (1997), 332 [331–6].

of Heidelberg, either Friedrich I (reg. 1449–76) or his nephew Philipp (reg. 1476–1508).[11]

The court of the Electors Palatine was a literary center of decidedly eclectic tastes, where courtly verse epics from the High Middle Ages were collected, along with humanist works in Latin and German and 'modern' prose histories based on French or Italian sources such as *Melusine* or *Pontus*. Then there were amateurish copies of Dutch verse compositions, which used thematic material from the Charlemagne cycle and demonstrated that the traditional rhyming couplet was certainly not obsolete.[12]

The Heidelberg *Lancelot* manuscript appears at first to be a homogeneous work, but codicological examination shows that it consists of three distinct parts. The first part (= PI) goes from Lancelot's childhood to the episode of the cart, though not to the very end. The second part (= PII) does not follow on directly; it begins with the *Agravain*, which is where the second half of the multi-volume French cyclic manuscripts begins. It goes right to the end of the *Lancelot*. The third part (= PIII) contains the *Queste* and the *Mort Artu*. The three parts also differ significantly in their textual structure. PI is superior to the other two parts: the translation is superior, the transmission is of higher quality, and the language is closer to classic Middle High German. The differences between PII and PIII are less marked and indicate several different translators at work, and perhaps different times of production. PIII may even have been translated before PII.[13]

The most likely explanation for all of these differences is that the *Lancelot* was translated in stages. The first stage (before 1250) ended at a break that was still visible in the fifteenth-century manuscripts. The final part (*Queste* and *Mort Artu*) must have come into existence before the middle of the fourteenth century, judging from the oldest manuscripts. This could have occurred independently of the oldest translation, especially if we accept that the middle part was not completed until sometime later: since the oldest evidence of the transmission of this part is Heidelberg MS P, we cannot rule out the possibility that its translation was connected with the production of this manuscript. The middle part is missing in the later Heidelberg manuscript (p, after 1500).

If we want to find the reason for the presumed break in the earlier translation, we cannot look for evidence in the assertion that this part of the text, with its extremely strong courtly features and its scant references to the Grail, was considered a self-contained work. It is not a counterpart to the non-cyclic *Lancelot do Lac*, not a 'Lancelot without the Grail,'[14] but rather a core narrative that breaks off in mid-sentence in the middle of an episode. All the same, it is remarkable that the text of the Heidelberg manuscript ends with the first line of an otherwise blank page (fol. 140r), as if the scribe was surprised by the sudden

11 Georg Steer, 'Der Heidelberger *Prosa-Lancelot*-Codex Pal.germ.147,' *Wolfram-Studien*, 9 (1989), 10–16.
12 Hartmut Beckers, '*Der püecher haubet, die von der Tafelrunde wunder sagen*: Wirich von Stein und die Verbreitung des *Prosa-Lancelot* im 15. Jahrhundert,' *Wolfram-Studien*, 9 (1986), 17–45.
13 Kari Keinästö, *Studien zu Infinitivkonstruktionen im mittelhochdeutschen Prosa-Lancelot* (Frankfurt, 1986), pp. 287–95.
14 The expression comes from Elspeth Kennedy, *Lancelot and the Grail* (Oxford, 1986), p. 3.

halt in his original or was somehow prevented from completing his work. Was there more to his original than his copy provides? Or did he hope to add the missing material at a later date?

One indication of attempts to complete the *Cycle* in the Heidelberg court milieu comes from a short piece of text also found in a Rheno-Franconian manuscript (k, before 1476).[15] It begins precisely at the break and was obviously intended to follow on from the missing text. But it does not go as far as the *Agravain*, only to the end of the Cart episode. It lacks Lancelot's abduction by a mysterious old woman and the subsequent departure of Arthur's knights on a great quest for Lancelot; this quest is crucial because it motivates the plot of the second part and it is already well under way when P resumes. Missing segments include the first visit of a knight of the Round Table (Gawain) to the Grail castle, and the description of Gawain and his four brothers which is of some importance to later events. According to the colophone, the Rheno-Frankish text is of Flemish origin: 'Diß buchelin zu einer stonden/ Hain ich inn flemische geschrieben fonden' [Some time ago I found this little book written in Flemish].[16] This connects it with the poems the Heidelberg court imported from Flanders, which indicate their provenance with remarkably similar phrasing.[17] It arrived too late to complete the Heidelberg manuscript. However, the subsequent history of the text shows that it was in fact inserted into the German *Lancelot*.

The only visible literary effect of the German *Prosa-Lancelot* came from the Heidelberg court and its dependence, the residence of Friedrich's widowed sister Mechthild in the Swabian town of Rottenburg. The Archduchess Mechthild definitely owned no less than *fünfe Lanzelunt* (five *Lancelots*),[18] and some of the verse narratives produced in the milieu of her court contain scattered references to names and motifs from the German *Prosa-Lancelot*.

From the Rottenburg of the Wittelsbachers, the romance may have also found its way to Munich, where Ulrich Füetrer, who served as master painter to the city and the Duke from 1453 onwards, wrote an abridged version for Duke Albrecht IV.[19] It is based on the same translation as the Heidelberg *Lancelot* and also includes MS k's additional part. Füetrer reduced the original text drastically but skillfully to just under 180 folios. The result resembles the prose histories in vogue at the time, but this was obviously not the desired objective of Füetrer or his patron. Indeed he rejected prose for a later work: between 1487 and 1495, when he went back to the *Prosa-Lancelot*, he transposed his *Lannzilet* into verse and used it as the concluding part of the *Buch der Abenteuer* that he had been

---

[15] See Kluge's edition, II, 3–115.

[16] Kluge, II, 115.

[17] Beckers, 'Der püecher haubet,' 39.

[18] Beckers, 'Der püecher haubet,' suggests this is a case of 'several manuscripts of parts of the Heidelberg *Prosa-Lancelot*-Corpus' (p. 42).

[19] Ulrich Füetrer, *Prosaroman von Lanzelot*, ed. Arthur Peter (1885; rpt. Hildesheim, 1972). On his life, work, and chronology, see Bernd Bastert, *Der Münchner Hof und Fuetrers Buch der Abenteuer* (Frankfurt, 1993), pp. 139–51 and 289–96.

composing.[20] Like the *Buch*, his *Lannzilet* is composed in the highly sophisticated form of the Titurel-type stanza:

> Do er die küniginne
> so wunnigklichen dort sach,
> nu sehet her, fraw Mynne,
> das sind aber ewr tuck, der ich ye jach:
> er hielt an witz, alls ob er wär entschlaffen
> dem geleich, wie dort her Parzival
> im sne. sunst gund er gen der rainen gaffen.   (stanza 925)

> [When he (Lannzilet) beheld the queen in all her beauty, then you see, Lady Love, this is your trickery at work again, of which I have always spoken: he stood there entranced, just like Perceval in the snow. Thus he gazed upon the noble lady.]

Not only did Füetrer reject the prose form which was so central to the *Cycle*, he also provided his work with a narrator characteristic of courtly verse romance: in the tradition of Wolfram's *Parzival* and the *Jüngere Titurel*, a seemingly incompetent narrator acts as questioner and critic in a disputation with *fraw Mynn*, *fraw Awentewr* and other personifications. This allows him to comment on events within the narrative for his public and simultaneously bring out its fictionality. The reference to Parzival in the above quotation reveals Füetrer's technique of inserting into his *Lannzilet* direct intertextual references to the works he was compiling for the *Buch der Abenteuer*.

With its 6,009 stanzas, the *Lannzilet* is longer than the first two parts of the *Buch der Abenteuer* combined (5,646 stanzas). Füetrer had compiled Wolfram's *Parzival* and the *Jüngere Titurel* with the romance of Troy (after Konrad von Würzburg), a *Merlin*, sections of Heinrich von dem Türlin's *Crône*, and *Lohengrin*. He added seven more Arthurian romances to make the *annder püech* (second book). The addition of *Lannzilet* makes this enormous work even larger than the *Cycle*'s summa of Arthurian literature: in addition to the story of Arthur's world and the Grail world, it also tells the story of the world of knighthood from its origins in Troy to the fall of Arthur's realm.

Füetrer left the plot basically unchanged, even when it deviated factually or conceptually from the first two books. For example, the story of the abduction of Ginover already existed in a different version (corresponding to Hartmann's *Iwein*); Lannzilet, whose childhood opens the third part, had already appeared as a knight of the Round Table in the first and second parts of the *Buch der Abenteuer*; and the role of Grail hero still belonged to Parzival.[21] At several key

---

20 Ulrich Füetrer, *Das Buch der Abenteuer*, parts I and II, ed. Heinz Thoelen (Göppingen, 1997); Ulrich Fuetrer, *Lannzilet*, ed. Karl-Eckhard Lenk (Tübingen, 1989), stanzas 1–1122; Ulrich Füetrer, *Lannzilet*, ed. Rudolf Voß (Paderborn, 1996), stanzas 1123–6009.
21 Rudolf Voß, 'Werkkontinuum und Diskontinuität des Einzelwerks – zum Ensemble von Ulrich Füetrers *Buch der Abenteuer*,' in *Cyclification: The Development of Narrative Cycles in the Chansons de Geste and the Arthurian Romances*, ed. Bart Besamusca et al. (Amsterdam, 1994), pp. 221–7.

points, however, Füetrer made consistent changes to his original.[22] For example, he does not allow Lancelot's adultery to be consummated. While Lancelot's love for the Queen remains the motivating source for his actions, it does not play a decisive role in his failure as Grail hero or in the destruction of Arthur's realm. In addition, Füetrer tones down the *Queste*'s exalted ideal of piety and tones down the contrast between spiritual and worldly knighthood. Arthurian knighthood continues to be judged positively in the parts of the *Lannzilet* that correspond to the *Queste*. As a result, the downfall of the Arthurian kingdom loses its external causality and its internal necessity. With the *Mort Artu*'s relentless intensification of the Fortuna theme, it comes across as chance, as the expression of inscrutable fate.[23]

Füetrer's verse *Lannzilet* was produced for an exclusive circle of literary connoisseurs. Apart from the dedication and a codex intended for Maximilian I, it only exists in one short fragment and two copies of the prose epitome.

It looked as if interest in the *Prosa-Lancelot* had died out – there is only one more manuscript (MS s, dated 1532) – when along came a new translation.[24] Although it begins as a revision of the older version, it soon changes to a different model and follows an independent, as yet unidentified French source (either one of the printed versions or one of the manuscripts closely related to them), and it fills the lacuna at the end of the Cart episode. It survives in a single Bavarian copy, dated 1576. It differs from the older version in its more restrained abridging and different style, which include the doublets that are so typical of Early New High German. Although the text itself is continuous, it is remarkable because it is peppered with words and bits of sentences in garbled French. These makeshift attempts to fill gaps in the text indicate this version could not have been intended for print and must have been produced exclusively for a limited circle of noblemen.

With this new version, the history of the *Cycle*'s texts and transmission in Germany comes to an end. It lacks continuity, yet it is a persistent and constant proposal for a 'German' *Lancelot*. The esthetic innovations of the *Cycle*, however, had no followers[25] – the history of German prose romance makes a fresh start in the second half of the fifteenth century.

[22] Rudolf Voß, 'Problematische Konstellationen: Zu Ulrich Füetrers Rezeption des *Prosa-Lancelot*,' *Zeitschrift für Literaturwissenschaft und Linguistik*, 70 (1988), 26–53.
[23] Hans-Joachim Ziegeler, '*fraw Fortun, fraw Wer, fraw Awentewr* und *fraw Mynne*: Darstellung und Interpretation von Konflikten und ihren Ursachen in Ulrich Fuetrers *Lannzilet*-Versionen,' in *Spannungen und Konflikte menschlichen Zusammenlebens in der Literatur des Mittelalters*, ed. Kurt Gärtner et al. (Tübingen, 1996), p. 336 [323–39].
[24] Partial edition in *Lancelot und Ginover*, ed. and trans. Hans-Hugo Steinhoff (Frankfurt, 1995), 2, 428–743, which corresponds to *LM* 2:81–267 (xxxix, 49–lii, 6).
[25] There is one brief fragment of a translation of the prose *Tristan* from the middle of the sixteenth century; compare *Die deutsche Literatur des Mittelalters: Verfasserlexikon*. 2nd ed., vol. 9 (Berlin, 1995), cols. 1060f.

II

Unlike Hartmann von Aue's and Wolfram von Eschenbach's adaptations of
Chrétien's romances, the German *Lancelot* is not an adaptation in its own right
but a strictly word-for-word translation.[26] Here and there the translator has
adjusted something to fit a more familiar world of values or experience, because
it struck him as foreign (or strange), particularly in the realm of courtly love. It
must be said that the adjustments are not systematic. Most of them are the result
of misreading or misinterpretation, which produces drastic shifts in emphasis.
These shifts occur primarily in the reflective parts of the narrative, for example
the long conversations about the conflicting values in the Lancelot-Ginover love,
and in the (rare) instances of narratorial intervention such as the commentary on
the conception of Galaad. Any interpretation of the *Cycle* based on the German
Lancelot therefore needs to be controlled with the exact wording of the French
original. This is not an easy task because, as we know, there is no such thing as
'the' *Lancelot-Grail Cycle*, only a confused medley of long versions and short
versions and combinations thereof. As transmitted by the Heidelberg manuscript, the German *Lancelot* can certainly be seen to represent one of those
redactions. In this view, not only does the German text require philological
attention, but it also justifies interpretive analysis.[27]

More vexing is the problem of methodology affecting research into the intellectual history and the history of the genre, for the *Cycle* is tied to French, not
German, literary history. It does not actually enter German literary history until
the fifteenth century, and then only sporadically. The fact that this has neither
hindered nor seriously harmed German philology, is a tribute to the fascination
of the *Cycle*.

It was Kurt Ruh who first brought a European focus to research on the
German *Lancelot*, with his 1959 essay,[28] but particularly with a later study of the
Queste that revived the controversy over the importance of Joachim of Fiore's
historical speculations for the conception of the *Cycle*.[29] Walter Haug crossed
over the national boundaries of scholarship with his study of the stages in which
the myth of the Queen's abduction was incorporated into the *Lancelot* stories. He

[26] Monika Unzeitig-Herzog, 'Zu Fragen der Wirkungsäquivalenz zwischen der altfranzösischen *Queste del saint Graal* und den deutschen Fassungen der *Gral-Queste* des
Prosa-Lancelot,' *Wolfram-Studien*, 14 (1996), 149–70.

[27] Cf. Cornelia Reil, *Liebe und Herrschaft: Studien zum altfranzösischen und mittelhochdeutschen
Prosa-Lancelot* (Tübingen, 1996), pp. 8–11. Reil's experiment is fascinating: she tries to analyze
the concept of love in the *Cycle* independently of its spiritual value in the *Queste*. Fritz Peter
Knapp has argued provocatively against using the German *Prosa-Lancelot* as the basis for
interpreting the *Cycle*. In his *Chevalier errant und fin'amor* (Passau, 1986) he cites the MHG text
'for convenience' (p. 10).

[28] Kurt Ruh, 'Lancelot,' *Deutsche Vierteljahrsschrift*, 33 (1959), 269–82.

[29] Kurt Ruh, 'Der Gralsheld in der *Queste del saint Graal*' (1970) in his *Kleine Schriften* (Berlin,
1984), I, 274–97 (also contains further works on *Lancelot*). For a rather different view, see Hans
Fromm, 'Zur Karrenritter-Episode im *Prosa-Lancelot*' (1979), in his *Arbeiten zur deutschen
Literatur des Mittelalters*, pp. 191–218. Klaus Speckenbach takes a different stand against Ruh's
view, in his article 'Endzeiterwartung im *Lancelot-Gral-Zyklus*,' in *Geistliche Denkformen in der
Literatur des Mittelalters*, ed. Klaus Grubmüller et al. (Munich, 1984), pp. 210–25.

used the *Prosa-Lancelot* as the paradigm for a literature that takes on the Chrétien-type courtly romance.[30] Elisabeth Schmid's structural analysis of the Grail Hero's genealogy in the *Queste* is set squarely in the context of the French Grail romances, from Robert de Boron to *Perlesvaus* (but influenced by Wolfram's *Parzival* and Heinrich von dem Türlin's *Crône*).[31] Schmid quotes the German text only to facilitate comparison. Christoph Huber's close textual analysis breaks the deadlock over the unity and 'double esprit' of the *Cycle*. He shows that two competing models provide meaning in the *Queste* at the narrative level, and he shows how they are interwoven but not harmonized.[32] This is a study that future discussion of the conception of the *Cycle* cannot afford to ignore.

Germanists have shed new light on the narrative structure of the *Cycle* in a whole series of studies that analyze specific aspects or individual motifs. Uwe Ruberg's comprehensive research into the representation of time and space in the *Cycle*; he picks up ideas from Ferdinand Lot and describes the function of time and space for the structure of the *Cycle*'s epic world and its construction of meaning.[33] The many dreams and their interpretations in *Lancelot* are the basis for Klaus Speckenbach's important conceptual insights.[34] Monika Unzeitig-Herzog's study compares the role of minor characters with those in Chrétien's *Chevalier de la charrette*.[35] The current debate on writing, image and the arts of memory has produced several studies on the episode of Lancelot's painting.[36]

The results of these and numerous other studies prove that it is possible to achieve meaningful results for the *Cycle*, even if the focus is on the German *Lancelot*. Therefore, these studies deserve also the attention of those working solely with romance texts based on the French original.

[30] Walter Haug, *Das Land, von welchem niemand wiederkehrt* (Tübingen, 1978). See also Haug's *Kleine Schriften: Strukturen als Schlüssel zur Welt* (Tübingen, 1989), pp. 672–86 (on the episode of the magic chessboard) and *Brechungen auf dem Weg zur Individualität* (Tübingen, 1995), pp. 288–300 (on the *Mort Artu* as the 'endgame' not only of the Arthurian world, but also of the conditions under which it can be narrated).

[31] Elisabeth Schmid, *Familiengeschichten und Heilsmythologie* (Tübingen, 1986), pp. 226–54.

[32] Christoph Huber, 'Von der *Gral-Queste* zum *Tod des Königs Artus*,' in *Positionen des Romans im späten Mittelalter*, ed. Walter Haug et al. (Tübingen, 1991), pp. 21–38; compare with Huber, 'Ritterideologie und Gegnertötung,' in *Spannungen und Konflikte*, pp. 59–73.

[33] Uwe Ruberg, *Raum und Zeit im Prosa-Lancelot* (Munich, 1965).

[34] Klaus Speckenbach, 'Form, Funktion und Bedeutung der Träume im *Lancelot-Gral-Zyklus*,' in *I sogni nel medioevo*, ed. Tullio Gregory (Rome, 1985), pp. 317–56; by the same author, 'Die Galahot-Träume im *Prosa-Lancelot* und ihre Rolle bei der Zyklusbildung,' *Wolfram-Studien*, 9 (1986), 119–33 (other *Prosa-Lancelot* articles in this volume).

[35] Monika Unzeitig-Herzog, *Jungfrauen und Einsiedler* (Heidelberg, 1990).

[36] Uwe Ruberg, 'Lancelot malt sein Gefängnis aus,' in *Erkennen und Erinnern in Kunst und Literatur*, ed. Dietmar Peil et al. (Tübingen, 1998), pp. 181–94; Klaus Ridder, 'Ästhetisierte Erinnerung – erzählte Kunstwerke,' *Zeitschrift für Literaturwissenschaft und Linguistik*, 105 (1997), 62–85.

III

In the *Lannzilet* prologue, Füetrer passes in review the names of poets before him who have praised and prized the chivalric heroes, poets whose work he can only hope to approximate. There is only one he feels sure to surpass:

> von Satzenhofen her Ulrich hat gesprochen
> ains tails von herren Lannzilet;
> wie er die awentewr hat ser zerprochen,
> do gib ich schullde kaine
> dem künsten reichen mann.
> vernembt, wie ich das maine!
> den grund der abentewr ich durch lesen han.
> wolt got, hiet ers zu end alls ich gelesen,
> er hiet es euch berichtet so,
> das mein kunst gen im werdt nicht wär ainer vesen. (stanza 109,5–110,7)

> [Sir Ulrich von Zatzikhoven has told us a few things about Sir Lannzilet; although he has cut the story into many fragments, I don't reproach the artful man for this. What I'm trying to say is: I have read through the basics of the story. I wish to God he had read it as thoroughly as I have, he would have presented it to you in such a way that my art wouldn't have been worth a jot compared to his.]

Ulrich von Zatzikhoven's *Lanzelet*, which Füetrer treats with condescension here, is a courtly romance of 9,444 rhyming couplets. If we believe the epilogue, it is really a *welschez buoch* (a French book). Its author claims to have obtained it in 1194 from a hostage whom Richard Lionheart offered in exchange for his own release from the prison of the Staufer Emperor Heinrich VI; we are assured that he did not add anything to the original or leave anything out.[37] Like the Lancelot of the prose romance, Lanzelet is kidnapped by a sea fairy (*merfeine*, v. 180), after his father Pant of Genewis, a *rex injustus*, falls victim to a rebellion of his vassals. The boy grows up in the care of his female rescuer on a remote island. He receives a courtly education and goes out into the world nameless and destitute. He succeeds in increasingly difficult adventures, then wins the favor and hand of three princesses. After he wins the third princess, Iblis, the sea fairy sends a messenger who reveals to him his name, his lineage, and his relationship to King Arthur and he soon becomes a knight of the Round Table. In the second part of the romance, Lanzelet proves his worth as a knight of Arthur's court. He

---

[37] Ulrich von Zatzikhoven, *Lanzelet*, ed. K. A. Hahn (1845; rpt. Berlin, 1965), lines 9322–49. The credibility of this story has recently been called into question by Wolfgang Spiewok: 'Der *Lanzelet* des Ulrich von Zatzikhoven – ein Werk Wolframs von Eschenbach?' in *Lancelot-Lanzelet hier et aujourd'hui*, ed. Danielle Buschinger et al. (Greifswald, 1995), pp. 329–39. The question in the title is answered in the negative. Spiewok considers the romance as the work of a Wolfram disciple. René Perennec has already shown conclusively that he presumes the existence of a French original because it is an *enfances* narrative ('Ulrich von Zatzikhoven: Lanzelet,' in *Interpretationen: Mittelhochdeutsche Romane und Heldenepen*, ed. Horst Brunner [Stuttgart, 1993], pp. 129–45). For an excellent account of research on the *Lanzelet*, see Ulrike Zellmann, *Lanzelet* (Düsseldorf, 1996), pp. 13–50.

disputes a foreign king's claim to Queen Ginover by defeating him in single combat. When the king later abducts the Queen, however, Lanzelet plays a very minor role in her rescue. In a series of very striking episodes, he proves his fidelity to Iblis and confirms his standing as the best knight. He returns to his father's realm and rules peacefully over four entire kingdoms.

There is no trace of Lanzelet's love for Ginover. The episode of her abduction is obviously still close to the mythical model, in which the King himself must get his Queen back.[38] The *welschez buoch* lacks the motifs that are characteristic of Chrétien's *Chevalier de la charrette*: the unfailing love for Ginover, the Cartride, and the Swordbridge crossing.

Lanzelet, however, could not be more different from the *Cycle*'s Lancelot: although they have the same beginnings (the childhood in the lake, the name-quest and identity-quest), they will go their separate ways. Lancelot loves Guinevere. He refuses to become a king in order to continue being her knight and he dies an exemplary but lonely death in the odor of sanctity, after the demise of Arthur's realm. Lanzelet loves all women, with the exception of Ginover; he brings stability to Arthur's realm, he makes his fortune and lives the rest of his days happily as a model ruler, surrounded by children and grandchildren.

Ulrich's original is later than Chrétien's *Erec*, whose basic motifs and atmosphere it presupposes. It can best be understood as a reaction to the complex problems posed by Chrétien's Arthurian romance, to which it provides a counter-model of thematic and narrative freedom.[39] The German romancer was not being naive; he took the parodic elements and expanded them in a congenial way.[40] In France, however, it was as if a Lancelot romance without the Lancelot-Ginover love could not exist alongside the *Chevalier de la charrette*: despite similarities of exposition, the *welschez buoch* disappeared and the French *Cycle* follows Chrétien's text. *Lanzelet* survived only where it faced no competition from the *Charrette* or the *Cycle*.

In Germany, its influence is small but enduring. Heinrich von dem Türlin makes use of *Lanzelet* in his *Crône*, Rudolf von Ems counts Ulrich von Zatzikhoven among his masters. Lanzelet and Iblis became proverbial as the ideal lovers,[41] and reading from the *Lanzelet* even became a subject for pictorial illustration. In the Manesse Codex a miniature shows the beloved lady reading to her knight from the *Lanzelet*, not from the infinitely more seductive *Prosa-Lancelot*.[42] The temptations of the *Lancelot*, though, are in tune with the time when the miniature was produced, as are the temptations to which Paolo and Francesca fell prey in the *Divine Comedy*. The Heidelberg court also owns a *Lanzelet* manuscript, dating from 1420. The author of *Persibein*, known to us only

---

[38] Haug, *Das Land*, pp. 10ff.

[39] Perennec, 'Ulrich von Zatzikhoven: *Lanzelet*,' pp. 142–4; Mertens, *Der deutsche Artusroman*, p. 99.

[40] Edith Feistner, 'er nimt ez allez zeime spil: Der *Lanzelet* Ulrichs von Zatzikhofen als ironische Replik auf den Problemhelden des klassischen Artusromans,' *Archiv für das Studium der neueren Sprachen*, 232 (1995), 241–54.

[41] See Kurt Ruh, 'Der *Lanzelet* Ulrichs von Zatzikhoven' (1975), in his *Kleine Schriften*, p. 63 [63–71].

[42] The miniature (fol. 311v) belongs to Waltram von Gresten.

through Füetrer's *Buch der Abenteuer*, constructed his work with motifs pillaged from the *Lanzelet*.[43] Füetrer was the only one who preferred the *Prosa-Lancelot* to the *Lanzelet*. But in skirting round the adultery issue, he somehow brought his hero closer to Ulrich's.

IV

Once Hartmann von Aue introduced the Arthurian romance into Germany, Lancelot the Arthurian knight became familiar, at least by name, as one of the great knights of the Round Table.[44] Clearly, people did not want to hear (or at least not speak) of his love for Ginover, even in Wolfram's *Parzival* and Heinrich's *Crône* which obviously knew Chrétien's *Charrette*.[45] Chrétien's *Erec*, *Yvain*, *Perceval*, and *Cligès* were adapted, but not the *Charrette*. Is this the result of the taboo that we also find in Ulrich Füetrer's work? Does this explain why the *Prosa-Lancelot* did not really stand a chance in Germany? All kinds of reasons have been offered to explain why it had so little appeal for the German public:[46] the Grail utopias in *Parzival* and *Jüngere Titurel* are less symptomatic of withdrawal from the world and would therefore be preferable to the utopia of the *Queste*; the stature of Parzival left no room for Galahad; the *Tristan* had a monopoly on the adultery theme, and the *Nibelungenlied* had a monopoly on catastrophic finales.

There are strong indications, however, that its esthetics were a liability, that it was indeed the 'materiality of the prose text itself' that gave it such limited appeal. The fact is that German poets had no ear (and no eye) for the new artistry of the prose *Lancelot*, which was for translation and not for adaptation, and consequently lacked the 'jolly gibberish' (*Kauderwelsch*) of verse romance and its 'grandiloquent orality.'[47]

As a result, the 'ripest fruit of the literary Arthurian world,' in all its brilliance, in all its melancholic loveliness, has, to all extents and purposes, remained a stranger to German literature to this very day.[48]

---

43 Mertens, *Der deutsche Artusroman*, pp. 319–24.
44 Danielle Buschinger, 'Le personnage de Lancelot dans la littérature allemande du Moyen Age,' in *Lancelot*, ed. Danielle Buschinger (Göppingen, 1984), pp. 17–28.
45 Christoph Cormeau, *Wigalois und Diu Crône* (Munich, 1977), pp. 178–89.
46 Walter Blank, 'Zu den Schwierigkeiten der *Lancelot*-Rezeption in Deutschland,' in *Chrétien de Troyes and the German Middle Ages*, ed. Martin H. Jones et al. (Cambridge, 1993), pp. 121–36; Neil Thomas, 'The Reception of the Prose *Lancelot* in France and Germany,' in *Nouveaux Mondes*, ed. Richard Maber (Durham, 1994), pp. 19–35. On the faint echoes of Arthurian romance particularly in modern German literature, see Mertens, *Der deutsche Artusroman*, pp. 341–53.
47 Ulrich Wyss, 'Auf der Suche nach dem arthurischen Prosaroman im deutschen Mittelalter,' in *Kultureller Austausch und Literaturgeschichte im Mittelalter*, ed. Ingrid Kasten et al. (Sigmaringen, 1998), pp. 225–7; a connection with the delayed literacy of the German high aristocracy is also suggested by Klaus Speckenbach, 'Prosa-Lancelot,' in *Interpretationen: Mittelhochdeutsche Romane*, p. 327 [326–52].
48 Max Wehrli, *Geschichte der deutschen Literatur vom frühen Mittelalter bis zum Ende des 16. Jahrhunderts* (Stuttgart, 1980), pp. 500 and 503.

Note

Since I wrote this chapter, several publications have appeared which are important because they complete the picture of Lancelot in Germany and because their interest goes beyond German-studies research on Lancelot. The most significant ones are:

Thordis Hennings, *Altfranzösischer und mittelhochdeutscher Prosa-Lancelot: Übersetzungs- und quellenkritische Studien* (Heidelberg, 2001). Using a reference in Elspeth Kennedy's article in *Romania*, 77 (1956), 104, she provides evidence of an Old French *Lancelot* manuscript (Paris, BNF fr. 751) that is very close to the text of the first part of the MHG *Lancelot*. This allows, for the first time, methodologically reliable research into the practice of translation. It confirms that the German text is an abridged translation and not a 'courtly adaptation' of its model.

Michael Waltenberger, *Das große Herz der Erzählung: Studien zu Narration und Interdiskursivität im Prosa-Lancelot* (Frankfurt, 1999).

The Arthur of the Germans: The Arthurian Legend in Medieval German and Dutch Literature, ed. W. H. Jackson et al. (Cardiff, 2000). Includes the following articles, each with a generous bibliography: Silvia Ranawake, 'The Emergence of German Arthurian Romance: Hartmann von Aue and Ulrich von Zatzikhoven,' pp. 38–53; Elizabeth A. Andersen, 'The Reception of Prose: The *Prosa-Lancelot*,' pp. 155–65; Bernd Bastert, 'Late Medieval Summations: *Rappoltsteiner Parzifal* and Ulrich Füetrer's *Buch der Abenteuer*,' pp. 166–80.

Valentina Sommer, *Der deutsche Prosa-Lancelot als ein posthöfischer Roman des späten Mittelalters: Eine textlinguistisch-stilistische Untersuchung* (Stuttgart, 2000).

Judith Klinger, *Der mißratene Ritter: Konzeptionen von Identität im Prosa-Lancelot* (Munich, 2001).

16

The Spanish Lancelot-Grail *Heritage*

MICHAEL HARNEY

There is no 'Spanish Cycle' to complement any of the branches of the French *Lancelot-Grail Cycle*. Rather, certain works from the latter population of texts were variously translated, adapted, modified, excerpted, or imitated, most of them anonymously, in Castilian and related dialects, and in Portuguese and Catalan. At the same time, and subsequently, many Arthurian elements and characters widely known in the cultural milieu of the Peninsula were incorporated, in more or less disguised form, into so-called pseudo-Arthurian works.

The earliest Peninsular reference to Arthurian matters is in a work by the Catalan troubador Guiraut de Cabrera, dating from around 1170, and clearly bespeaking Guiraut's knowledge of such well known characters as Erec, Tristan, 'Yceut' (Isolde), and 'Gualvaing' (Gawain).[1] Guiraut's fastidious analysis of a jongleur's handling of Arthurian material suggests that the *matière de Bretagne* was at first a prestigious import destined for elite Peninsular audiences.[2] Another early trace of Arthur in a Peninsular source occurs in a brief reference in the *Corónicas navarras*, dating from the last decade of the twelfth century.[3]

William Entwistle notes the intervention of several important historical personages in the early formation of Peninsular Arthurian tradition. These include Eleanor, daughter of Henry II of England and of Eleanor of Aquitaine, who married into a Spanish house and remained a patroness of troubadours.[4] Further evidence for the reception of Arthurian matter are the copies of several French romances known to have existed in the libraries of King Martin of Aragon (d. 1410), King Duarte of Portugal (d. 1438), and Prince Charles of Viana (d. 1461). Awareness of Arthurian legend and literature is revealed by the work

---

1 Manuel Milá y Fontanals, *De los trovadores en España*, in his *Obras completas*, 8 vols. (Barcelona, 1889), II, 272–84, with reference to Erec (p. 276), to Tristan (p. 282), to Yceut and Gualvaing (p. 283).

2 Henry Thomas, *Spanish and Portuguese Romances of Chivalry* (Cambridge, 1929), pp. 21–2; William J. Entwistle, *The Arthurian Legend in the Literatures of the Spanish Peninsula* (London, Toronto and New York, 1925), p. 12; María Rosa Lida de Malkiel, 'Arthurian Literature in Spain and Portugal,' in *Arthurian Literature in the Middle Ages*, ed. Roger Sherman Loomis (Oxford, 1959), p. 406 [406–18].

3 Antonio Ubieto Arteta, ed., *Corónicas navarras* (Milagro and Valencia, 1964), p. 40; discussed by Entwistle, 'Geoffrey of Monmouth and Spanish Literature,' *Modern Language Review*, 17 (1922), 383 [381–91], and *Arthurian Legend*, pp. 35–36. See also Lida de Malkiel, 'Arthurian Literature,' p. 407, and Alan Deyermond, *A Literary History of Spain: The Middle Ages* (London and New York, 1971), pp. 249–50.

4 Entwistle, *Arthurian Legend*, p. 33.

of Alfonso the Learned (d. 1284) and his grandson King Dinis of Portugal (d. 1325), both of whom mention Tristan in their poetry. King Dinis's bastard son Pedro, Count of Barcellos (d. 1354) includes in his *Livro das Linhagens* a genealogy of English kings adapted from Geoffrey of Monmouth's Latin Chronicle. The Vatican manuscript of the *Canzioniere portoghese Colocci-Brancuti* contains *Lays de Bretanha* which confirm a familiarity, among thirteenth-century Galician and Portuguese troubadors, with the *matière de Bretagne*.[5]

The *Libro del caballero Zifar*, the earliest extant chivalric romance in Castilian (c. 1300), alludes to King Arthur in describing a battle: 'ca non se vio el rey Artur en mayor priesa e en mayor peligro con el Gato Paul que nos viemos con aquellos maldichos'[6] [for King Arthur didn't find himself in greater difficulty or greater danger with Cat Palug than we did with those miscreants]. The 'Gato Paul' mentioned in this passage is very probably a deformation of 'Cath Palug,' from the episode of the Battle of Lake Lausanne in the *Lancelot-Grail's Merlin*.[7] In chapter 206 of the *Zifar*, the hero's son sojourns in the realm of the Ynsolas Dotadas, ruled over by the Empress Nobleza whose mother had watched over and rescued 'don Yuan, fijo del rey Orian . . . quando don Yuan dixo a la reyna Ginebra que el auie por señora vna dueña mas fermosa que ella'[8] [don Yvain, son of King Orian . . . when Don Yvain said to Queen Guinevere that his lady was more beautiful than she was]. Lida de Malkiel observes that the *Zifar's* Yván (Yuan) evokes Chrétien's *Yvain*, although the incidents referred to correspond to Marie de France's *Lanval* and *Graelent*.[9]

Sir Henry Thomas maintained that the interludes of the Dauntless Knight and the Enchanted Isles demonstrate the influence of the *matière de Bretagne* on the *Zifar's* anonymous author.[10] In the first episode, the Dauntless Knight is conducted by a Lady of the Lake to an underwater kingdom, where he becomes her consort and the sovereign over her magical realm. After seven days, the Lady bears the knight's son who, in turn, grows to maturity in seven days. When a beautiful woman tempts the knight, the Lady of the Lake turns into a monstrous demon who drives the knight and his son from the magical kingdom. The *Zifar's* second magical episode sees Roboán, Zifar's son, conveyed by magical boat to the Enchanted Isles. There he marries the beautiful Empress Nobleza, with whom he enjoys a preternaturally happy existence. After he is three times tempted by a beautiful woman, whom we know to be the Devil in disguise, he is instantly ferried back to the real world, there to repent his loss of Nobleza and the happiness he had known with her.

The Arthurian character of these episodes has been questioned by Lida de Malkiel.[11] Whether or not we agree with the Celtic hypothesis concerning them,

5   See Thomas, *Spanish and Portuguese Romances*, pp. 22–7.
6   *El Libro del cauallero Zifar*, ed. Charles Phillip Wagner (Ann Arbor, 1929), p. 215.
7   Noted by Lida de Malkiel, 'Arthurian Literature,' p. 408.
8   *Zifar*, p. 458.
9   Lida de Malkiel, 'Arthurian Literature,' p. 408n.
10   Thomas, *Spanish and Portuguese Romances*, 19–20. The relevant episodes are found in *Zifar*, 226–42 and 456–80.
11   Lida de Malkiel, 'Arthurian Literature,' 413n. Also discussed by A. H. Krappe, 'Le Mirage celtique et les sources du *Chevalier Cifar*,' *Bulletin Hispanique*, 33 (1931), 99–101 [97–103], and 'Le lac enchanté dans le *Chevalier Cifar*,' *Bulletin Hispanique*, 35 (1933), 110–113 [107–25].

it must be allowed that the *Zifar*'s reference to very specific incidents and personages from Arthurian works indicates the author's expectation of a knowledgeable appreciation on the part of his readers. The fact that this romance seems thoroughly bourgeois in spirit – 'its protagonists,' notes Lida de Malkiel, 'are moral and middle-class, with stray gleams of humour' – intimates a broad reception of Arthurian literature by the turn of the fourteenth century.[12]

By the middle of the fifteenth century, knowledge of the Arthurian romances and their contents had penetrated all circles of Peninsular society. This dissemination is confirmed by the frequency of Arthurian allusions in such lyrical collections as the famous *Cancionero de Baena* (mid-fifteenth century), and by the popularity of Arthurian themes and personages in the Peninsular ballad tradition.[13] However, actual works on Arthurian themes do not appear to have widely circulated in the Peninsula until well after the second half of the thirteenth century, with the following century witnessing a sharp increase in the number of translations and adaptations.[14]

Peninsular adaptations and translations were mostly based on versions of the Tristan tale, and on works from the *Lancelot-Grail* and *Post-Vulgate* cycles. Since the precise French manuscripts from which Peninsular versions were derived are not extant, it is impossible to verify whether or not the presumed differences between the corresponding French works and their Hispanic analogues were present in the original manuscripts (thus, as presumable variants of extant French texts), or were introduced by the Peninsular adapters. Moreover, the presumed original Hispanic versions of the *Post-Vulgate Cycle* being lost, we do not know in which of the Peninsular languages or dialects such primordial adaptations were written. These lost originals, in any event, gave rise to texts and fragments of texts written in both Castilian and Portuguese. The Catalan texts represent an independent reception of Arthurian sources.[15]

Three branches of Arthurian material are represented by the Castilian and Portuguese adaptations/translations. The *Libro de Josep Abarimatía*, of which versions in Castilian and Portugese exist, was probably based on Robert de Boron's *Roman du Graal* and was probably written in the second decade of the fourteenth century.[16] The *Estoria de Merlín*, and two versions called *Baladro del sabio Merlín*, all in Castilian, contain, in addition to modified Arthurian characters and episodes, much additional material from various sources and traditions. In Castilian we also have a version narrating the Grail quest and the death

---

12 'Arthurian Literature,' 414. On the middle-class spirit of the *Zifar*, see also Michael Harney, 'Law and Order in the *Libro del caballero Zifar*,' in *Society and Culture in the 'Libro del Caballero Zifar'*, ed. Vincent Barletta and Michael Harney, special issue of *La corónica*, 27.3 (1999), 134–9 [125–44].

13 On the *Cancionero de Baena*'s references to Grail themes, see Thomas, *Spanish and Portuguese Romances*, pp. 26–7. See also Lida de Malkiel, 'Arthurian Literature,' pp. 412–13, and María Cruz García de Enterra, 'Libros de caballerías y romancero,' *Journal of Hispanic Philology*, 10 (1985–86), 104–7 [103–15].

14 *Amadís de Gaula*, ed. Juan Manuel Cacho Blecua, 2 vols. (Madrid, 1987), pp. 126–35.

15 Deyermond, *History*, p. 150.

16 Pedro Bohigas Balaguer, *Los textos españoles y gallego-portugueses de la 'Demanda del santo grial'*, Revista de Filología Española, Anejo 7 (Madrid, 1925), p. 78; Lida de Malkiel, 'Arthurian Literature,' p. 407; José María Viña Liste, ed., *Textos medievales de caballerías* (Madrid, 1993), pp. 315–16.

of King Arthur, *La Demanda del Sancto Grial*. In addition to these works, all fragmentary, there exist fourteenth-century Catalonian fragments corresponding
more or less to books II and III of the French prose *Lancelot*, as well as fragments
of Castilian versions of the Lancelot story, one of them extensive, which apparently are not based on the same version of the French prose *Lancelot* as the
Catalan fragments.[17] Versions of the Tristan story are represented by mid- and
late-fourteenth-century fragments in Catalan, Castilian and Galaico-Portuguese.
An extensive but incomplete Castilian and Aragonese manuscript of a version of
the *Tristán de Leonís*, in the Vatican library, is the basis of George Tyler Northup's
1928 edition.[18] The only extant printed version of the Castilian *Tristán de Leonís*,
from 1501, represents, in Sharrer's opinion, 'an early state of the Castilian
Tristan,' with some material included from the sentimental romance *Grimalte y
Gradissa*.[19]

The analysis of manuscripts and stemmae carried out by Entwistle has been
thoroughly supplemented by Lida de Malkiel and updated by Harvey Sharrer.
Little new can be added to what must be regarded as an authoritative body of
philological work already accomplished in this area, other than the occasional
readjustment of our knowledge regarding the date or authorship or provenance
of this or that specific manuscript, or the details of the stemmae of manuscripts.[20]

Because there are no recognized original Peninsular masterpieces overtly
devoted to Arthurian themes, and because surviving Arthurian works, or lost
works whose existence can be plausibly demonstrated, are derivative or fragmentary or both, discussion of the *matière de Bretagne* in the Peninsula – as a
problem in literary history and literary criticism – requires consideration of
post-Arthurian works whose theme, plot, and characters can only be explained
as derivations from and imitations of the patterns set by various branches of the
Grail Cycle.

On the one hand, the Peninsula is an Arthurian backwater, with no independent masterpieces directly based on Arthurian themes or directly adapted
from Arthurian prototypes. There is nothing comparable in the peninsula to
Wolfram von Eschenbach's *Parzival*, Hartman von Aue's *Erec*, or Gottfried von
Strassburg's *Tristan und Isolde*. Straightforwardly Arthurian works in the Peninsula are all, again, translations or condensed adaptations, and all are fragmentary.[21] Such innovation as may be detected among the adapters of texts derived

---

17 That is, to vols. I, II, III of *The Vulgate Version of the Arthurian Romances*, ed. H. Oskar Sommer
    (Washington, D.C., 1908–13; rpt. New York, 1979). See also Harvey Sharrer, *A Critical Bibliog-
    raphy of Hispanic Arthurian Material, I. Texts: The Prose Romance Cycles* (London, 1977),
    pp. 18–19.
18 Discussed and critiqued by Sharrer, *Critical Bibliography*, pp. 28–9; but see *El cuento de Tristán
    de Leonís, edited from the Unique Manuscript Vatican 6428*, ed. George Tyler Northup (Chicago,
    1928), pp. 19–25, which remains a very cogent and useful discussion of the provenance of the
    Vatican manuscript and its relationship to other versions in French and Italian.
19 Sharrer, *Critical Bibliography*, p. 30.
20 See Lida de Malkiel, 'Arthurian Literature,' and Sharrer, *Critical Bibliography*, 'Spain and
    Portugal.' See also Fanni Bogdanow's thorough examination of the complex history of the
    Portuguese and Spanish versions of the Post-Vulgate *Queste del Saint Graal*, 'The Spanish
    Baladro and the *Conte du brait*,' *Romania*, 83 (1962), 383–99.
21 Deyermond, *History*, pp. 279–82.

from French Arthurian originals involves, for example, suppression of intro-spective passages in favor of action scenes, or ideological bowdlerization.[22]

On the other hand, if we expand our purview to include what has been called pseudo-Arthurian literature, 'neo-Arthurian literature' or the 'sub-Arthurian romances of chivalry,' we discover some very significant works which enjoyed international popularity and extraordinary historical influence in subsequent lit-erary history. These works must be considered a prolongation of the Arthurian legacy without which they could not have come into existence.[23]

Juan de Castrogeriz's mid-fourteenth-century free translation and gloss of the *De regimine principum* of Aegidius Romanus, in a passage first detected by Raymond Foulché-Delbosc, deplores the character and temperament of 'malos caballeros' (bogus knights), who habitually recount the 'maravillas de Amadís e de Tristán e del Caballero Cifar' [wonders of Amadís and of Tristan and of the Knight Cifar]. Such phony knights 'no facen fuerza de cosa del mundo, sino de parescer e semejar caballeros e no lo son, ca sus caballerías cuentan entre las mugeres'[24] [they pay no heed to anything in the world but resembling and imitating knights, but they are nothing of the kind, for their deeds are recited among women]. Martín de Riquer points out a possible uncertainty as to the date of this passage. Only one of the manuscripts, the latest, expresses this opinion, raising the possibility that the sentiment referring to the three famous fictional knights was a later interpolation.[25]

Regardless of the precise date of the now-famous passage from Castrogeriz's gloss on Aegidius, the quote would seem to confirm the evolutionary sequence proposed by Lida de Malkiel and echoed by Williamson, in which a predomi-nantly aristocratic Peninsular readership for the earlier, purely Arthurian trans-lations and adaptions, gives way to the bourgeois and sentimental themes of *Amadís* and its later continuations, imitations, and affines.[26]

This model, however, is perhaps too simple. For one thing, there is no clear evidence of generic supersession. Pero López de Ayala's *Rimado de Palacio* (late

---

22 As when passages expressing ambivalence toward chivalric ethics or prerogatives are expur-gated; see J. B. Hall, '*Tablante de Ricamonte* and Other Castilian Versions of Arthurian Romances,' *Revue de Littérature Comparée*, 48 (1974), 182 [177–89], who notes that the French prose *Lancelot*, with its tragic outcome and frequent ambivalence concerning chivalry, was not popular in Castile (188), while spiritual and anti-chivalric elements, so prevalent in the French original, are suppressed in the *Demanda del sancto Grial* (189). See also J. B. Hall, 'La Matière arthurienne espagnole: The Ethos of the French Post-Vulgate *Roman du Graal* and the Castilian *Baladro del sabio Merlin* and *Demanda del Sancto Grial*,' *Revue de Littérature Comparée*, 56 (1982), 426–31 [423–36].

23 See Deyermond, *History*, p. 279, and Edwin Williamson, *The Half-Way House of Fiction: Don Quijote and the Arthurian Romance* (Oxford, 1984), p. 37, for their terminological contributions on this question.

24 Juan García de Castrogeriz, *Glosa castellana al 'Regimiento de principes' de Egidio Romano*, ed. Juan Beneyto Pérez, 3 vols. (Madrid, 1947), III, 361–2. See also Raymond Foulché-Delbosc, 'La plus ancienne mention d'Amadís,' *Revue Hispanique*, 15 (1906), 815 [806–15].

25 Martín de Riquer, *Estudios sobre el Amadís* (Barcelona, 1987), pp. 12–13. He refers to Sylvia Roubaud, 'Les manuscrits du "Regimiento de Príncipes" et l'"Amadís",' in *Mélanges de la Casa de Velázquez*, 5 (1969), 218 [202–22]. An exhaustive and up-to-date listing of references to versions of *Amadís* or to the hero himself is provided by Riquer, followed by an illuminating discussion of the allusions to *Amadís* in various works (*Estudios*, pp. 8–35).

26 Lida de Malkiel, 'Arthurian Literature,' pp. 415–17; Williamson, *Half-Way House*, p. 37.

fourteenth century) tells of his youthful penchant for listening to readings of chivalric novels:

> Plógome otrosí oír muchas vegadas
> libros de deuaneos, de mentiras prouadas,
> Amadís e Lançalote, e burlas es[c]antadas,
> en que perdí mi tienpo a muy malas jornadas.[27]

> [It pleased me as well to listen very often
> to books full of nonsense, of conspicuous lies,
> Amadís and Lancelot, and insidious quackery,
> on which I wasted my time, day after idle day.]

López de Ayala's years are 1332–1406.[28] Assuming that the youthful listening habits he deplores were indulged during his teens and twenties (the passage cited occurs in a section devoted to sins committed by means of the sense of hearing), the years implied are around the middle of the fourteenth century, the same period indicated by the reference in Castrogeriz.[29] The *Amadís* and its arguably bourgeois congeners did not, therefore, supersede the older French-inspired romances; rather, the latter persisted and coexisted with the *Amadís* and romances that imitated it.

Aristocratic and even royal audiences, including the emperor Charles V, read *Amadís* and other supposedly bourgeois romances, while bourgeois audiences read or listened to versions of the Tristan and Lancelot stories.[30] Keith Whinnom points out that works dedicated to aristocrats may still be of interest 'to all levels of society,' while Sara Nalle has argued that the assumption of a uniquely upper-class audience for such genres as the chivalric romance fails to account for 'the steady aristocratization of Spanish culture and values' and a general 'fascination [with] noble status and values.' Although she is referring to the early sixteenth century, the social trends and class structure she mentions orig-inated centuries before.[31]

As Grace Williams pointed out nearly a century ago, the plot of *Amadís* shows a very close correspondence to that of the prose *Tristan* and, especially, the French prose *Lancelot*. In addition to striking similarities in style (extreme length, episodic narration, interlaced parallel plots, etc.), there are many resemblances in storyline and subject matter. Williams demonstrates, for example, analogies in the opening sections of the Spanish romance and the prose *Tristan*, a close paral-

---

[27] Pero López de Ayala, *Rimado de palacio*, ed. Germán Orduna (Madrid, 1987), stanza 163.

[28] López de Ayala, *Rimado*, p. 9.

[29] See also Riquer, *Estudios*, p. 15.

[30] See Daniel Eisenberg, 'Who Read the Romances of Chivalry?' in his *Romances of Chivalry in the Spanish Golden Age* (Newark, DE, 1982; rpt. from *Kentucky Romance Quarterly*, 20 [1973], 209–33), p. 90 [89–117]; also Jan-Dirk Müller and Valérie Minchin, 'Le Roman de chevalerie à la cour de l'Empereur Maximilien 1er,' in *Le Roman de chevalerie au temps de la Renaissance*, ed. Marie-Thérèse Jones-Davies (Paris, 1987), pp. 155ff. [153–66].

[31] Keith Whinnom, 'The Problem of the "Best-Seller" in Spanish Golden Age Literature,' *Bulletin of Hispanic Studies*, 67 (1980), 195 [189–98]; Sara T. Nalle, 'Literacy and Culture in Early Modern Castile,' *Past and Present*, 126 (1989), 87–8 [65–95]. See also Luis García de Valdeavellano, *Orígenes de la burguesía en la edad media española* (Madrid, 1969), pp. 179–216; José Luis Romero, *Crisis y orden en el mundo feudoburgués* (Mexico City, 1980), pp. 16–51 and 251–96; and Hall, 'La Matière arthurienne,' p. 435.

lelism in toponymic styles, and very similar onomastic patterns in the French romances and their later Spanish counterpart (e.g. Fr. Agravain/Sp. Agrajes; Belays/Belaís; Brisane/Brisena; Galahaut, Galaad/Galaor; Gauvain/Galvanes; Nascien/Nasciano). Above all, many episodes in the *Amadís* seem clearly to imitate passages in the French prose *Lancelot*, the Prose *Tristan*, and other French Arthurian works.[32]

The *Amadís* pertains, in a literal sense, to the Matter of Britain. Chiefly set in Great Britain and neighboring lands, the action, like that of the prose *Tristan* and the *Lancelot-Grail Cycle*, begins only a few years after the time of Christ.[33] The hero's maternal grandfather is Garinter, King of Lesser Britain; his father is King Perion of Gaul. Amadís, like Lancelot (whose father is Ban of Benoic, 'a region vaguely placed in western France'), is from the continent ('Gaul' probably equating more or less with France). Amadís's beloved Oriana is a princess of Great Britain; the king of that country is her father, Lisuarte.[34]

What Frappier says of the French prose *Lancelot* is true of the *Amadís* as well: both works are 'a maze of tourneys, strange encounters, perilous forests.'[35] In both the French and the Spanish works, a youth of unknown parentage is received into the court of a king famous for his personal chivalry and patronage of knights. The youth serves the monarch faithfully, but falls in love with the ruler's wife or daughter. The liaison is quickened by the youth's heroic rescue of his beloved from the clutches of abductors, and entangled by the lady's subsequent jealousy, aroused by false rumors of the hero's inconstancy (an important role is played, in both cases, by courtly interlopers). In both works his lady's rejection reduces the hero to despondency and near-madness, and induces his self-exile in a remote locale. In both works the jealous lady relents, and the lovers eventually reconcile. The hero obtains control, in both cases, of a fabulous domain (Joyeuse Garde in the prose *Lancelot*, Insula Firme in the *Amadís*). Finally, the heroes of both works enjoy magical protection, with the *Amadís*'s sorceress Urganda the Unknown corresponding to Lancelot's Dame du Lac.[36]

The *Amadís*, like the French prose *Lancelot*, reveals 'a system of forecasts and concordances [that] binds the mass of adventures together.'[37] These prophecies

32 Grace S. Williams, 'The *Amadís* Question,' *Revue Hispanique*, 21 (1909), 40, 42–5, 50–60, 60–145 [1–167]. See also Bohigas Balaguer, 'La novela caballeresca, sentimental y de aventuras,' in Guillermo Díaz-Plaja, ed., *Historia general de las literaturas hispánicas*, 6 vols. (Barcelona, 1949–53), II, 222–5 [187–236]; Lida de Malkiel, 'Arthurian Literature,' p. 415, and 'El desenlace del *Amadís* primitivo,' *Romance Philology*, 6 (1953), 285–7 [283–9], as well as Antonio Rodríguez Moñino, 'El primer manuscrito del *Amadís de Gaula*,' *Boletín de la Real Academia Española*, 36 (1956), 215 [199–216], who argues (vindicating Lida de Malkiel) that Montalvo, the *remanieur* of the 1508 *Amadís*, condensed rather than expanded on the medieval original.

33 Williams, '*Amadís* Question,' 40.

34 Jean Frappier, 'The Vulgate Cycle,' in *Arthurian Literature in the Middle Ages*, ed. Loomis, p. 297 [295–318]. See also, on the *Amadís*'s contradictory representation of Gaul, Williams, '*Amadís* Question,' 46; also Edwin B. Place, 'Amadís of Gaul, Wales or What?' *Hispanic Review*, 23 (1955), 100–103 [99–107].

35 Frappier, 'Vulgate Cycle,' pp. 300–301.

36 Lida de Malkiel, 'Arthurian Literature,' p. 415. See also Bohigas Balaguer, 'Novela caballeresca,' p. 228; Edwin B. Place, 'Fictional Evolution: The Old French Romances and the Primitive *Amadís* reworked by Montalvo,' *PMLA*, 71 (1956), 528 [520–9]; and, for comparison with the *Prose Lancelot*, Frappier, 'Vulgate Cycle,' pp. 296–302.

37 Frappier, 'Vulgate Cycle,' pp. 295–6.

chiefly correlate the careers of Amadís and of his son Esplandián, a relationship highly reminiscent of that between Lancelot and Galahad. In its original form, before the presumed reworking of Montalvo, the author/adaptor who produced the extant first printed edition of 1508, the *Amadís* had a tragic outcome, analogous to the cataclysmic war between Arthur and Lancelot in the *Mort Artu*.[38] The *Amadís*, in short, methodically substitutes Arthurian personages, episodes, and plot devices, while subtly departing from the model. What might have prompted this methodical recasting of Arthurian materials?

Both the prose *Lancelot* and the *Amadís* betray an equivocal attitude toward sexual love. The Spanish romance, like its French model, regards amorous passion as the 'source of all good,' despite the fact that it occasions 'adultery, deceit, and disloyalty.'[39] Although both works sympathize with the lovers, they reveal ambivalence toward their respective transgressions: the *Lancelot* with regard to adultery, the *Amadís* with regard to filial impiety. James Fogelquist, expanding on the contrast discussed by Williams, Bohigas Balaguer, and Lida de Malkiel, notes that lovers in the *Amadís* and other Peninsular chivalric romances live in fear not of jealous husbands but of controlling fathers.[40] The *Amadís* and its imitators replace the earlier adulterous triangle of the knight, his beloved, and her husband with that of the knight, his lady, and her paramount male kin. These kinsmen in *Amadís* and *Tirant lo blanch* are fathers; in *Curial and Güelfa*, an elder brother; in the *Zifar*, both fathers (in the case of Zifar himself, books 1 and 2) and uncles (the case of Roboán and his eventual consort, the Princess Seringa, book 4).[41]

The shift in the locus of control over the female converts the triangle of the jealous husband (Arthur), his wife (Guinevere) and her lover (Lancelot), into that of the domineering father (Lisuarte), his daughter (Oriana), and her suitor (Amadís). A similar contrast could be made between the triangle formed by King Mark, Isolde, and Tristan (Mark's brother's son), and that represented by the Greek Emperor, Carmesina, and Tirant lo blanch. The sentimental romance, as in the fifteenth-century *Cárcel de Amor*, presents a triangle similar to the one we encounter in the Spanish chivalric romances, in the form of Leriano's love for Laureola, daughter of King Gaulo of Macedonia.[42]

The adultery of the Arthurian stories is replaced, in the Spanish chivalric

---

38 Lida de Malkiel, 'El desenlace,' 286–8; Rodríguez Moñino, 'Primer manuscrito,' 215. See also Juan Bautista Avalle-Arce, 'Tirant lo Blanc, Amadís de Gaula y la caballeresca medieval,' in *Studies in Honor of Sumner M. Greenfield*, ed. Harold L. Boudreau and Luis T. González del Valle (Lincoln, NB, 1985), pp. 25–30, and J. B. Avalle-Arce, *Amadís de Gaula: el primitivo y el de Montalvo* (Mexico, 1990), ch. 1, et passim.

39 Frappier, 'Vulgate Cycle,' p. 302.

40 James Donald Fogelquist, *El 'Amadís' y el género de la historia fingida* (Madrid, 1982), p. 103; cited by Harry Sieber, 'The Romance of Chivalry in Spain: From Montalvo to Cervantes,' in *Romance: Generic Transformations from Chrétien de Troyes to Cervantes*, ed. Kevin Brownlee and Marina Scordilis Brownlee (Hanover and London, 1985), p. 206.

41 See Michael Harney, *Kinship and Marriage in Medieval Hispanic Chivalric Romance* (Turnhout, 2001), p. 145.

42 Diego de San Pedro, *Cárcel de Amor*, ed. Keith Whinnom, 3rd ed. (Madrid, 1985), pp. 88–9. A late-medieval Spanish version of the Tristan triangle – therefore one presumably contemporary to earlier, lost versions of the *Amadís* – is found in *El cuento de Tristán de Leonís*, ed. Northup, pp. 122–4 (containing the episodes of Mark's marriage to Isolde, and the wedding-night substitution of a handmaiden, called Branjen, for the Queen).

romances, by the domestic allegiance of the monogamous couple. R. Howard Bloch, interpreting the 'economics of romance,' explains how emphasis on the *ménage* as opposed to the *maison* (i.e. the lineage) leads to the formation of a 'fundamentally new *patrimoine*,' belonging to 'the newly formed conjugal couple, definitively separated from the lineage of birth.' The earlier rule, of patrilineal 'autonomy of maternal and paternal lines . . . is abrogated so as to effect the continual cognatic alienation of that which . . . was considered the inalienable right, the proper, of dynastic succession.'[43]

This focus on the household, ultimately supported by an ideology of individual marital consent fomented by the Church, both reflects and accelerates a bourgeoisification of real-world society. This illuminates why, in later romances, the 'principal subject . . . is heterosexual love and its relationship to the social convention of marriage.'[44] F. L. Critchlow's study of French *romans d'aventure* of the late twelfth and thirteenth centuries cogently summarizes the genre's typical plot as one in which a woman's preferences are 'seldom respected or consulted' in the arrangement of her marriage. To evade her father's marital strategy, 'she connives with her lover, who has been thrust aside by her unwilling parent for another, to defeat her lord's purposes by a resort to ruse.'[45]

The romances analyzed by Critchlow – the *Comte de Poitiers*, *Escanor*, *Floris et Liriope*, *Joufrois*, etc. – present a notable contrast with the Tristan and Lancelot romances. Those earlier stories accentuate the injustice of the forced marriage, the quandary of the *mal mariée*. Many readers of such works could have construed the adultery as a legitimate response to a repressive system that victimized women in the name of status, property, and patrilineal continuity. The essentially supportive depiction of adultery in the Tristan and Lancelot romances sympathizes with female defiance of patriarchal despotism, within the context of the on-going social transformation that originates in the adoption of the consensual model of marriage by ever-broader segments of society. Where the *Tristan* and *Lancelot* romances exonerate adultery in terms of a flawed marriage contract, later romances justify amorous autonomy as a thwarting of nuptial constraint.[46]

We may understand the advent of the original, medieval *Amadís* as a response to this bourgeois, consensual environment. An anonymous author/adapter, modeling his work on the paradigm offered by some version or versions of the French prose *Lancelot*, devised an analogue in which the husband-wife-lover triangle was replaced by another triangle, that of the father-daughter-suitor. López de Ayala's reference confirms that the two versions, the adulterous and the consensual, coexisted into early-modern times. This conjunction of the two modes is additionally confirmed by the ongoing popularity of the Tristan theme

---

43 R. Howard Bloch, *Etymologies and Genealogies. A Literary Anthropology of the French Middle Ages* (Chicago, 1983), pp. 162–4.

44 Harney, *Kinship and Marriage*, pp. 146–7. See also Dafydd Evans, 'Wishfulfilment: The Social Function and Classification of Old French Romances,' in *Court and Poet: Selected Proceedings of the Third Congress of the International Courtly Literature Society, Liverpool, 1980*, ed. Glynn S. Burgess et al. (Liverpool, 1981), p. 129 [129–34].

45 Frank L. Critchlow, 'On the Forms of Betrothals and Wedding Ceremonies in the Old French *Romans d'aventure*,' *Modern Philology*, 2 (1904–05), 502 [497–537].

46 Harney, *Kinship and Marriage*, pp. 241–4.

and its various manifestations. The two literary treatments of marriage and consent coexist, we might argue, because the generalized social effects of the ideology of consent take many centuries to manifest themselves; indeed, familial conflict over the marriage arrangement remains a social issue and a literary theme down to the present day.

Meanwhile, the many sequels of the *Amadís*, as well as such works as the *Palmerín de Oliva*, its continuation, *Palmerín de Inglaterra*, and their sequels, are explicable in their maintenance of the pseudo-Arthurian profile in that they are obvious emulations of *Amadís*.[47] The same may be said – as to century of composition and imitative nature – of such Portuguese romances as *Clarimundo*, and of the large number of chivalric romances in Castilian surveyed by Daniel Eisenberg in his study of this genre in its sixteenth-century heyday.[48]

---

[47] Thomas, *Spanish and Portuguese Romances*, pp. 85–91; Sieber, 'The Romance of Chivalry in Spain,' p. 205.

[48] Eisenberg provides a very thorough survey of scholarship on the chivalric romances, of the late medieval background and earlier versions before their sixteenth-century popularity, and of the sixteenth-century genre ('Who Read the Romances?' pp. 9–54).

17

Neither Sublime nor Gallant:
The Portuguese Demanda *and the New Destiny of Man*

HAQUIRA OSAKABE

[Translated by Elspeth M. Ferguson]

The *Demanda do Santo Graal*[1] (Quest for the Holy Grail) exists as a fifteenth-century copy of a manuscript from the preceding era consisting of the Portuguese translation (possibly direct) of a French original. It is thought that the latter, in its most complete form, has disappeared. The integral state of the text in its current manuscript form (MS 2594 of the National Library of Vienna) allows us to discuss the transformation processes (and the reasons for them) through which the matière de Bretagne must have passed to arrive at this point, for it contains numerous modifications when compared with its sources, both recent and remote. The Christian intervention, taking advantage of the power of the myth conveyed by the story of the Grail from its origin, was without doubt one of the main factors in these changes. The creation of a lineage from Joseph of Arimathia to chivalric times and the attribution of a eucharistic nature to the object called the Grail are confirmation of this process of transformation of the story and the myth by intellectually active sectors of the Church in the first centuries of this millennium.

But the Christianisation did not stop there. The thirteenth century saw the configuration of two great cycles in which the chivalric matière was subjected to more profound organisation and unification. Its very structure passed through the sieve of increasingly strong religious intervention.

Let me recapitulate. The first of these cycles, now known as the *Vulgate Cycle* (1215–35) or *Lancelot-Grail*, centres around the journey of Arthur's greatest hero, from infancy through his adventures at court until his death, including the tensions between Lancelot and King Arthur and culminating in the downfall of the kingdom. Between the beginning (*Lancelot*) and the end (*Mort Artu*) of this trajectory is the narrative (*Queste del Saint Graal*) of the figure of Galahad, the great knight's son whose moral consistency distinguishes him from his father (in the context of the *Cycle*, of course) without eclipsing his father's importance or worth. Thus the *Lancelot–Queste del Saint Graal–Mort Artu* trilogy, which forms the fundamental and innovative part of this ensemble, cannot free itself from the

---

[1] The text used is *A Demanda do Santo Graal*, ed. Irene Freire Nunes (Lisbon, 1995). See also *A Demanda do Santo Graal*, ed. Joseph Piel, completed by Irene Freire Nunes (Lisbon, 1988).

196 HAQUIRA OSAKABE

powerful presence of the greatest hero of earthly chivalry, despite the moralising nature of the second book.

In spite of the apparent architectonic unity of this great whole, it is not difficult to accept Jean Frappier's thesis that three distinct individuals hold authorial responsibility for the trilogy.[2] In our opinion, two facts justify this hypothesis. The first is the non-episodic nature of the second book (hereafter referred to as the *Vulgate Queste*) compared to the other romances. The second is the melancholy tone of the third book. If, on the one hand, the third book has a certain closeness to the *Lancelot* in terms of its episodic nature, on the other hand its clearly elegaic tone sets it apart – and at the same time its more detailed style and its greater preponderance of episodic plot differentiate it from the second book. The third book also distances itself from the second through a less committed and, to a certain extent, spiritually resigned world vision in which the re-evaluation of chivalric ideals continues to confront religious values. To be more precise, although the *Mort Artu* ends with the downfall of the chivalric kingdom of Logres, the whole romance never fails to defend its pre-eminent hero, as will be seen further on.

The second cycle, known as the *Post-Vulgate*, was composed immediately after the first. It consists of fragments only and forms the basis of the Portuguese document mentioned above (hereafter referred to as the Portuguese *Demanda*). The second cycle consisted hypothetically of three parts: the *Estoire del Saint Graal*, *Merlin* and *Queste del Saint Graal*. Everything would indicate a major alteration in this cycle compared to the earlier version: in the hypothetical original of the last part (hereafter referred to as the *Post-Vulgate Queste*) the basic plot of the romance of the same name in the *Vulgate* was fused with its sequel, the *Mort Artu*. The Portuguese *Demanda do Santo Graal* and the Spanish *Demanda del Sancto Grial* are derived from that text.

At the present stage of research into Arthurian texts, the conclusions which can be drawn about the Portuguese *Demanda*, its innovations and its specific features, are always provisional because, as aforementioned, we have only fragments of the text or texts from which it appears to originate. The monumental work of Fanni Bogdanow in re-establishing the text of the romance by articulating diverse fragments, has, to date, been published only in part.[3] A comparison of the Portuguese *Demanda* and the *Post-Vulgate Queste* will not only have to await the publication of all the final half, but will also have to accept that a large part of the episodes which constitute the first half are only comprehensible in conjunction with the Portuguese text. This means that everything which could be said about a hypothetical underlying text is, for the moment, only verifiable in the Portuguese text except in those sections where we are fortunate to have the French original. In any case, while all the labour of textual archaeology being carried out, particularly by Bogdanow, is of fundamental importance, another field of enquiry is already open: the elaboration of hypotheses on the reasons for the changes which a possible definitive text of the *Post-Vulgate Queste* could

2 *La Mort le roi Artu*, ed. Jean Frappier, 3rd ed. (Geneva and Paris, 1964), Introduction.
3 Fanni Bogdanow, *La version Post-Vulgate de la Queste del Saint Graal et de la Mort Artu* (Paris, 1991).

prove. In this task, the importance of the Portuguese *Demanda*, the sole complete witness to the existence of the final book in the *Cycle*, is that it can underpin that which the original fragments cannot yet authorise at the present stage of research. Beyond that, and most importantly, its significance is immeasurable if we consider it less as a document and more as a literary work, given its providentially complete and integral state. It is from this point of view that we will attempt to consider it.

Let us begin our analysis by considering the effects on meaning arising not only from the fusion or combination of the *Vulgate Queste* and *Mort Artu*, but also from the elimination of everything relating to Lancelot in the previous cycle. In this connection, it should be noted that the *Post-Vulgate Cycle* omits all the narration of great chivalric deeds, passing directly from the pre-history of the Grail (Joseph of Arimathia and Merlin) to the account of the *Demanda* and the downfall of the Arthurian kingdom. This consideration guarantees the prime importance of the *Post-Vulgate Queste* in the corpus of great transformations undergone by the Arthurian story. Taking as our starting point the prime testimony supplied by the Portuguese *Demanda*, we can make the following observations:

1. The *Post-Vulgate Queste* is far from being a translation, even a free translation, of its *Vulgate* namesake.

2. Conversely, because of the deliberate suppression of the *Lancelot*, there are several important discursive transformations. In the first place, episodes and themes linked to Lancelot either pass through a process of diminution or suffer a kind of dislocation. For example, in this work, allusions to facts relating to the excessively worldly character of Lancelot are consigned to a past supposedly familiar to the reader and are retained only as referential support for the new information in the narrative. The author moves from what we might call transformation of the previous story to simple episodic allusion, for the sole purpose of making the current work autonomous. The hero's birth, his deeds of valour, his love affair with Guinevere and even his paternity of Galahad are scarcely mentioned. It is quite clear that the narrative scope and also the desired emphasis are quite different. Besides this, the *Post-Vulgate Queste* carries out a similar procedure with the episodes concerning Tristan which its author has extracted from the original context of the Tristan tradition, introducing into them innovations and interpolations which take on new meaning in this work.

Having established this, let us consider two questions before making a closer examination of the romance. The first of these, already indicated in the preceding lines, concerns its autonomy as a work in the structural scheme in which it is presented. The second, which also concerns the question of autonomy, refers to the problem that the Portuguese *Demanda* is a translation, not an original text.

The first question does not seem to present major problems. The Portuguese *Demanda* has referential autonomy, although it harks back to a whole preceding discursive context and, as has been seen, it is made up not only of the *Vulgate Queste* and the *Mort Artu* but is also indebted for a good many of its episodes to the version of the quest in the *Prose Tristan*. Besides this, it introduces episodes which did not exist in that context (unless there is a gap in the document). Examples of this are the famous episode of Galahad and Bohort in the castle of Brutus and Lancelot's nightmares (different from his dreams in the *Vulgate Queste*); these justify fully what we have just stated. Dealing with the particular case of the *Post-Vulgate Queste*, and more specifically with the Portuguese *Demanda*, it must be allowed that it constitutes a new, autonomous work to be regarded as a complete entity in the eyes of the reader. In this respect, it must be considered one of the most representative extant documents of the late Middle Ages. As we have seen, it is a late work (whether the hypothetical French original or our definitive version) and contains content highly revealing of its crepuscular nature.

The autonomy of the Portuguese *Demanda* as a literary work conceived as a whole, leads to a second question, which is the fact that it is a translation. This raises some interesting problems. In the first place, we cannot talk of an authorial style or authorial invention in this case, except in those parts where a documentary comparison allows us to prove it. However, in a great many medieval texts, the intervention of copyists or translators was common. This can authorise (if the comparison of fragments allows it) the idea of a certain autonomy, at least stylistic, for the *Demanda*. The researcher Colette Storms, of the University of Louvain, recently presented an analysis comparing fragments which relate to the episode of Galahad at the castle of Brutus, and observed that the Portuguese translation accentuated the condemnatory character of the original text.[4]

To proceed, given the lack of a complete base text to be used in stylistic comparison, the parameters for analysis of the Portuguese text must come from the text itself. Thus it is necessary to assume criteria which take into account the coherence of the stylistic options as well as their appropriateness within the linguistic patterns of Galician-Portuguese at the time of its translation.

Thus we believe that it is legitimate to work from the hypothesis, even if provisional, that the Portuguese *Demanda* is justified and explained in the context of the heightened moral tension of the end of the medieval period. At that time, within the discourse of spiritual edification, transgressions signified a rupture in the loving union which emanated from God. Because of this, the notion of guilt then occupied an important place. And the notion of punishment too.

We will begin with the examination of a fairly obvious procedure: the Portuguese *Demanda* adds a second ending onto the one represented by the death of Galahad and the news Bohort receives about the kingdom of Logres before he reaches Camelot. To recapitulate: the *Vulgate Queste* ends with the episode of the death of Galahad (and of Perceval) in Sarraz. These deaths had not only been announced previously but, most importantly, the death of Galahad was a desired death, the culmination of the grace which would be

---

4   Colette van Coolput-Storms, 'Souillure, indignité et haine de soi: l'impossible rachat dans la *Demanda do Santo Graal*,' in *Atlas do I Seminário Internacional de Trabalho Filológico sobre Textos Medievais Portugueses* (São Paolo, forthcoming).

granted to him through the contemplation of the Grail. The only survivor of the three is Bohort, to whom falls the mission of recounting what has happened to Arthur and what remains of his court. The *Mort Artu* begins exactly at this point and its central action revolves around the destinies not only of the king but, especially, of Lancelot. As we said before, the moral preoccupation of this romance is to dignify a content reminiscent of the chivalric ideal of vassalage, the attribute of Lancelot which moves the betrayed king and prevails over the lust so roundly condemned in the previous book.

In the architecture of the *Cycle*, the *Vulgate Queste* constitutes almost a suspension of the episodic plot, a kind of temporal lapse, in which the earthly adventure and the illusions of chivalry are replaced by a purely spiritual purpose. It is an adventurous pilgrimage in which the heroes are called to abandon material arms and to submit to a succession of temptations, purifications and sorrows which finally lead to a strange event. The *Vulgate Queste* is a concentratedly doctrinaire and spiritualising work with a pessimistic ending with respect to expectations of earthly success, proposing to man a difficult life of spiritualisation whose recompense is not in any way in accordance with human logic which links effort to reward. In that sense, the *Vulgate Queste*, more than the account of an adventure, which, in itself, results in human failure, constitutes a kind of doctrinal-didactic fiction which points out primarily the initial mistake which set in motion the earthly search for the Grail. In fact, Arthur's sad premonitions of the outcome of that adventure show clearly that the substance to which it aspired was not compatible with the human, gallant world of the court. But this is obvious. Beyond relating success or failure, the whole of the *Vulgate Queste* stems from the unfolding of an emblematic discourse through its doctrinal content. This is the source of its synthetic or sparse character in which the destiny of the hero culminates in the glory of its own impossibility. That is, Galahad is the hero of another dimension, a dimension glimpsed with the utmost difficulty by his closest companions: the *Queste* maintains a victorious but extremely selective doctrine.

The *Mort Artu*, in its turn, marks the return to earthly reality and tries to reduce the weight of Lancelot's sins, failures and betrayals. This is its purpose, much more than narrating the end of the Arthurian kingdom. Finally, surprisingly, the narrative manages to separate and grade qualities and defects in such a way that there is a clear division between the sins on one hand and the chivalric virtues on the other. Thus earthly chivalry redeems its sinful hero through profane merits.

Seen as a whole, the Portuguese *Demanda* is structured as a series of episodes within episodes. Its beginning and its ending have Arthur and Lancelot as their main characters and, as concrete setting, the kingdom of Logres from whence the knights set out for adventures and to which those who remain return. Inside this outer compartment, which deals with all the human tensions surrounding the love affair of Lancelot and the queen and the great dissensions within the kingdom, fits the great adventure of Galahad, and, inside that, the episodes in which both the lovers of Camelot and Tristan himself expiate their lust. In comparison with the *Vulgate Queste*, the plots of the Portuguese *Demanda* are richer and the transition to the outcome is therefore slower. The inclusion of the

episodes inherited from the Tristan tradition and the more substantial appearance of Lancelot's '*crises de conscience*' are signs of the greater episodic
complexity of this work. We may recall the long parallel adventure undertaken
by Palamedes in his pursuit of the Questing Beast; and the conflict between that
character and Tristan which occasions a sort of lover's quest which causes
Tristan to deviate even more from the straight way of the celestial quest.

Because of this structuring, it is possible and justifiable to claim that the
Portuguese *Demanda* is a romance with a double (or perhaps triple) ending, one
giving rise to another. (The significant impact of this will be further discussed
later on.) The first of the endings goes a little beyond the ending of the *Vulgate
Queste*, which finishes with the arrival of Bohort in Logres:

> Quant Boorz vit qu'il ert remés tot seuls en si loingteinnes terres com es parties de
> Babiloine, si se parti de Sarra tot armez et vint a la mer et entra en une nef. Si li
> avint si bien que en assez poi de tens ariva el roialme de Logres. Et quant il fu
> venuz el pais, si chevalcha tan par ses jornees qu'il vint a Camaalot, ou li rois
> Artus estoit. Si ne fu onques si grant joie fete come il firent de lui, qar bien le
> cuidoient avoir perdu a touz jors mes, por ce que si longuement avoit esté fors
> del pais.[5]

> [When Bohort saw that he was completely alone in such distant lands as regions
> of Babylon, he left Sarraz, completely armed, came to the sea and boarded a ship.
> He was extremely fortunate and arrived quickly in the kingdom of Logres. And
> when he arrived in the country, he rode without stopping until he came to
> Camelot where King Arthur was. And never was there such great rejoicing as at
> this return as they had thought him lost for ever as he had been out of the country
> for so long.]

This passage exists in the Portuguese *Demanda* but an intermediary episode
separates it from the account of the arrival of Bohort at King Arthur's castle. It is
the moment when he is informed of the dissension in the realm and learns of the
desire to tell the king of the queen's betrayal with Lancelot:

> 'E como vai, disse el, na corte aa linhagem de rei Bam?
> – Mui bem, disse ele, fora duas cousas: a ña, porque rei Artur ha queixume já
> quanto de Estor de Mares, que retou Galvam pola morte de Erec depois que se
> tormarom da demanda do Santo Graal. E outrossi pola morte de Palamedes; e
> quer provar que nom deve seer cavaleiro nem haver a companha da Távola
> Redonda. E houvera ende a seer a batalha, ca nom ficara por Estor, mas a raña e
> dom Lançalot meterom i paz. Mas nunca se pois amarom, onde a linhagem de rei
> Artur vai posfaçando acá em poridade, mas nom sei se dizem verdade, ca dom
> Lançalot jaz com a raia e qurem-no dizer a el-rei por meterem mortal desamor
> entre el-rei e a linhagem de rei Bam.'[6]

> [And, he said, how is it with the lineage of King Ban at court?
> – Very well, he said, apart from two things: firstly, King Arthur is displeased
> with Hector de Mares, who challenged Gawain over the death of Erec after they
> returned from the quest for the Holy Grail, and also over the death of Palamedes;

5 *La Queste del Saint Graal*, ed. Albert Pauphilet (Paris, 1949), p. 274.
6 *A Demanda do Santo Graal*, p. 458, para. 630.

wishing to prove that he should not be a knight and not belong to the fellowship of the Round Table. And the contest would already have taken place if Hector had had his way, but the queen and Sir Lancelot made peace between them. But they never cared for each other after that. Secondly, the purity of the lineage of King Arthur is being stained, as they say (although I do not know if they are telling the truth) that Sir Lancelot lies with the queen and they want to tell the king in order to provoke mortal enmity between the King and King Ban's lineage.]

In our opinion, this is the first ending of the *Post-Vulgate Queste* and the *Demanda*. Only after this does Bohort arrive in Camelot.

The second ending of the romance could, in its turn, be unfolded into a third. That is the account of the death of Arthur, which reproduces in general terms the text of the *Mort Artu*, but with substantial alteration concerning the death of the king himself. Remember that in the text of the *Vulgate*, after the episode of the sword, Girflet, on the insistence of the king, leaves him and goes to a nearby hill, from where he sees the arrival of Morgain who, with other ladies, invites the king to go aboard her ship. The king accepts and the craft moves away. Days later the same Girflet returns to the Black Chapel to find out if Lucan has been buried and there finds two tombs, one of Lucan, the other of Arthur. Girflet asks the hermit if it is true that the king is buried there and receives confirmation from the hermit. In the Portuguese *Demanda*, we read, first of all, that Arthur's insistence that Girflet depart is justified by the king himself: ' "nom quero que fiquedes comigo ca mia fim se achega. E nom. é cousa posta que nenuu saiba verdade de mia fim" '[7] ['I do not want you to remain with me as my end is near. And it is ordained that no one shall know the truth about my end']. In the second place, in the narration of the Portuguese *Demanda*, it is not confirmed that the body of Arthur is actually buried in the Black Chapel. Girflet discovers that the tomb attributed to the king is empty and instead of his body there is only his helmet. (We will return to the importance of this change later on.) But this second dénouement has its counterpart in the narration of the death of Lancelot. Here too the episode is based on the narrative of the *Mort Artu* but with the addition of a significant ingredient. It is the account of the episode of the death of the queen which establishes the link between the death of Arthur and the death of Lancelot. The Portuguese *Demanda* draws the aforementioned episode, omitted from the *Mort Artu*, from a Tristanian source: the queen, having taken the veil, cannot bear the rigours of the religious life and falls mortally ill. She is helped by a maiden who had loved Girflet and who sends word to Lancelot from the queen in the hope that he will arrive and save her. Meanwhile, another maiden, who had loved Lancelot, for the sake of vengeance announces that he will not come as his ship has been lost at sea. The queen is overcome and dies, not without previously wishing that her heart be sent to her beloved as proof of her passion. Lancelot does not receive it but he does learn of her death with great grief. What follows is an almost exact reproduction of the *Mort Artu* in respect of the fate of Lancelot: the struggle and revenge against the descen-

7   *A Demanda do Santo Graal*, p. 493, para 684.

dants of Mordred, his withdrawal to the hermit life with Blioberis and the Archbishop of Canterbury, where he dies and is afterwards buried in the Joyous
Guard. It should be remembered, however, that the *Mort Artu* ends with Bohort
abandoning his own kingdom (Gaunes) and dedicating himself, in the place of
Lancelot, to the hermit life together with the same Blioberis, the Archbishop of
Canterbury, and also Meraugis, who has recently become a hermit. However,
the *Demanda* continues beyond this reference, and this is fundamental. Onto the
scene comes King Marc of Cornwall who orders the complete devastation of the
kingdom of Logres and all its symbols, and the destruction of 'all the churches
and monasteries' which Arthur had built. Furthermore, King Marc orders the
destruction of the tomb of Lancelot and the burning of his body. This devastation only stops with the killing of Marc by a descendant of the family of Ban. The
survivor of all this is Bohort.

Let us pick up here the order of the two great endings. In the first, after the
death of Galahad, Bohort decides to return to Logres. As we have already said,
on the way to Camelot, he learns of the great moral misery which threatens the
unity of the kingdom. In the second ending, firstly everything points to the
death of Arthur, especially after the return of the sword to the lake. He is
survived by the queen, Lancelot and, among few other companions in arms,
Bohort. But then the queen dies, affirming, despite all, the great passion which
united her to Lancelot and him to her. Giving himself up to the virtues of the
hermit's life, the 'Chevalier de la Charrette' dies in an aura of holiness. His tomb
remains to perpetuate his name and valour. With King Marc, however, there
comes a definitive twist in the romance with the devastation not only of the
entire kingdom but of the remains of its best knight. Once again it is Bohort who
survives, this time as a hermit.

It is important to note that, although he is never a salient character in the
Demanda, Bohort always ends up appearing as the great survivor of all the
adventures. Particularly in this version when he is the sole survivor of the great
devastation unleashed by King Marc of Cornwall. For what reasons would the
author of this last *Demanda*, as he re-wrote it, once again keep this character,
since, with the addition, it would be normal to believe that nothing at all would
remain of the kingdom? Let us try to answer.

When he decided to merge the *Vulgate Queste* and the *Mort Artu*, the author of
the *Demanda* was re-telling stories from the point of view of one who already
had a vision of the whole of the preceding romances and thus understood the
necessity of stressing certain aspects. We already mentioned that allusive references were used to fill gaps arising from the elimination of certain episodes from
the cycle. However, in the case of the joining together of the *Mort Artu* and
Vulgate Queste, the author seems to have wanted to insert the central plot into an
episodic development which provoked a much more dramatic impact than the
separate reading of the two texts. The ending of the *Vulgate Queste*, let us
remember, is gently melancholic compared to the corresponding ending of the
Portuguese *Demanda* where Logres already appears threatened by the dissensions which will take place. And instead of allowing the icons of the Arthurian
kingdom to survive with the symbolic grandiosity of the resting places of
Arthur and Lancelot, the *Demanda* creates in the first place the enigma of the

disappearance of Arthur's body and then presents the disoriented reader with the decimation of the kingdom and, above all, the disappearance of the remains of its most emblematic knight. Thus it can be considered that, in the episodic plan, the *Demanda*, for its own purposes, rewrites the adventures of the Round Table in a climate of almost total discouragement, with nothing surviving the moral and physical downfall of the kingdom. Except Bohort. In his extraordinary article on the *Vulgate Queste*, Etienne Gilson sees in the figure of this unfortunate knight the most obvious manifestation of the lower level of Grace.[8] He suffers the most cruel trials and yet is the least rewarded of the three knights of the Grail. It is his humanity without grandeur which brings him the prize and the task of surviving Galahad, Perceval, Arthur, Lancelot and the very kingdom of Logres at the end of everything.

Let us elaborate a little on the reflections of Gilson: the Portuguese *Demanda* seems to alert its reader to the surprising fact that what survives the idyllic, adventurous dreams of earthly chivalry and the mystical aspirations of heavenly chivalry is the amazing strangeness of a completely ordinary man. Without the outbursts of Lancelot and without the impetuosity of Galahad, it falls to Bohort, legitimate expression of humanity, to accept from here on a common, anonymous life. Beyond any ambition, what is left to him is the simple exercise of humility.

We said above that the Portuguese *Demanda* 'creates' the enigma of Arthur's empty tomb in the Black Chapel, a fact which follows directly from the preceding speech of Arthur: ' "And it is ordained that no one shall know the truth about my end." ' This episode leaves something hanging in the air. The tomb which would establish the definitive truth about the death of Arthur is found to be empty. And, finally, no one saw him die, although he was seen retiring in the ship of his sister Morgain.

Thus, in the rewriting of the story, the *Demanda*, on the one hand, prepares the reader for a very clear lesson: the destiny of man is neither sublime nor heroic but simply prosaic. But on the other hand, something turns this destiny a little more mysterious, like the final destiny of Arthur, who was born under the sign of a redeeming promise.

---

8   Etienne Gilson, 'La Mystique de la Grâce dans la *Queste del Saint Graal*,' *Romania*, 51 (1925), 321–47.

18

The Lancelots of the Lowlands

FRANK BRANDSMA

Introduction

What could be more natural than translating an Old French prose text into Middle Dutch prose? Two small fragments from a fourteenth-century manuscript illustrate precisely this, for they contain a Middle Dutch prose translation of the French prose *Lancelot*. And yet in the Low Countries there is far more manuscript evidence of translations of the same text in rhymed couplets: *Lantsloot vander Haghedochte* (c. 1260), and the *Lanceloet–Queeste van den Grale–Arturs doet* trilogy (c. 1280) preserved in the *Lancelot* Compilation (c. 1320).[1] It is generally assumed that the two rhymed versions preceded the prose version, although there is as yet no conclusive evidence for this. The three independent translations of the Old French prose *Lancelot* might therefore represent a gradual introduction of its literary innovations, such as the use of prose and the use of *li contes* as an impersonal narrator, into Middle Dutch literature.

---

1 On *Lantsloot*, see W. P. Gerritsen, ed., *Lantsloot vander Haghedochte: Fragmenten van een Middelnederlandse bewerking van de Lancelot en prose*, with intro. and commentary by Gerritsen, Middelnederlandse Lancelotromans, 2 (Amsterdam, 1987); see also F. P. van Oostrom, *Lantsloot vander Haghedochte: Onderzoekingen over een Middelnederlandse bewerking van de Lancelot en prose* (Amsterdam, 1981). The full text of the Compilation is in W. J. A. Jonckbloet, ed., *Roman van Lancelot (XIIIe eeuw)*, 2 vols. ('s-Gravenhage, 1846–49). One third of the *Lanceloet–Queeste–Artus doet* trilogy and a number of the inserted romances have yet to be edited. The new partial editions are: Bart Besamusca and Ada Postma, eds., *Lanceloet. De Middel-nederlandse vertaling van de Lancelot en prose overgeleverd in de Lancelotcompilatie: Pars 1 (vs. 1–5530, voorafgegaan door de verzen van het Brusselse fragment)*, Middelnederlandse Lancelotromans, 4 (Hilversum, 1997); Bart Besamusca, ed., *Lanceloet. De Middelnederlandse vertaling van de Lancelot en prose overgeleverd in de Lancelotcompilatie: Pars 2 (vs. 5531–10740), met een inleidende studie over de vertaaltechniek*, Middelnederlandse Lancelotromans, 5 (Assen and Maastricht, 1991); Frank Brandsma, ed., *Lanceloet. De Middelnederlandse vertaling van de Lancelot en prose overgeleverd in de Lancelotcompilatie: Pars 3 (vs. 10741–16263), met een inleidende studie over de entrelacement- vertelwijze*, Middelnederlandse Lancelotromans, 6 (Assen, 1992); Ada Postma, ed., *Lanceloet. De Middelnederlandse vertaling van de Lancelot en prose overgeleverd in de Lancelotcompilatie: Pars 4 (vs. 16264–26636)*, Middelnederlandse Lancelotromans, 7 (Hilversum, 1998). For discussion of the three translations, see W. P. Gerritsen, Orlanda S. H. Lie and F. P. van Oostrom, 'Le *Lancelot-en-prose* et ses traductions moyen-néerlandaises,' in *Langue et littérature françaises du Moyen Age*, ed. R. E. V. Stuip (Assen, 1978), pp. 39–49, and in *Arturistiek in artikelen: Een bundel fotomechanisch herdrukte studies over Middelnederlandse Arturromans*, ed. F. P. van Oostrom (Utrecht, 1978), pp. 137–47, with a bibliography of Middle Dutch arthuriana since 1945. A guide to recent Arthurian research in the Low Countries can be found in Bart Besamusca, 'The Low Countries,' in *Medieval Arthurian Literature: A Guide to Recent Research*, ed. Norris J. Lacy (New York and London, 1996), pp. 211–37.

Whether this idea is completely convincing is debatable, but first we must consider the texts themselves, starting with the prose fragments. Then we will focus on the famous Middle Dutch *Lancelot* Compilation.

The Middle Dutch Prose Lancelot

The prose manuscript fragments belong to the Rotterdam Gemeentebibliotheek collection (hence the name 'Rotterdam Fragments' and the initial *R*) and are dated c. 1340–50; the original prose translation may have been done in the thirteenth century, after or about the same time as the verse translations. They consist of two non-consecutive parchment folios with two columns of prose on each side, eight columns of forty-one lines in all, with four red and blue initials two lines high; the end of sentences is usually marked with a dot. The dialect is predominantly Brabantine. Both folios contain episodes belonging to the so-called 'Préparation à la Queste' section of the French prose *Lancelot*. The first fragment describes how Gawain is invited to take part in the tournament at the 'Chastel del Moulin.' In the second fragment Lancelot lies ill after drinking from a poisoned well and the damsel who can cure him wants to know what her reward will be for restoring him to health.[2] In her groundbreaking study and edition of the fragments, Orlanda Lie calls this episode (*R* II) the 'Virgin Love Covenant,' and the other episode (*R* I) the 'Chastel del Moulin.'[3] Her comparison of the fragments with their nearest extant French relatives shows that the prose translator followed his source almost word for word, sometimes even giving a more succinct account by omitting superfluous explanatory phrases or tightening the syntax. We can see this in the lines describing Thanaguin's request for help from Gawain in the tournament. This moment in the narrative is important because it also provides examples of the translation techniques of the *Lantsloot* and *Lanceloet* translators; the French text is represented by the short version (*LS* IV, 336.10–15):

> si li requiert quil li ait . Et mesires Gauuain dist quil li aidera volentiers . Grans mercis sire fet li cheualiers . Dont ne doute iou mie . que iou naie lonor del tornoiement .
>
> A tant sassistrent au souper . si furent moult lie cil de laiens de la promesse que mesires Gauuain lor auoit faite . Car grant fiance auoient en lui de uaintre le tornoiement.

> [and he (Thanaguin) implored him (Gauvain) to help him. And my lord Gauvain said he would help him gladly. 'Thank you very much, sir,' the knight said, 'now I do not doubt at all that I will have the honour of the tournament.'

---

[2] The first fragment corresponds to *LS* (*The Vulgate Version of the Arthurian Romances*, ed. H. Oskar Sommer, 7 vols. [(Washington, D.C., 1908–13); rpt. New York, 1979]) IV, 335.36 – 338.39, and *LM* (*Lancelot: roman en prose du XIIIe siècle*, ed. Alexandre Micha, 9 vols. [Geneva, 1978–83]) 2:357–62 (lxv, 7–17); the second to *LS* V, 81.28 – 83.35, and *LM* 4:153–8 (lxxvi, 30–36).

[3] O. S. H. Lie, *The Middle Dutch Prose Lancelot: A Study of the Rotterdam Fragments and their Place in the French, German, and Dutch Lancelot en prose Tradition*, Middelnederlandse Lancelotromans, 3 (Amsterdam, 1987).

Then they sat down to supper and were very glad of the promise my lord Gauvain had made them, for they had great faith that he would win the tournament.][4]

The Middle Dutch prose text (*R* I, lines 14–20) follows the French closely (differences are in italics):

Ende hi bat hem *op grote vrienscap* dat hi hem holpe. Ende mijn here Walewein seide dat hijt gerne doen soude. '*Danc* hebt,' seit hi (*die riddere*) '*ende* ic duchte mi dan lettel, ic en sal hebben den prijs van den tornoie.'

Doe ghingense sitten ten etene. Ende alle die van daer binnen waren blide van den gelove dat mijn here Walewein gelovet hadde, bedi sie hadden grote hope dat *sie* den tornoi verwinnen souden.

[And he implored him to help him for the sake of their great friendship. And my lord Gauvain said he would gladly do so. 'Thank you,' the knight said, 'now I am not afraid that I shall not win the prize of the tournament.'

Then they sat down for the meal. And all the people who were inside the castle were happy with the promise that my lord Gauvain had made, because they cherished hopes that they would win the tournament.][5]

Overall, the differences are few and far between. What is really striking is that the prose translator has often achieved a word for word correspondence with the French original. He works at the level of the word. He is able to do so because he is not constrained by rhyme or stress which would require him to think and express himself in verse and couplets. His various emphases also belong to the word level, as when he qualifies Thanaguin's request ('op grote vrienscap') with a more sober word of thanks and with the bystanders' confidence that they (and not just he) will win the tournament. The more explicit inquit-formula could also be explained by a dittography in the French exemplar ('fet li li chevaliers') caused by misreading the first 'li' as 'il,' but this seems unlikely: the Dutch translator must have preferred this atypical construction to indicate the speaker, for he uses it three more times in the fragments.[6]

A Rhymed Adaptation: Lantsloot vander Haghedochte

The prose translator's work contrasts starkly with the adaptation of the French text by the poet of *Lantsloot vander Haghedochte* (*LH*), but before we turn to his version of this same episode, it is important to note that the three Dutch translations are based on three different French manuscripts which belong to different strands in the complicated prose *Lancelot* tradition.[7] This tells us that the transla-

---

4 For a translation of the long version (*LM* 2:357–8 [lxv, 9]) see *Lancelot-Grail: The Old French Arthurian Vulgate and Post-Vulgate in Translation*, ed. Norris J. Lacy (New York and London, 1993–97), III, 95.

5 Translations are from Lie, *The Middle Dutch Prose Lancelot*, p. 195.

6 Cf. *R* I, lines 34 and 36, and *R* II, line 34.

7 Lie shows that for the Chastel del Moulin episode the prose text follows one group of manuscripts of the short version, whereas the exemplar of *Lanceloet* (the text in the Compilation)

tions were made independently, an idea that is corroborated by a parallel
reading of the texts. Fortunately, the Chastel del Moulin episode exists in the
prose fragments as well as in *LH* and in the Compilation manuscript, so we have
three versions of the same passage. A comparison clearly shows that the translators did not use one anothers' text(s). Each worked independently from his own
French exemplar, translating according to his own guidelines. The prose translator focused on the word and the *LH* poet focused on the paragraph, as his
version of the meeting of Thanaguin and Gawain/Walewein shows:

	Doe die dienst was gedaen	[When the serving was done
6036	Entie maeltijt vergaen	And the meal was over
	Bat die here sinen gast	The lord asked his guest
	Met goeder herten harde vast,	Wholeheartedly and sincerely,
	Entie ridders allegader	And the knights all together
6040	Badens des aventuren vader,	Asked the father of adventures
	Waleweine, die bi hem sat,	Gawain, who was sitting next to him,
	Entie vrouwe mede bat,	And the lady also asked,
	Dat hi wapine droeghe,	That he would carry arms,
6044	Dur sine genaden, oft hem voege,	Through kindness, if it pleased him,
	Opten anderen dach daer naer	On the next day
	Metten gonen die waren daer,	With those present,
	Ende helpen behouden haer ere.	And help them keep their honour.
6048	Des baden si Waleweine sere,	They earnestly asked Gawain this,
	Diet node soude hebben ontseit	Who would not have liked to refuse
	Ende sprac hi waers ghereit	And who said he was ready
	Alte doene dat hi wiste,	To do the best he could
6052	Beide met crachte ende met liste,	Both with strength and with cunning,
	Dat goet ridder soude bestaen	As a good knight would do
	Over die hem ere hadden gedaen.	For those who did him honour.
	Des waren si alle toe gemake	This pleased all of them
6056	Ende dancten hem sere dier sake.[8]	And they greatly thanked him for it.]

Although the narrative outcome is the same – Gawain will fight in
Thanaguin's party – this passage is much longer and shows numerous differences in wording, phrasing and even in the sequence of the events narrated. If
we italicised the differences between this text and the French original or the
Middle Dutch prose translation, every word and every line would be in italics.[9]

---

belonged to another group of the same version, and *LH* is closer to the long version (*The
Middle Dutch Prose Lancelot*, pp. 39–72). Van Oostrom has pointed to the manuscripts of 'group
BN 1430' which, like *LH*, switch from the long to the short version at *LS* IV, 123; they follow
the ß version of the prose *Charrette* and the long version of the 'Préparation à la Queste'
(*Lantsloot vander Haghedochte*, pp. 9–47). It is impossible to compare the Virgin Love Covenant
episode with *LH* because the *LH* fragments do not contain this episode, but *Lanceloet* and *R* II
follow different redactions of the short version, cf. Lie, *The Middle Dutch Prose Lancelot*, pp.
73–138. Besamusca has shown that in the *Lanceloet* section corresponding to *LS* V, the oscil-
lating 'BN 122' group is closest to the translator's exemplar (*Lanceloet. Pars 2*, pp. 15–34); see
also *Lanceloet. Pars 1*, pp. 24–7.

8 *Lantsloot*, lines 6035–56 (ed. Gerritsen).
9 As mentioned above in n. 7, *LH* generally follows the long version in this section. The text of
the long version differs from the above short version of the passage mainly in its more elaborate wording of Thanaguin's gratitude ('et si m'aït Diex, je vos en sai meillor gré que se vos me
donissiés le meillor chastel que vostre oncle li rois ait,' *LM* 2:358 [lxv, 9]), which does not
however appear in the *LH* translation.

This translator seems to take a whole paragraph from his French source and to translate it by retelling it in his own words and couplets. He produces an adaptation rather than a translation.[10] Taking the text paragraph by paragraph, he created the space he needed to transform prose into rhyming couplets and thereby to adapt the text to the needs of his assumed aristocratic audience. 'Father of adventures,' Walewein's epithet in Middle Dutch, is coined by this text, and is only one of many aspects of the passage that deserve further discussion but cannot realistically be dealt with here, so I will focus instead on one aspect that reveals the nature of the *LH* translator's work.

There are three major tendencies in the adaptation. The most striking change in the above passage demonstrates one of them. In the French text, Gauvain is asked to sit beside Thanaguin before dinner is served, whereas in the Dutch text the request is made after the meal. Hospitality is an important convention in *LH*: van Oostrom found several examples and showed that they belong to a category of changes concerning manners and courtliness.[11] The text holds the courtly code in high esteem and tends to idealise the behavior of the characters and the world in which they live.

A second major category of changes made by the *LH* poet is his elimination of the chronicle-like setting that characterises the prose *Lancelot*; he achieves this by omitting many chronological and geographical details, which leaves the narrative with the rather vague and universal setting of Arthurian verse romance that we know from Chrétien de Troyes. Similarly, he changes the innovative narrative perspective of the prose *Lancelot*, in which *li contes* functions as an impersonal narrator, by using a traditional, first-person narrator.[12] The adaptor's third and final major tendency is rationalisation: he 'must have been intensely preoccupied with the need to tell a tale in which all events have an obvious and plausible rational explanation. With this aim in mind, he frequently makes motivation explicit that is merely implicit in the Old French.'[13] For instance, when the enchantress Camille commits suicide by jumping out of a castle window, he explains that the window was as large as those in a church and therefore big enough for her to leap through.[14]

---

10 See W. P. Gerritsen and F. P. van Oostrom, 'Les relations littéraires entre la France et les Pays-Bas au Moyen Age: quelques observations sur la technique des traducteurs,' *Actes du septième congrès national de la Société Française de Littérature Comparée, Poitiers, 27–29 mai 1965* (Paris, 1967), p. 34: 'adaptation, le type de version étrangère dont l'auteur a abrégé, amplifié ou alteré, dans le dessein d'y mettre ses propres accents, le texte de son original, aussi longtemps qu'il s'en tient, dans ses écarts à la "fable" de cet original.' On the *LH* translator's technique see van Oostrom, *Lantsloot*.

11 Van Oostrom, *Lantsloot*, pp. 132–4, where the translator's omission of instances of kissing to bid farewell is discussed as an example of different conventions in France and the Low Countries

12 Cf. W. P. Gerritsen and van Oostrom, 'Les adapteurs néerlandais du 'Lancelot-(Graal)' aux prises avec le procédé narratif des romans arthuriens en prose,' in *Mélanges de Langue et de Littérature Françaises du Moyen Age et de la Renaissance offerts à Charles Foulon* (Rennes, 1980), II, 105–14, and Bart Besamusca and Frank Brandsma, 'Between Audience and Source: The First-Person Narrator in the Middle Dutch *Lanceloet*,' in *Conjunctures: Medieval Studies in Honor of Douglas Kelly*, ed. Keith Busby and Norris J. Lacy (Amsterdam and Atlanta, 1994), pp. 15–29.

13 Van Oostrom, *Lantsloot*, p. 238.

14 Van Oostrom, *Lantsloot*, p. 94.

Van Oostrom connects such tendencies to the adaptation's presumed audience, the courtly elite: 'by depicting the Arthurian world as a courtly Utopia, *LH* holds up a mirror to the reality of its public's court and inspires the pursuit of courtly perfection.'[15] Confronted with the innovative prose *Lancelot*, the poet apparently 'aims to blur the revolutionary elements of the original by moving back from prose to verse, from disillusionment to idealisation, from realism to vagueness.'[16] Such conservatism might reflect the listening audience's need to be introduced gently to Arthurian cyclic romance: the familiar conventions of the verse romances would make it more accessible. By this time, translations of Thomas's *Tristan*, Chrétien's *Conte du Graal*, and romances such as *Fergus* and the *Vengeance Raguidel* were available in Middle Dutch.

Another Version in Verse: Lanceloet–Queeste–Arturs doet

And there was more to come. The second half of the thirteenth century was the heyday of Arthurian romance in Middle Dutch: in addition to 'home-grown' romances such as *Walewein, Moriaen* and the *Ridder metter mouwen*, a second verse translation of the *Prose Lancelot* was made by a Flemish poet. This rendition survives in a number of smaller fragments and as part of the *Lancelot* Compilation.[17] Since the fragments contain passages from all three parts of the trilogy, and the Compilation also contains the *Queeste* and *Arturs doet*, this Flemish version consisted of at least the last three romances in the *Lancelot-Grail Cycle*. It is possible that some of the fragments belong to a manuscript based on the Compilation, as they all have the same three-column layout.[18] Van Oostrom has even suggested that the two *Lanceloet*-fragments represent a dedication copy made for Gerard van Voorne, a nobleman from Zeeland,[19] but the exact status of the fragments – one of them was discovered quite recently – awaits full investigation. Since the first editions of the prose translation and *LH* appeared in 1987, work has begun on a new edition of the *Lancelot* Compilation's *Lanceloet*.[20] A

---

15 Van Oostrom, *Lantsloot*, p. 242.

16 Van Oostrom, *Lantsloot*, p. 243.

17 On the 'Brussels' fragment of the *Lanceloet*, see *Lanceloet. Pars 1*; the 'Hague' fragment of the same text is edited by Maartje Draak, 'The Workshop behind the Middle Dutch Lancelot Manuscript, The Hague K.B. 129 A 10,' in *Neerlandica manuscripta: Essays presented to G. I. Lieftienck*, vol. 3, *Litterae textuales* (Amsterdam, 1976), pp. 18–37; on the *Lanceloet* fragments, see also M. Draak, *Oude en nieuwe Lancelot-problemen en de noodzakelijkheid van lezen* (Amsterdam, 1976). The *Queeste* fragment is discussed in Bart Besamusca and Hans Kienhorst, 'Een onbekend fragment van de Middelnederlandse vertaling van *La Queste del Saint Graal*,' *De nieuwe taalgids*, 76 (1983), 496–500. The recently discovered fragment of *Arturs doet* is edited by G. Croenen and J. D. Janssens, 'Een nieuw licht op de Lancelotcompilatie? De betekenis van het pasgevonden fragmentje van *Arturs doet*,' *Queeste*, 1 (1994), 3–11 and 108–25. Cf. also Jos A. A. M. Biemans, '*Arturs Doet* op papier of perkament,' *Queeste*, 2 (1995), 72–3.

18 Cf. Jan-Willem Klein, 'De status van de *Lancelotcompilatie*: handschrift, fragmenten en personen,' *Tijdschrift voor Nederlandse Taal-en Letterkunde*, 114 (1998), 105–24.

19 Van Oostrom, 'Maecenaat en Middelnederlandse letterkunde,' in *Hoofsheid en devotie in de middeleeuwse maatschappij*, ed. J. D. Janssens (Brussels, 1982), pp. 21–40; see also his *Aanvaard dit werk: Over Middelnederlandse auteurs en hun publiek* (Amsterdam, 1992).

20 See n. 1 for the volumes published.

comparison of the Compilation text and the fragments shows that it is a faithful copy of the existing Flemish translation. Before delving into the complications of the Compilation, let us take a closer look at the second verse translation, which is usually called *Lanceloet*.

The Walewein-Thanaguin [Taganas] meeting reads:[21]

ende	Hi bat Waleweine dat hi woude	[(And) He asked Walewein
3045	Hem ten tornoye in staeden staen	To help him in the tournament
	Ende Walewein belovet hem saen.	And Walewein promised him to do so.
ende	Hi dankets hem dat hijt hem behiet.	(And) He thanked him for his promise.
ende	Hi seide hine ontsage hem do niet	(And) He said he had no worry now
	Hine soude hebben die ere	That he wouldn't have the honour
3050	Van dien tornoye in allen kere.	Of the tournament in any case.
	Si gingen sitten eten tier tijt	They sat down to eat then
	Ende si waren alle verblijt	And they were all pleased
	Vanden belove dat hem dede	With the promise Walewein made.
	Walewein. Si hopeden daer mede	They hoped to win with that
3055	Te verwinnen sonder waen.	Promise without a doubt.
	Des ander dages sijn si op gestaen	The next morning they rose]

The three words in the margin were written by a contemporary corrector, whose activities will be discussed later. The *Lanceloet* translator works in couplets, whereas words and paragraphs were the basic units in the prose text and *LH*. The text is full of rhyme-fillers (e.g. 'sonder waen,' 'daer mede,' 'in allen kere,' 'saen'), words or phrases that have little meaning but do provide the rhyme word. The translation stays quite close to the French text. It differs mainly from the *LS*-text quoted earlier in that Taganas' gratitude (lines 3047–50) is expressed here in indirect speech (probably for rhyme-related reasons), whereas the French text quotes his words directly. These four lines close with a filler, 'in allen kere,' to complement the word 'ere' (honour) which translates one of the key words in the French phrase.

This is the *Lanceloet* translator's modus operandi, as Besamusca has shown: a phrase is translated, producing a rhyme word which is then paired with its partner by means of a standard filler.[22] Sometimes it is the couplet's first rhyme-word that comes from the French, at other times it is the second one, as in lines 3054–5: 'sonder waen' is the rhyme-filler for 'opgestaen' in the next line. It is rare for neither of the two rhyme-words to come from the French original. In about a quarter of the couplets both rhyme words come from the source text, as in lines 3051–2 where both 'tijt' and 'verblijt' correspond to words in the original. Compared with *LH*, whose translator created more poetic freedom for his retelling of the paragraph and filled out his story with creative additions to the story, the *Lanceloet* poet's desire to adhere to his source frequently led to the use of stylistically dull rhyme-fillers.[23] On the other hand, enjambment (e.g. 3053–4) is more common in *Lanceloet* and it makes the text flow more smoothly (at least

---

[21] *Lanceloet. Pars 1*, lines 3044–56.
[22] *Lanceloet. Pars 2*, pp. 51–73.
[23] Van Oostrom, *Lantsloot*, pp. 55–62.

for the modern reader; we do not know whether the device was problematic for a medieval performer).[24]

The *Lanceloet* translator follows his French exemplar closely. Although he writes in verse, tends to reduce its verbosity and is more vague in his geographical and chronological details, he has embraced the innovations of his source (e.g. the narrative perspective of 'li contes').[25] His faithfulness to the French text produced innovation in the Middle Dutch context: of the three works, the prose translation must have been the most foreign to traditional taste, whereas the *LH* adaptation seems primed for it and *Lanceloet* occupied the middle ground. We can speculate that the three Middle Dutch Lancelot-romances were stages of development in the literary education of the Low Countries; the idea is appealing but also problematic because it assumes that all three texts were meant for more or less the same audience. This is unlikely because of their textual independence from one another (and from their French exemplars), and because of the dialectical differences between the two Flemish verse texts and the Brabantine prose; unlikely also because the likelihood of one patron (or court) financing three voluminous translations of the same text is remote. It is more likely that the three texts were made for different patrons. In Flanders the French *Lancelot* was very popular at the francophone court, but we can surmise that the lesser nobility had a greater affinity with Flemish and therefore wanted to and were able to afford translations of this romance that upholds aristocratic models and morals. *LH* and the translation of the trilogy featuring *Lanceloet* could then be the result of patronage by two different noblemen in Flanders, whereas the prose translation with its Brabantine dialect may have been made for a patron in that region (although a poet's dialect is not necessarily synonymous with the patron's origin, of course). The texts themselves provide no clues to the identity of these hypothetical patrons, no prologues or epilogues have come down to us (those in the *Lanceloet* trilogy belong to the Compilation version), and so much remains unclear that perhaps, as Stephen Jaeger has pointed out, we should not allow the patronage paradigm to raise these issues rather than solve them.[26]

Things may in fact have been far more complicated, since there are indications that two more Middle Dutch translations existed which have not come down to us directly but may be hidden within German versions. The epilogue of a 1476 manuscript of the *Karrensuite* in prose states: 'Diss buchelin zu einer stonden Hain ich inn flemische geschrieben fonden Von eyme kostigen meister verricht, Der es uss franczose darczu hait gedicht' [I found this little book at a given time written in Flemish, made by a clever master who translated it from the French]. This means that there was another Flemish translation, which, as

---

24 On the versification of Middle Dutch texts and its development (used as a means to date texts), see Evert van den Berg, *Middelnederlandse versbouw en syntaxis: Ontwikkelingen in de versifikatie van verhalende poëzie ca. 1200 – ca. 1400* (Utrecht, 1983).

25 *Lanceloet. Pars 2*, pp. 75–124; also Besamusca and Brandsma, 'Between Audience and Source.'

26 'Patrons and the Beginnings of Courtly Romance,' in *The Medieval Opus: Imitation, Rewriting and Transmission in the French Tradition*, ed. Douglas Kelly (Amsterdam and Atlanta, GA, 1996), pp. 45–58.

Lie has shown, does not relate directly to any of the three Middle Dutch texts.[27] And then there is the possibility that the German Heidelberg *Prosa-Lancelot* had a Middle Dutch intermediary which was related to the prose translation. This idea was first proposed by the Finnish scholar Pentti Tilvis.[28] Thus there could have been even more translations of the *Lancelot-Grail Cycle* into Middle Dutch than those represented by the extant Middle Dutch manuscripts.

The Lancelot *Compilation*

The Compilation manuscript (The Hague, Koninklijke Bibliotheek, MS 129 A 10) dates from the first decades of the fourteenth century and contains over 60,000 lines of the second verse translation of the trilogy. Its contents could be characterised as a full-scale prototype of what may have been the flagship of Middle Dutch Arthurian romance. Diagram I shows the romances in, and the making of, the Compilation.

The entire Compilation runs to well over 87,000 lines on 241 folios with three columns of 60 lines or so, recto and verso. Five scribes wrote various parts of the manuscript; the most important among them is called B. He seems to have coordinated the scribal activities – at one point he takes over when the parchment becomes very thin and scribe C perhaps did not dare write on it – and he sometimes adds authorial remarks in order to connect texts or correct omissions. From fol. 99, all the leaves are in his hand, so he is responsible for penning all the inserted romances. Given the range of his activities, it has been suggested by Besamusca that B is the compiler, the maker of the Compilation.[29] Scribe B has even written down the name of the owner, for the final leaf states in his hand: 'hier indet boec van lancelote dat heren lodewijcs es van velthem'[30] [here ends the book of Lancelot that belongs to Sir Lodewijk van Velthem].

Lodewijk van Velthem was a parish priest in the hamlet of Velthem near Leuven, and a well-known Middle Dutch poet. He translated part of the fourth section and is the author of the fifth section of the *Spiegel historiael* (a translation, begun by Jacob van Maerlant, of Vincentius' *Speculum historiale*).[31] In 1326 he completed his translation of the *Suite-Vulgate du Merlin*, yet another continuation

---

27 O. S. H. Lie, 'The Flemish Exemplar of MS W, f° 46* Blankenheim, a Fifteenth-Century German Translation of the *Suite de la Charrette*,' in *Arturus Rex II: Acta conventus Lovanensis*, ed. W. van Hoecke, G. Tournoy and W. Verbeke (Leuven, 1991), pp. 404–18.
28 See *The Middle Dutch Prose Lancelot*, pp. 22–5; Thomas Klein, 'Zur Sprache des Münchener Prosa- Lancelot-Fragments,' in *Mittelalterliches Schauspiel: Festschrift für Hansjürgen Linke zum 65. Geburtstag*, ed. U. Mehler and P. A. H. Touber (Amsterdam and Atlanta, GA, 1994), pp. 223–40.
29 *Lanceloet. Pars 2*, pp. 125–84.
30 *Lanceloet. Pars 1*, pp. 16–22.
31 Velthem's patron for the fifth section may have been Gerard van Voorne, hence van Oostrom's suggestion that the dedication copy of the Compilation was made for him; see also Bart Besamusca, 'Het publiek van de Middelnederlandse Artursromans,' in *Op avontuur: Middeleeuwse epiek in de Lage Landen*, ed. J. D. Janssens et al. (Amsterdam, 1998), pp. 149–50.

DIAGRAM I

Old French *Lancelot-Grail* trilogy:

| *Lancelot*: 'Préparation' | *Queste* | *Mort Artu* |

* Flemish translation in verse (c. 1280):

| *Lanceloet* | *Queeste* | *Arturs doet* |

* First phase of the compilation:

| *Lanceloet*   1 | *Queeste* | *Arturs doet* |

* second phase (the configuration proof-read by the corrector):

| *Lanceloet*   [1] | *Queeste* | *Arturs doet* |

Lancelot Compilation (The Hague, K.B., 129 A 10):

| *Lanceloet* | 1 | 2 | *Queeste* | 3 | 4 | 5 | 6 | 7 | *Arturs doet* |

1: *Perchevael* (adaptation of existing translation of Chrétien's *Conte du Graal*)
2: *Moriaen* (adaptation of existing Middle Dutch romance)
3: *Wrake van Ragisel* (adaptation of existing translation of *Vengeance Raguidel*)
4: *Riddere metter mouwen* (adaptation of existing Middle Dutch romance)
5: *Walewein ende Keye* (original, composed especially for the Compilation?)
6: *Lanceloet en het hert met de witte voet* (original, influenced by the Old French *Lai de Tyolet* [composed specially for the Compilation?])
7: *Torec* (adaptation of existing translation of lost Old French romance)

of a translation by Jacob van Maerlant (who, around 1262, translated prose versions of Robert de Boron's *Joseph d'Arimathie* and *Merlin* for Albrecht van Voorne). Velthem thus provided the missing part of the *Cycle* in Middle Dutch. This meant that the entire Arthur-Grail narrative was available: it began with the Grail story in the *Historie van den Grale* (albeit in Maerlant's rendering of the *Joseph* rather than the *Estoire dou Saint Graal*), it moved through the tales of Merlin and Lancelot into the *Queeste* and *Arturs doet*, and it was enriched with seven more romances in the Compilation. Velthem's name connects all of this material, as owner of the Compilation and translator of the *Suite-Vulgate*.

There is, however, no manuscript evidence that the entire Middle Dutch cycle ever existed in a single (two- or three-volume) manuscript.[32] Fragments exist of both Maerlant's and Velthem's translations, but they differ in layout from the Compilation manuscript. An almost complete version of the Grail-Merlin texts is

---

32 See Draak, *Oude en nieuwe Lancelot-problemen.*

available only in a Middle Low German manuscript ('Burgsteinfurt,' dated c. 1420).[33] This manuscript belonged (and still belongs) to the library of the counts of Bentheim. Its final leaf states which books were in the possession of Eberwin II of Güterswijck at the end of the fifteenth century, mentioning among other romances, 'twe nye boke van lantslotte vnde eyn olt boeck van lantslotte' [two new books of Lancelot and one old book of Lancelot]. This intriguing remark indicates that at least in this library the Grail-Merlin volume was accompanied by Lancelot texts (in German or Middle Dutch?) at the beginning of the fifteenth century. And there seem to have been an old and a new Lancelot, but rather than speculate which version of the Middle Dutch texts could be considered old (*LH*?) or new (*Lanceloet*? the prose versions in Dutch and German?), let us return to Velthem and the Compilation.

Lodewijk van Velthem might even have been scribe B. The main argument against this identification is a manuscript fragment traditionally considered a Velthem autograph, written in a hand different from B's, but its autograph status has been called into question.[34] This weakens the case against identification, and Jan-Willem Klein has recently argued that Velthem must be the compiler.[35] Still, there is as yet no irrefutable proof that Velthem was scribe B and the compiler. And there is another role, incompatible with that of scribe B, that Velthem the owner may have played in the making of the Compilation. Writing in a different hand from B's, a corrector has proof-read parts of the texts and inserted marginal additions that facilitate the oral delivery of the text to a listening audience.[36] The *Lanceloet* passage quoted above will illustrate his activities. The scribe here is A, his work is notoriously sloppy and this leads to frequent corrections. A minor error is found in line 3055, where scribe A forgot the abbreviation mark for the final *n* of the word 'verwinnen,' and wrote 'verwinne.' The corrector, recognisable by the ductus of his tilde, added the abbreviated *n*. It is generally assumed that he did not check the scribal text against the exemplar, but read the text before him carefully, correcting textual and syntactical errors, and faults in the logic of the sentences. An example of the latter category is the

---

33 Timothy Sodmann, ed., Jacob van Maerlant, *Historie van den Grale und Boek van Merline; nach der Steinfürter Handschrift* (Cologne, 1980) is an edition of Maerlant's translations (see also Bart Besamusca and Frank Brandsma, 'Jacob van Maerlant, traducteur vigilant, et la valeur didactique de son *Graal-Merlijn*,' in *Miscellanea Medievalia: Mélanges offerts à Philippe Ménard* [Paris, 1998], I, 121–31); Johannes van Vloten, *Jacob van Maerlants Merlijn, naar het eenig bekende Steinforter handschrift* (Leiden, 1880) gives both Maerlant's and Velthem's texts but in a reconstructed Middle Dutch version.

34 See Jos A. A. M. Biemans, 'Onsen Speghele Ystoriale in Vlaemsche, codicologish onderzoek naar de overlevering van de Spiegel historiael van Jacob van Maerlant, Philip Utenbroeke en Lodewijk van Velthem,' Diss. Utrecht 1995, I, 183–5.

35 J.-W. Klein, 'De status van de *Lancelotcompilatie*,' 114–18.

36 See W. P. Gerritsen's articles, 'Corrections and Indications for Oral Delivery in the Middle Dutch Lancelot Manuscript, The Hague, K.B. 129 A 10,' in *Neerlandica manuscripta: Essays presented to G. I. Lieftinck*, vol. III, *Litterae textuales* (Amsterdam, 1976), pp. 39–59; 'A Medieval Text and its Oral Delivery,' in *Talks on Text: Papers Read at the Closing Session of the NIAS Theme Group 'Orality and Literacy' on May 27th, 1992*, ed. W. P. Gerritsen and C. Vellekoop (Wassenaar, 1992), pp. 72–81; 'Van oog tot oor: De Lancelotcompilatie als voorleesboek,' *Nederlandse letterkunde*, 1 (1996), 45–56; and Brandsma, 'Gathering the Narrative Threads: The Function of the Court Scenes in the Narrative Technique of Interlace and in the Insertion of New Romances in the *Lancelot* Compilation,' *Queeste*, 7 (2000), 1–18.

corrector's addition of 'do' (then) in line 3048; it indicates a causal relationship (between Taganas' confidence and Walewein's promise) that is absent from the scribal text. Without recourse to the French text, the corrector thus restored a logical connection which was present in the French ('Dont ne doute iou mie'), but lost in the scribal rendition of the translation.

Even more important than these textual improvements are the remarkable marginal additions in the same passage, which add the standard abbreviation for 'ende' (a Z with a horizontal stroke through it) in front of lines 3044, 3047 and 3048. The corrector also writes other words in the margin, e.g. 'mer,' 'ay,' and 'here' or 'joncfrouwe,' and uses the last two in dialogues to indicate the addressee of a speech that is about to begin. Gerritsen has shown that the marginal additions help a performer who is reading the text aloud by showing him where one sentence (or speech) ends and the next one begins. Like most medieval manuscripts, especially verse texts, the Compilation uses punctuation sporadically and inconsistently. Particularly when the two-line rhythm of the couplet-sentence is broken, the reader can usually see where a new sentence begins by relying on the use of a temporal adverb (e.g. the equivalent of 'then' or 'now'), a name ('Walewein') or similar phrases indicating a character (e.g. king or queen), a personal pronoun (he, she, they) or a word like 'ende.'[37] The corrector has reinforced this system, making it more visible for the performer and more audible for the audience (we assume the marginal remarks such as 'ende' and the addressee indicators, were 'voiced,' i.e. read aloud as an integral part of the scribal text). Thus in lines 3047–8 the beginning of new sentences is signalled by the word 'Hi' and highlighted by the two marginal additions, probably because the second line of this couplet forms a separate sentence and should be read as such. 'Ende,' of course, has a remarkable parallel in the (corrector-less) Middle Dutch prose version and in the French source: si, et.

The corrector's intervention in the Compilation manuscript offers a unique opportunity to look over the shoulder of a medieval performer, to understand the difficulties of his task and to appreciate the assistance offered to him: help from someone who knew the performer's job. If we add to this the possibility that the poet Velthem was the manuscript's owner, it produces a fascinating idea: Velthem could have made these remarks in preparation for his own performance of parts of the text. It must be said however that an overview of where the corrections do and do not appear shows no clear divisions indicating units of performance. It rather looks as if the deficiencies of A's scribal work in the first half of the Lanceloet text led to more than just textual correction: while combing through this fault-ridden text, the corrector may have prepared it for oral delivery as well. But even within this section the intensity of his activity is erratic, and even changes: after some 11,000 lines, marginal dots become far more common, especially to indicate a change of speaker in a dialogue. Generally speaking, the number of corrections drops as the text progresses. As

---

[37] The Lanceloet passage seems to contain an exception to this general statement: the name 'Walewein' at the beginning of line 3054 is the last word of a sentence, not the first. Here, however, the scribe or corrector used punctuation (a period) to indicate that the sentence stopped after this name.

more of the corrector's work becomes available in the new edition of the *Lanceloet–Queeste–Arturs doet*, research into his activities will perhaps reveal whether he was or could not have been Lodewijk van Velthem.

The presence or absence of the corrector's pen in parts of the manuscript does not seem to indicate performance units, but it does identify one of the phases in the making of the Compilation: the second phase in Diagram 1. Only the *Lanceloet–Perchevael–Queeste–Arturs doet* tetralogy has corrections and marginal additions; it may be that the other six texts did not need correcting, but it is much more likely that they were not inserted until the manuscript came back from the corrector's table.[38] This second phase (which has many stages, too detailed for the scope of this chapter) involved a change of position for the *Perchevael*: the text was placed initially within the interlace of the final quest in the *Lanceloet*, then taken out and placed after the *Lanceloet* before the manuscript went to the corrector.[39] When the manuscript came back to the compiler, then, the *Perchevael* and the *Moriaen* formed a duo as the two texts that had to precede the *Queeste* because one of their principal characters (Perceval) does not survive the Grail quest. Unfortunately, the last leaves of the *Lanceloet* translation are lost and the precise linkage between this text and *Perchevael* is an enigma.

The connections between *Perchevael* and *Moriaen*, and between *Moriaen* and *Queeste* illustrate the compiler's clever use of the court scenes which invariably open and close (sections of) Arthurian romances.[40] The meeting at 'Carlioen' at the end of *Perchevael* is linked to the court scene at the beginning of *Moriaen*. A brief prologue is the only sign of the beginning of a new text. The *Moriaen* epilogue describes how its protagonists return to Arthur's court, where Galahad and the Grail will appear at Whitsuntide, so it provides the link to the *Queeste*. The texts inserted after the *Queeste* do not even have prologues as linkage and the interlaced tale seems to move on continuously, while the meeting and parting of the narrative threads are dictated by the court scenes at regular intervals. The compiler has used specific elements of the interlace technique to forge his compilation: the court scenes enabled him to insert new texts unobtrusively, and the 'formal switches' made it possible for him to insert extra narrative threads (like the one describing Lancelot's adventures in *Moriaen*) and to give the whole textual patchwork the same outlook.[41] He combined two kinds of texts – verse and prose romances – in the rhymed format of the former and the narrative structure of the latter. The original Middle Dutch verse romances to be

---

38 See J.-W. Klein, 'De genese van de *Lancelotcompilatie*,' in *Lanceloet. Pars 1*, pp. 94–110; Frank Brandsma, 'A Voice in the Margin: The Corrector of the Middle Dutch *Lancelot* Compilation,' in *King Arthur in the Medieval Low Countries*, ed. H. M. Claassens and D. F. Johnson (Leuven, 2001), pp. 69–86.

39 See Draak, 'The Workshop,' and J.-W. Klein, 'Codicologie en de *Lancelotcompilatie*: de invoeging van de *Moriaen*,' in *De nieuwe taalgids*, 83 (1990), 526–39.

40 See Brandsma, 'Gathering the Narrative Threads.'

41 On the 'formal switches,' see Elspeth Kennedy, *Lancelot and the Grail: A Study of the Prose 'Lancelot'* (Oxford, 1986), pp. 161–78; *Lanceloet. Pars 3*, pp. 53–63, and Besamusca and Brandsma, 'Between Audience and Source,' 15–29; for Lancelot's narrative thread in *Moriaen*, see Besamusca, 'The Influence of the *Lancelot en prose* on the Middle Dutch *Moriaen*,' in *Arturus Rex II*, pp. 352–60.

inserted did not have formal switches, but the compiler introduced them into his versions of these texts, thus creating the illusion of a whole, of one long narrative told by the impersonal narrative voice of 'Davonture,' stating 'Nu gewaget davonture das' [Now the story speaks of] or 'Davonture seget hier ter steden' [the story states here].[42]

Conclusion

The expansion of the *Lancelot-Grail Cycle* in the Low Countries takes two forms. On the one hand there were at least three, maybe five, independent translations, on the other hand the Lancelot-trilogy forms the core of the Compilation to which seven verse romances are linked. Only the fragmentary *Tristan*, Penninc and Vostaert's *Walewein* and the *Ferguut* have escaped absorption into the Lancelot sphere; whereas the latter two texts are focal points of research in their own right, the bulk of Arthurian studies in the Netherlands is dedicated to the Lancelot romances.[43] The edition of the Compilation, under the patronage of the Constantijn Huijgens Institute in The Hague, is in full swing and various aspects of the Compilation are being studied, such as the insertion and adaptation of texts like *Perchevael* and *Walewein ende Keye*, and the process of cyclification, while a team led by David Johnson is working on an English translation of the entire Compilation.[44] To conclude this essay and simultaneously whet the appetite of literary scholars eager to read the Compilation, the compiler's prologue paradoxically provides a perfect ending:[45]

	Mar wildi vort int lesen duren,	[If you continue to read
10	Ghi sult nu horen scone die jeesten,	You will hear beautiful stories,
	Bede van rouwen ende van feesten,	Both of sorrows and delights,
	Van ridderscape groete daet,	Of great deeds of chivalry,
	Van selsienehede menich baraet,	Great tales of wondrous things,
	Die dese partie hevet in.	That this part of the book contains.]

---

[42] 'Davonture' (the adventure, the story) is the Middle Dutch equivalent of *li contes*. See *Lanceloet. Pars 3*, pp. 174–201, and Gerritsen and van Oostrom, 'Les adapteurs néerlandais.' The two examples are in lines 2565 and 5075 of *Lanceloet. Pars 1*.

[43] See Besamusca, 'The Low Countries,' and his 'The Medieval Dutch Arthurian Material,' in *King Arthur of the Germans: The Arthurian Legend in Medieval German and Dutch Literature*, ed. W. H. Jackson and Sylvia A. Ranawake (Cardiff, 2000), pp. 187–229.

[44] See Marjolein Hogenbirk, 'Gauvain, the Lady and her Lover,' in *Bibliographical Bulletin of the International Arthurian Society*, 48 (1996), 257–70, and 'A Perfect Knight: The Character of Walewein in the Middle Dutch *Walewein ende Keye*,' in *King Arthur in the Medieval Low Countries*, pp. 163–72. On cyclification see *Cyclification: The Development of Narrative Cycles in the Chansons de geste and the Arthurian Romances*, ed. Besamusca et al. (Amsterdam, Oxford, New York, and Tokyo, 1994).

[45] *Lanceloet. Pars 1*, lines 9–15.

19

Manuscripts of the Lancelot-Grail Cycle in England and Wales: Some Books and their Owners

ROGER MIDDLETON

Manuscripts of the *Lancelot-Grail Cycle* were widely available throughout Europe during the Middle Ages. They were produced in large numbers from the first half of the thirteenth century, when the individual texts were composed and the *Cycle* brought into being, until the first years of the sixteenth century, by which time they were being superseded by the succession of printed editions that had begun with the *Lancelot* of 1488. As one would expect, most of the manuscripts were written in northern France, but significant numbers were made on the fringes of French-speaking territory, in areas such as England, southern France and Italy, where part of the population had French as their native language and part did not. The manuscripts circulated freely within France itself (north and south) and frequently passed to neighbouring areas, including those that were not French-speaking. The movement of manuscripts in the opposite direction, from surrounding regions to northern France, was doubtless much less common, and there is virtually no evidence for it until the very end of the medieval period.

The manuscripts themselves were of various types, some relatively small, much the same size as modern books, others extremely large and in several volumes. Some were written in haste, others with great care. Many of the survivors are richly decorated with miniatures and other artwork, whilst others are entirely plain. The high proportion of extant manuscripts with miniatures is not likely to be an accurate reflection of the original state of affairs. Their status as luxury items, as well as any interest aroused by the paintings themselves, will have tended to preserve the illustrated books in greater numbers, whereas the copies containing nothing but text (in a language that was becoming increasingly difficult to understand) could be discarded with few qualms, or replaced by the more convenient printed editions.

There are approximately 220 surviving manuscripts and larger fragments of the various texts that make up the *Lancelot-Grail Cycle*. The majority are in France and have probably been there ever since they were written, but 42 (including 3 fragments) are now in England or Wales, 2 now in France were probably in England during the Middle Ages, and a further 25 were in England during the nineteenth century before returning to the Continent or moving on to the United States or Japan. Thus, nearly a third of the survivors have been in England or Wales at some time.[1]

---

[1]   The numbers given count each volume separately regardless of the shelfmarks assigned by

It is safe to assume that there were many more manuscripts of the *Lancelot-Grail* in England during the Middle Ages, and although specific evidence is not plentiful, it is not entirely lacking.[2] Monasteries may not be the most obvious places to look for vernacular romances of love and chivalry, but there are examples of such books being donated and then kept by the recipients (probably more as a memorial to the donor than out of any interest in the texts themselves). An early example is Bordesley (Worcestershire) where amongst forty books bequeathed to the abbey in 1305 by Guy de Beauchamp, Earl of Warwick, we find 'Un Volum en le quel est le premer livere de Launcelot'; 'un Volum del Romaunce Iosep ab Arimathie e deu Seint Grael' and 'Un Volum de la Mort ly Roy Arthur e de Mordret' (possibly a set of the complete *Cycle* despite the apparent gaps). Somewhat later, Nicholas of Hereford, Prior of Evesham (Worcestershire) 1352–92, gave a large number of books to his monastery including 'Mort de Arthor cum Sankreal in eodem uolumine.' The catalogue of the library of St. Augustine's Abbey at Canterbury yields 'Liber de launcelet in gallico (fol. 2: *tun fren*)', 'Liber qui vocatur Graal in gallico (fol. 2: *qe eles*)' and 'Lib' del Rex Htus [i.e. Artus] in gallico (fol. 2: *issierent*)', all given by Thomas Arnold (who became a priest in 1370).[3] A surviving *Lancelot* from an unidenti-fied monastic library is Oxford, Bodleian Library MS Rawlinson Q.b.6, which has a note with the telltale format 'launselot in gallico 2° f° *que nous.*'

In crown documents the first mention of *Lancelot-Grail* manuscripts is for Isabella of France, queen of Edward II. A record for 10 December 1357 refers to 'John of Paris, coming from the King of France to the Queen at Hertford, and returning with two volumes, of Lancelot and Sang Réal, sent to the same King by Isabella.'[4] At her death in 1358 some of her books went to her son Edward III, but others went (in theory at least) to her daughter Joan, including 'Vnus magnus liber coopertus cum corio albo de gestis Arthuri' and 'Vnus liber consimilis de sanguine regali' (which are probably the two volumes of 1357). Although she was Queen of Scotland, Joan remained in England until her death in 1362, and it looks as though the books she had inherited then reverted to

the libraries that now own them. For various reasons it is not possible to give an exact total, the principal difficulties being the classification of the fragments and of the manuscripts whose text is not consistently that of the *Lancelot-Grail Cycle.*

2   A fundamental resource is Susan H. Cavanaugh, 'A Study of Books Privately Owned in England: 1300–1450,' diss. University of Pennsylvania 1980, with an alphabetical list of owners but no index of titles.

3   See, respectively, Madeleine Blaess, 'L'abbaye de Bordesley et les livres de Guy de Beauchamp,' *Romania*, 78 (1957), 511–18, and the Corpus of British Medieval Library Cata-logues, 3: *The Libraries of the Cistercians, Gilbertines and Premonstratensians*, ed. David N. Bell (London, 1992), pp. 4–10, nos. 2, 9 and 22; Madeleine Blaess, 'Les manuscrits français dans les monastères anglais au moyen âge,' *Romania*, 94 (1973), 321–58, and the Corpus of British Medieval Library Catalogues, 4: *English Benedictine Libraries: The Shorter Catalogues*, ed. R. Sharpe, J. P. Carley, R. M. Thomson and A. G. Watson (London, 1996), pp. 131–50, no. 69 (though a 'Sankreal' bound with a *Mort Artu* is more likely to be a *Queste* than the *Estoire* suggested by the editors); Montague Rhodes James, *The Ancient Libraries of Canterbury and Dover* (Cambridge, 1903), pp. 373–4, nos. 1528, 1529 and 1534. All also in Cavanaugh, 'Study of Books,' under the names of the donors.

4   Edw. A. Bond, 'Notices of the Last Days of Isabella, Queen of Edward the Second, drawn from an Account of the Expenses of her Household,' *Archaeologia*, 35 (1854), 468 [453–69]. See also Cavanaugh, 'Study of Books,' under 'Isabella of France.'

Edward. Some of them (having passed to Richard II) are identifiable in a document of 1384–85 (wrongly interpreted as a list of Richard's library). This later list
mentions 'vne Romance de Roy Arthure,' 'vn liure appelle Galaath' (i.e. a
Queste) and 'vn autre liure comensant *Apres ce que Henriz*' (possibly a *Mort Artu*
if we allow for a scribal error in the name?). There is a good chance that the first
two of these are the volumes returned from France in 1357 and handed down
the generations.[5]

When Sir Simon Burley, a former tutor of Richard II, was executed in 1388, an
inventory of his confiscated property included 'I liure du Romans du Roy
Arthur couere de blanc.'[6] More important, however, is the inventory of goods
belonging to Thomas of Woodstock, Duke of Gloucester, seized at Pleshey in
1397, which records 'un gros livre Fraunceys de Merlyn,' 'un large livre en
Fraunceis appellez le Romance de Launcelot,' and 'un large livre rouge del Tretiz
de Roy Arthur ove iiij claspes de laton.'[7] Since the castle of Pleshey was a part of
the Bohun inheritance of his wife, it may be that these books were originally
from her family. Thus, by the end of the fourteenth century the crown possessed
(in name at least) some six or seven *Lancelot-Grail* manuscripts (but by inheritance and confiscation rather than active interest). A somewhat later inventory is
that of Sir John Fastolf whose goods in his castle of Caister, Norfolk, in about
1450 included amongst the French books a 'liber de Roy Artour.'[8]

In wills and testaments we find a number of items that may be manuscripts of
the *Lancelot-Grail* (though we cannot be sure that all are in French). In a will of
1269 William de Beauchamp refers to a book of Lancelot; in 1380 Elizabeth la
Zouche left to her husband a 'Lanchelot'; in a will of 1391 Margaret Courtenay,
Countess of Devon, left to one of her daughters her 'Artur de Britaigne' (not
necessarily a *Lancelot-Grail* text), and to Anneys Chambernon her 'merlyn'; in
1392 Isabella, Duchess of York, bequeathed to her son Edward her 'launcelot'; in
1412 Elizabeth Darcy left to her husband her 'Lanselake' and her 'Sainz Ryall'; in
1435 Thomas Hebbeden left to Isabella Eure 'unum librum gallicum vocatum
Launcelot.'[9] The most interesting case, however, is that of Sir Richard Roos who
in a will made in March 1481/2 left his 'grete booke called saint Grall bounde in
boordes couerde with rede leder and plated with plates of laten' to his niece
'Alianore hawte.' This is almost certainly the volume that is now in the British
Library as MS Royal 14 E. iii, containing *Estoire*, *Queste* and *Mort Artu* and

---

5   For the text of these lists see Edith Rickert, 'King Richard II's Books,' *The Library,* fourth series
    13 (1932–33), 144–7. For the correct interpretation of the documents of 1384–85 see Richard F.
    Green, 'King Richard II's books revisited,' *The Library,* fifth series 31 (1976), 235–9.
6   V. J. Scattergood, 'Two Medieval Book Lists,' *The Library,* fifth series 23 (1968), 236–9.
7   See Viscount Dillon and W. H. St. John Hope, 'Inventory of the Goods and Chattels Belonging
    to Thomas, Duke of Gloucester, and seized in his castle at Pleshy, co. Essex, 21 Richard II
    (1397); with their values, as shown in the escheator's accounts,' *The Archaeological Journal,* 54
    (1897), 300, 301 and 302 [275–308].
8   H. S. Bennett, *The Pastons and their England* (Cambridge, 1932), p. 111.
9   These wills are mentioned by various authors, but most are conveniently collected by Carol
    M. Meale, ' "all the bokes that I haue of latyn, englisch, and frensch": Laywomen and their
    Books in Late Medieval England,' in *Women and Literature in Britain, 1150–1500,* ed. Carol M.
    Meale (Cambridge, 1993), p. 139 [128–58]. For William de Beauchamp see Nicholas Harris
    Nicolas, *Testamenta vetusta,* 2 vols. (London, 1826), p. 51.

bearing the signatures (amongst others) of Richard Roos and Eleanor Haute. It is probably the book that appears in the Richmond Palace inventory of 1535 as no. 103 'Le St. Gral, donné a la Royne' for it also has the signature of 'E[lizabeth] Wydevyll,' queen of Edward IV, a kinswoman (by marriage) of Eleanor Haute.[10]

The existence of other lost manuscripts may be deduced from the surviving copies that were written in England (which will have required their exemplars to be in England) and from translations into English and Welsh that have French *Lancelot-Grail* manuscripts amongst their sources. Best known of these is the work of Malory who made use of more than one French manuscript for his compilation.[11] Another important text to have used a *Lancelot-Grail* manuscript is the stanzaic *Le Morte Arthur* (in contrast to the alliterative *Morte Arthure* which follows the chronicle tradition of Geoffrey of Monmouth and Wace). Also from French manuscripts are the anonymous prose *Merlin* of Cambridge University Library MS Ff. 3. 11, and the *Merlin* and *Holy Grail* by Henry Lovelich. The Scottish *Lancelot of the Laik* is the only evidence of a *Lancelot-Grail* manuscript north of the border during the Middle Ages. The text almost certainly had a written French source, and the political content of the text implies that the intended audience was Scottish, but whether the adaptation was actually done in Scotland is impossible to say. In the only surviving copy (in Cambridge University Library MS Kk. 1. 5) the dialect is inconsistent, mixing Lowland Scots with southern forms, but the relevant part of the manuscript (formerly a composite volume) contains several texts with clear Scottish connections.[12]

The Welsh version of the *Queste del Saint Graal*, preserved as the first part of *Y Seint Greal*, implies the presence of a French manuscript in South Wales, probably in the circle of Hopcyn ap Thomas, during the latter part of the fourteenth century. From the same period is a fragmentary Welsh version of the birth of Arthur that seems to be based upon the French prose *Merlin*.[13] Other scattered references in Welsh literature show a knowledge of the French texts, but do not necessarily imply the use of manuscripts.

For the surviving manuscripts, a major distinction is to be drawn between those that were in England during the Middle Ages and those that came to England or Wales at some later stage. The evidence available for distinguishing between the two categories is of various kinds and of varying solidity. In some

---

[10] Ethel Seaton, *Sir Richard Roos, c. 1410–1482, Lancastrian Poet* (London, 1961), pp. 547–8. See also Carol Meale, 'Manuscripts, Readers and Patrons in Fifteenth-Century England: Sir Thomas Malory and Arthurian Romance,' *Arthurian Literature*, 4 (1985), 103 [93–126], and P. W. Fleming, 'The Hautes and their "Circle": Culture and the English Gentry,' in *England in the Fifteenth Century: Proceedings of the 1986 Harlaxton Symposium*, ed. Daniel Williams (Woodbridge, 1987), p. 90 [85–102].

[11] See, for example, P. J. C. Field, 'Malory and the French Prose *Lancelot*,' *Bulletin of the John Rylands University Library of Manchester*, 75 (1993), 79–102.

[12] Information on the manuscripts and sources of these English (and Scottish) versions is conveniently collected by Helaine Newstead in *A Manual of the Writings in Middle English 1050–1500*, ed. J. Burke Severs (New Haven, 1967), sec. 2, 'Arthurian Legends,' pp. 38–79 and 224–56.

[13] See two studies by Ceridwen Lloyd-Morgan: 'Perceval in Wales: Late Medieval Welsh Grail Traditions,' in *The Changing Face of Arthurian Romance: Essays on the Arthurian Prose Romances in Memory of Cedric E. Pickford*, ed. Alison Adams et al. (Cambridge, 1986), pp. 79–81 [78–91]; and '*Breuddwyd Rhonabwy* and later Arthurian literature,' in *The Arthur of the Welsh*, ed. Rachel Bromwich, A. O. H. Jarman and Brynley F. Roberts (Cardiff, 1991), pp. 193–205 [183–208].

cases there is a clear history for a given manuscript (placing it either in England or in France), whereas at the other end of the spectrum we are left with not much more than an educated guess (though few are much in doubt).[14] Of the forty surviving *Lancelot-Grail* manuscripts now in England or Wales, nineteen were in England during the Middle Ages, and at least six of them are likely to have been written there. The two most straightforward cases are British Library MSS Royal 20 A. ii and Egerton 2515, both written in a script that uses long-stemmed *r* (not always an absolute guarantee of English origin, but evidence enough in the present context). Almost as clear are British Library MS Royal 19 C. xiii (in which omitted text added on fols. 51v and 52 uses long-stemmed *r*) and MS Royal 20 C. vi. This is described in the catalogue as 'written in England (West of England?),' but this view may have been influenced by the text added at the end in a slightly later hand; this added text and some added titles use long-stemmed *r*. We may also include Cambridge, Corpus Christi College MS 45, identified as English by Gweneth Hutchings, and British Library MS Royal 19 B. vii which was copied from it (or from a direct descendant of it).[15]

A further nine manuscripts exhibit clear signs of having been in England during the Middle Ages, and the first two may have been written there (though the evidence from the script is inconclusive); the rest were probably written in France and brought to England soon after. These nine are: British Library MSS Lansdowne 757 (the text added in the lower margins of fols. 40 and 40v uses long-stemmed *r*), Additional 32125 (the notes in the margins sometimes use long-stemmed *r*, good examples being on fols. 179v and 214), Royal 14 E. iii (the Roos and Haute signatures mentioned above), Royal 20 D. iv (Bohun family) and Royal 15 A. xi (used as flyleaves in a manuscript that had fifteenth-century English owners); Bodleian Library MSS Digby 223 (fifteenth-century marginalia in English) and Rawlinson Q.b.6 (English names from the fifteenth and early sixteenth centuries, English spelling of *launselot* in the monastic catalogue description on the flyleaf); Nottingham University Library MS Middleton L. M. 7 (fourteenth-century note concerning the bishop of Coventry and Lichfield); Cambridge University Library MS Additional 7071 (from Ribston Hall, in Yorkshire, and probably there since the sixteenth century; annotations in English from the early sixteenth century, including one that refers to Caxton's Malory).

To these may be added without serious reservations the other manuscripts from the royal collection (MSS Royal 19 C. xii, 20 B. viii, 20 D. iii). It is highly improbable that Renaissance (or later) kings would have procured manuscripts

14 Since the aim of the present study is to distinguish between those manuscripts that were in England or Wales during the Middle Ages and those that came to England or Wales at a later stage, only such evidence as will sufficiently establish that distinction will be cited. Limitations of space preclude giving all that is known of the history of the sixty-seven manuscripts with which we are concerned (excluding from the discussion the two smaller fragments: British Library MS Cotton, Julius A i, and Bodleian Library MS Douce 379). A more detailed historical study of the surviving *Lancelot-Grail* manuscripts will be published in due course.

15 Gweneth Hutchings, 'Two Hitherto Unnoticed Manuscripts of the French Prose *Lancelot*,' *Medium Aevum*, 3 (1934), 189–94. For the relationship between these two manuscripts see Elspeth Kennedy, 'Le *Lancelot* en prose (MS 45),' in *Les manuscrits français de la bibliothèque Parker: Actes du Colloque 24–27 mars 1993*, ed. Nigel Wilkins (Cambridge, 1993), pp. 23–38.

of this type from abroad. Much more likely is that they had been in the royal collection for some time or that they were more or less accidental acquisitions at the time of the Dissolution. A similar observation applies to Bodleian Library MS Ashmole 828. The few brief annotations in English are difficult to date, but the library of Elias Ashmole (1617–92) reflects his professional concerns as Windsor herald, his particular interests in astrology and alchemy, and his general antiquarianism. There is very little literature, and even less French. It is most unlikely that he would have had any great desire to own a copy of an Old French chivalric romance, except as part of a general wish to preserve manuscripts from destruction. All of which implies a chance discovery in England rather than a deliberate import from France.[16]

Another important category is that of manuscripts now in France that were in England during the Middle Ages. The two identified so far (but there may be more) are Bibliothèque nationale de France MSS fr. 123 and 749. The first of these was apparently made in England towards the end of the thirteenth century, though there is also some evidence for connections with Artois, so perhaps we should not entirely exclude the possibility of English scribes and artists working in northern France.[17] The second (BNF, fr. 749) has a note of its contents in English on its final leaf. This is in the gathering that was separated from the rest of the manuscript, found again amongst the fragments of BNF, n.a.fr. 5237 and now reincorporated. Since the note records the contents it must have been written when the last eight leaves were still in place. By the end of the fifteenth century both these books had entered the library of the well-known bibliophile Louis de Bruges, whose collection passed more or less intact to the royal library at Blois. In 1466 Louis was one of the ambassadors sent to negotiate the treaty that was to be sealed by the marriage of Charles the Bold and Margaret of York. Four years later he rescued the fleeing Edward IV and entertained him for several weeks, first in Holland and then in Bruges. After Edward was restored to his throne, another diplomatic mission brought Louis de Bruges to England in 1472, and he was well received by the grateful king who made him Earl of Winchester. These visits would have provided obvious opportunities for Louis to acquire manuscripts (by purchase or donation), and there is reason to believe that he did obtain a number of his books in England.[18]

Manuscripts of the *Lancelot-Grail* not in England in the Middle Ages began to arrive in the early eighteenth century, no doubt as a result of the growing interest in collecting for its own sake. The earliest arrival was probably what is now Manchester, John Rylands University Library MS French 1, acquired from an unknown source by Charles Spencer, 3rd Earl of Sunderland (who died on

---

[16] On the other hand, Martine Meuwese informs me that fragments of the *Estoire* in Bologna have miniatures by the same artist as Ashmole 828, and almost certainly represent the remains of a companion volume; see Monica Longobardi, 'Ancora nova frammenti della *Vulgata*: L'*Estoire du Graal*, il *Lancelot*, la *Queste*,' *Giornale Italiano di Filologia*, 46 (1994), 197–228.

[17] See François Avril and Patricia Danz Stirnemann, *Manuscrits enluminés d'origine insulaire VIIe–XXe siècle* (Paris, 1987), pp. 109–13.

[18] See in general J. B .B. Van Praet, *Recherches sur Louis de Bruges, seigneur de La Gruthuyse* (Paris, 1831). For books that may have been obtained in England, see Léopold Delisle, *Le Cabinet des manuscrits de la bibliothèque impériale*, 4 vols. (Paris, 1868–81), I, 145–6.

19 April 1722). This is the last volume (now divided into two) of a four volume set of the complete *Cycle*. There are missing gatherings from the Rylands volumes in Bodleian Library MS Douce 215 (from the La Vallière sale in Paris of January 1784), and the other three volumes of the set are now Amsterdam, Bibliotheca Philosophica Hermetica MS 1 (formerly Phillipps 3630). The first volume has the arms of La Rochefoucauld on fol. 1, and the flyleaves of several volumes use paper watermarked with the arms of Amsterdam and the name 'P IOLLY,' indicating that it was made in France for the Dutch market by the Pierre Jolly who died in 1713, or by a namesake who was active in 1710, both with mills near Limoges. Thus, if the other volumes and the missing gatherings were on the Continent at the beginning of the eighteenth century, it is fair to assume that Sunderland obtained his volumes abroad rather than in England.[19]

Other early arrivals were those in the Harleian collection, the first being British Library MS Harley 4419 (with the arms and bookplate of Nicholas-Joseph Foucault).This was one of several manuscripts that came from a sale conducted by Thomas Ballard on 20 February 1721. Those bought on commission were received by Humfrey Wanley, Harley's librarian, three days later, but the *Lancelot* was one of those offered by the bookseller Nathaniel Noel at the beginning of March.[20] Harley's other *Lancelot-Grail* manuscripts, British Library MSS Harley 6340 and 6341–42, came from the collection at Anet (sold in Paris in November 1724). All three volumes bear one or other of the two convoluted marks that are found on manuscripts that had been at Anet, and they can be identified with items in the catalogue amongst the 'Manuscrits sur papier.'[21] There are no entries for them in Wanley's diary (which continues until 23 June 1726), suggesting that they did not reach the library until after his death in July 1726. The latest possible date of acquisition would be the death of Edward Harley in 1741.

Other early eighteenth-century imports are amongst the manuscripts that Richard Rawlinson (1690–1755) bequeathed to the Bodleian Library at Oxford. As already indicated, MS Rawlinson Q.b.6 was in England during the Middle

19 See Cedric E. Pickford, 'An Arthurian Manuscript in the John Rylands Library,' *Bulletin of the John Rylands Library*, 31 (1948), 318–44; M. A. Stones, 'Short Note on Manuscripts Rylands French 1 and Douce 215,' *Scriptorium*, 22 (1968), 42–5; Alison Stones, 'Another Short Note on Rylands French 1,' in *Romanesque and Gothic: Essays for George Zarnecki*, ed. Neil Stratford (Cambridge, 1987), pp. 185–92 (with plates); Martine Meuwese, 'Twelve Bleeding Tombs and Seven Flaming Hands: Text and Image in the Amsterdam *Estoire*,' *The Arthurian Yearbook*, 2 (1992), 135–58.

20 See *The Diary of Humfrey Wanley 1715–1726*, ed. C. E. Wright and Ruth C. Wright, 2 vols. (London, 1966), I, 87–9 and 90–1. Foucault had died in Paris on 7 February 1721 (27 January by the English calendar), but this was not the reason for the dispersal of his collection. All the Foucault manuscripts sold by Ballard, and a good few more that did not come to London, had been sold in The Hague in June of the previous year; see *Bibliotheca Menarsiana, ou catalogue de la bibliothèque de feu Messire Jean Jacques Charron, Chevalier Marquis de Menars . . .* (The Hague, 1720). For details of English book sales (cited here by seller and date only), see the indispensable *List of Catalogues of English Book Sales 1676–1900 now in the British Museum* (London, 1915).

21 *Catalogue des manuscrits trouvez après le décès de Madame la Princesse, dans son Château Royal d'Anet* (Paris, 1724), edited in Ernest Quentin Bauchart, *Les femmes bibliophiles de France (XVIe, XVIIe & XVIIIe siècles)*, 2 vols. (Paris, 1886), I, 309–40. In the sale catalogue the Harleian manuscripts are the eighth item on p. 21 and the first on p. 22 (p. 322, nos. 8 and 12, in Bauchart's edition).

Ages, but his other two *Lancelot-Grail* manuscripts seem to have come from France. The provenance of MS Rawlinson D. 899 is suggested by the fleur-de-lys watermark in an end flyleaf and several marginal notes in French of the sixteenth century, whilst the history of MS Rawlinson D. 874 is revealed by the note on fol. 355 ('pauye: au Roy Loys XII'), marking it as one of the books taken from the library of the Duke of Milan at Pavia after the French conquest of 1499–1500. It is to be identified with no. 943 in the Pavia inventory of 1426. Like others with similar inscriptions it would have been taken to the royal library at Blois.[22]

After these seven volumes at the beginning of the century there seems to have been nothing further until the influx of manuscripts that began in the 1780s and continued during the first half of the nineteenth century. Many manuscripts came on to the market and crossed the Channel as a result of the French Revolution and the Napoleonic wars, but very few of the *Lancelot-Grail* manuscripts imported at this time came to England for that reason. The three that did were those described in the *Bibliotheca Parisiana*.[23] Included in the sale were a number of manuscripts that the catalogue claims to have been owned by Claude d'Urfé, but which in fact came from Cardinal Loménie de Brienne, Archbishop of Sens. The cardinal had obtained them in 1788 from the Minimes of Tonnerre, to whom they had been given by the founder of their house, Charles-Henri de Clermont, Count of Clermont-Tonnerre (who died in 1640).[24] The *Lancelot-Grail* manuscripts in the *Bibliotheca Parisiana*, are nos. 367, 371 and 372 of which 371 is as yet unidentified amongst surviving manuscripts. The others came eventually to Sir Thomas Phillipps, and were both lost to England with the dispersal of his collection (see below). One is now New Haven, Yale University, Beinecke Library MS 227, and the other is in a private collection near Paris.

Much more significant, however, for the importing of Arthurian manuscripts at the end of the eighteenth century are the two crucial figures of the Duke of La Vallière and Pierre-Antoine Bolongaro-Crevenna. The first of these is well known, the second almost entirely ignored, but both played an important role. La Vallière's library in Paris was one of the largest hitherto collected, and after

---

22 See Elisabeth Pellegrin, *La Bibliothèque des Visconti et des Sforza ducs de Milan, au XVe siècle* (Paris, 1955), pp. 71 and 282, but note that the editorial intervention in the text of the inventory entry is unwarranted; there is an error in the manuscript itself and it is the (partial) reflection of it in the inventory that confirms the identification.

23 Almost everything about this sale has given rise to confusion of one sort or another, most of it unnecessary. The French catalogue, *Bibliotheca elegantissima, parisina* (London and Paris, 1790) advertises the sale for 'le lundi 28 mars 1791' (which is correct). The English version of this catalogue, *Bibliotheca Parisiana* (n.p., n.d.), gives the date of the sale as 'Monday the 26th of March, 1791,' but some copies have a cancel title page with the correct date (one is reproduced by Arthur Rau, 'Bibliotheca Parisina,' *The Book Collector*, 18 (1969), 307–17; another is Bodleian Library Douce C 167). The collector was a 'Mr. Paris' referred to by most bibliographers as 'Pâris de Meyzieu,' but this identification is easily contested by Rau, 'Bibliotheca Parisina,' though he is unable to propose a suitable alternative. The seller was in fact Antoine-Marie Pâris d'Illins (1746–1809), later to be a general in Napoleon's army, who was a son of Antoine Pâris d'Illins (1712–77) and a nephew of the Jean-Baptiste Pâris de Meyzieu (1718–78) whose library was sold in 1779.

24 J. B. B. Van Praet, *Recherches sur Louis de Bruges*, p. 210. The provenance is confirmed by those bindings that have (or had) heavy brass centrepieces with the crossed keys of Clermont that often leave an identifiable impression in the velvet even when removed.

his death in 1780 the sale of the manuscripts and the early printed books was entrusted to De Bure. A catalogue in three volumes (compiled very largely by Van Praet) appeared in 1783 in readiness for the sale that took place from January to May 1784. The Bibliothèque du Roi took nearly all the Old French manuscripts that were in verse but none of the prose romances, judging no doubt that their holdings of these were already more than sufficient. The buyer of all but one of the manuscripts of prose romances was Crevenna, and it was the sale of his collection in Amsterdam (26 April 1790) that made them available to English collectors. Without La Vallière there would have been no collection, but without Crevenna these manuscripts or at least the majority of them would have remained in France.

At the Amsterdam sale the prose romances (lots 5129 to 5143) were divided more or less equally between only two buyers, Payne and Vandenberg, and all but one came to England.[25] The six bought by Payne went to the Duke of Roxburghe, the one *Lancelot-Grail* being La Vallière 3989 (Crevenna 5130), a three-volume set of the complete cycle. At the Roxburghe sale (18 May 1812, lot 6093) it passed to the Marquess of Blandford, and at his White Knights sale (7 June 1819, lot 3799) to Richard Heber, at whose sale (10 February 1836, lot 1488) it was acquired by the British Museum (now British Library MSS Additional 10292–4). It is the manuscript from which Sommer printed his *Merlin* in 1894 and his *Vulgate Version* in 1909, twice giving an account of its history.[26] Like most writers, however, he makes no mention of Crevenna, supposing Roxburghe to have acquired it at the La Vallière sale of 1784.

Of the seven bought by Vandenberg, all containing *Lancelot-Grail* texts, two went to Francis Douce, one to John Louis Goldsmid, one to George Galwey Mills, one to the British Museum, one is lost from view until it reappears in the collection of George Folliott, and one remains untraced. La Vallière 3991 (Crevenna 5132) is now British Library MS Additional 5474, having been acquired no later than 1796 (as can be deduced from the handwritten catalogue preserved as British Library MS Additional 5015, where the description falls well within the section prepared by Joseph Planta).[27] The inserted *Mémoire* purporting to give part of the manuscript's earlier history should be treated with caution. La Vallière 3993 (Crevenna 5133) was acquired by Francis Douce who bequeathed his collection to the Bodleian Library in Oxford where the manuscript is now MS Douce 303. La Vallière 3995 (Crevenna 5134), an incomplete

---

25 The names of the purchasers at the Crevenna sale are to be found in a copy of the catalogue in the Bodleian Library, Oxford: Mus. Bibl. III. 8° 406–8. There is no problem in identifying 'Payne' as the well-known London booksellers Thomas Payne and son. The identity of 'Vandenberg' is not so straightforward but, given that the books came to England, a possible candidate is the London bookseller S. Vandenbergh who issued a number of catalogues at about this time, those in the Bodleian being for 1779, 1780, 1794 or 1795, and 1796 (none with Crevenna manuscripts, the first two being too early).

26 *Le Roman de Merlin or the Early History of King Arthur*, ed. H. Oskar Sommer (London, 1894) and *The Vulgate Version of the Arthurian Romances*, ed. H. Oskar Sommer, 8 vols. (Washington, D.C., 1909–16), I, xxiii–xxiv (both reproducing entries from the sale catalogues, both with incorrect number for Roxburghe).

27 See the *Catalogue of Additions to the Manuscripts 1756–1782: Additional Manuscripts 4101–5017* (London, 1977), under MS Add. 5015 (with further references).

Joseph and *Merlin* in thirty-seven leaves, is the one that is untraced. La Vallière 4003 (Crevenna 5135) went to John Louis Goldsmid, to be bought at his sale (11 December 1815, lot 158) by Edward Vernon Utterson. The book next appeared as lot 534 in a sale held by Evans on 28 May 1832, when the unnamed seller was in fact Utterson and when the buyer was Richard Heber. At Heber's sale (10 February 1836, lot 970) it was acquired by Sir Thomas Phillipps (8230 in his catalogue). With the final dispersal of the Phillipps collection it was amongst the 'remainder' bought by H. P. Kraus (Catalogue 153, no. 44). It is now in a private collection in Japan. La Vallière 4004 (Crevenna 5136) was in the collection made by George Folliott during the latter part of the nineteenth century, and eventually sold by his descendants (Sotheby's, 12 May 1930, lot 81). It is now Chicago, Newberry Library, f 21. The account of the manuscript's earlier and later history by Paul Saenger contains nothing that throws any light on the years between Crevenna and Folliot.[28] La Vallière 4005 (Crevenna 5137) went to George Galwey Mills, to be bought at his sale (24 February 1800, lot 1193) by David Thomas Powell, and at his sale (31 July 1848, lot 220) by the British Museum (now British Library MS Additional 17443). The arms on fol. 1 should be described as those of 'Granson' because there is no warrant, heraldic or otherwise, for adopting the form 'Grandison' and thereby implying the English branch of this Swiss-French family. La Vallière 4006 (Crevenna 5138), fragments from the last volume of a complete cycle (subsequently identified as the missing gatherings of the Rylands manuscript), is now MS Douce 215.

The one La Vallière manuscript of a prose romance that escaped Crevenna in 1784 was La Vallière 3994, bought by De Bure for Count MacCarthy. This too soon came to England, however, rejoining other La Vallière manuscripts in the Roxburghe collection. At the famous sale (18 May 1812) it was lot 6092 and went to Richard Heber. Acquired at the Heber sale (10 February 1836, lot 1490) by Techener it returned to Paris, but came to England again in 1849 when the Earl of Ashburnham purchased the manuscript collection of Joseph Barrois (see below). It is now New York, Pierpont Morgan Library, M. 207–8.[29]

Mention has already been made of Francis Douce (1787–1834) who was not only a collector but also a scholar (Assistant Keeper of Manuscripts at the British Museum for a time, from 1807 until he resigned in 1811). Apart from his La Vallière/Crevenna manuscripts (MSS Douce 215 and 303) he had four others. His *Mort Artu* (MS Douce 189) came from the Soubise library (presumably from the Paris sale of 1789, probably lot 5351); his *Estoire, Merlin* (MS Douce 178) had belonged to Anne de Graville, who had also owned the *Lancelot* now in Chicago.

---

[28] Paul Saenger, 'Un manuscrit de Claude d'Urfé retrouvé à la Newberry Library de Chicago,' *Bibliothèque de l'école des chartes*, 139 (1981), 250–2. Alison Stones informs me that the gatherings that are in a later hand have decoration that is English, though this does not necessarily mean that the book was then in England. At the end of the fifteenth century (or very soon after) it was in Normandy in the library of Louis Malet de Graville.

[29] I have not yet seen the Morgan manuscript to confirm the La Vallière provenance, and the identification relies upon the assumption that there is an error in the La Vallière catalogue when it describes lot 3994 as being in two columns (Morgan, M. 207–8 being in three). However, the identification made by Seymour de Ricci in his *Census* (see note 39) is likely to be correct. Sale catalogues with buyers and prices confirm the history from Roxburghe onwards.

The Douce manuscript for which there is least evidence of previous history is MS Douce 199, the only hint being the instructions in rather odd Middle French that accompany an elaborate system of signs indicating the correct order of the leaves (now rebound). This probably implies that the book was in France at the time, but is no guarantee. On fol. 323 (the first end flyleaf) there is a date in English, '5th. July 1794,' apparently in the hand of Francis Douce, though it is always difficult to be sure from such a small sample.

Douce is also important for other reasons. He knew other collectors and had studied their manuscripts, sometimes comparing them closely with his own. It is to Douce that we owe the information that two of the *Lancelot-Grail* manuscripts from the *Bibliotheca Parisiana* (nos. 367 and 372) were acquired by his friend John Adair Hawkins. In a list of *Lancelot-Grail* manuscripts Douce attributes two copies of the *Estoire* to 'Mr. Hawkins,' and two of the *Merlin* to 'J. A. Hawkins' (MS Douce f. 21, pp. 1–2). The identity of the two manuscripts (each containing both texts) is revealed by Douce's notes in his copy of the *Parisiana* sale catalogue (Douce C 167) where both 367 and 372 are marked in pencil 'now Mr. H.' and by his annotation in his own copy of these texts (MS Douce 178, fol. 315v: 'So far this Ms agrees with Mr. H's no. 372').

As well as being knowledgeable about the manuscripts of his friends and rivals in the sale room, Douce was generous in lending his books, printed and manuscript. Thus, on 22 May 1814 he lent Goldsmid his 'Ms. Saint Graal' and on 27 October his 'Ms. Merlin' (recorded in MS Douce e. 75, p. 44). These manuscripts are probably MSS Douce 303 (*Estoire*) and 178 (*Estoire* and *Merlin*), but Douce also had part of an English *Merlin* (MS Douce 236, previously owned by Edward Llwyd) and a modern transcript of part of the *Merlin* in the Auchinleck manuscript (MS Douce 124). By May of the following year Goldsmid had acquired two volumes of a *Lancelot* at an anonymous sale (Evans, 16 May 1815, lot 143). Douce knew these volumes because he later identifies them as from the same set as his MS Douce 215 (though he does not mention that Goldsmid was the purchaser in 1815). When Goldsmid died only a few months later, these volumes were lot 159 at his sale (11 December 1815); they were bought by Dulau, and Douce saw them in his shop in July 1817 (notes by Douce inserted in MS Douce 215). They next appear in Robert Lang's sale (17 November 1828, lot 1305) to be bought by Phillipps, who in due course reunited them with their missing first volume, itself identified by Douce (in his notes in MS Douce 215) as the *Grail* at the sale of P. C. Parris (18 May 1815, lot 1035). Thus, by a remarkable coincidence, the separated volumes of the set were sold in London in different rooms within a few days of each other. As already mentioned, vols. 1, 2 and 3 (Phillipps 3630) are now in Amsterdam, and vol. 4 (apart from the gatherings that came to Douce) is now in Manchester.

There are two manuscripts that were in British collections in the early years of the nineteenth century where the assumption that they were late imports is not supported by specific evidence.[30] The first of these is the one *Lancelot-Grail* known to have been in Scotland, at Hamilton Palace, in the collection formed by

---

[30] I have not yet had the opportunity of examining either of these manuscripts at first hand, so there may be clues not recorded in published descriptions.

Alexander Douglas (1767–1852), Marquess of Douglas until 1818, then 10th Duke of Hamilton. He bought books in Italy, France and England, but even those bought in England had often come from abroad.[31] Despite the lack of precise information, it is probably reasonable to assume that his *Lancelot* (Hamilton 49) was not in England during the Middle Ages. It was produced in Italy, early in the fourteenth century, and the simplest assumption is that Hamilton obtained it in Italy, along with his many other manuscripts of known Italian provenance.[32] In 1882 the Hamilton collection was put up for sale, and Sotheby's prepared a catalogue for the forthcoming auction. However, before the sale could take place, and even before the catalogue was published, the collection was bought by the Berlin museum.[33] The purchase was subsequently divided between the museum's Kupferstichkabinett and the Prussian State Library (with Hamilton 49 going to the library). This part of the collection was removed to Schloss Wolkenburg during the last war, and returned to East Berlin in 1946 (Deutsche Staatsbibliothek, Preussischer Kulturbesitz, Hs. Hamilton 49).

The second manuscript for which we lack specific information on provenance is one that was in the collection of the Duke of Newcastle under Lyne, at Clumber Park (Nottinghamshire). At the sale of this library (Part III, Sotheby's, 6 December 1937) it was lot 937, and was bought by Maggs for Martin Bodmer. It subsequently came back on the market with H. P. Kraus (Catalogue 165, no. 9), sold in 1986 to Tenschert (Catalogue 16, nos. 6 and 7, divided into two volumes). It is last recorded for sale in 1995 by Jörn Günther of Hamburg (Catalogue 3, no. 11, both volumes). The binding is by 'H. E. Stamper,' presumably the Henry Stamper who was in business as a binder at 17 Frith Street in London until 1866. The cover is described as having the arms of the 4th Duke of Newcastle (died 1851), but his son, the 5th Duke (died 1864), probably used the same stamp. Many of Newcastle's Old French manuscripts came from the library of Thomas Johnes of Hafod with the duke's acquisition of the Hafod estate (including the library) in 1832, but there is no specific indication that this is the origin of Newcastle 937. The miniatures are attributed to the Parisian workshop of the *Cité des Dames* in the first decade or so of the fifteenth century, and its inclusion of the *Vie de Bertrand du Guesclin* will not have recommended it to the English market at this time. So the provisional assumption would be that it did not come to England or Wales until after the Middle Ages, probably between 1790 and 1860.

Throughout the first half of the nineteenth century the dominant figure was that greatest of all collectors Sir Thomas Phillipps, who bought some of his

---

31 See the introduction to *Die lateinischen Handschriften der Sammlung Hamilton zu Berlin* beschrieben von Helmut Boese (Wiesbaden, 1966), pp. xiii–xvii, to which may be added the observation that 'Marq. of Douglas' (or simply 'Douglas') is often enough to be found in the margins of English sale catalogues.

32 Hamilton spent much of his youth in Italy, and his acquisition of numerous manuscripts from Italian collections is documented by Boese, pp. xiii–xv. For evidence that Hamilton 49 was made in Italy see Leonardo Olschki, *Manuscrits français à peintures des bibliothèques d'Allemagne* (Geneva, 1932), p. 35 and plate XXXIX.

33 This unpublished catalogue is the source of the Hamilton numbers still in common use. Copies of it are extremely rare; the one in the British Library is not catalogued, but kept in the Department of Manuscripts.

Lancelot-Grail manuscripts abroad, and some in England. However, all those that he bought in London had probably come from France in the last forty years, and all eventually left England again with the dispersal of the collection. Phillipps 130 (now New Haven, Yale University, Beinecke Library MS 229) and Phillipps 4377 (now Berkeley, California, Bancroft Library MS UCB 73) were both bought (at different times) from the bookseller Royez in Paris. Phillipps 1045 (now Yale, Beinecke Library MS 227) and Phillipps 1047 (now in a private collection near Paris) are the Clermont-Tonnerre manuscripts that Phillipps bought at an anonymous sale at Evans (27 May 1825, lots 855 and 856).[34] Phillipps 1046 (now Cologny-Geneva, cod. Bodmer 147) was lot 857 in the same sale, its earlier provenance being unknown, but probably continental to judge from an inserted note in French (reproduced in the Evans sale catalogue). The name on fol. 159 transcribed as 'Antoney de Racygnano' (fourteenth century) is unidentified, but presumably French or Italian rather than English. Phillipps 1279 (now Berkeley California, Bancroft Library MS UCB 107) was one of eight manuscripts bought in 1825 from Pierre-Philippe-Constant Lammens, librarian to the University of Ghent, and Phillipps 3643 (now Berkeley California, Bancroft Library MS UCB 106) was acquired at the Lang sale (17 November 1828, lot 1962). Lang had probably obtained it from Payne and Foss (their 1825 catalogue, no. 9153), no doubt acquired by them at the Motteley sale in Paris in 1824 in which it was lot 875, easily recognized by its unique contents.[35] The complex history of Phillipps 3630 (now Amsterdam, Bibliotheca Philosophica Hermetica MS 1) has been outlined above (thanks to Douce).[36] Phillipps 8230 (La Vallière 4003) has also been discussed above.

A manuscript that Phillipps must have been offered, but which he declined, is now Cologny-Geneva, cod. Bodmer 105. That this manuscript was in France during the Middle Ages is confirmed by the arms of Guyot le Peley of Troyes (died 1485), but it has made a number of visits to England. In 1834 it was twice offered at auction by Wheatley (sales of 17 March, lot 931, and 23 June, lot 1003)

---

34 At the dispersal of the collection, Phillipps 130, 1045, 1046 and 1047 were in Sotheby's sale of 1 July 1946 (lots 6, 14, 8 and 10), the first two being acquired by Dudley Colman (and later by Charles Stonehill), whilst Phillipps 1046 went to Maggs for Bodmer, and Phillipps 1047 to Scheler in Paris. These last three are sometimes said to have belonged to Charles Yarnold, but this is not so. Despite the heading in the Phillipps catalogue the manuscripts bought at the Yarnold sale (Southgate, 6 June 1825) were Phillipps 1048–56 only; Phillipps 1036–47 were bought at the anonymous sale at Evans just over a week earlier (27 May 1825), and Phillipps records the relevant catalogue numbers (though he confuses 856 and 857).

35 See Paul Meyer, 'Notices sur quelques manuscrits français de la bibliothèque Phillipps à Cheltenham,' *Notices et Extraits des manuscrits*, 34.1 (1891), 156 [149–58].

36 Despite the Phillipps numbers on its spine (see Meuwese, 'Twelve Bleeding,' 136) vol. 1 never had a number in the Phillipps catalogue. No doubt '1045' was changed to '1047' as Phillipps tried to find which of his manuscripts corresponded to the Evans sale catalogue (cf. his confusion over the Evans numbers 856 and 857, noted above). Once he had recognized that this volume belonged with the two bought in 1828 he added it to Phillipps 3630, making this three volumes instead of two (but too late to change the entry in the catalogue). The history given for vol. 1 in 1979 by H. P. Kraus (Catalogue 153, no. 31) is in error on two counts: this volume was never Phillipps 1046 and the manuscript that was Phillipps 1046 never belonged to Charles Yarnold (see note 34). However, the confusion goes back to Phillipps himself as there is a note in his hand on the second flyleaf, 'Bought I believe in Yarnold's sale or of Longman & co' (information kindly supplied by Martine Meuwese). 'Longman & co' is likely to be correct; Longman was the buyer at the Parris sale in 1815 at the high price of £20.

to be acquired by the bookseller Thomas Thorpe (no. 473 in his 1834 catalogue of manuscripts). In each case it is easily recognized by the fact that it is in four volumes, on paper, with additional paintings on vellum. By 1864 at the latest it was in Florence, the property of Baron Seymour Kirkup.[37] However, it returned to England for the sale of his library in London (6 December 1871, lot 2338), after which it is lost from view until sold by the Galerie Charpentier in Paris as part of the library of Dr. Lucien-Graux (26 January 1957, lot 64), acquired by Martin Bodmer.

In the middle of the nineteenth century the principal English buyer of *Lancelot-Grail* manuscripts was the Earl of Ashburnham, but mainly by accident. The first of his eight volumes was acquired in 1847 when he bought the collection of Guglielmo Libri (Ashburnham-Libri 121, now Florence, Biblioteca Mediceo-Laurenziana MS Ashburnham 48). The addition of a French poem in the fifteenth century and the name 'Gaufroy Duchastel' indicate that it remained in France during the Middle Ages (always assuming that these are not one of Libri's notorious forgeries to disguise an illicit provenance). The next six of Ashburnham's *Lancelot-Grail* volumes were acquired in 1849 when he bought the manuscripts of Joseph Barrrois. These were Ashburnham-Barrois 35 (2 vols.), 36 (3 vols.) and 398. The previous history of Barrois 35 has already been outlined: first recorded at the La Vallière sale (lot 3994), it had later spent time in England in the Roxburghe and Heber collections before returning to Paris in 1836, where it was offered for sale by Techener.[38] At the sale of the Ashburnham-Barrois manuscripts (Sotheby's, 10 June 1901) it was lot 536, and is now New York, Pierpont Morgan Library, M. 207–8. The three volumes of Barrois 36 are not a true set. The first two belong together and had been owned by Jehan de Brosse, 'seigneur de sainte Sevère et de Boussac et Mareschal de France'; the third volume was added later, but all three were at Anet in 1724. In the Barrois sale of 1901 they were lot 537, and are now Pierpont Morgan Library, M. 805–7. The single volume of Barrois 398 was written at Bruges in 1479, belonged to the family of Rolin, and came to Barrois via the cathedral library at Tournai. At the sale in 1901 it was lot 535, and it too found its way to New York where it is Morgan, M. 38. Thus, all the Ashburnham-Barrois copies of the *Lancelot-Grail* have come by different routes to the Pierpont Morgan Library.[39]

---

37 Mentioned in *La Tavola Ritonda o L'Istoria di Tristano*, ed. Filippo-Luigi Polidori, 2 vols. (Bologna, 1864–65), I, xlii–xliii, n. 1.

38 *Bulletin du bibliophile*, 2 (1836), no. 141 of the catalogue, and vol. 5 (1842), no. 588.

39 For more details of their earlier and later history see *Census of Medieval and Renaissance Manuscripts in the United States and Canada* by Seymour de Ricci with the assistance of W. J. Wilson, 3 vols. (1935–40; rpt. New York, 1961), pp. 1371, 1404 and 1658–59; *Supplement to the Census of Medieval and Renaissance Manuscripts in the United States and Canada* originated by C. U. Faye, ed. W. H. Bond (New York, 1962), pp. 338 and 359. It is known that Morgan, M. 805–6 were originally bound in one volume, and François Avril recognized them as having been at Anet: *L'Art au temps des rois maudits: Philippe le Bel et fils 1285–1328, exposition, Paris, Galeries nationales du Grand Palais, 17 mars–29 juin 1998* (Paris, 1998), p. 303, no. 204. From additional information kindly supplied by Alison Stones it appears that M. 807 was also at Anet, and I am inclined to think that all three volumes were then bound as one, in the unexpected order 805–807–806, representing the *Lancelot* on p. 16 of the sale catalogue referred to in note 21 (no. 127 in Bauchart's edition), but the whole question requires further investigation.

The one *Lancelot-Grail* manuscript acquired by Ashburnham from choice was Appendix 223, obtained in 1863 (the note 'A. 1863' is written on the flyleaf, and the presumption that this represents the year of acquisition is supported by the fact that the two preceding numbers in the Appendix were bought at the Libri sale of 1862). It had previously been in the sale of P. N. Menin des Pinssarts in Paris (J. F. Delion, 30 November 1843, lot 1459), and was bought at that time by Labarq on behalf of an owner who has written a note to that effect on the flyleaf (in French and signed 'M. P.'). When the Ashburnham Appendix was acquired en bloc by Henry Yates Thompson, the *Lancelot* was amongst the many manuscripts discarded in a sale at Sotheby's (1 May 1899, lot 153). Acquired by Sir John Williams, it came with the rest of his collection to the National Library of Wales at Aberystwyth (MS 445-D).

The other *Lancelot-Grail* manuscript at Aberystwyth (National Library of Wales MS 5018-D) entered the library with the acquisition of the collection of F. W. Bourdillon in 1922. When the manuscript had come to England is not known. There is a Latin ex libris of 'Claudio Thomassin' (partly erased), and that of the 'Bibliotheca Sedanensis' (founded 1607) can be read under ultra-violet light. Clearly legible, however, is that of Peter Frolov, the Russian mining engineer who gave books and manuscripts to the Imperial Library in St. Petersburg. This latter (in Russian) is dated 1817.

The most recent import to England, but perhaps the most famous, is the Huth *Merlin* (British Library MS Additional 38117), which had formerly belonged to the great seventeenth-century scholar Du Cange. This was acquired from the Parisian booksellers Bachelin-Deflorenne in the early 1870s by the English collector Henry Huth.[40] On the death of his son, Alfred Henry Huth, in 1910 it was included in the bequest of fifty manuscripts and printed books chosen by the Trustees of the British Museum.[41]

The most obvious feature of the surviving *Lancelot-Grail* manuscripts that were in England during the Middle Ages, whether written there or imported, is that they are all relatively early. The characteristic period for their production, is the late thirteenth to early fourteenth century. There is no example clearly later than 1350, and certainly none from the fifteenth century (even amongst those with miniatures). It is also worth noting that Edward IV, who did commission luxurious manuscripts in French in the latest Flemish style, both before and after his brief exile in Bruges in 1470, included no chivalric romances amongst his purchases.[42] In court circles this no doubt reflects a change of interests, but in the

---

[40] For a more detailed history see *The Huth Library: A Catalogue of the Printed Books, Manuscripts, Autograph Letters, and Engravings, collected by Henry Huth, with collations and bibliographical descriptions*, 5 vols. (London, 1880), III, 954–7, and *Merlin*, ed. Gaston Paris and Jacob Ulrich, 2 vols. (Paris, 1886), I, i–v.

[41] See *Catalogue of the Fifty Manuscripts & Printed Books Bequeathed to the British Museum by Alfred H. Huth* (London, 1912).

[42] See Janet Backhouse, 'Founders of the Royal Library: Edward IV and Henry VII as Collectors of Illuminated Manuscripts,' in *England in the Fifteenth Century: Proceedings of the 1986 Harlaxton Symposium*, ed. Daniel Williams (Woodbridge, 1987), pp. 39–41 [23–41], and Anne F. Sutton and Livia Visser-Fuchs, 'Choosing a Book in Late Fifteenth-Century England and

country at large the change is one of language, for the later fourteenth century onwards is the time of the English and Welsh adaptations.

Another notable characteristic of the surviving manuscripts, is that a higher-than-expected proportion of those written in England, and even of those that were brought here during the Middle Ages, are severely utilitarian in appearance. One is a hotchpotch of scribal hands (Lansdowne 757), and another is an assembly of parts from different manuscripts (Royal 20 A. ii); several are significantly defective or in a poor state of repair (particularly the fragments in Royal 15 A. xi, the *Lancelot* section of Royal 20 A. ii, Lansdowne 757 and Notting-ham, L. M. 7). More important, however, is that just over half are relatively small, containing individual texts (or the virtually inseparable *Estoire* and *Merlin*) rather than the complete *Cycle*, and even more (mostly the same manu-scripts) have little or no decoration.[43] The notable exceptions are Rawlinson Q.b.6, Royal 14 E. iii, Royal 20 D. iv, Ashmole 828 and Digby 223, whilst others fall between the extremes, but the general point still holds. In contrast, the manuscripts brought in later by collectors are nearly always larger and more carefully produced, often of high quality and with extensive programmes of miniatures (the most obvious exception being Aberystwyth, National Library of Wales MS 445-D). One conclusion that might be drawn from the 'utilitarian' manuscripts is that they were produced for, and subsequently owned by, people who had an interest in the text itself. There is certainly no question of their ever having been used for the purposes of display. It is also more common for the manuscripts that were in England to show signs of having been read, and of having been read with close attention. Several of them have notes in the margin (sometimes in French, sometimes in English), and several have corrections or additions to the text. These manuscripts were not only 'utilitarian' in appear-ance, they really were put to use. This may also account for their state of repair. A book may just as easily be damaged by constant use as by careless neglect.

The notes in English are of interest for other reasons. They show that the manuscripts were being read by people whose first language was not French, and from the date of the handwriting (and sometimes from the content) it appears this was at a time well into the fifteenth century and even later. The sixteenth-century note on Cambridge University Library MS Additional 7071 that refers to the printed edition of Malory takes us into a period when a manu-script in French was outmoded both in its language and in its means of produc-tion. Although this reminds us that even as late as this there were people still taking an interest in these outdated French books, we should not overlook the fact that by this time the general movement is in the direction of English, and in

---

Burgundy,' in *England and the Low Countries in the Late Middle Ages*, ed. Caroline Barron and Nigel Saul (Stroud and New York, 1995), pp. 84–6 [61–98].

[43] There are six manuscripts that are both small (300mm or less) and with no more than coloured capitals for decoration: Royal 15 A. xi, 19 B. vii, 20 A. ii, 20 B. viii, Lansdowne 757 and Addi-tional 32125; three others are small but with one or two miniatures: Royal 19 C. xiii, 20 C. vi, Egerton 2515; five are larger but without miniatures: Royal 19 C. xii, 20 D. iii, Nottingham, L. M. 7, Cambridge Additional 7071 and Corpus Christi College MS 45.

the direction of other types of literature. One has only to look at the productions of Caxton to grasp where the market lay (his Malory being something of an exception).[44] Nor should we forget that by the time of these notes it may be little more than fifty years to the very different world of Shakespeare.

---

[44] See Sutton and Visser-Fuchs, 'Choosing a Book,' p. 70.

20

Towards a Modern Reception of the Lancelot-Grail Cycle

CAROL DOVER

The large number of films either inspired by Arthurian themes (modern in scope) or drawn more closely from Arthurian works of literature is testimony to the continuing power of the Arthurian legends to fascinate and inspire, in the true spirit of the medieval tradition of continuation.[1] The change of medium is not restricted to feature films, since television producers have adapted the cinematic art to the small screen with serializations and made-for-television movies.[2] Kevin Harty lists 564 medieval movies produced since the first film was made in 1897,[3] two years after the Lumière brothers invented the medium, to the present day, and a total of 79 Arthurian movies,[4] the earliest of which were French. But if the sheer quantity of output is evidence of the modern vitality of the medium, a rapid breakdown of the films reveals that the English-speaking world has a proprietary hold, and in the words of a recent author, 'overall quality does not seem to be on the upswing in Arthurian films.'[5] The medieval sources most frequently exploited for Arthurian film, insofar as sources can be adduced, tend to be of anglophone origin, especially Malory's *Death of Arthur*, but the Perceval story, based on Chrétien de Troyes's *Le Conte du Graal* or Wolfram von Eschenbach's *Parzival*, the Tristan and Isolde story, and *Le Chevalier de la Charrette* also have their place. Medieval Arthurian literature sprang from a common Celtic heritage – the matter of Brittany as well as Britain – which was actively exploited at a time when the English court's official language was the Norman variety of French,[6] but in the domain of film, there is a linguistic and cultural divide. Anglophone directors understandably have a predilection for the English medieval tradition, French directors tend to take the French tradition, and German directors the German tradition, but it has been suggested that

---

1   The material has been conveniently catalogued by Kevin J. Harty, *The Reel Middle Ages* (Jefferson, NC, and London, 2002); Harty's 'A Complete Arthurian Filmography and Selective Bibliography,' chapter 12 of his edited volume, *King Arthur on Film: New Essays on Arthurian Cinema* (Jefferson, NC, 1999); also Bert Olton, *Arthurian Legends on Film and Television* (Jefferson, NC, and London, 2000). For a more restricted, narrative treatment of Arthurian film, see Rebecca A. Umland and Samuel J. Umland, *The Use of Arthurian Legend in Hollywood Film* (Westport, CT, and London, 1996).
2   Serialized films preceded television serials; see Bert Olton, *Arthurian Legends*, pp. 3–16.
3   *The Reel Middle Ages*.
4   'A Complete Arthurian Filmography.'
5   Olton, *Arthurian Legends*, p. 2.
6   King Henry II promoted Arthurian literature for political ends.

anglophone audiences view the Arthurian legends through a different lens from that of francophone audiences because of historically-determined differences in cultural perception. For native English speakers, King Arthur is not only a literary figure but also a historical figure, and this linkage influences the significance they would attach to Arthurian legends. French audiences, in contrast, perceive the Arthurian world as myth, endowed with literary but not historical reality, and King Arthur as a mythical creation of the literary imagination.[7] To *Lancelot-Grail* readers, then, it should be no surprise that the *Cycle*'s version of the Arthurian legends is conspicuous by its absence in English-language and German-language Arthurian movies, particularly if we remember the size and complexity of the *Cycle*.

This chapter has a narrow focus: movies that are clearly based on all or part of the *Lancelot-Grail Cycle* and are significantly faithful to the medieval original. This narrows the coverage quite drastically, rejecting Grail-centered movies such as Richard Blank's *Parzival* (1980) and Eric Rohmer's *Perceval le Gallois* (1979) because they follow a literary tradition that makes Perceval the Grail hero, not Galahad.[8] Although Perceval does appear in the *Cycle*, he enters late and is a minor player, for the authors of the *Cycle* were intent on developing a Grail hero of their own.[9] For this reason I have excluded all movies having Perceval as their hero, and selected three movies that intersect with the *Lancelot-Grail Cycle* in very specific ways.

Les Chevaliers de la Table Ronde (1990)

To find a substantial reliance on the *Lancelot-Grail Cycle* we must go to French cinema and Denis Llorca's *Les Chevaliers de la Table Ronde*,[10] which a serious viewer would surely honor with the label of 'most authentically medieval example of cinema Arthuriana.'[11] The credits express thanks to 'Chrétien de Troyes et ses continuateurs,' on the strength of which some have assumed that Llorca used Chrétien as his primary source, yet the film seems to owe much more to the *continuateurs*, primarily the anonymous authors of the *Lancelot-Grail Cycle*, who recycled Chrétien's Lancelot story in the *Lancelot* together with aspects of the Tristan legend and Chrétien's Perceval poem. It is the

---

7   See Jeff Rider et al., 'The Arthurian Legend in French Cinema: Robert Bresson's *Lancelot du Lac* and Eric Rohmer's *Perceval le Gallois*,' in *Cinema Arthuriana: Twenty New Essays*, rev. ed., ed. Kevin J. Harty (Jefferson, NC, 2002), pp. 149–62.

8   Blank's movie is based on Wolfram von Eschenbach's *Parzival* (thirteenth century).

9   See Annie Combes, 'From Quest to Quest: Lancelot and Perceval in the Prose *Lancelot*,' *Arthuriana*, 12.3 (Fall 2002), 7–31, and E. Kennedy, *Lancelot and the Grail* (Oxford, 1986).

10   Directed by Denis Llorca; produced by Pierre Braunberger; 3hrs. 28mins.; distributed by Les Films du Jeudi; Alain Macé (Arthur), Valérie Durin (Guinevere), Denis Llorca (Lancelot), Jean-François Prévaud (young Merlin), Alain Cuny (old Merlin), Michel Vitold (Fisher King), Catherine Rétoré (young Viviane), Maria Casarès (old Viviane), François Berreur (Galahad), Benoit Brione (Gawain), Gilles Geisweiler (Perceval).

11   Harty, 'Cinema Arthuriana: An Overview,' in *Cinema Arthuriana*, rev. ed., applies this label to Rohmer's *Perceval le Gallois*, echoing the fact that Rohmer's film was produced at a time when *authenticité* was a watchword of New Wave cinema.

Lancelot-Grail that provides Llorca's film with its plot, its characters, its narrative texture, and its tone.

The film received mixed reviews when it came out in 1990. On the positive side, 'Denis Llorca ne s'est pas contenté de filmer son spectacle théâtral; il l'a enrichi, il l'a rendu plus envoûtant, plus magique, plus mystérieux. La réussite est totale.'[12] Yes, the film came out of Llorca's twelve-hour stage play, *Quatre Saisons pour les chevaliers de la table ronde* (1989), condensed to three and a half hours for the screen, which put his actors before the camera by day and on stage by night. The difficulty of passing from stage to screen and vice versa is not to be underestimated, for theater requires an actor to project, an enterprise in which the quality of script and voice and gesture are large and crucial, whereas in the cinematic art the camera takes over the projection, zooming in, moving back, following close or at a distance, capturing intimately that which theater must evoke, but the end result in both cases must be a question of the imagination and power of the production. Other reviews berated *Les Chevaliers de la Table Ronde* as an overambitious project: 'La "recherche" de Llorca ne va pas beaucoup plus loin que la seule puissance du texte. Le reproche n'est pas d'avoir fait du théâtre filmé, ce n'est pas le cas, mais quelque chose qui tient du simple récit monté en image. La quête est dite plutôt que montrée.'[13] Given the vast size of the *Lancelot-Grail*, Denis Llorca might be forgiven the exorbitant length of his film but it fits his reputation as a director of large-scale mythic productions and adaptations of long, complex literary masterpieces.[14]

The play's title, *Quatre Saisons pour les chevaliers de la table ronde*, confers on the Arthurian world the unremitting structure of the four Ages of Man (infancy, youth, maturity, old age). If the film's title suggests a focus on Arthur's knights only, its four seasons are assigned to the *Cycle*'s four Arthurian works: *Merlin* is the springtime promise, *Lancelot* is the summer with its flower of chivalry, the *Queste* is the last fruits of autumn, and the *Mort Artu* is the wintry finale of the Arthurian world. But the cinematic challenge facing Llorca was, how to pare down and select from such a vast and complex narrative source, and still capture the epic proportions of its written form. His solution is to create tableaux rather than a neatly evolving storyline or the grandiose glamor associated with Hollywood movies. He retains the general reshaping of his written source and the two worlds of Arthurian chivalry and the Grail that Chrétien suggested in *Le Conte du Graal*. Llorca retains the general chronology of the *Cycle*, but with some notably creative exceptions. My intention here is not to provide a detailed intertextual analysis of the film in relation to the *Cycle*, but to show how the director has shaped his film for modern audiences while retaining key elements of the prose work.

As Sandra Gorgievski has shown, the storyline is structured around four geographical locations: the Holy Land, the forest, the Arthurian realm (a lake,

---

12 *L'Année du Cinéma* (Paris, 1999).
13 *Cahiers du Cinéma*, 437 (1990), p. 85.
14 Sandra Gorgievski, 'From Stage to Screen: The Dramatic Compulsion in French Cinema and Denis Llorca's *Les Chevaliers de la Table Ronde* (1990),' in *Cinema Arthuriana*, ed. Harty, p. 163 [163–76].

Tintagel Castle, Camelot), and the Grail Castle.[15] The Holy Land is the first and shortest segment of the narrative, indeed its tools are intensely tactile, for it relies solely on images and unspoken sound to convey the story of Christ's Passion in the briefest and most powerful terms possible. A man rides through a sunny tranquil meadow on a donkey with the crawl title, 'Voici que ton roi vient assis sur un âne de petitesse,' then the camera cuts to red darkness and a dark spearhead raised against an increasing din of grating, jarring, sound, then cut to a pair of women's hands raised up like a cup to catch blood that drips at first, then flows freely down over them. Then women enact the Deposition, with the camera's final focus resting on the marble-like features of the man awaiting resurrection in the tomb. The idyllic innocence of the ride on the donkey was the road to Calvary and the beginning of the Grail. This is Llorca's *Estoire* narrative, condensed into an evocation of the origin of the Grail.

The four-part Arthurian narrative is framed ingeniously by Galahad's night in the forest, where he is lost on his way back to his grandfather's castle. Supernatural voices reassure him, telling him not to be afraid and to follow his own path, he is lost because he has 'lost his memory' (echoes of Chrétien's Perceval). The first three parts of the Arthurian narrative are presented as the visions Galahad has in his sleep. They are separated from one another by two parallel episodes that project out into the Grail world: first Gawain's unsuccessful visit to the Grail castle, then Lancelot's visit to the Grail castle where he is deceived into sleeping with the Fisher King's daughter, Amite, and Galahad is conceived. The third narrative part (corresponding very loosely to the *Queste*) closes with Galahad sitting on the Perilous Seat at the Round Table (thereby fulfilling Merlin's prophecy); the narrative incorporates the Grail quest through two flashbacks, with Gawain remembering his visit to the Grail castle and Perceval remembering the child Galahad. The fourth part of the Arthurian narrative, corresponding loosely to the *Mort Artu*, is what Galahad remembers or dreams at night in the forest. With the death of Arthur and his knights, a boy returns the sword to the lake and Galahad awakes.

Llorca's frame is a felicitous invention that keeps Galahad ever present but in the background. When he resumes his journey in the morning light, the action cuts to a playful interlude. When we discover where he goes, he becomes, physically and symbolically, the link that joins the beginning and the end of the film, the known but unseen resurrection of the crucified man in the opening sequence and the healing of the Fisher King that signals the resurrection of the land and the completion of the Grail quest. But here Llorca plays significantly with the chronology of the *Cycle* by leaving Galahad alive on earth after the collapse of the Arthurian world (unless his memories of the Grail quest by Arthur's knights and key episodes from the *Mort Artu* are in fact foresight). Galahad's own quest for the Grail is the event that is missing from the framed episodes, as is his journey home. The Fisher King's despair at his own suffering and waiting in the tender care of his daughter, Amite, is suddenly broken by the sound of the

---

[15] 'From Stage to Screen,' p. 165. I have made very slight modifications to her very useful layout of the structure of the narrative; what I call 'Holy Land' is labeled 'Bible,' and I prefer to call 'four geographical locations' what she calls 'four levels.' I use her layout freely in this essay.

grandson's voice calling: 'Grandpère!' – the word confidently resonates in sound and appears in written form on a luminous white screen. This device suggests that the experience of the Grail is beyond mortal sight and 'reserved for a higher vision,' as it is in the *Cycle* where Galahad takes the revelation of the Grail with him at his passing over, but Llorca roots his Galahad firmly in family love. Unlike Chrétien's Perceval, he does apparently find his way home to his mother and his grandfather, and this in itself brings a message of hope for the Grail family. And hope for a new world of chivalry?

Given the length of Llorca's film, it would be pointless to try to account for all the modifications the director has made to his primary source. One of the most notable of them, however, is the absence of the fierce battles that are crucial to Arthur's establishment as a worthy warrior king in the *Merlin* text. Indeed there is very little warfare in the narrative; gone are Lancelot's parents, King Ban and Queen Elaine, and his cousin's parents, and with them the pseudo-historical connection that makes Ban Arthur's vassal in the *Cycle*. The infant Lancelot is taken by a young damsel called Viviane as she bathes in a lake and sees a knight kidnap the child's mother (echoes of the German *Lanzelet*, perhaps). The episodes at the lake are skillfully developed; Viviane and the Lady of the Lake, who are the same character in the *Lancelot*, are two separate characters, mother and daughter, in the film. The mother prophesies that her daughter will become 'une mère vierge,' and she sends her to Merlin. Hence the child Lancelot is conveniently referred to as her son, whom she calls 'fils de roi' and 'beau fils,' as in the *Cycle*. The young Arthur is portrayed as a veritable simpleton, a naive, carousing youth who catches sight of the beautiful Guinevere in her father's courtyard from his vantage point on the ground, where he is recovering from a bout of drinking. Arthur is a pitiful, indecisive figure who never rises to regal stature and maintains throughout a child-like attachment to Merlin.

Most of the film's decor is naturalistic: castles, fields, a cave, forest, country interiors, clearly intended to provide a realistic rendering of the medieval Arthurian world but the rendering of certain marvelous events is decidedly Gothic; for example, when Lancelot raises the lid of the tomb in the Cemetery of the Future he descends into the tomb and makes a dark, subterranean journey into Gorre. Thus it contrasts sharply with the sparse, symbolic visualization of the world of the Grail family. The Grail castle has a minimalist decor, a white table for discussion between the Fisher King and first Gawain, then Lancelot. White and red dominate. The Fisher King is frequently shown lying in the center of a bare room on his bare pallet, which the camera fixes from high above, then circles round slowly as it descends and closes in. The camera captures the fact that his wound is sexual: his loins are draped in a red cloth that flows like blood between his thighs when he stretches his old, pain-racked body or tries to rise from his bare pallet. This is a symbolic world, suggestive of a transcendent reality.

The frame Llorca gives to his film enhances the thematic emphasis he seeks, but within the frame certain episodes have particular structural value. He develops the *Cycle*'s Merlin into the fascinating figure of an alchemist dabbling in the medieval equivalent of science, in search of the origins of human life in a manner that anticipates human cloning today. His experiments, conducted in a laboratory, are aimed at creating a man with sulphur and mercury. 'C'est l'union qui fait la force' is the theme not only of his experiments but also of his relations with women. The unions he seeks are sexual and he scoffs at womanly talk of love, but Viviane's resistance to his sexual advances inflames him all the more and makes him fall in love with her. A viewer familiar with the *Lancelot-Grail* will be aware of how close Llorca stays to the literary text. Viviane's love for her son is emphasized, the teaching he receives from her in preparation for knight-hood is retained almost verbatim, although the splendiferous procession from lake to Arthur's court is omitted. Llorca innovates by creating for Galahad a corresponding education in knighthood, whereas the *Lancelot-Grail* merely mentions that the child was raised in an abbey. Galahad's education comes not from his mother but from his grandfather, the Fisher King. It echoes in lyrical terms the evangelical message of Love:

> 'Ecoute mes paroles, grave-les dans ton coeur et ne les oublie pas:
> les grands devoirs du chevalier tiennent en amour,
> amour est son devoir,
> amour est son droit,
> amour est son courage,
> amour est sa prouesse,
> amour est son courage,
> amour est sa grandeur,
> amour est sa quête.'

But it links up with the concept of Love and knighthood conveyed by Lancelot's visit to the Grail castle and the conception of Galahad. Do you know what God created you for? is a recurring question in the film, asked of Lancelot and Gawain – but not of Arthur. It underpins the conversation between King Pelles (Fisher King) and his guest, Lancelot, which Llorca develops into a lengthy exchange about woman, man, love, and the purpose of sons: the son accom-plishes what the father leaves undone, he is therefore necessary to life itself. The King's response to Lancelot's ignorance of what still remains to be accomplished is both didactic and lyrical:

> 'L'amour, car jusqu'ici l'homme n'a accompli que la haine.
> La connaissance, car jusqu'à présent l'homme n'a accompli que l'erreur.
> La joie, car jusqu'à présent l'homme n'a accompli que le plaisir et la douleur.
> La vie, car jusqu'à présent l'homme n'a accompli que la naissance et la mort.
> L'unité, car jusqu'à présent l'homme n'a accompli que la division et la guerre.'

The King's moralizing replaces the vituperative tirades that Lancelot attracts from many of the hermit figures that crop up on his path in the forest in the *Cycle*, and it distills into actions the lesson of Love from the teaching of Christ in the gospels. Because Amite loves Lancelot, she wants to be loved by him in return but he is indifferent. However, her father reminds her that she must sleep with him because God created her to bear Lancelot's child: ' "Est-ce que tu l'aimes?" – "Oui" – "Alors c'est toi qui créera l'amour, comme un enfant." ' The body is not Love: ' "Le corps est souffrance, l'esprit est liberté. Sommes-nous libres?" – "Oui." '

The scene of the conception of Galahad is rendered indirectly with a delicacy at once comparable to and different from that of the written text: the drugged Lancelot is led to the chamber of the woman he believes is Guinevere, he finds a white lily on his pillow, he takes it, gradually draws the petal into his mouth. Then Amite appears, but with Guinevere's features; she takes the petal in her mouth and Lancelot accepts her as Guinevere. The defloration echoes the text's narratorial comment, 'through this flower of virginity which was then corrupted and violated another flower was recovered . . . from this lost flower was restored the virgin Galaad' (*LM* 4:210), that extols the act as divine intervention. But the film suppresses Lancelot's violent reaction to his discovery of the deception, which is a frequent subject for illustration in *Lancelot* manuscripts.

The final segment returns to where we first saw Galahad, in the forest. He leaves and crawl titles stand in for visual action:

> Et Galahad reprit son chemin
> vers le château de son grandpère
> Loin
> Très loin

After a small interlude, the camera returns to the Grail Castle for the final shots. It focuses on the Fisher King who wakes up on his pallet, raises himself with great difficulty. The camera turns round him in a circle, as it has done before, then zooms in on his despair. Amite arrives, washes his feet in silence once he is dressed and seated at the window, looking out. A voice sings, he asks who it is. She says he is alone. The movie risks ending on a tragic note with the old man suffering and waiting, like the row of sons of the Old Testament that Michelangelo painted in the Sistine Chapel, who wait for the time to be accomplished when their messiah will come, and with him generation and regeneration and the new beginning of history. But the painful silence is broken by the off-stage voice of young Galahad, calling 'Grandpère!' There is, it seems, a son returned to accomplish the deeds left undone by his father. Unlike Chrétien's Perceval, Galahad has found his way home. This, I think, is the point where we see clearly that the *Cycle*'s epic quality and its romance heritage have been built into the film: the epic is not invested in the battles, the politics, the ruler, it is in the reflective aspect, it is on the side of the Grail, of the simple and the faithful, and they survive the ashes of the Arthurian world.

Unlike the end of the *Cycle*, *Les Chevaliers de la Table Ronde* ends with a message of human hope that transcends the tragedy of Arthurian society. In its lyrical flights, Llorca's film achieves a sober majesty that renders with startling efficacy Etienne Gilson's assessment of the entire *Cycle* as 'a summa of love.'

Lancelot du Lac (1974)

In a 1960s interview Robert Bresson spoke of his desire to make a Lancelot film in two languages (French, English) and possibly three (German) because the legend is part of a mythology shared by all three,[16] but *Lancelot du Lac* was

---

16 'The Question,' interview by Jean-Luc Godard and Michel Delahaye, in *Robert Bresson*, ed.

twenty years in the making from conception to completion in 1974.[17] Although Bresson mentions Chrétien de Troyes' *Chevalier de la Charrette* in the same interview and context, it is *La Mort le roi Artu* that provides him with his narrative framework, characters, and motifs.

For his film, he simplifies the *Mort Artu*'s cast of characters and concentrates attention on a few: Lancelot, Guinevere, Arthur, and Gawain, with Lionel, Bohort, Agravain, Gaheriet, and Mordred. The *Mort Artu*'s internal feuding (Gawain's family vs Lancelot's) that poisons the fellowship of the Round Table is fueled by Gawain's brother Agravain, but Bresson concentrates it all in Mordred. He develops the friendship between Lancelot and Gawain, the man of action who trusts Lancelot and looks up to him as the guide and protector of them all. There are no epic panoramas, no lengthy military campaigns in the film, and any glamor we might want to attach to Arthur's court is reduced to the austerity of a farmhouse. Bresson's Arthur is a more competent leader than Llorca's, but while he relies on Lancelot to maintain fellowship among his knights, he is blind to the consequences of the factional strife within the camp. Bresson omits two important events that, in the *Mort Artu*, depict Arthur's rage at discovering the true relationship between Lancelot and the Queen. Firstly, the Mador (the Poisoned Apple) episode, one of several court intrigues used to ensnare Guinevere, which ends in her being tried, found guilty, and condemned to be burned at the stake, for Arthur is determined she must die because he cannot avenge himself on Lancelot. But the Church intervenes . . . Secondly, the episode of Lancelot's wall paintings, which Morgain maliciously reveals to Arthur as irrevocable proof that Lancelot and the Queen are lovers. In the film, Guinevere's sphere of action is reduced almost entirely to the private function of Lancelot's lover. Finally, the three tournaments that are key turning points in the *Mort Artu* are reduced to one, which Bresson uses as the crux on which the narrative turns.

Bresson's version bears a limited resemblance to the *Mort Artu* and yet the first half of the film is based on a short summary from the *Mort Artu*,[18] which refers back to the moment in the *Queste* where Lancelot sees the Grail, is healed by it, and promises a hermit to remain chaste and never again sin with the Queen. But Bresson's protagonist is the Lancelot of *Chevalier de la Charrette* whom the *Lancelot-Grail*'s prose romancers adopted, and it is highly likely that Bresson assumed his viewers were familiar with Lancelot as the knight whose heart was shaped by Love, for the knight's generosity to Mordred and Gawain in the film accords well with Chrétien's (and the *Lancelot-Grail*'s) characterization. Chrétien dramatized Lancelot's ability to reconcile his Love for the Queen

James Quandt, Cinematheque Ontario Monographs, 2 (Toronto, 1998), p. 481 [453–83], translated by Jane Pease.

[17] Direction and screenplay, Robert Bresson. Cast: Luc Simon (Lancelot), Laura Duke Condominas (Guinevere), Vladimir Antolek-Oresek (Arthur), Humbert Balsan (Gawain). Distributed by Mara Films. 80 mins.

[18] Kristin Thompson, 'The Sheen of Armour, the Whinnies of Horses: Sparse Parametric Style in *Lancelot du Lac*,' in *Robert Bresson*, p. 343 [339–71]. The summary passage is in Norris J. Lacy's translation of *The Death of Arthur*, vol. 4 of *Lancelot-Grail: The Old French Arthurian Vulgate and Post-Vulgate in Translation*, ed. Norris J. Lacy (New York and London, 1995), at p. 91.

with chivalry, but Bresson (like the *Lancelot-Grail* authors) adds love of God as a third, competing element.

The film opens with the clash of two swords in a dark forest, then the sight and sound of blood gurgling and gushing from two knights felled in quick succession. Riderless horses career through the dark forest. Two mounted knights pause to peer at two skeletons in armor hanging from a tree. A sword slashes across an altar, toppling the burning candles. The camera cuts to the title, *Lancelot du Lac*, against a background image of the Grail, and crawl titles are scrolled down to the sound of pipes and drums beating to the rhythm of a brisk military march: here, in the crawl titles, the Grail is mentioned repeatedly. Much has been made of the absence of the Grail in the film proper. Although the film's title follows the medieval romance tradition of naming a work for its hero, its original title was *The Grail*. This connects with the opening sequence, which visualizes the mother's stark assessment of chivalry to her son in Chrétien's Grail story: chivalry has lost its moral compass and been reduced to slaughter. Indeed, the crawl titles give a brief history of the Grail (not 'Holy Grail') in which Lancelot is mentioned only twice:

> Après une suite d'aventures qui relèvent du merveilleux dont Lancelot fut le héros, les chevaliers du roi Artus, dits 'Chevaliers de la table ronde,' se sont lancés à la quête du Graal . . . L'enchanteur Merlin, avant de mourir, voua les chevaliers à cette aventure sainte. Certains signes interprétés par lui, désignèrent, pour mener la quête non pas Lancelot, le premier chevalier du monde, mais un tout jeune chevalier, Perceval (Parsifal) le 'Très Pur.'

But Perceval disappeared. From the start Lancelot belongs, then, to a marvelous past and failure in the present. Our first glimpse of him (the recognition is retroactive) brings a sense of foreboding and fate: ' "Celui dont on entend les pas mourra dans l'année," ' prophesies an old peasant woman in the forest who gives him directions on his way home from the quest. The Grail never appears in the film itself and figures only as an object of discussion between Lancelot and Guinevere.

Others have pointed out that all of Bresson's films are about confinement and freedom, and *Lancelot du Lac* is no exception. Arthur confines his knights to camp out of fear that their failure in the Grail quest is a sign that they have offended God, and fear that further action might increase the long casualty list of his knights. They are men of action deprived of action: no military activity, no quest, no mission, no access to the Round Table where the knights met in fellowship and equality. Their confinement 'poisons the air,' as Gawain puts it. Arthur looks to Lancelot to keep the peace for him, but in the new atmosphere of physical constraint, factional strife breaks out between Lancelot's family and Gawain's family, fanned by Mordred, although lack of clarity about the relations between characters makes it hard to identify the factions.

This is physical confinement, but Bresson's interest is in Lancelot's inner confinement, although it is not obvious at the first viewing because of Bresson's style, or rather 'form,' with its emphasis on the ordering of the narrative. It has often been called 'elliptical' because it provides only partial shots of events and things, leaving the viewer to pay especially close attention to the narrative in order to fill in the gaps. Although the narrative is linear, the action progresses visually by repeated gestures or words which the viewer does not catch immediately.[19] Bresson's refusal to explain his characters' behavior through psychology,[20] reduces their conduct to a kind of study in behaviorism that denies us access to what we would consider their thoughts and emotions, and yet he considers the human voice to be 'the most revealing thing that exists.'[21] This is interesting, because expressionlessness is the hallmark of speech in his films. All of the dialogues pass information across a divide rather than convincing the interlocutor, but the very lack of expressiveness has the effect of making the words stand out, inviting us to concentrate on words and gestures which, though isolated, join to form a pattern. In *Lancelot du Lac* Bresson uses his customary technique: 'hide the ideas, but so that people find them. The most important will be the most hidden.'[22] I will try here to show briefly how the motif of confinement comes into play in *Lancelot du Lac*, and link it to Bresson's so-called Jansenism. Given Bresson's legendary austere treatment of the protagonists of his films, Lancelot, the knight whose heart chose Love over reason seems to me the perfect candidate for Pascal's aphorism, 'le coeur a ses raisons que la raison ne connaît point.' The film's Lancelot-Guinevere love narrative begins with Lancelot telling Guinevere they cannot be lovers any more – he no longer wears her ring – and ends with him handing her over to King Arthur at her request because there is no other option.

I have already mentioned that Bresson viewed the Lancelot legend as part of a mythology common to French, English, and German cultures. It should be no surprise, then, that he treats Lancelot as a mythical character. In myth, the character traits are already fixed, the outcome of the tale is already known and cannot be changed, which restricts innovation to *how* the ending comes about. This means that as long as Lancelot's thoughts and actions conform to those of Chrétien's mythical knight who served Arthur because his every action was inspired by his love for Arthur's Queen, the pattern is set, like an automatic template: he has to safeguard the Queen at all costs, and serve Arthur. Lancelot is generous and loving, but he has sworn to change his way of life. Lancelot's inner confinement is caused initially by his oath, which has created an apparent paradox for himself: he truly loves the Queen, and yet has sworn to renounce all carnal contact with her for love of God. In the claustrophobic space of Arthur's camp he cannot escape her intense gaze: when he goes to church, she is there with Arthur. The rest is the story of a predestined death that is foreshadowed ironically in apparently inconsequential expressions thrown out by other characters. To Gawain, Lancelot's conduct is that of a saint, 'Lancelot est devenu un

19 See P. Adams Sitney, 'The Rhetoric of Robert Bresson,' in *The Essential Cinema: Essays on Film*, ed. P. Adams Sitney (New York, 1975), pp. 182–207.

20 R. Bruce Elder, 'What I Admire in Robert Bresson's Film is his Method,' in *Robert Bresson*, p. 533 [532–43].

21 'The Question,' p. 471. On the poetic quality of the voice in *Lancelot du Lac*, see Lindley Hanlon, 'Chansons et Gestes: Voice and Verse in *Lancelot du Lac*,' in *Fragments: Bresson's Film Style* (London and Toronto, 1986), pp. 157–87.

22 Robert Bresson, *Notes on the Cinematographer*, trans. Jonathan Griffin (London, Melbourne, and New York, 1986), p. 34.

saint. Il aura son nom dans le calendrier,' to which Guinevere replies in jest. Arthur commands his knights 'Perfectionnez-vous,' words that secretly resonate in Lancelot because of the tension between God and the Queen. His efforts to keep the peace by offering friendship to Mordred (it is refused), and by calming Gawain's impatience for action with the gift of a jeweled harness, reveal his duty to Arthur and his love for Arthur's knights.

Bresson delineates Lancelot's path with two repeating structural markers. The first is the prophetic words of the peasant woman who gives him directions in the forest. When she reappears much later, Lancelot has resumed wearing Guinevere's ring, he has fought in the Escalot tournament and won, and the peasant woman is nursing the wounds he sustained in the tournament. Like Perceval's mother in the *Conte du Graal*, she tries to protect him from certain death by keeping him from chivalry, but he returns to rescue the Queen. From this point on the march of fate is inexorable. It's too late. He leaves just in time to rescue Guinevere from prison because that is his mythical pattern of behavior – the quintessential act that identified Chrétien's Lancelot before the *Cycle* took him over.

Bresson imagines the process by which Lancelot tries to renounce the Queen and keep God. It is the dialogues between the lovers that spell out the conflict of incompatibilities. Lancelot returns from the Grail quest resolved to end his love affair with the Queen because a mysterious voice reproached him his lying, double conduct. ' "Tu as fait ça?" ' is Guinevere's response, the nearest her voice comes to expressiveness in the film. Yet his love for her remains unchanged. She believes him, but he has stopped wearing her ring. She defends their love on the grounds of the solemn oath he swore to her as her lover, which must take precedence over any other oath because it came first. Clearly, she believes their love is just as sacred. She evokes the common destiny they share of being made for one another to help one another.

Bresson vocalizes Lancelot's torment as a tristanesque conflict between what he must do (*devoir*), what he wants to do (*vouloir*), and what he can do (*pouvoir*). His duty is to bring back the Grail, he says, but Guinevere points out that it is God he wanted, not the Grail, ' "Et Dieu n'est pas un objet qu'on rapporte." ' Knowing Lancelot as she does, she believes his oath to God was based on an imaginary cause-and-effect relationship between their love and the failure of the Grail quest, when the real cause was the failure of Arthurian chivalry: ' "Vous étiez acharnés. Vous avez tué, pillé, incendié, et puis vous vous êtes retournés les uns sur les autres sans vous reconnaître. Et c'est notre amour que vous accusez de ce désastre?" ' At this stage Guinevere's words identify the Grail quest with the search for God, which threatens Lancelot's love for her, so for her the conflict is between Lancelot's will and God's will, Lancelot's love for her and love of God, but she refuses to believe God can separate them. Calm and generous as always, Lancelot is still resolved to keep his oath to God because he believes his love for Guinevere and God are compatible, and she does eventually release him from his oath to her, leaving him free to devote himself to God, Lancelot goes to the chapel alone and prays God to keep him from temptation because his resistance is weak.

Quite by chance, the tournament brings a welcome return to action for

Arthur's knights. When Guinevere arranges a final farewell meeting with
Lancelot, however, the prospect of the Queen being exposed publicly
(Guinevere thinks someone has taken her scarf, Lancelot knows Mordred has)
puts her in mortal danger. This throws him back into his role as the Queen's
lover, for he has always protected her because he adores her, body and heart. He
has her heart, but it is the absence of her body that makes him suffer. How can
she live without him and he without her? The Queen arranges a rendezvous
with him while the others are at the tournament, Lancelot lets it be known that
he will not participate (to give Mordred's spies false hopes of catching him in
Guinevere's bedchamber), yet he rides off to the tournament secretly, incognito,
but not before we see one of the most significant gestures of the film: Lancelot
puts the Queen's ring back on his finger and promises himself to come back for
her. His act has the virtue of protecting the Queen's reputation, fighting for love
of her (as his every act has been), restoring morale to the camp, and serving the
King, but he does not voice this. Lancelot's resounding success at the tournament betrays his concealed identity as the White Knight, but he is seriously
wounded and is nursed by the old peasant woman in the forest. Despite her
efforts to keep him from chivalry (echoes of Perceval's mother) in order to keep
him alive, he insists on leaving to return to court. Her words are prophetic:
' "Vous devriez être mort . . . Vous êtes bête et vous ne cesserez de ne jamais
apprendre rien." ' Lancelot's reply, ' "Je pars pour vivre," ' underscores the
freedom that he feels Love gives him. The Queen is his life. Lancelot returns to
rescue the Queen dramatically from Arthur, who has imprisoned her, and takes
her to his castle.[23] Yet the final irony is that, having rescued the Queen from
Arthur, Lancelot has to unwillingly return her to him, because there is no other
option. Only by losing her can he protect her, and then he dies protecting Arthur
(unsuccessfully) in order to safeguard the woman to whom he swore eternal
love.

The lovers' dialogues reveal that Bresson also modeled his Lancelot's situation and conduct on the Celtic legend of Tristan and Yseut, which Chrétien used
as the model for his Lancelot story, and which forms the common Celtic mytho-
logical heritage at the basis of the Lancelot story. It enacts Bresson's belief 'that
our lives are made of predestination and of chances [hasard]': by the age of six or
seven we are already formed, and it becomes obvious in the early teen years.
Thereafter, we simply 'continue to be what we have been, making use of the
different chances.'[24] Henceforth chance (it is not even choice) determines what
we do and the direction we take in life. Like Tristan, Lancelot dies for Love.

One of Bresson's signal departures from the Mort Artu deserves mention here
in the context of Lancelot's sacrificial journey. He omits the religious figures
(hermits) who reprimand the knights in the Mort Artu, and more particularly the
Church with its human hierarchy of bishops, archbishops and Pope, who in the
Mort Artu offer key characters refuge, in order to provide a 'happy ending.' This
does not mean that there is no place for religion in the film. There certainly is
religious observance because we see the knights in church, but there are no

---

[23] In the Lancelot the castle is Lancelot's Joyeuse Garde.
[24] 'The Question,' p. 480.

visible human intermediaries between man and God. In the *Queste* and in the *Mort Artu*, Lancelot swears his oath to 'a holy man,' 'a hermit in the forest,' but in the film he heard a voice and 'j'ai juré cela à Dieu sur mon épée nue.' In the film, when Lancelot goes to the chapel to ask God for communal protection and for personal strength to withstand temptation, it is a simple Celtic cross that he faces, not a priest or a monk or bishop. In the film, Lancelot is alone with God.

Bresson remarked that monks and religious men were responsible for changing the Celtic legends, rewriting them to make them incorporate an ideological viewpoint. He omits them because he believed they wrote themselves into a myth to give it hope, but in the process they falsified the myth by offering a way out that fudged the issue of choice and free will and instead gave false hope in the service of ideological window-dressing. And I am reminded that during the time *Lancelot du Lac* was in production, Bresson described himself as a 'Christian atheist' in revolt against the Catholic Church's hypocrisy. His view of the human condition in *Lancelot du Lac* is bleak, based on his own austere observation of the world. It shows Lancelot confined by the habits of his heart and the Love that shaped it. If the crawl titles announce between the lines the futility of Lancelot's quest for the Grail, it is because Lancelot's Grail is and remains Guinevere. Like Yseut, she returns to her lord and husband, submitting to a fate that cannot be changed. And Lancelot responds to the call of chivalry, to rescue Arthur from death at the hands of his son Mordred. The final clunk of Lancelot's armor that signals his death is the last we hear or see of Arthurian chivalry. His mythical self reveals itself in his death.

Monty Python and the Holy Grail (1975)

Don Hoffman observes that 'the Pythons are most surprising when they are most medieval.'[25] It is difficult not to be surprised by a film whose vision is conveyed in a comic, irreverent mishmash stocked with so many memorable sights, sounds, and effects. First, the sound of horses' hooves suggests a mounted knight approaching, that is, until we actually see the means of production: the sound is made by King Arthur's squire, Patsy, clapping together two coconut halves to the rhythm of horses' hooves, as he and the King move along with the shuffling gait of a child on a hobby horse. The sight undercuts the sound and our expectations as well. It undercuts Arthur's regal status by presenting him as a king without a horse, a king who traipses around on foot wearing a white robe to travel through muddy pastures, but always wears a crown because that is what identifies a king. Second, the episode of Arthur's encounter with the Black Knight, who insists on having his limbs cut off, one by one, rather than admit defeat in one-on-one combat, explodes the chivalric romance convention of the Arthurian knight whose heroism is hyperbolic and

---

[25] Donald L. Hoffman, 'Not Dead Yet: *Monty Python and the Holy Grail* in the Twenty-First Century,' in *Cinema Arthuriana*, ed. Harty, p. 143 [136–48]. The film is directed by Terry Gilliam and Terry Jones; distributed by Python Pictures. Cast: Graham Chapman, John Cleese, Terry Gilliam, Eric Idle, Terry Jones, Michael Palin.

fearless to the death.[26] But for spectators unfamiliar with the convention, the film's visualization of the gore and grotesque senseless of such conduct has a dark side.[27]

Some of the greatest surprises come when the Pythons juxtapose the medieval with the modern, creating surprise through incongruity, which in turn undercuts the possibility of seriousness because there is no middle ground, only the clash of two irreconcilable extremes. The Pythons' irrepressible humor has been gently called 'undergraduate, juvenile, sophomoric'[28] and 'comic anarchy.'[29] Their unmistakable style – anti-seriousness, anti-dogma, anti-authority – mocks the pretentiousness of all things reverential, including 'the high style artsiness of the French film,'[30] and the Holy Grail by bonding the sacred object to scatology in the film's title. When they made the film in 1974–75, their limited cinematic experience was bolstered by their interest in the medieval period and the hours spent in lecture halls as undergraduates. Knights were one of Terry Gilliam's obsessions and, as he later explained in the context of early preparations for the film, 'I was in my Chaucer period . . . Terry [Jones] and I were great medievalists, so we couldn't wait to get in there.'[31] The Pythons appear to have relied on Sir Thomas Malory's Arthuriad for much of their live Arthurian narrative, although it has been suggested that some of the troupe were familiar with the *Lancelot-Grail*.[32] But this film, for all its buffoonery and hilarious excesses, and deliberately false historical pretensions,[33] claims a special place in the current volume because it is the only Arthurian film I know in which an illustration from an extant medieval manuscript of the *Cycle* plays an active role in the telling of the narrative.

In addition to having live characters and narrative, the film has animation sequences. Some are modern while others give the film a 'medieval flavor,' such as the pages of an ancient book that are turned with the sugar-sweet nostalgia of a family photo album. As Martine Meuwese points out, animation sequences

---

26 See Raymond H. Thompson, who attributes the film's success to the 'ironic techniques so central to their vision of the Arthurian legend,' in 'The Ironic Tradition in Four Arthurian Films,' *Cinema Arthuriana*, ed. Harty, p. 111 [110–117].
27 See the reaction of audiences at its New York premiere, described in Bob McCabe, *Dark Knights and Holy Fools: The Art and Films of Terry Gilliam* (New York, 1999), p. 35.
28 Terry Gilliam, in an interview with Bob McCabe, *Dark Knights and Holy Fools*, p. 38.
29 Howard H. Proudy, 'Monty Python and the Holy Grail,' in Frank N. Magill, ed., *Magill's Survey of Cinema: English Language Films*, Series 2, 6 vols. (Englewood Cliffs, NJ, 1981), 4:1634.
30 Hoffman, 'Not Dead Yet,' p. 140.
31 *Dark Knights and Holy Fools*, p. 48.
32 See Thompson, 'Ironic Tradition,' p. 114, and Hoffman, 'Not Dead Yet,' p. 140.
33 See Hoffman, 'Not Dead Yet,' p. 137: 'The film begins with the title in Gothic script: England, 932 A.D . . . The year 932 is just not memorable; indeed, for Arthurians it is significantly insignificant. It is roughly four centuries too late for an attempt at pseudo-historicism, an attempt to situate the narrative in the period of the Germanic invasions of England against which a possibly historical Arthur may have fought. It is, on the other hand, more or less three centuries too soon for the efflorescence of Arthurian literature inspired by Geoffrey of Monmouth and slightly more than half a millennium too early for a setting appropriate for Sir Thomas Malory, the most direct Arthurian source for the film. At best, it is more or less accidentally halfway between 1469, when Malory claims to have completed *Le Morte* and 542, when, according to the Vulgate *Queste del Saint Graal*, the Quest of the Holy Grail was undertaken . . . a date so completely certain to reverberate soundlessly, to evoke associations with absolutely nothing.'

serve as framing devices or interludes for the tales of individual knights – 'The Quest for the Holy Grail,' 'The Tale of Sir Galahad,' 'The Tale of Sir Launcelot,' 'Season Animation' – and some of the original sketches for the animation sequences contain visual motifs that were inspired by illuminations from four-teenth-century manuscripts.[34] Meuwese identified one of the motifs as belonging to the Manchester manuscript of the *Lancelot-Grail*, Rylands Fr.1, which contains the second half of the *Lancelot*, the *Queste del Saint Graal*, and the *Mort Artu*.[35] The visual motif in question occurs in the first volume of the manu-script at f. 82, which has a miniature and profuse marginal decoration.[36] In the top left margin a brown-robed monk-sciapod reads an open book; at the top right corner a musician-sciapod plays a violin to a little white dog who sits up begging. Halfway down the right margin an angel, in a long gray dress, with multi-colored wings and a golden halo, looks over her shoulder towards the text as she plays a large hand organ. In the right corner of the lower margin, a baboon dressed in a pink cowl, with his striped buttocks exposed, plays a harp and looks up at a smaller baboon sitting on the grass, who winds thread on a frame. He in turn looks ahead to a female baboon, naked except for her draped headgear, who rides on a sheep and spins yarn with a distaff. Below her, a white dog and a white rabbit run along the margin.

This is a complex web of illustration made of conventional figures that recur over and over in the pages of Gothic manuscripts. The precise significance of marginal decoration in Gothic manuscripts is difficult to pin down,[37] but there is usually a humorous element and 'the frequent juxtaposition of unrelated themes in a totally incongruous context heightens the chaotic effect.'[38] Birds, baboons, monsters, dragons, fantastic creatures, sciapods, human or semi-human figures

---

34 Martine Meuwese, 'The Animation of Marginal Decorations in *Monty Python and the Holy Grail*,' forthcoming in *Arthuriana*. I thank Martine for generously providing me with a pre-publication copy of her article.

35 The three works are distributed in the two-volume manuscript as follows: vol. 1 fol. 1 – vol. 2 fol. 181v, second part of *Le livre de Lancelot*; vol. 2 fols. 182–211v, *Les aventures del saint graal*; vol. 2 fols. 212–257v, *La mort al roi artus*. I thank the Rylands Library for allowing me to examine this manuscript.

36 The text corresponds to *LM* 4:339. The miniature, located at the top left of fol. 82, shows King Claudas, with his dwarf, asking a damsel for news of Lancelot. In the *Lancelot-Grail*'s Gothic manuscripts, the opening page of each work is where the marginal decoration is traditionally most dense and fully developed. Although Rylands Fr. 1 fol. 82 is not an opening page, it seems to be treated as one because of a scribal and content break at fol. 81v.

37 Lilian M. C. Randall, *Images in the Margins of Gothic Manuscripts* (Berkeley and Los Angeles, 1966), shows that some medieval marginal illustration, particularly the more developed compositions found in bas-de-page, clearly serve a didactic purpose by recalling folk wisdom from proverbs or well-known moralizing tales, whether sacred or profane in origin, while others apparently evoke medieval ethnic slurs, or comment on the text they accompany, or comment on the more official form of illustration found in nearby miniatures (pp. 3–20). See also Michael Camille, *Image on the Edge* (Cambridge, MA, 1993), who discusses the marginal decoration in Gothic manuscripts as an exuberant, alternative discourse that comments upon or contests that of the written text. For an example of marginal illustration that plays off the accompanying text while commenting on a miniature, see Carol R. Dover, ' "Imagines Historiarum": Text and Image in the French Prose *Lancelot*,' in *Word and Image in Arthurian Lit-erature*, ed. Keith Busby (New York and London, 1996), pp. 79–104. On the work of medieval miniaturists, see Jonathan J. G. Alexander, *Medieval Illuminators and their Methods of Work* (New Haven, 1992).

38 *Images in the Margins*, p. 19.

engage in acts of defecation, copulation, weaving, chasing, spearing, playing music. The marginal decoration of Rylands 1 f. 82 certainly conforms to these criteria with its mixture of higher life and lower life.

The use of the film's visual animation was the brainchild of the Pythons' animation artist and co-director, Terry Gilliam, but he did not have to deal with the complexity of the manuscript page. He describes how he did the artwork in the early days of Monty Python, 'in Regent Street, . . . I was getting all these pictures from art books photographed, and they'd blow them up to the size I wanted them. Then I'd cut them out and colour them in with felt-tip markers, then I'd airbrush a body, and so on.'[39] Meuwese has identified his source as Lilian Randall's *Images in the Margins of Gothic Manuscripts*, which reproduces black and white photographs of marginal figures and arrangements from medieval Gothic manuscripts. Gilliam's sketches for the film are reproduced in the book of the film, accompanied by the numbers Randall used to identify the medieval motifs in her book.[40] It is thanks to her illustrations that Gilliam re-cycled marginal motifs from a variety of types of manuscripts, both sacred and profane, in Latin and French, just as medieval miniaturists did.

Gilliam took the Rylands Fr. 1 motif of the angel with hand organ. In the manuscript it occurs in the *Lancelot* section, but in the film he uses it on the title page of 'The Quest for the Holy Grail' animation:

The Quest for the Holy Grail opens with naked trumpeters [from Randall] who stand with their heads between their legs playing trumpets literally anally. Then two identical mirror-imaged angels with a portable organ come flapping their wings, rising from the bottom to the top of the picture, followed by little souls borne up in a cloth, and a Romanesque Christ, his hand raised in blessing, set in a mandorla surrounded by sunbeams. Trumpeting angels rise through the picture, and then comes the title picture containing the text, with medieval initials: 'The Quest for the Holy Grail', which is hoisted up, rattling, by a winged holy woman on the right and yet another angel with a portable organ on the left. The angel with the portable organ, which repeatedly appears in this animation, is taken from Randall.[41]

Gilliam's angel figure, whose presence in the Rylands manuscript seems to call attention to the higher, religious element of the Grail quest through singing to the greater glory of God, is juxtaposed in the film with the anal antics of the naked trumpeters, in a game of incongruity that juxtaposes the heavenly and the earthly, the refined and the grotesque. But does it reinforce the sacred? In the *Lancelot-Grail* the purity of Galahad is never in question, he succeeds in adventures which other knights either fail or are not allowed to attempt. In *Monty Python and the Holy Grail*, however, the juxtaposition in this animation sequence echoes the live narrative's treatment of the hero Galahad, whose quest leads him to Castle Anthrax where he finds ravishing damsels and ladies, all waiting to be

---

[39] *Dark Knights and Holy Fools*, p. 34.
[40] Graham Chapman et al., *Monty Python's Second Film: A First Draft* (London, 1977).
[41] Meuwese, 'Animation of Marginal Decorations.'

ravished, and the naive pure knight has to be dragged away against his will by his more worldy-wise companions. The Pythons' Galahad is a very secular hero!

Terry Gilliam's animation from the Rylands manuscript parallels the work of the illuminators of medieval manuscripts. As Martine Meuwese so aptly puts it, 'Terry Gilliam not only had a perfect understanding of how medieval marginal decoration works; he also set to work himself as a miniaturist and thus continued a tradition whose origins lie in the Middle Ages,' and he worked 'entirely in keeping with the spirit and humour of his medieval predecessors, thus breathing new life into their creations . . . The nature of his medium made it possible for him to bring a new dimension to the medieval sources.'[42] He captures what we take to be the true spirit of marginalia, which might make us wonder indeed whether 'this film is simply the product of too much research to be dismissed lightly.'[43]

If this film 'set movie making back 900 years,' as its initial publicity boisterously claimed in 1975, it is appropriate that it should commandeer visual material from a 700-year-old manuscript, because that leaves a mere 200-year gap for the rest of the film to fill.

Three directors who transfer parts of the *Lancelot-Grail Cycle* to the screen in three very different ways. The Pythons and Bresson made their films in 1975 and 1974 respectively, Llorca made his in 1990. If medievalism 'takes the long view in which the present and the future can be studied in light of the past and the past can be re-imagined in light of the present and the future,'[44] these three films offer three responses for their present. Llorca reorders the *Cycle*'s sequence of events to send society a positive message of rebirth and spiritual renewal, through the hope that the Christian message of Love and family can provide. In the mid-seventies, when profound societal changes have loosened the old fabric of European society and yet war rages in Vietnam, Bresson tries to see the present through the past in an uncompromising view of man imprisoned by his inability to have a critical perspective on himself. The Pythons' contemporaneous response is humor that spoofs the past and present, yet captures in one corner of their work the venerable medieval tradition of continuation in which they themselves dabbled: the marginal form it takes elicits the saving grace of laughter in the face of the sometimes violent contradictions of their times.

42 Meuwese, 'Animation of Marginal Decorations.'
43 Mark Burde, 'Monty Python's Medieval Masterpiece,' *The Arthurian Yearbook*, III, ed. Keith Busby (New York and London, 1993), p. 4 [2–20].
44 Harty, *The Reel Middle Ages*, p. 3.

21

A Select Bibliography of the Lancelot-Grail Cycle

CAROL DOVER

Given the great size of the *Lancelot-Grail Cycle* itself, and the range and diversity of its influence, this bibliography is very selective, aiming to provide readers with the primary resources for the French text itself. More detailed bibliographical references can be found in the individual chapters.

EDITIONS

Bogdanow, Fanni, ed. *La version Post-Vulgate de la Queste del Saint Graal et de la Mort Artu: Troisième partie du Roman de Graal.* Vols. I, II, IV.1. Paris, 1991.

Frappier, Jean, ed. *La Mort le roi Artu: roman du XIIIe siècle.* 3rd. ed. Geneva, 1964.

Hucher, Eugène, ed. *Le Saint Graal.* 3 vols. Le Mans, 1875.

Hutchings, Gweneth. *Le roman en prose de Lancelot du Lac: le Conte de la Charrette.* Paris, 1938.

Kennedy, Elspeth, ed. *Lancelot do Lac: The non-cyclic Old French Prose Romance.* 2 vols. Oxford, 1980.

Micha, Alexandre, ed. *Lancelot: roman en prose du XIIIe siècle.* 9 vols. Geneva and Paris, 1978–83.

———, ed. *Merlin: roman du XIIIe siècle.* Geneva, 1979.

Paris, Gaston, and Jacob Ulrich, eds. *Merlin: roman en prose du XIIIe siècle.* Paris, 1886.

Pauphilet, Albert. *La Queste del Saint Graal.* Paris, 1921.

Ponceau, Jean-Paul, ed. *L'Estoire del Saint Graal.* 2 vols. Paris, 1997.

Sommer, H. Oskar, ed. *The Vulgate Version of the Arthurian Romances.* Vols. 1–7. Washington, D.C., 1908–13. Reprinted New York, 1979.

ENGLISH TRANSLATIONS

Cable, James, trans. *The Death of King Arthur.* Harmondsworth, 1971.

Carman, J. Neale, trans. *From Camelot to Joyous Guard: The Old French 'La Mort le roi Artu.'* Ed. with intro. by Norris J. Lacy. Lawrence, KS, 1974.

Corley, Corin, trans. *Lancelot of the Lake*, with introduction by Elspeth Kennedy. Oxford, 1989.

Lancelot-Grail: The Old French Arthurian Vulgate and Post-Vulgate in Translation. General ed. Norris J. Lacy, with intro. by E. Jane Burns. New York and London, 1996. Vol. I: *The History of the Holy Grail* (trans. Carol J. Chase) and *The Story of Merlin* (trans. Rupert T. Pickens). Vol. II: *Lancelot*, part I (trans. Samuel N. Rosenberg); *Lancelot*, part II (trans. Carleton W. Carroll); *Lancelot*, part III (trans.

Samuel N. Rosenberg). Vol III: *Lancelot*, part IV (trans. Roberta L. Krueger); *Lancelot*, part V (trans. William W. Kibler); *Lancelot*, part VI (trans. Carleton W. Carroll). Vol. IV: *The Quest for the Holy Grail* (trans. E. Jane Burns); *The Death of Arthur* (trans. Norris J. Lacy); The Post-Vulgate, part I: *The Merlin Continuation* (intro. and trans. by Martha Asher). Vol. 5: The Post-Vulgate, parts I–II: *The Merlin Continuation* (cont.), *The Quest for the Holy Grail*, *The Death of Arthur* (trans. Martha Asher). Also Chapter Summaries and Index of Proper Names.

Matarasso, Pauline, trans. *The Quest of the Holy Grail*. Harmondsworth, 1969.

Paton, Lucy Allen, trans. *Sir Lancelot of the Lake: A French Prose Romance of the Thirteenth Century*. New York, 1929.

MANUSCRIPTS

Micha, Alexandre. 'Les manuscrits du *Lancelot* en prose.' *Romania*, 84 (1963), 28–60 and 478–99.

———. 'La tradition manuscrite du *Lancelot* en prose.' *Romania*, 85 (1964), 293–318 and 478–517.

Stones, M. Alison. 'The Earliest Illustrated Prose *Lancelot* Manuscript?' *Reading Medieval Studies*, 3 (1977), 3–44.

Woledge, Brian. *Bibliographie des romans et nouvelles en prose française antérieurs à 1500*. Geneva, 1954.

———. ———: *Supplément 1954–1973*. Geneva, 1975.

CRITICAL STUDIES

Baumgartner, Emmanuèle. *L'Arbre et le Pain: Essai sur la Queste del Saint Graal*. Paris, 1981.

———. 'From Lancelot to Galahad: The Stakes of Filiation.' In *The Lancelot-Grail Cycle: Text and Transformations*, ed. Kibler, pp. 14–30.

———. 'Temps linéaire, temps circulaire et écriture romanesque (XIIe–XIIIe siècles).' In *Le Temps et la durée dans la littérature au Moyen Age et à la Renaissance: Actes du Colloque organisé par le Centre de Recherche sur la Littérature du Moyen Age et de la Renaissance de l'Université de Reims (Novembre 1984)*. Ed. Yvonne Bellenger. Paris, 1986. pp. 7–21.

———. 'Remarques sur la prose du *Lancelot*.' *Romania*, 105 (1984), 1–15.

Besamusca, Bart, et al. *Cyclification: The Development of Narrative Cycles in the Chansons de Geste and the Arthurian Romances*. Koninkliijke Nederlandse Akademie van Weterschappen: Verhandelingen, Afd. Letterkunde, N.S. 159. Amsterdam, Oxford, New York, Tokyo, 1994.

Besamusca, Bart. *The Book of Lancelot: The Middle Dutch Lancelot Compilation and the Medieval Tradition of Narrative Cycles*. Trans. Thea Summerfield. Cambridge, Eng., 2003.

Burns, E. Jane, *Arthurian Fictions: Rereading the Arthurian Cycle*. Columbus, Ohio, 1988.

Chase, Carol. 'Des Sarrasins à Camelot.' *Cahiers de Recherches Médiévales (XIIIe–XIVe s.)*, 5 (1998), 45–53.

Combes, Annie. 'From Quest to Quest: Perceval and Galahad in the Prose *Lancelot*.' *Arthuriana*, 12.3 (Fall 2002), 7–30.

Dover, Carol. 'From Non-Cyclic to Cyclic *Lancelot*: Recycling the Heart.' In

Transtextualities: Of Cycles and Cyclicity in Medieval French Literature. Ed. Sara Sturm-Maddox and Donald Maddox. Binghamton, NY, 1996. pp. 53–70.

———.' "*Imagines historiarum*": Text and Image in the French Prose *Lancelot*.' In *Word and Image in Arthurian Literature*. Ed. Keith Busby. New York, 1996. pp. 89–113.

Dufournet, Jean, ed. *Approches du Lancelot en prose*. Paris, 1984.

Frappier, Jean. 'Le Graal et la chevalerie.' In *Autour du Graal*. Geneva, 1977. pp. 89–128.

———. *Etude sur la Mort le roi Artu*. 3rd ed. Geneva, 1972.

——— and Reinhold R. Grimm. *Le Roman jusqu'à la fin du XIIIe siècle. Grundriss der romanischen Literaturen des Mittelalters*. Vol. IV, parts 1 and 2. Heidelberg, 1978.

Freeman-Regalado, Nancy. 'La chevalerie celestielle: Spiritual Transformations of Secular Romance in *La Queste del Saint Graal*.' In *Romance: Generic Transformations from Chrétien de Troyes to Cervantes*. Ed. Kevin Brownlee and Maria Scordilis Brownlee. Hanover, NH, and London, 1985. pp. 91–113.

Gilson, Etienne. 'La mystique de la grâce dans la *Queste del Saint Graal*.' *Romania*, 51 (1925), 321–47.

Kelly, Douglas. *The Art of Medieval French Romance*. Madison, WI, 1992.

Kennedy, Elspeth. *Lancelot and the Grail*. Oxford, 1986.

———. 'Variations in the Pattern of Interlace in the *Lancelot-Grail*.' In *The Lancelot-Grail Cycle: Text and Transformations*, pp. 31–50.

Kibler, William W., ed. *The Lancelot-Grail Cycle: Text and Transformations*. Austin, TX, 1997.

Lacy, Norris. 'Spatial Form in the *Mort Artu*.' *Symposium*, 31 (1977), 337–45.

Leupin, Alexandre. *Le Graal et la littérature*. Lausanne, 1982.

Lot, Ferdinand. *Etude sur le Lancelot en prose*. Paris, 1918. Reprinted 1954.

Matarasso, Pauline. *The Redemption of Chivalry: A Study of the Queste del saint Graal*. Geneva, 1979.

Méla, Charles. *La Reine et le Graal: La conjointure dans les romans du Graal de Chrétien de Troyes au Livre de Lancelot*. Paris, 1984.

Pauphilet, Albert. *Etudes sur la Queste del saint Graal attribuée à Walter Map*. Paris, 1921.

Szkilnik, Michelle. *L'Archipel du Graal: Etude de l'Estoire del Saint Graal*. Geneva, 1991.

Trachsler, Richard. *Merlin l'enchanteur. Etude sur le 'Merlin' de Robert de Boron*. Paris, 2000.

Valette, Jean-René. *La Poétique du merveilleux dans le Lancelot en prose*. Paris, 1998.

Index

Numbers in bold refer to illustrations and their captions

ARTHURIAN STUDIES

Printed and bound by CPI Group (UK) Ltd, Croydon, CR0 4YY

09/06/2025

14685718-0004